Tokyo TARAREBA GIRLS

7

AKIKO HIGASHIMURA

TODAY'S RECOMMENDATIONS

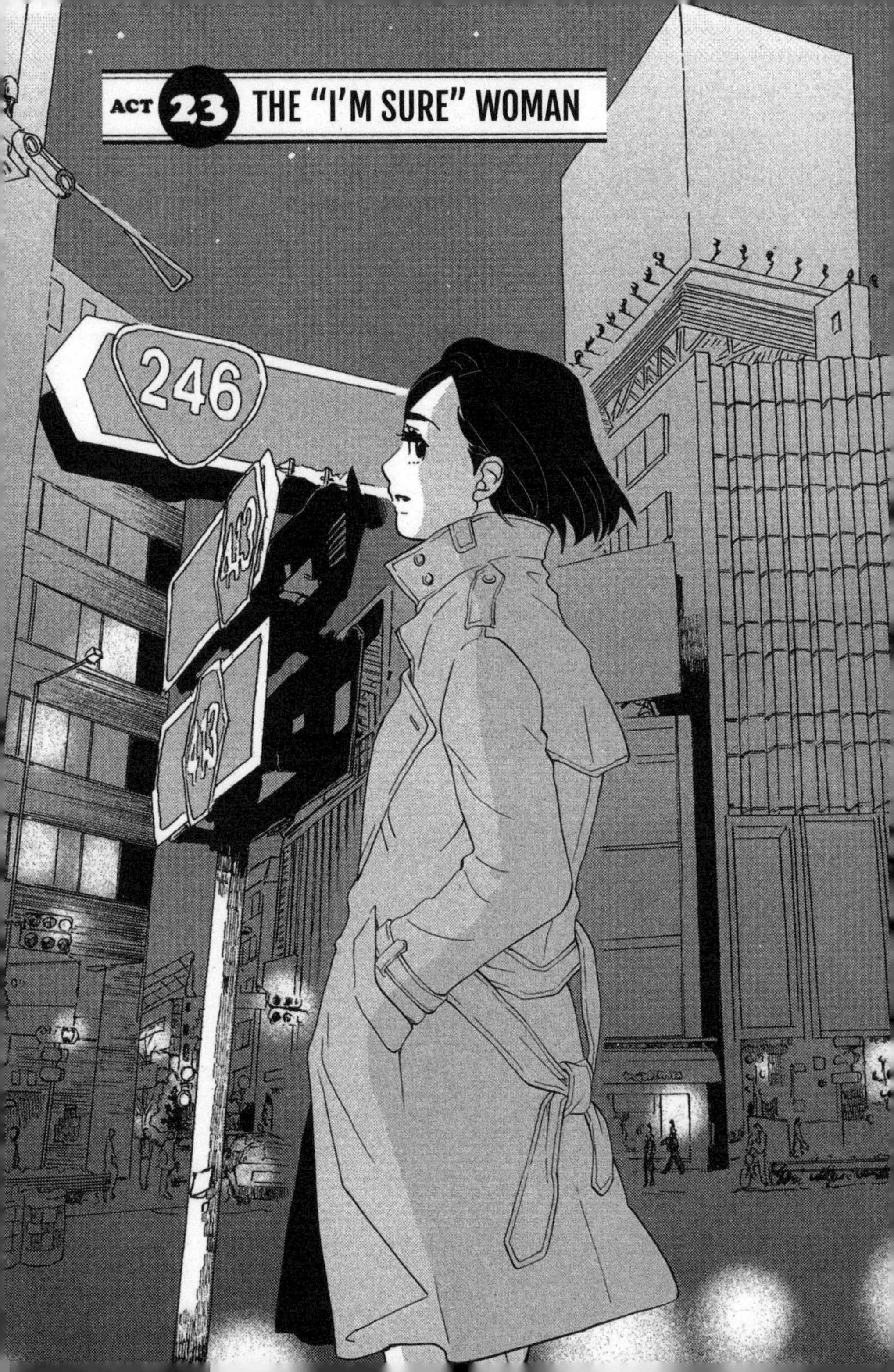
ACT 23 THE "I'M SURE" WOMAN
246

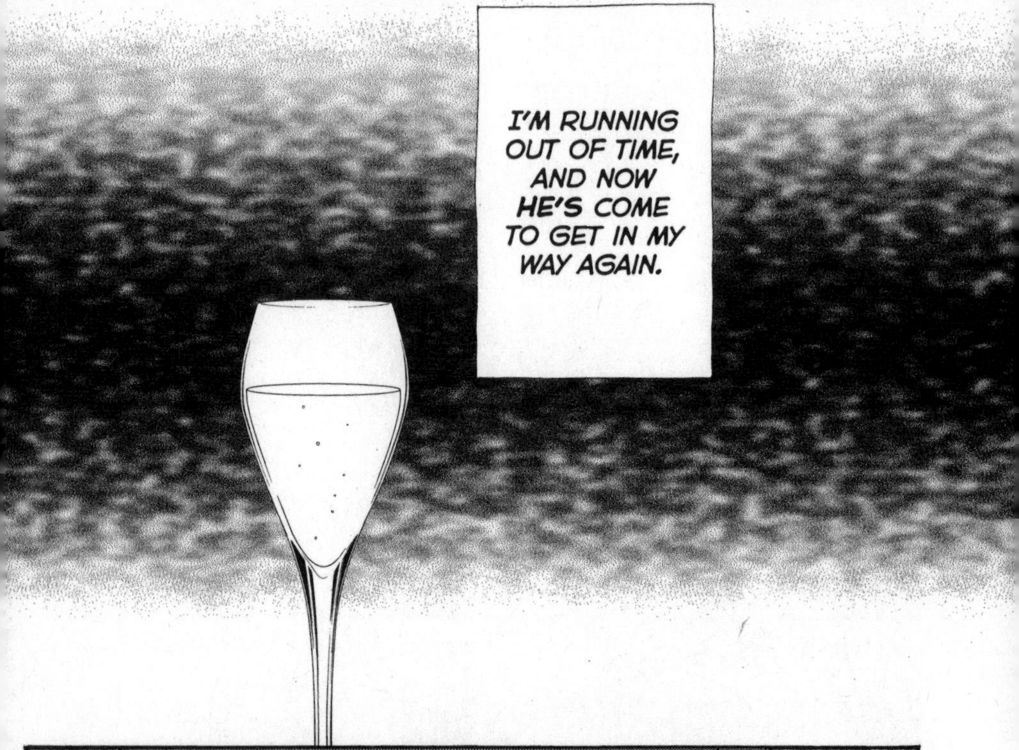
I'M RUNNING OUT OF TIME, AND NOW HE'S COME TO GET IN MY WAY AGAIN.

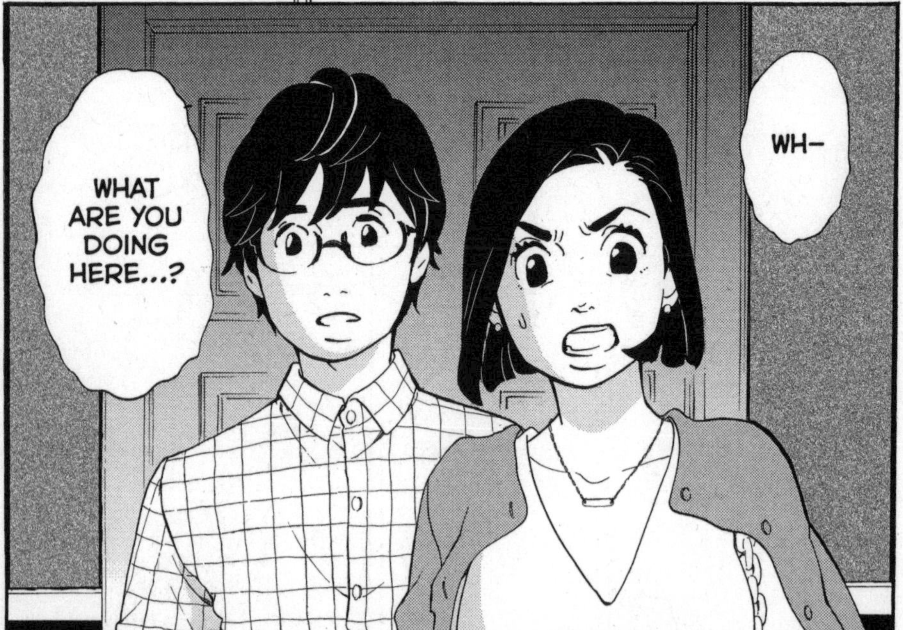
WH–
WHAT ARE YOU DOING HERE...?

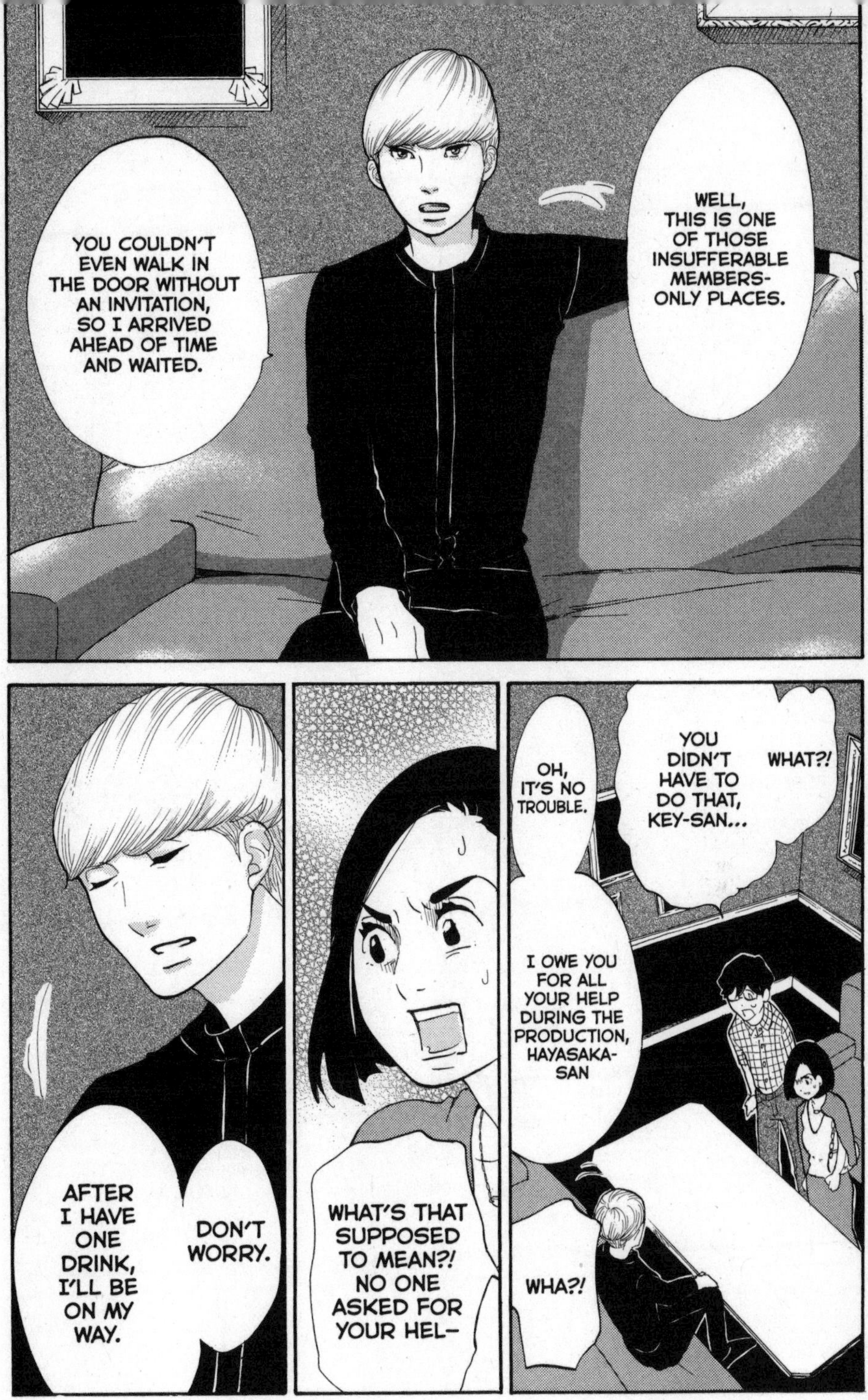
WELL, THIS IS ONE OF THOSE INSUFFERABLE MEMBERS-ONLY PLACES.
YOU COULDN'T EVEN WALK IN THE DOOR WITHOUT AN INVITATION, SO I ARRIVED AHEAD OF TIME AND WAITED.
WHAT?!
YOU DIDN'T HAVE TO DO THAT, KEY-SAN...
OH, IT'S NO TROUBLE.
I OWE YOU FOR ALL YOUR HELP DURING THE PRODUCTION, HAYASAKA-SAN
WHA?!
WHAT'S THAT SUPPOSED TO MEAN?! NO ONE ASKED FOR YOUR HEL-
DON'T WORRY.
AFTER I HAVE ONE DRINK, I'LL BE ON MY WAY.

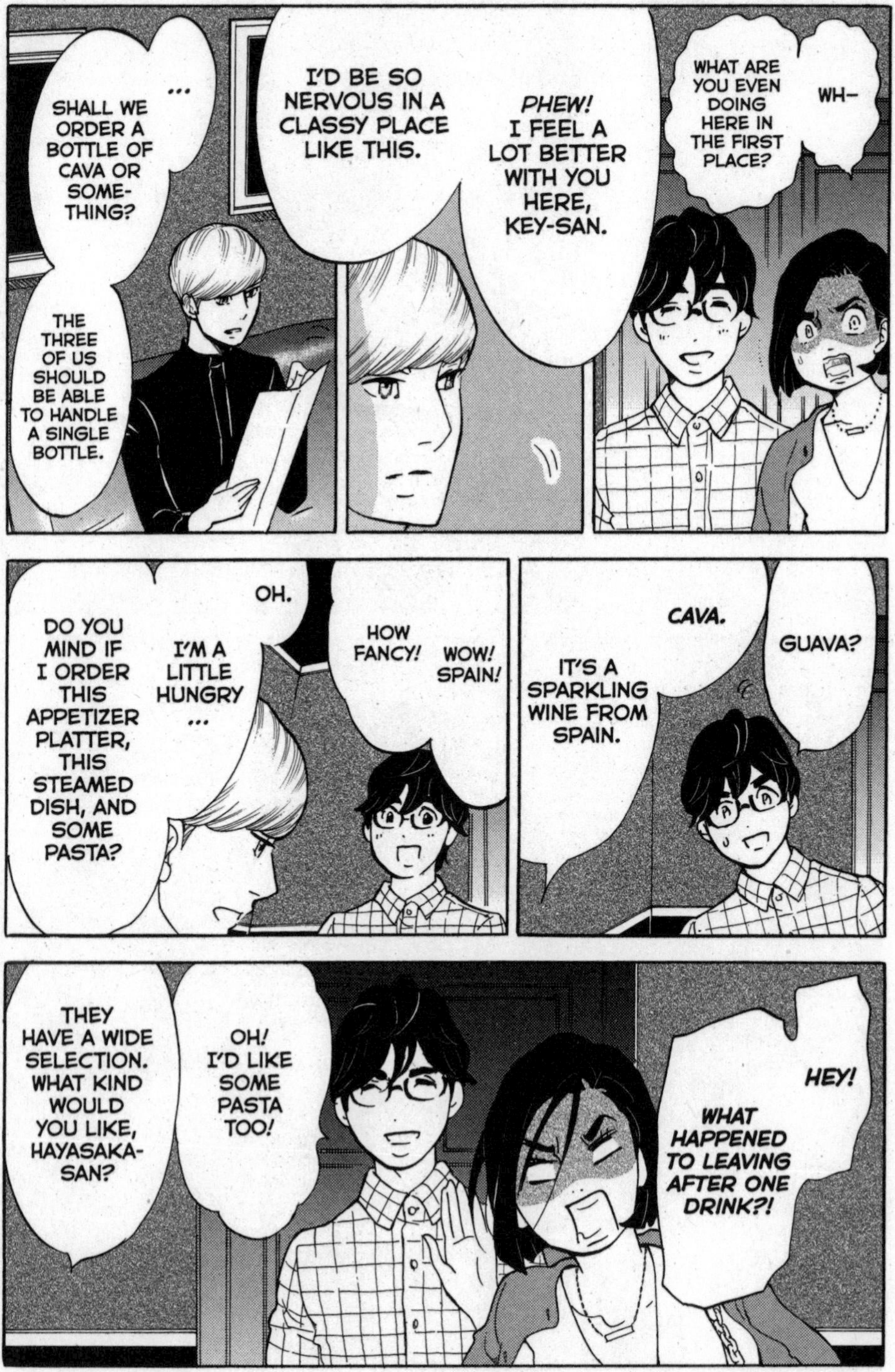
WH–
WHAT ARE YOU EVEN DOING HERE IN THE FIRST PLACE?
PHEW! I FEEL A LOT BETTER WITH YOU HERE, KEY-SAN.
I'D BE SO NERVOUS IN A CLASSY PLACE LIKE THIS.
...
SHALL WE ORDER A BOTTLE OF CAVA OR SOME-THING?
THE THREE OF US SHOULD BE ABLE TO HANDLE A SINGLE BOTTLE.
GUAVA?
CAVA.
IT'S A SPARKLING WINE FROM SPAIN.
WOW! SPAIN!
HOW FANCY!
OH.
I'M A LITTLE HUNGRY...
DO YOU MIND IF I ORDER THIS APPETIZER PLATTER, THIS STEAMED DISH, AND SOME PASTA?
HEY!
WHAT HAPPENED TO LEAVING AFTER ONE DRINK?!
OH! I'D LIKE SOME PASTA TOO!
THEY HAVE A WIDE SELECTION. WHAT KIND WOULD YOU LIKE, HAYASAKA-SAN?

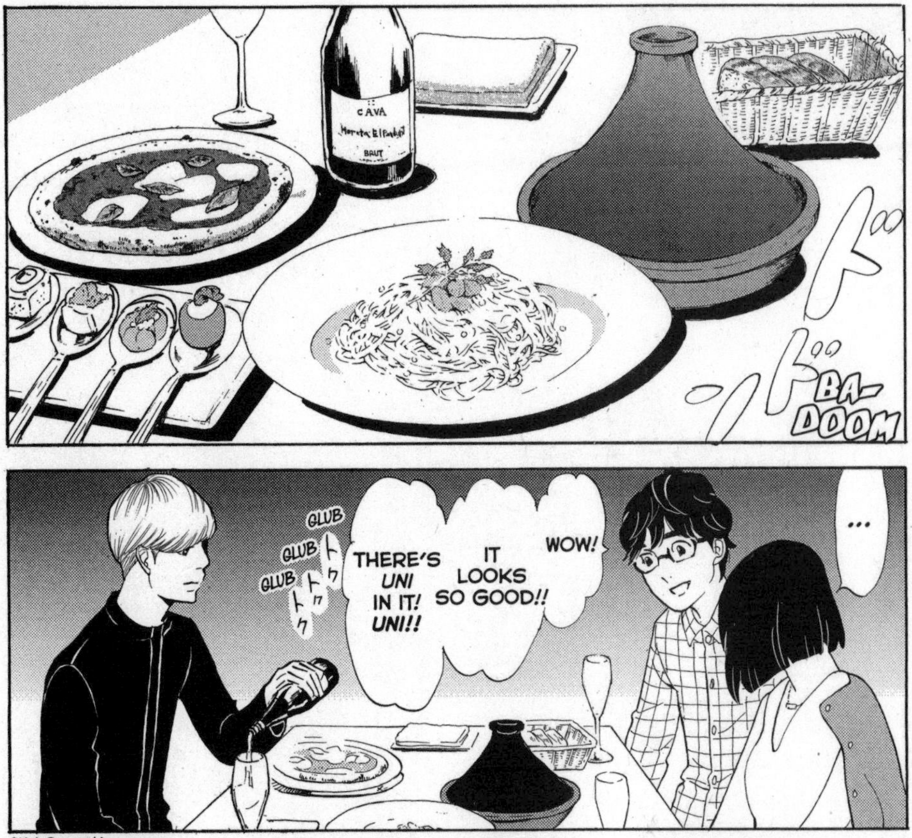
BA-DOOM
...
WOW!
IT LOOKS SO GOOD!!
THERE'S *UNI* IN IT! *UNI*!!
GLUB
GLUB
GLUB

**Uni*: Sea urchin

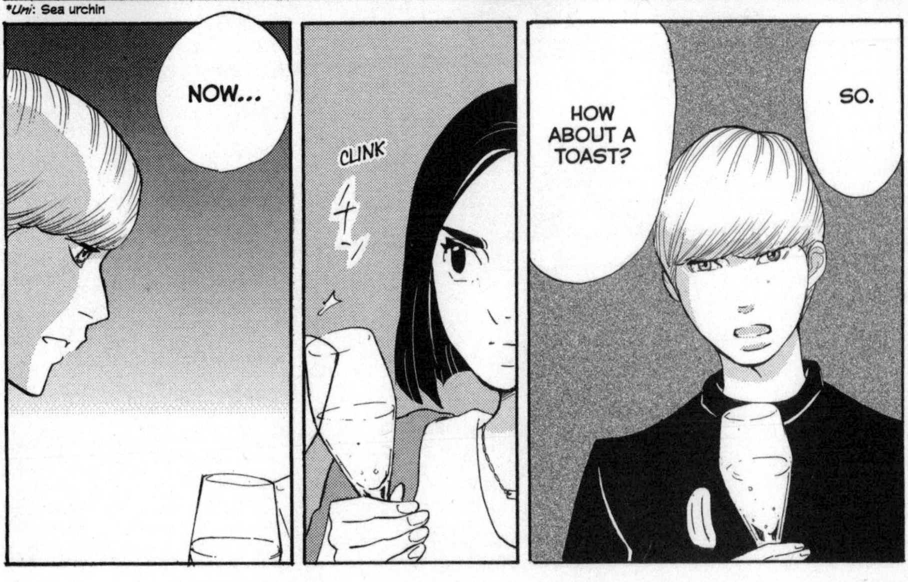
SO.
HOW ABOUT A TOAST?
CLINK
NOW...

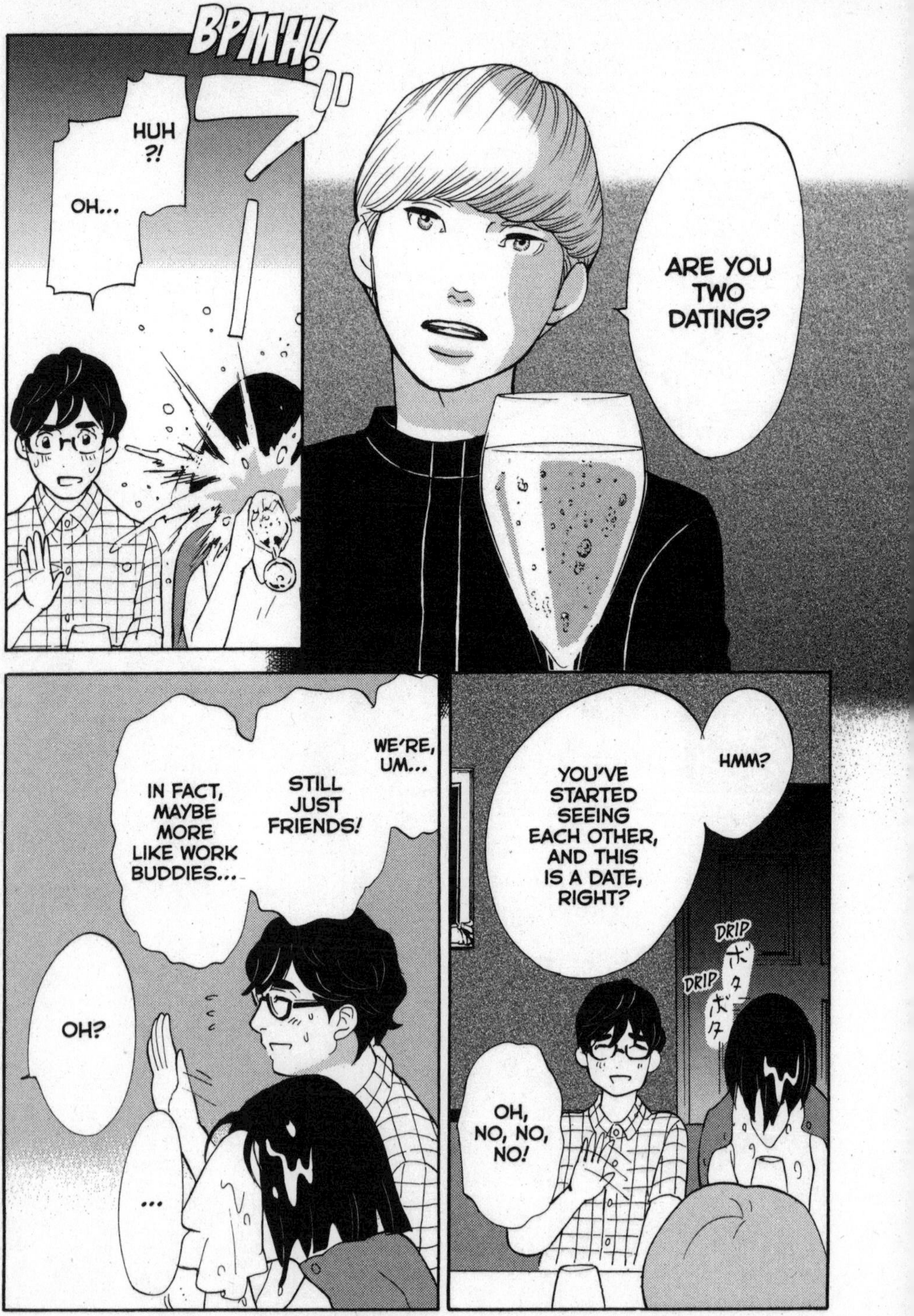

ARE YOU TWO DATING?
BPMH!
HUH ?!
OH...
HMM?
YOU'VE STARTED SEEING EACH OTHER, AND THIS IS A DATE, RIGHT?
DRIP
DRIP
ボタ
ボタ
OH, NO, NO, NO!
WE'RE, UM...
STILL JUST FRIENDS!
IN FACT, MAYBE MORE LIKE WORK BUDDIES...
OH?
...

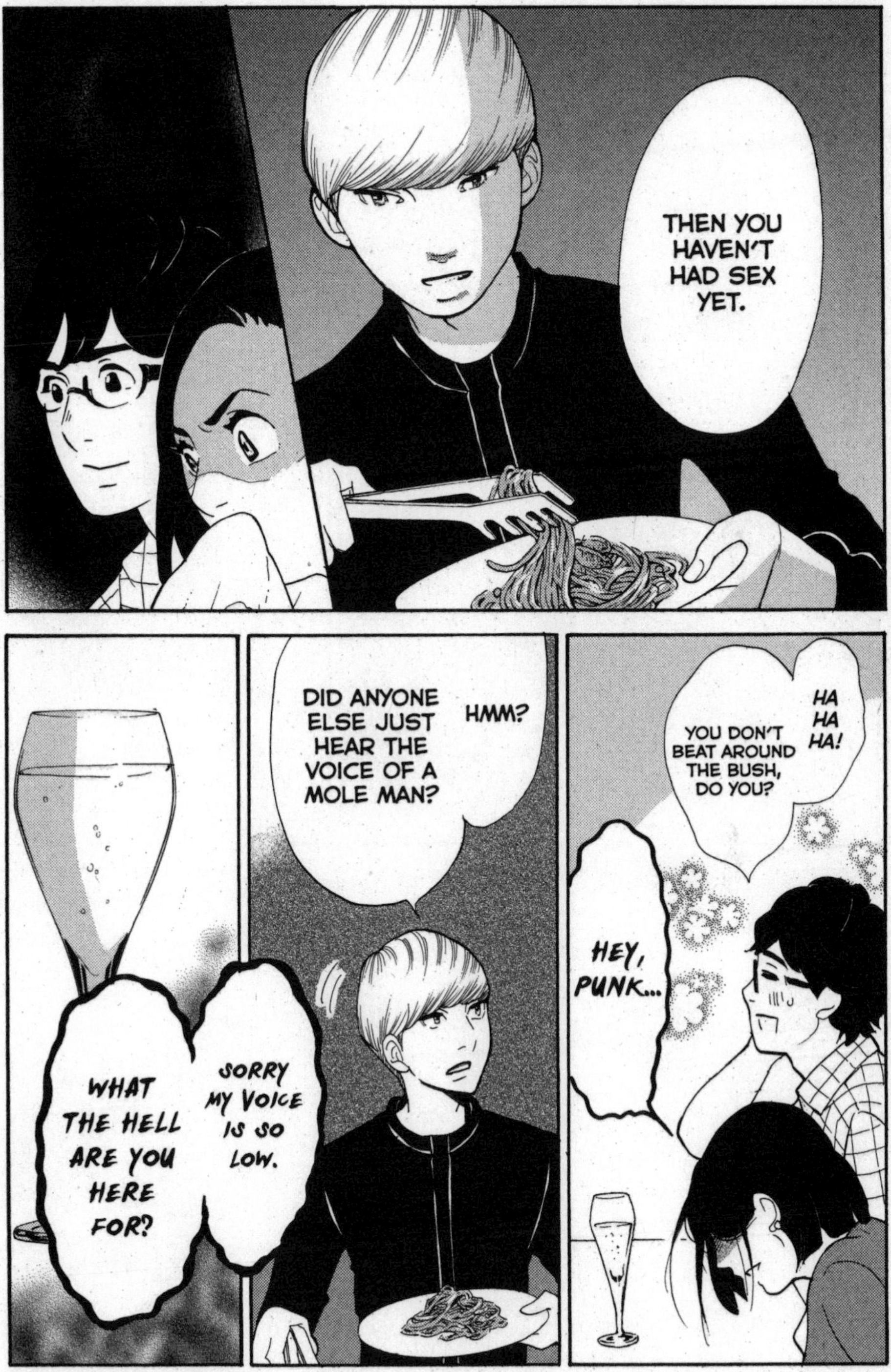
THEN YOU HAVEN'T HAD SEX YET.
HA HA HA!
YOU DON'T BEAT AROUND THE BUSH, DO YOU?
HEY, PUNK...
DID ANYONE ELSE JUST HEAR THE VOICE OF A MOLE MAN?
HMM?
SORRY MY VOICE IS SO LOW.
WHAT THE HELL ARE YOU HERE FOR?

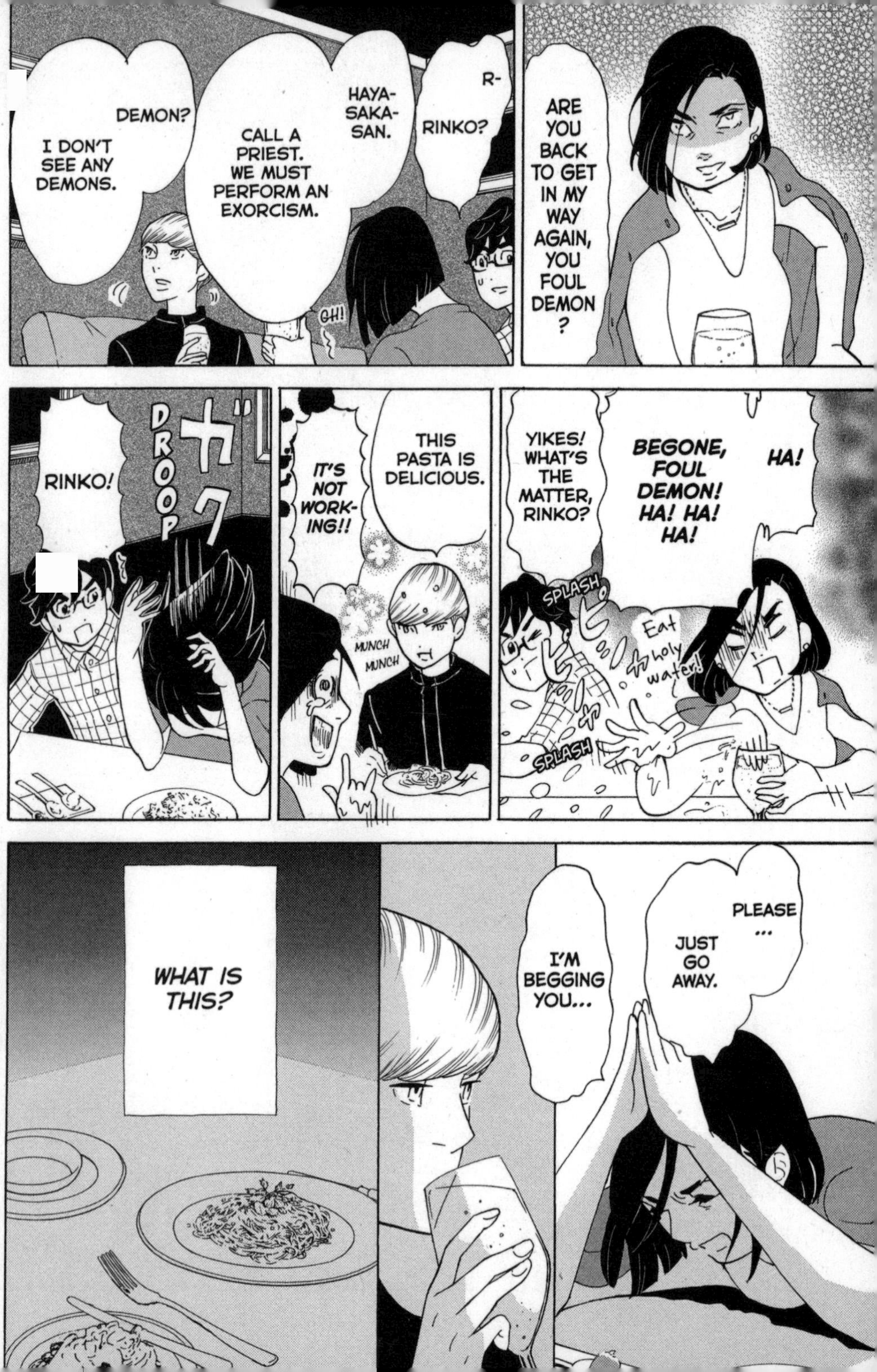
ARE YOU BACK TO GET IN MY WAY AGAIN, YOU FOUL DEMON?
R- RINKO?
HAYA-SAKA-SAN.
CALL A PRIEST. WE MUST PERFORM AN EXORCISM.
DEMON? I DON'T SEE ANY DEMONS.
GH!
HA!
BEGONE, FOUL DEMON! HA! HA! HA!
YIKES! WHAT'S THE MATTER, RINKO?
SPLASH
Eat holy water!
SPLASH
THIS PASTA IS DELICIOUS.
IT'S NOT WORKING!!
MUNCH MUNCH
ガク
DROOP
RINKO!
PLEASE... JUST GO AWAY.
I'M BEGGING YOU...
WHAT IS THIS?

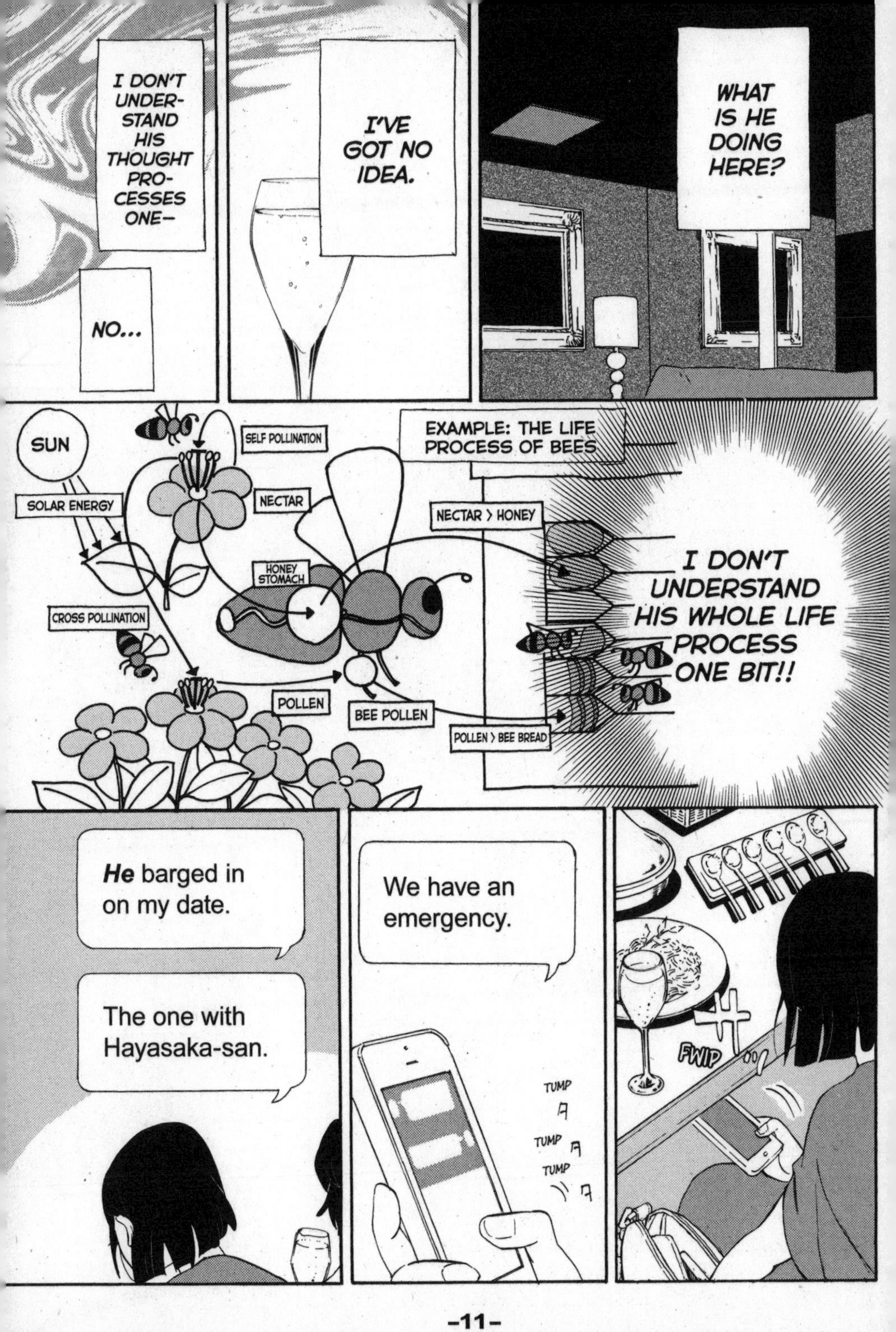
WHAT IS HE DOING HERE?
I'VE GOT NO IDEA.
I DON'T UNDERSTAND HIS THOUGHT PROCESSES ONE—
NO...
I DON'T UNDERSTAND HIS WHOLE LIFE PROCESS ONE BIT!!
EXAMPLE: THE LIFE PROCESS OF BEES
NECTAR > HONEY
POLLEN > BEE BREAD
BEE POLLEN
SELF POLLINATION
NECTAR
HONEY STOMACH
SUN
SOLAR ENERGY
CROSS POLLINATION
POLLEN
FWIP
We have an emergency.
TUMP
TUMP
TUMP
He barged in on my date.
The one with Hayasaka-san.

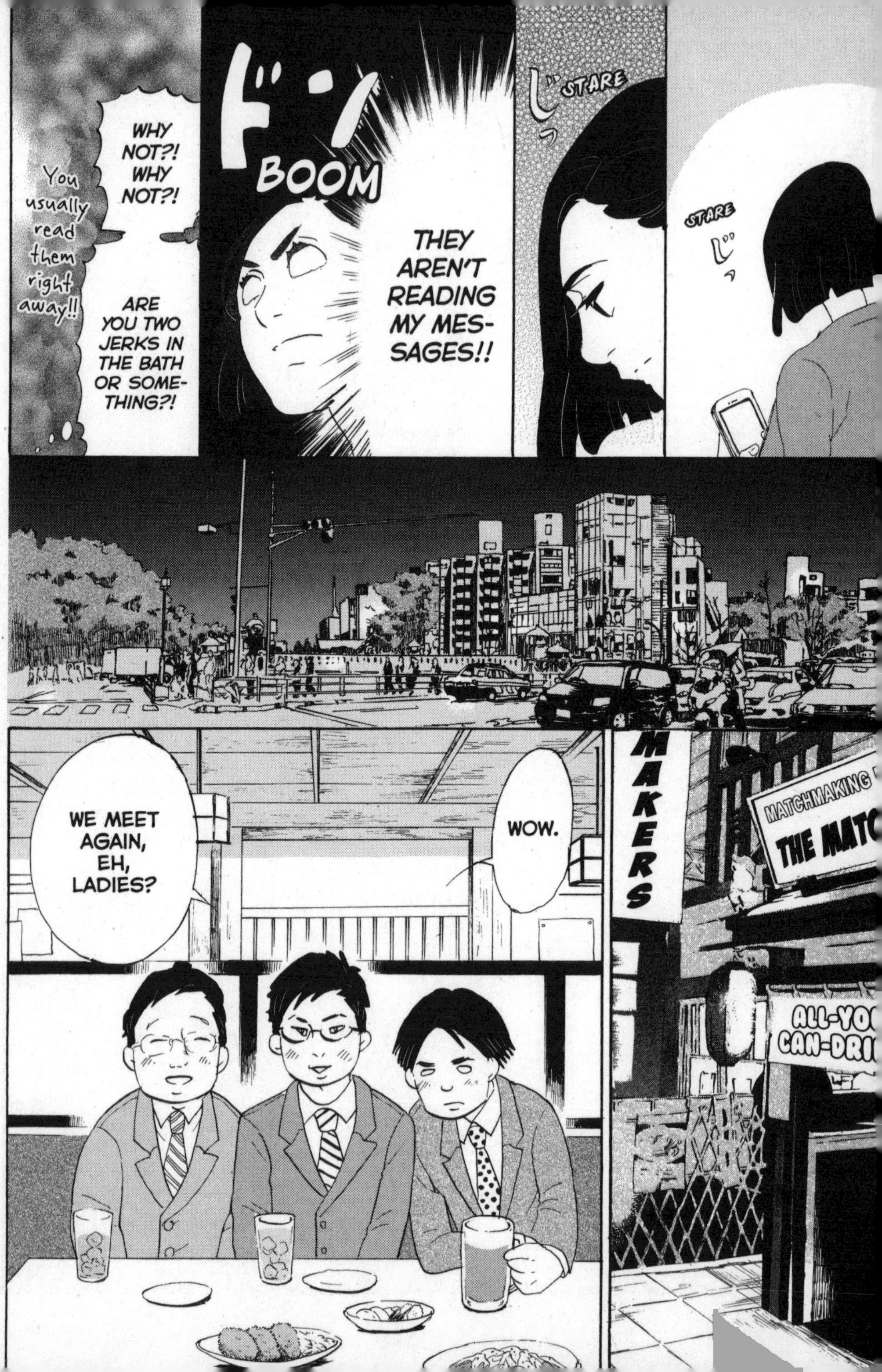

じっ
STARE
じっ
STARE
ドーン
BOOM
THEY AREN'T READING MY MES-SAGES!!
WHY NOT?! WHY NOT?!
You usually read them right away!!
ARE YOU TWO JERKS IN THE BATH OR SOME-THING?!
MAKERS
MATCHMAKING
THE MATC
ALL-YO
CAN-DRI
WOW.
WE MEET AGAIN, EH, LADIES?

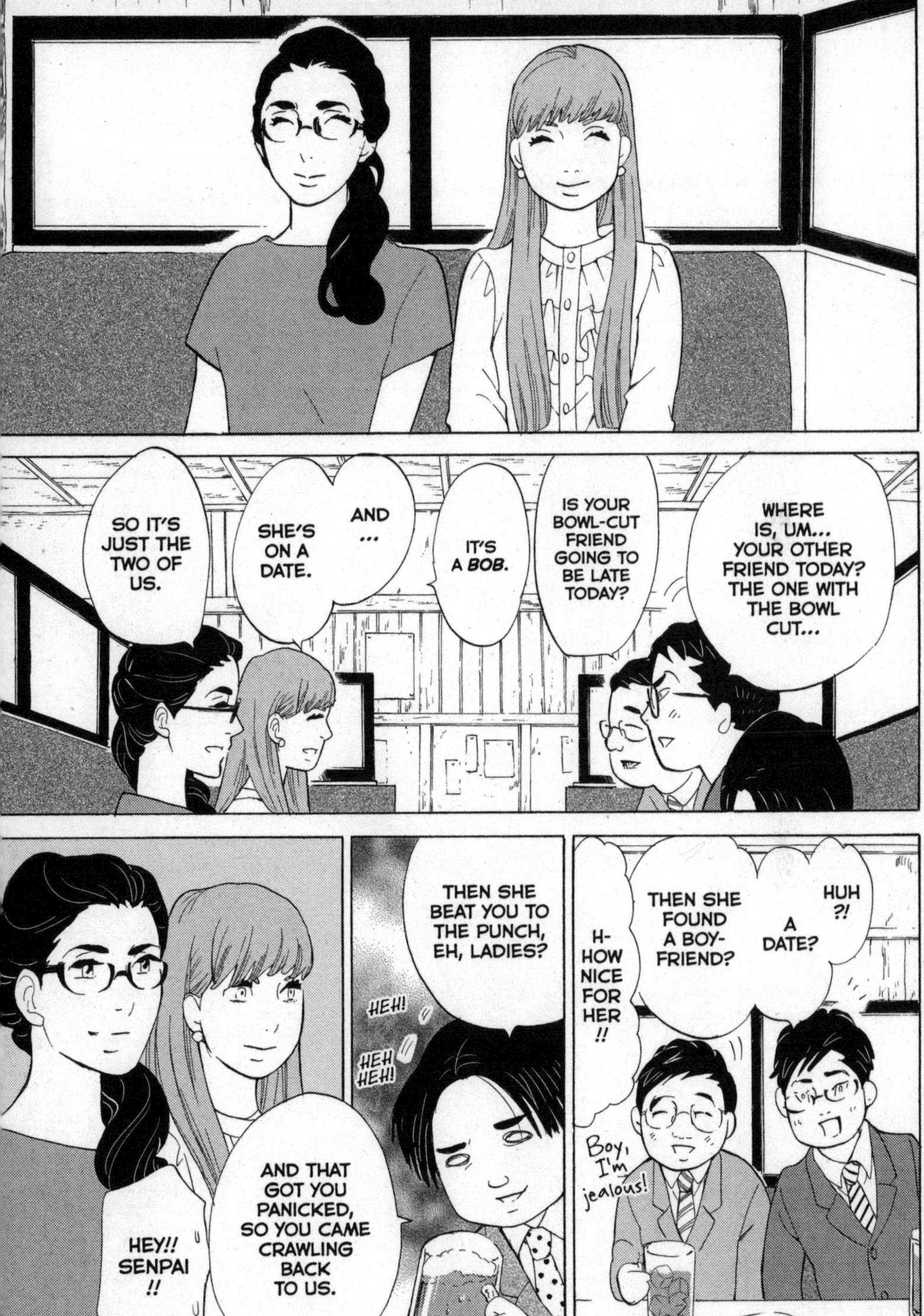

WHERE IS, UM... YOUR OTHER FRIEND TODAY? THE ONE WITH THE BOWL CUT...
IS YOUR BOWL-CUT FRIEND GOING TO BE LATE TODAY?
IT'S A *BOB*.
AND ...
SHE'S ON A DATE.
SO IT'S JUST THE TWO OF US.
HUH ?!
A DATE?
THEN SHE FOUND A BOY-FRIEND?
H- HOW NICE FOR HER !!
Boy, I'm jealous!
THEN SHE BEAT YOU TO THE PUNCH, EH, LADIES?
HEH!
HEH HEH!
AND THAT GOT YOU PANICKED, SO YOU CAME CRAWLING BACK TO US.
HEY!! SENPAI !!

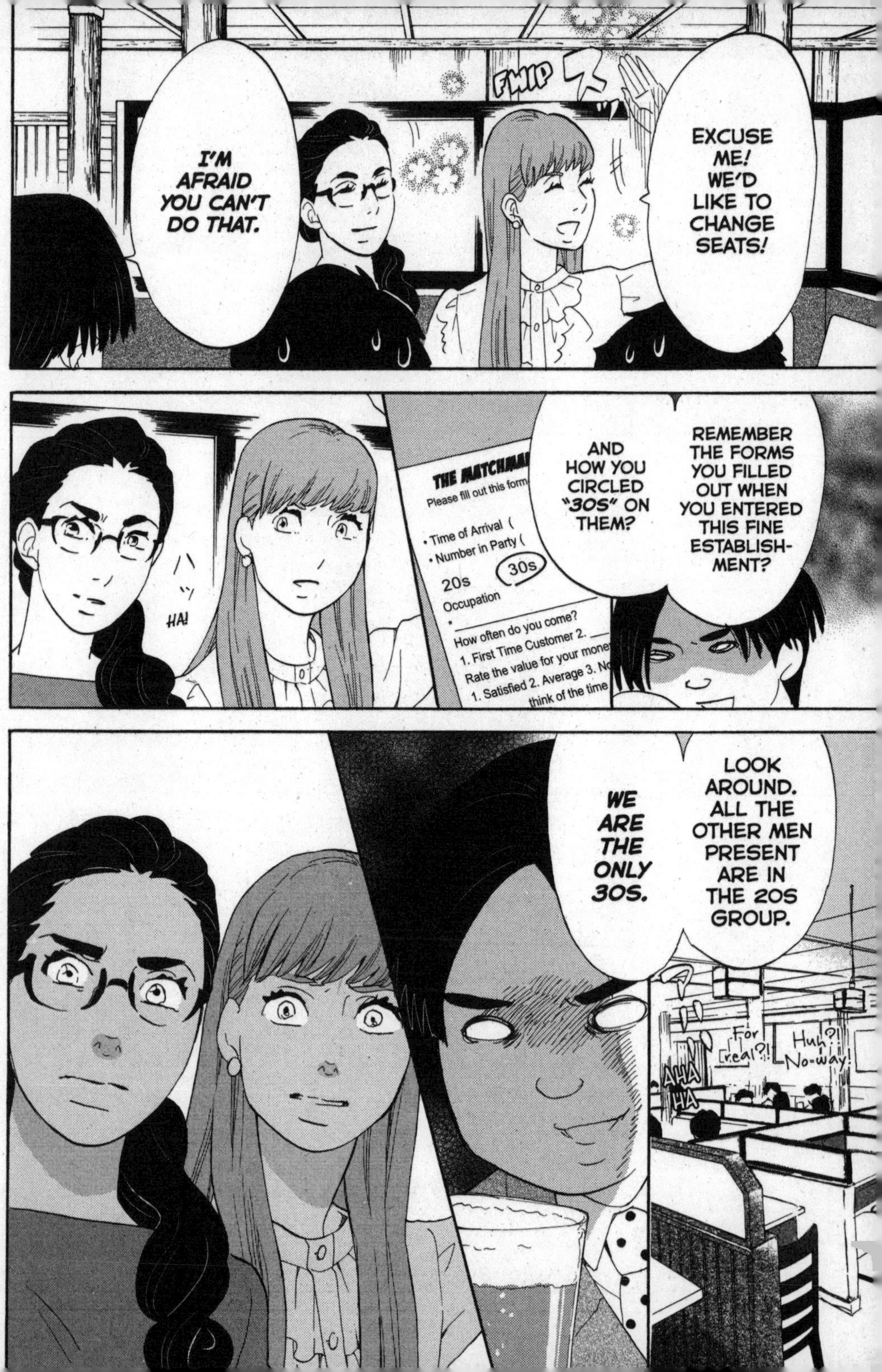
EXCUSE ME! WE'D LIKE TO CHANGE SEATS!
FWIP
I'M AFRAID YOU CAN'T DO THAT.
REMEMBER THE FORMS YOU FILLED OUT WHEN YOU ENTERED THIS FINE ESTABLISHMENT?
AND HOW YOU CIRCLED "30S" ON THEM?
Please fill out this form
• Time of Arrival (
• Number in Party (
20s
30s
Occupation
How often do you come?
1. First Time Customer 2.
Rate the value for your mone
1. Satisfied 2. Average 3. No
think of the time
HA!
LOOK AROUND. ALL THE OTHER MEN PRESENT ARE IN THE 20S GROUP.
WE ARE THE ONLY 30S.
Huh?! No-way!
For real?!
AHAHA

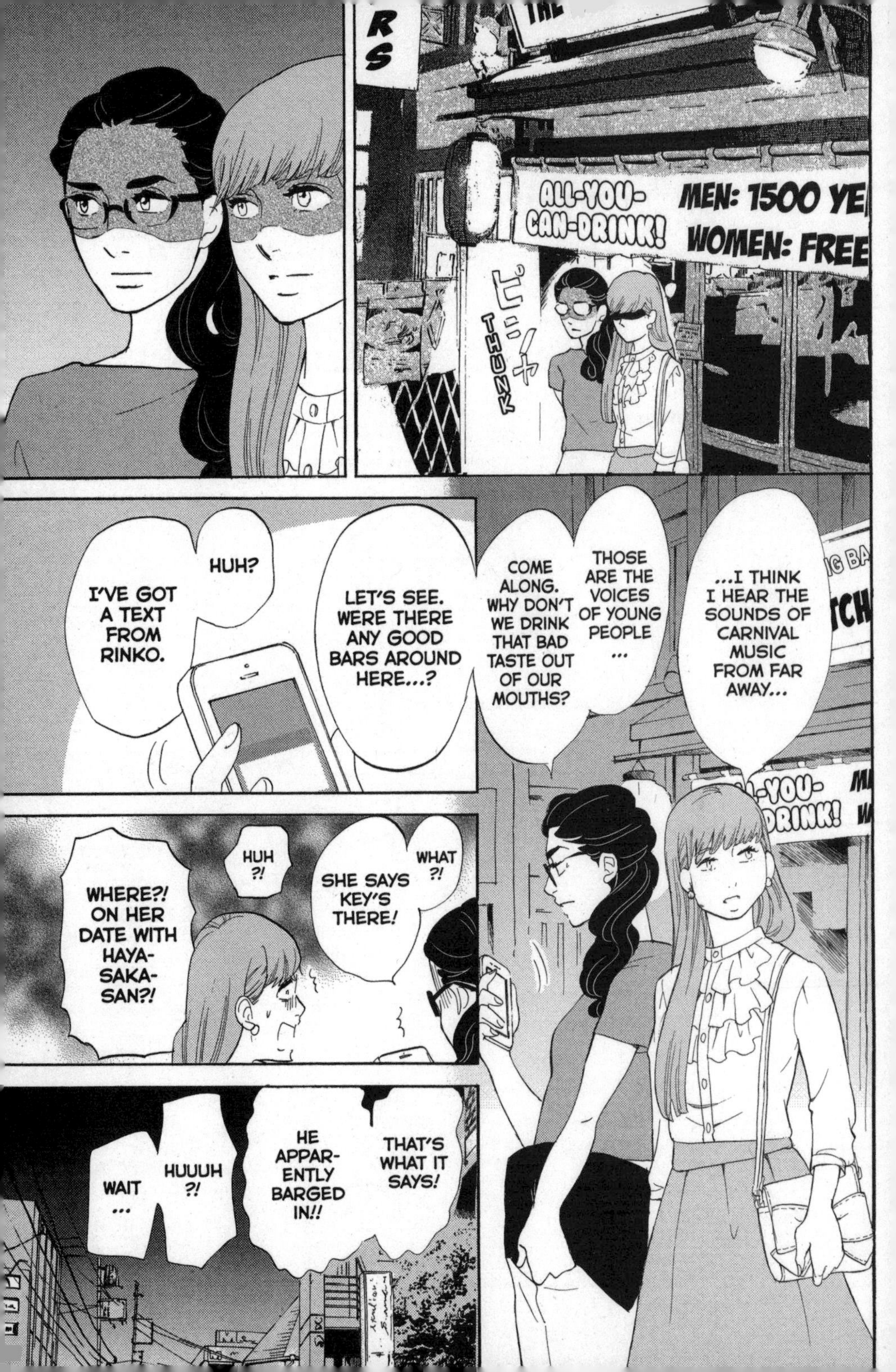
THE
RS
ALL-YOU-CAN-DRINK!
MEN: 1500 YE
WOMEN: FREE
ピシャ
THUNK
...I THINK I HEAR THE SOUNDS OF CARNIVAL MUSIC FROM FAR AWAY...
THOSE ARE THE VOICES OF YOUNG PEOPLE...
COME ALONG. WHY DON'T WE DRINK THAT BAD TASTE OUT OF OUR MOUTHS?
LET'S SEE. WERE THERE ANY GOOD BARS AROUND HERE...?
HUH?
I'VE GOT A TEXT FROM RINKO.
WHAT?!
SHE SAYS KEY'S THERE!
HUH?!
WHERE?! ON HER DATE WITH HAYA-SAKA-SAN?!
THAT'S WHAT IT SAYS!
HE APPARENTLY BARGED IN!!
HUUUH?!
WAIT...

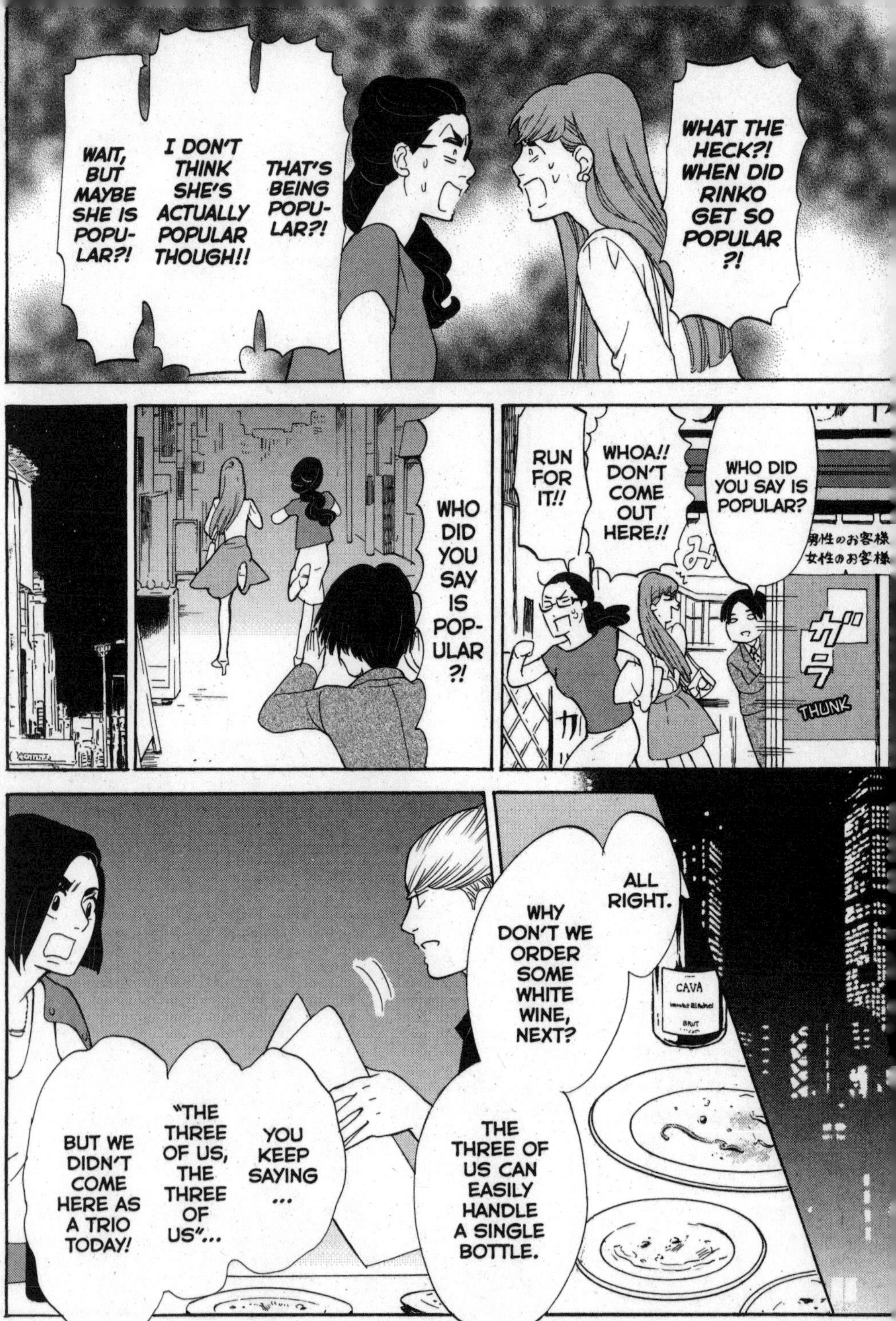
WHAT THE HECK?! WHEN DID RINKO GET SO POPULAR?!
THAT'S BEING POPULAR?!
I DON'T THINK SHE'S ACTUALLY POPULAR THOUGH!!
WAIT, BUT MAYBE SHE IS POPULAR?!
男性のお客様
女性のお客様
WHO DID YOU SAY IS POPULAR?
WHOA!! DON'T COME OUT HERE!!
RUN FOR IT!!
ガラ
THUNK
WHO DID YOU SAY IS POPULAR?!
ALL RIGHT.
WHY DON'T WE ORDER SOME WHITE WINE, NEXT?
CAVA
BRUT
THE THREE OF US CAN EASILY HANDLE A SINGLE BOTTLE.
YOU KEEP SAYING ...
"THE THREE OF US, THE THREE OF US"...
BUT WE DIDN'T COME HERE AS A TRIO TODAY!

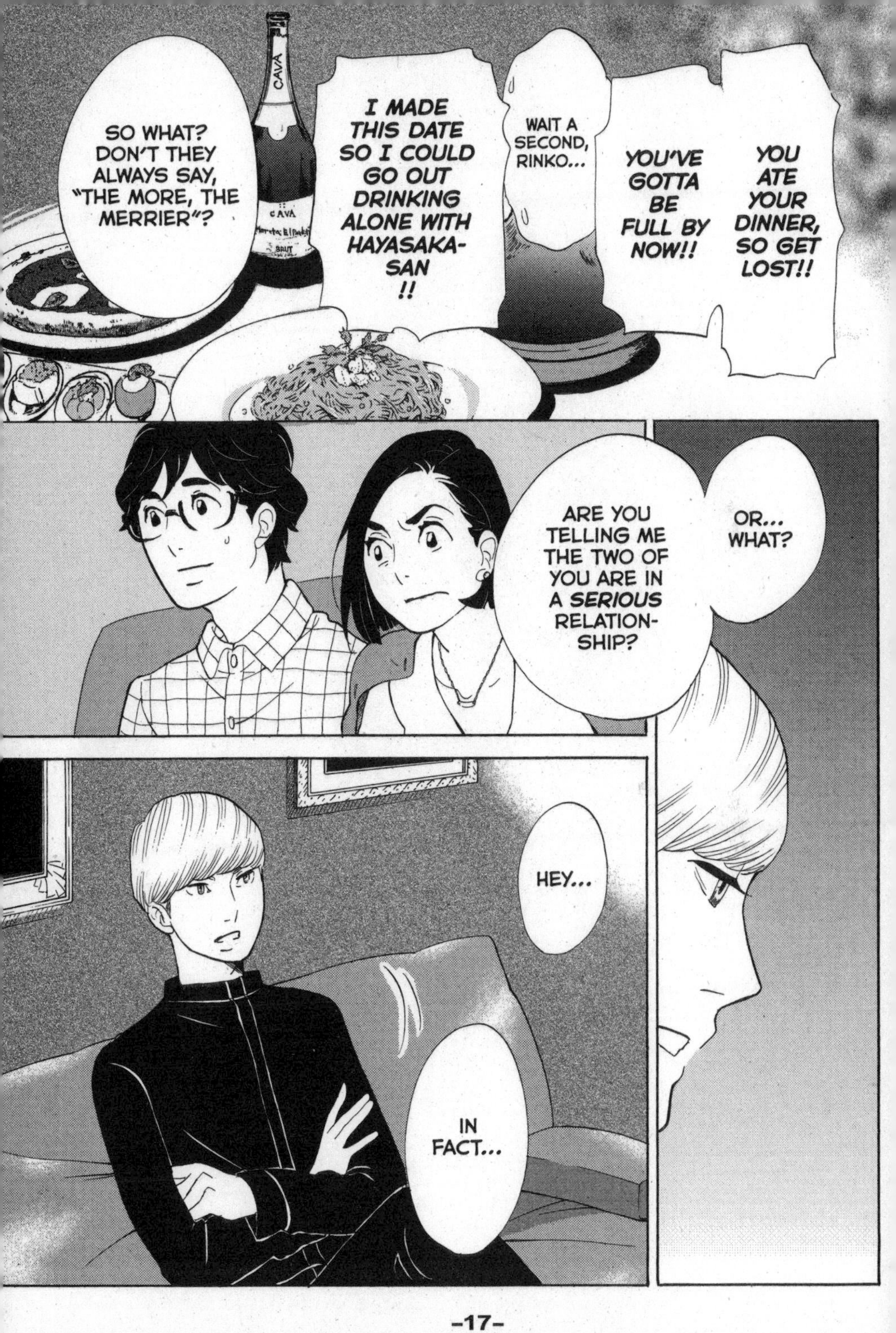
YOU ATE YOUR DINNER, SO GET LOST!!
YOU'VE GOTTA BE FULL BY NOW!!
WAIT A SECOND, RINKO...
I MADE THIS DATE SO I COULD GO OUT DRINKING ALONE WITH HAYASAKA-SAN !!
SO WHAT? DON'T THEY ALWAYS SAY, "THE MORE, THE MERRIER"?
ARE YOU TELLING ME THE TWO OF YOU ARE IN A *SERIOUS* RELATIONSHIP?
OR... WHAT?
HEY...
IN FACT...

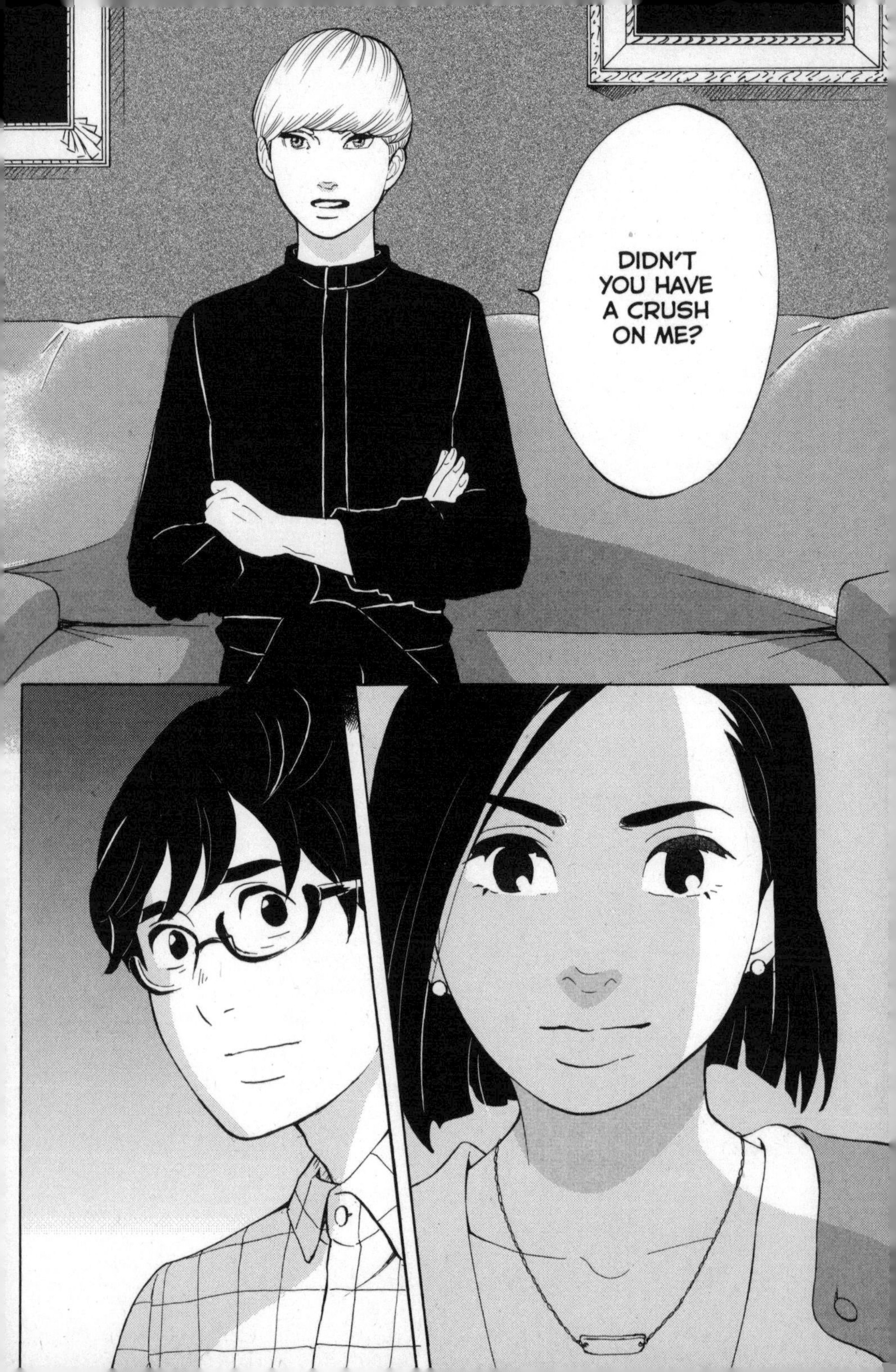
DIDN'T YOU HAVE A CRUSH ON ME?

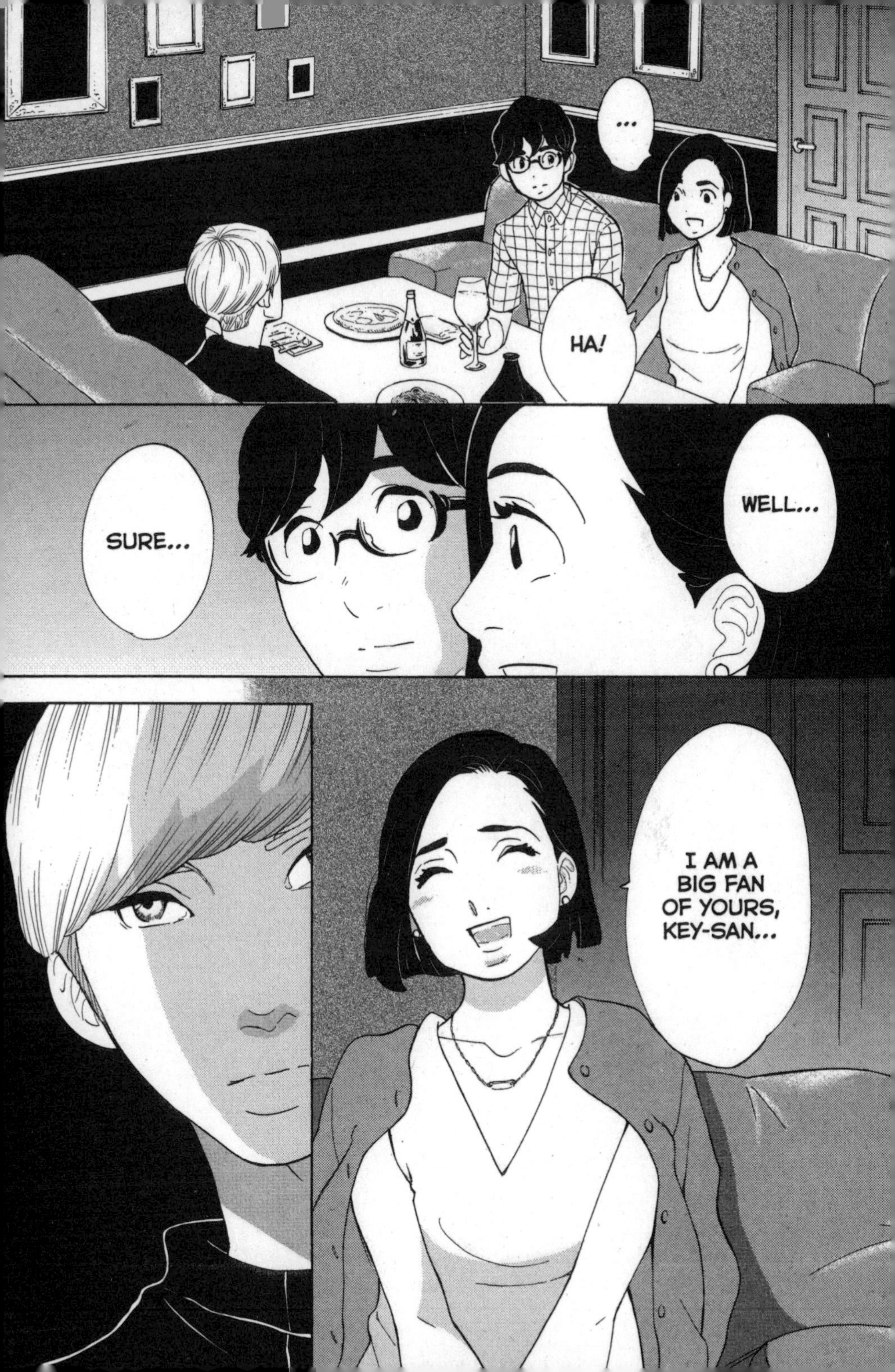
...
HA!
WELL...
SURE...
I AM A BIG FAN OF YOURS, KEY-SAN...

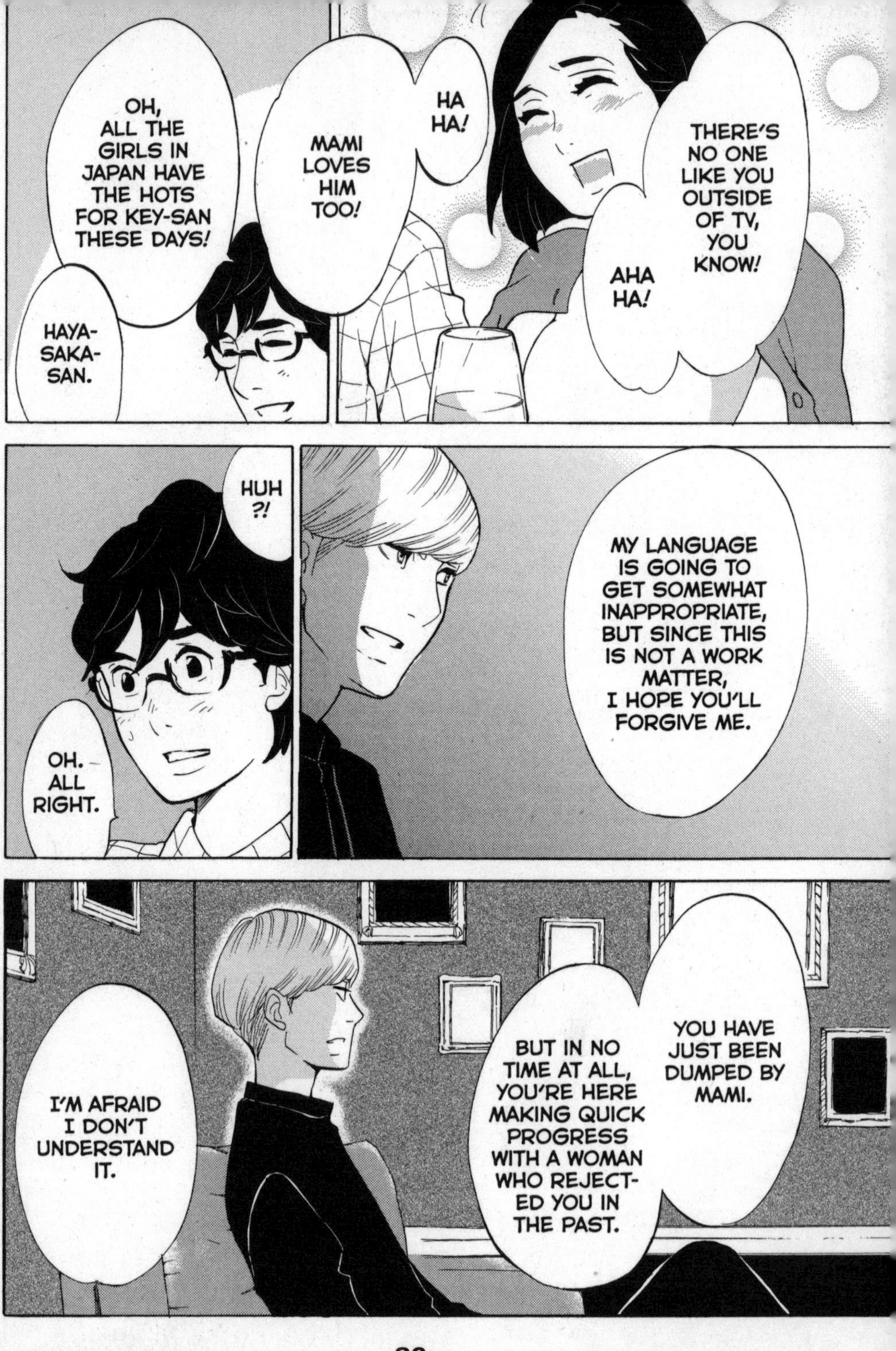
THERE'S NO ONE LIKE YOU OUTSIDE OF TV, YOU KNOW!
AHA HA!
HA HA!
MAMI LOVES HIM TOO!
OH, ALL THE GIRLS IN JAPAN HAVE THE HOTS FOR KEY-SAN THESE DAYS!
HAYA-SAKA-SAN.
MY LANGUAGE IS GOING TO GET SOMEWHAT INAPPROPRIATE, BUT SINCE THIS IS NOT A WORK MATTER, I HOPE YOU'LL FORGIVE ME.
HUH ?!
OH. ALL RIGHT.
YOU HAVE JUST BEEN DUMPED BY MAMI.
BUT IN NO TIME AT ALL, YOU'RE HERE MAKING QUICK PROGRESS WITH A WOMAN WHO REJECT-ED YOU IN THE PAST.
I'M AFRAID I DON'T UNDERSTAND IT.

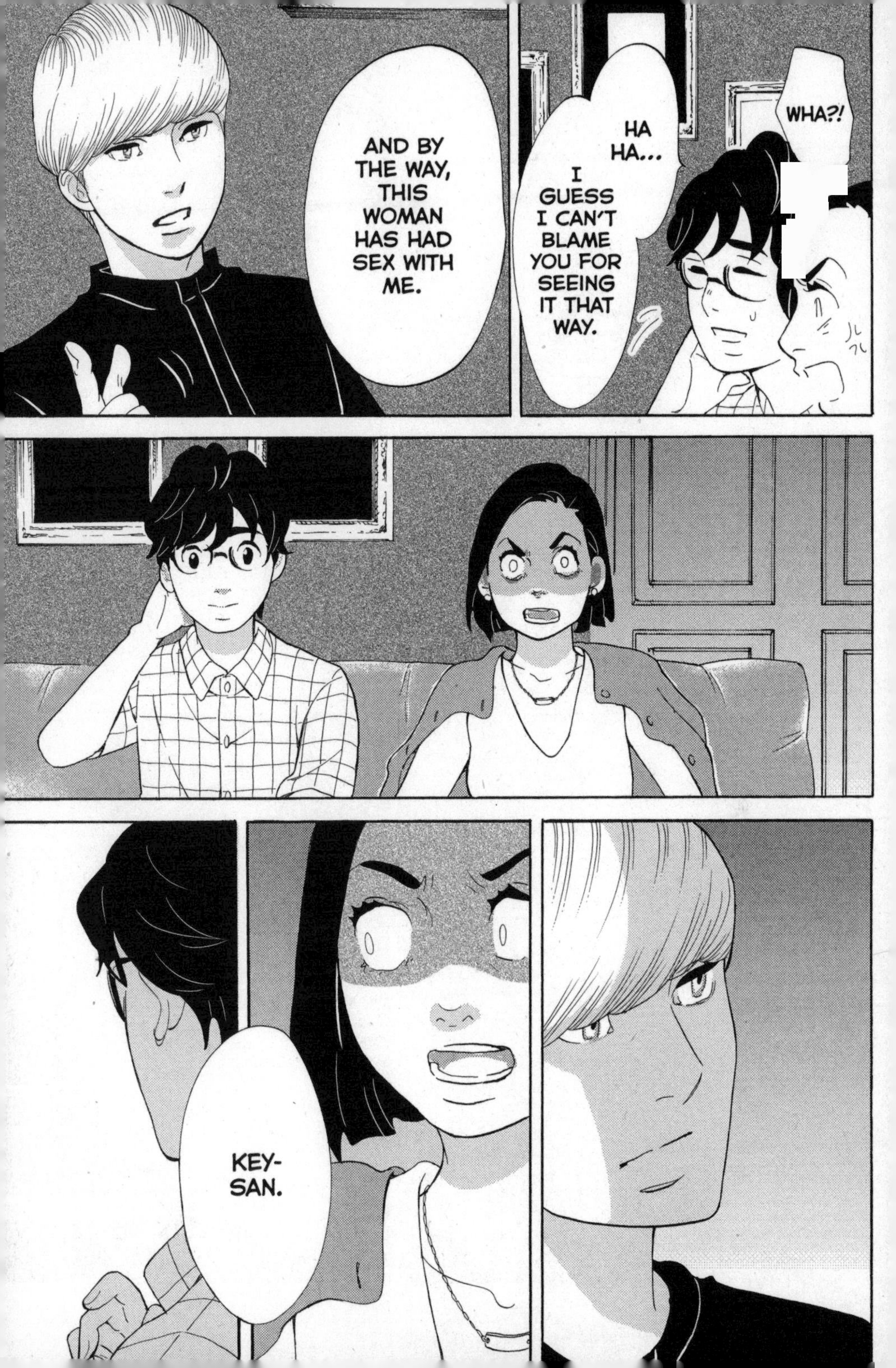
WHA?!
HA HA...
I GUESS I CAN'T BLAME YOU FOR SEEING IT THAT WAY.
AND BY THE WAY, THIS WOMAN HAS HAD SEX WITH ME.
KEY-SAN.

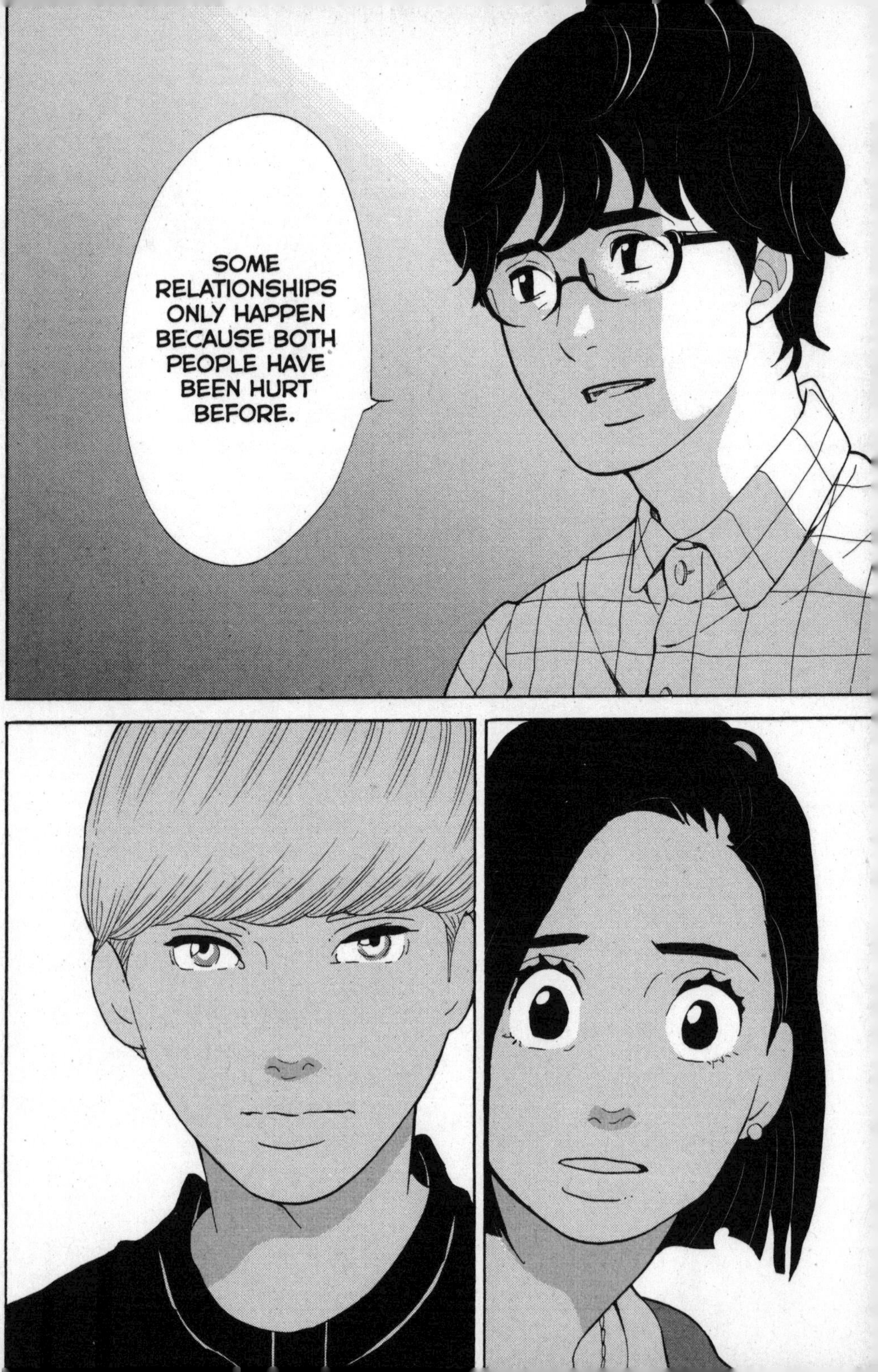
SOME RELATIONSHIPS ONLY HAPPEN BECAUSE BOTH PEOPLE HAVE BEEN HURT BEFORE.

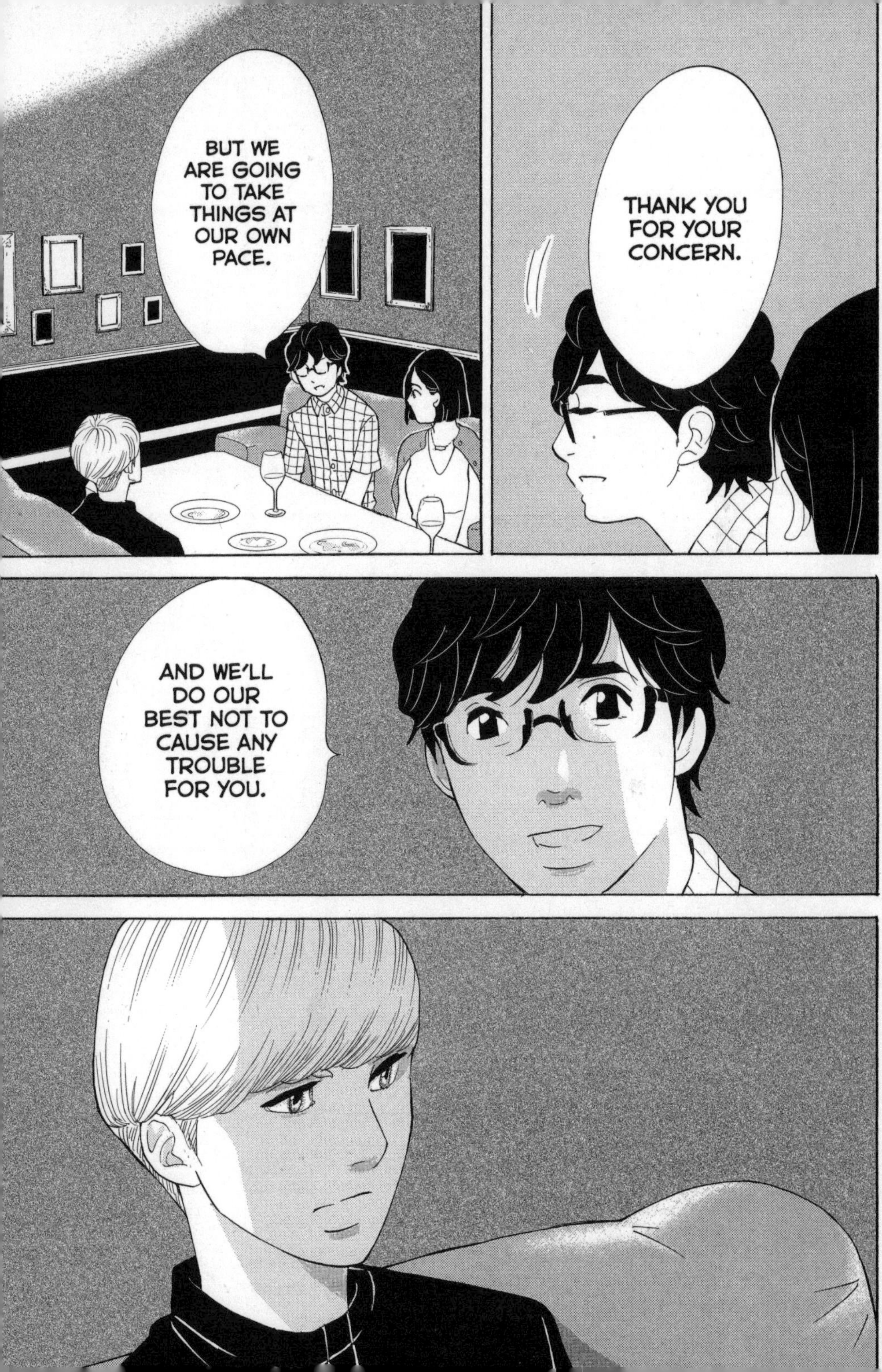
THANK YOU FOR YOUR CONCERN.
BUT WE ARE GOING TO TAKE THINGS AT OUR OWN PACE.
AND WE'LL DO OUR BEST NOT TO CAUSE ANY TROUBLE FOR YOU.

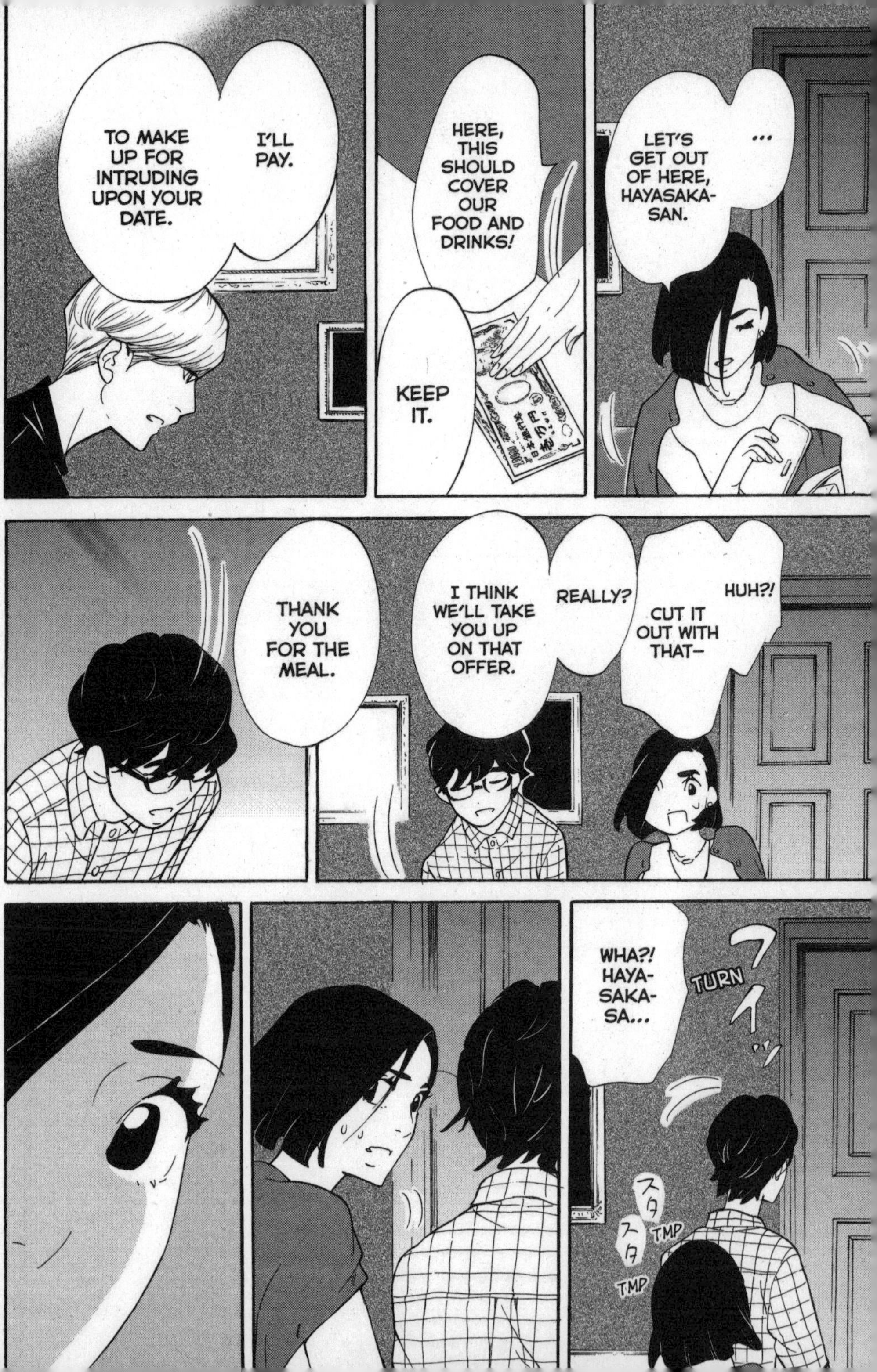
...
LET'S GET OUT OF HERE, HAYASAKA-SAN.
HERE, THIS SHOULD COVER OUR FOOD AND DRINKS!
KEEP IT.
I'LL PAY.
TO MAKE UP FOR INTRUDING UPON YOUR DATE.
HUH?!
CUT IT OUT WITH THAT—
REALLY?
I THINK WE'LL TAKE YOU UP ON THAT OFFER.
THANK YOU FOR THE MEAL.
WHA?! HAYA-SAKA-SA...
TURN
TMP
TMP

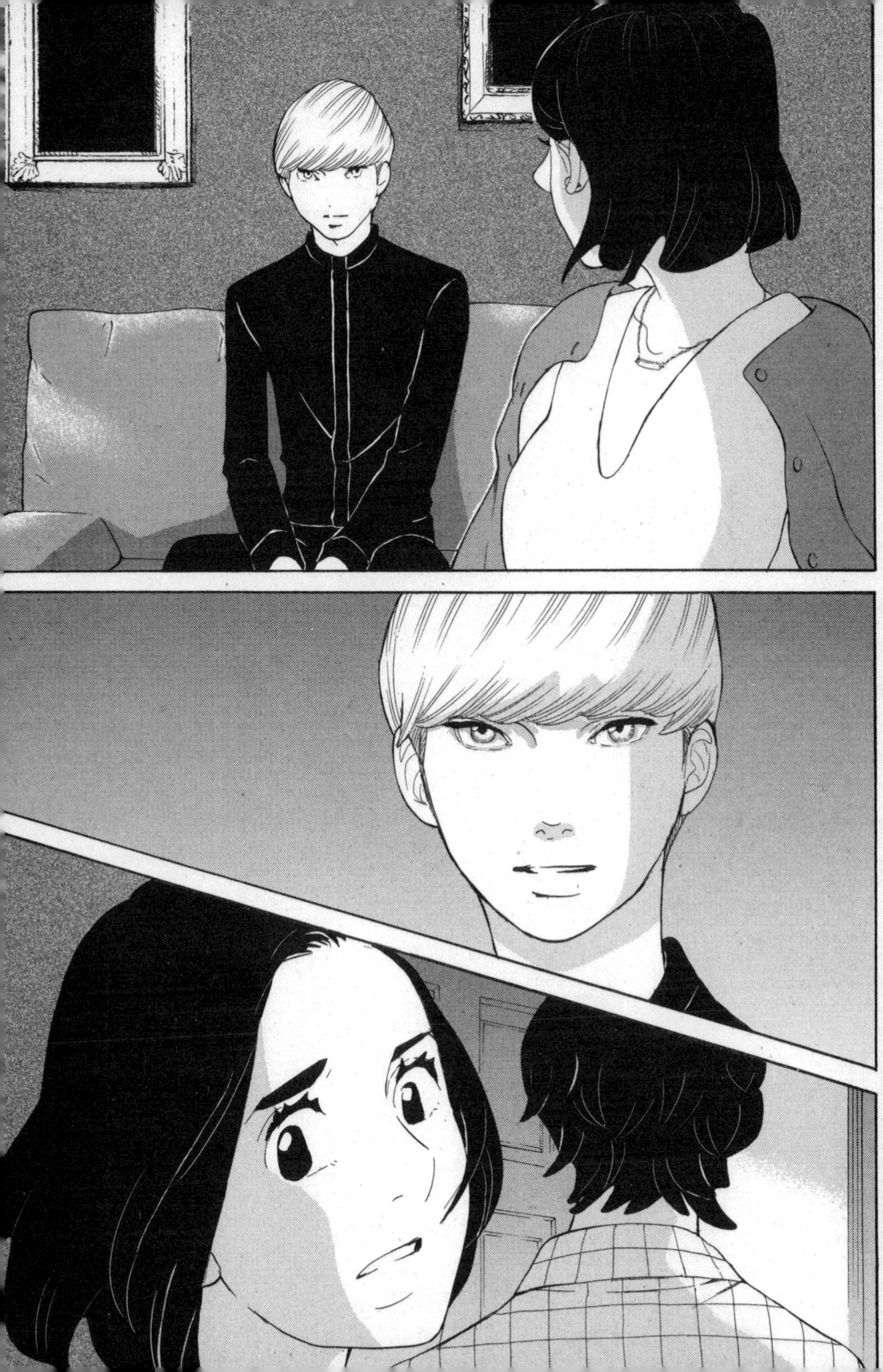

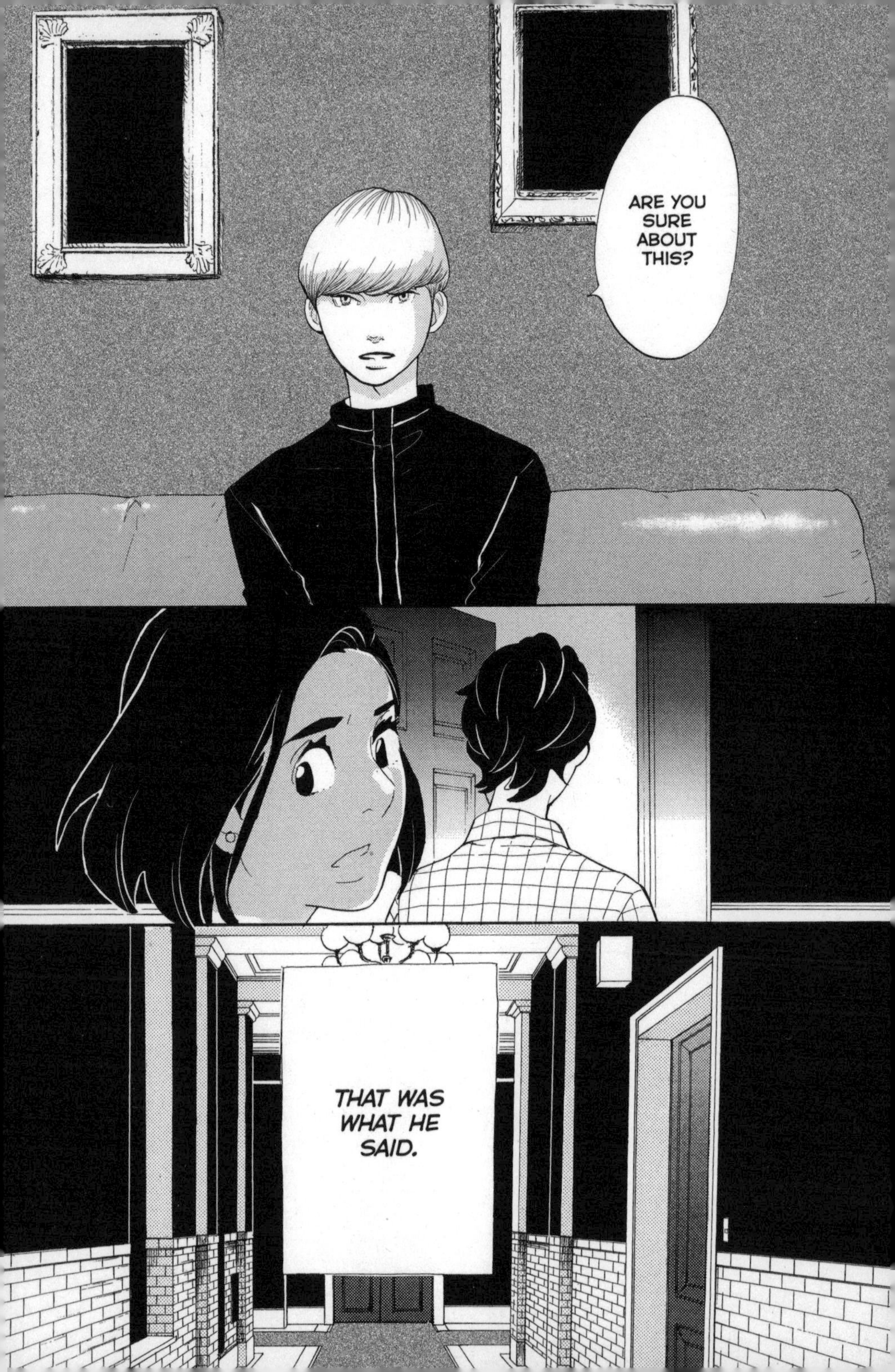
ARE YOU SURE ABOUT THIS?
THAT WAS WHAT HE SAID.

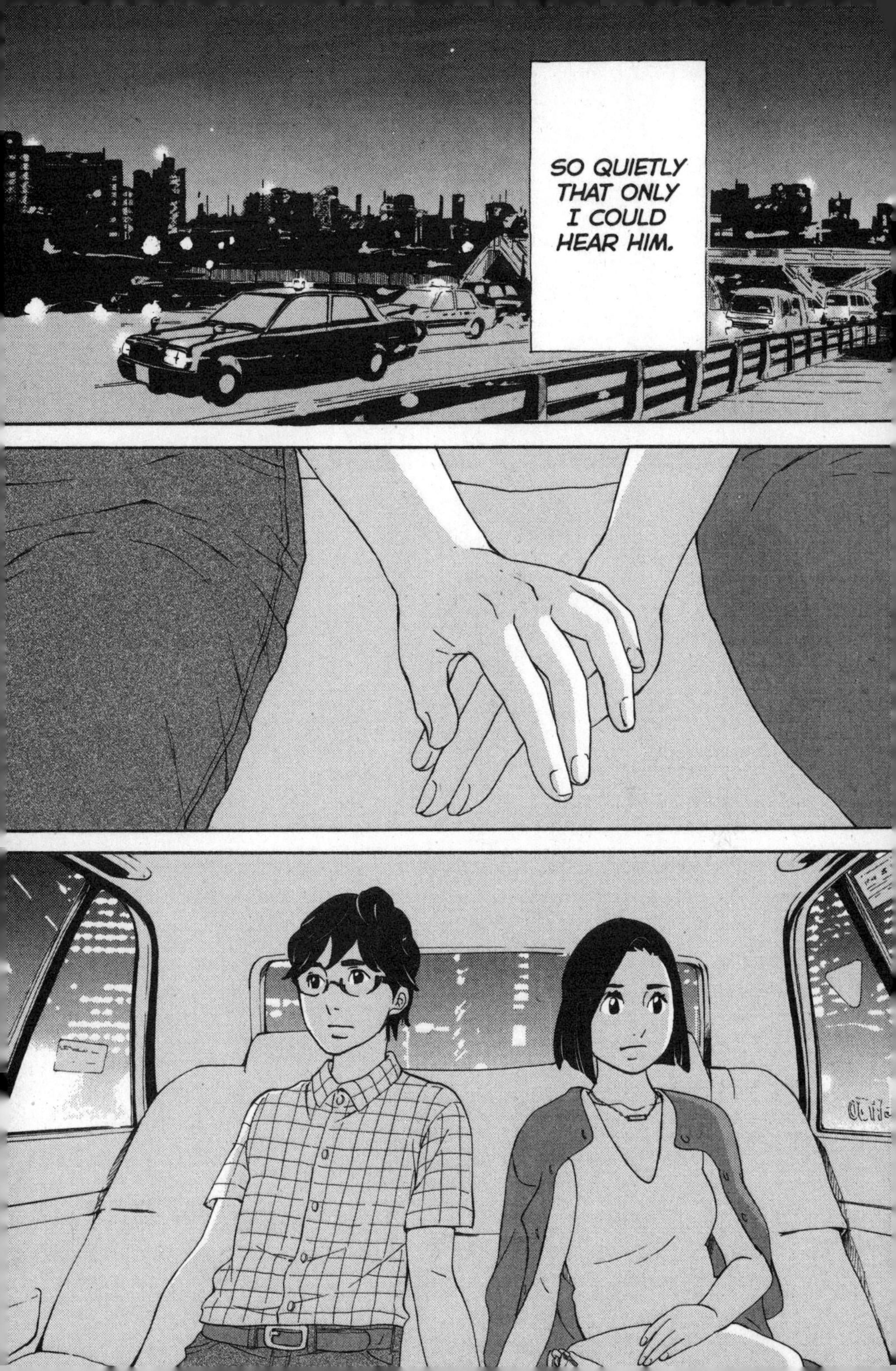
SO QUIETLY THAT ONLY I COULD HEAR HIM.

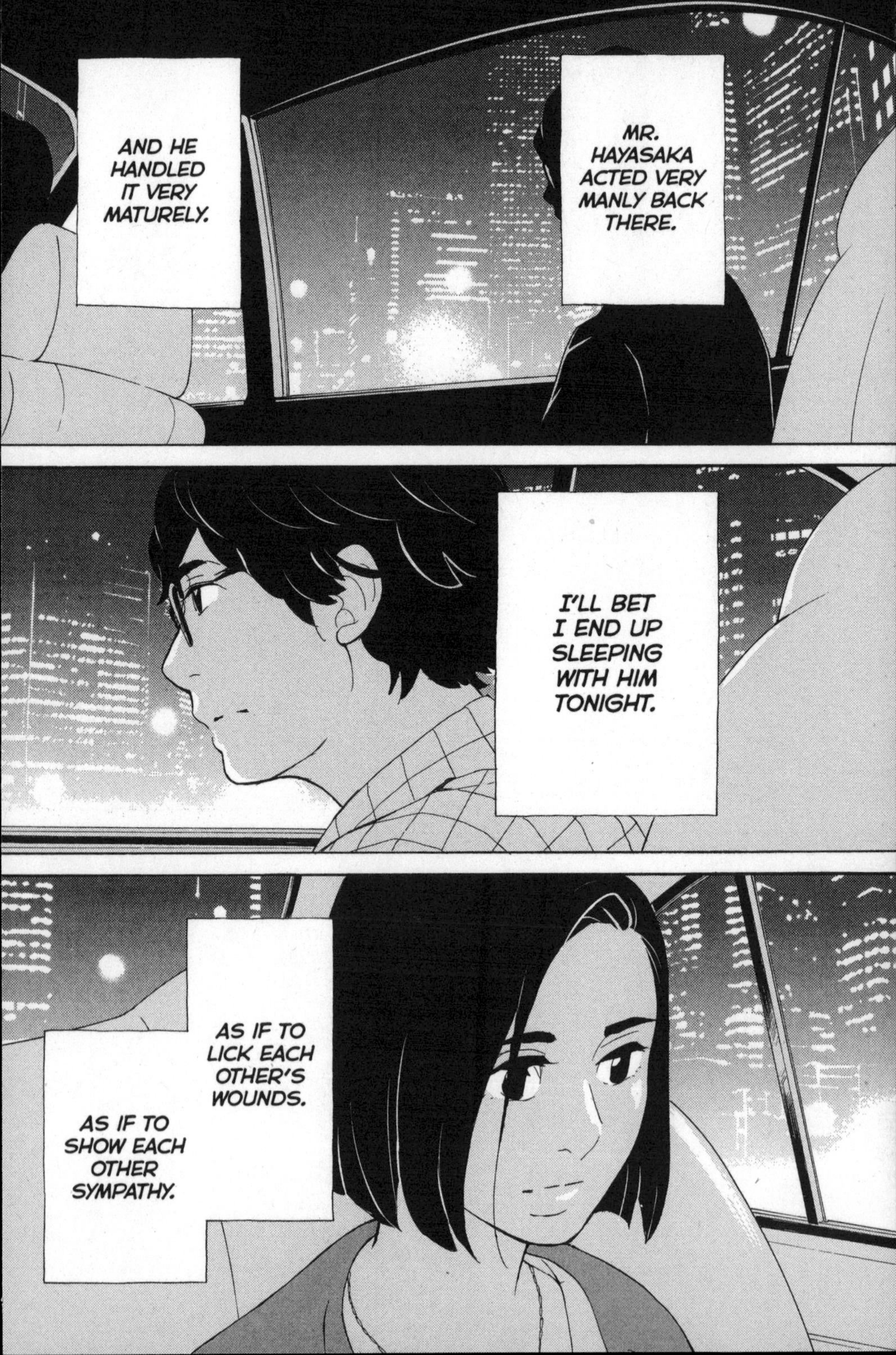
MR. HAYASAKA ACTED VERY MANLY BACK THERE.
AND HE HANDLED IT VERY MATURELY.
I'LL BET I END UP SLEEPING WITH HIM TONIGHT.
AS IF TO LICK EACH OTHER'S WOUNDS.
AS IF TO SHOW EACH OTHER SYMPATHY.

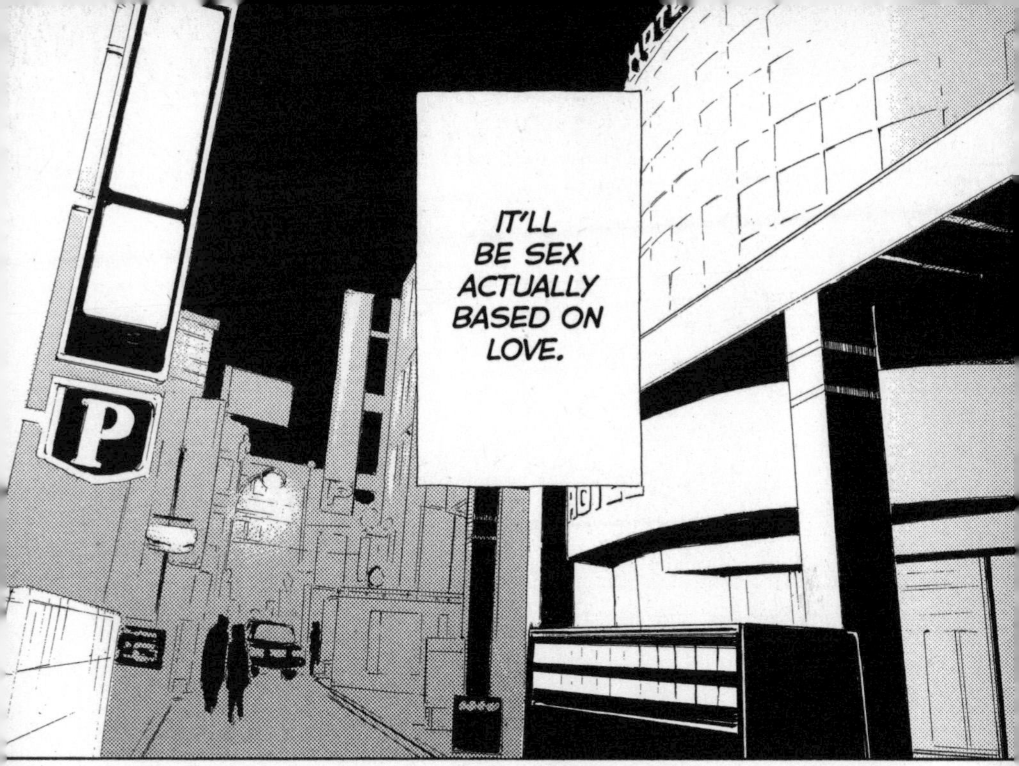
IT'LL BE SEX ACTUALLY BASED ON LOVE.
P

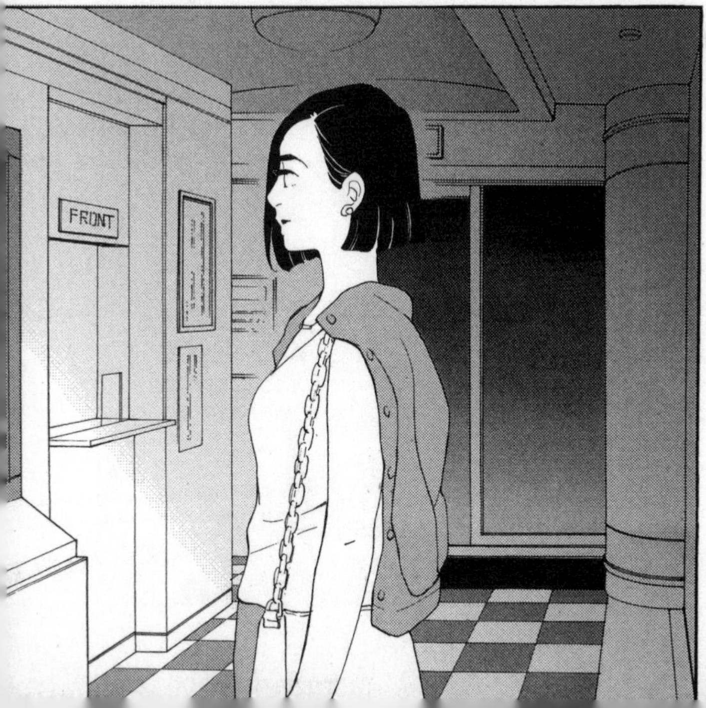
FRONT

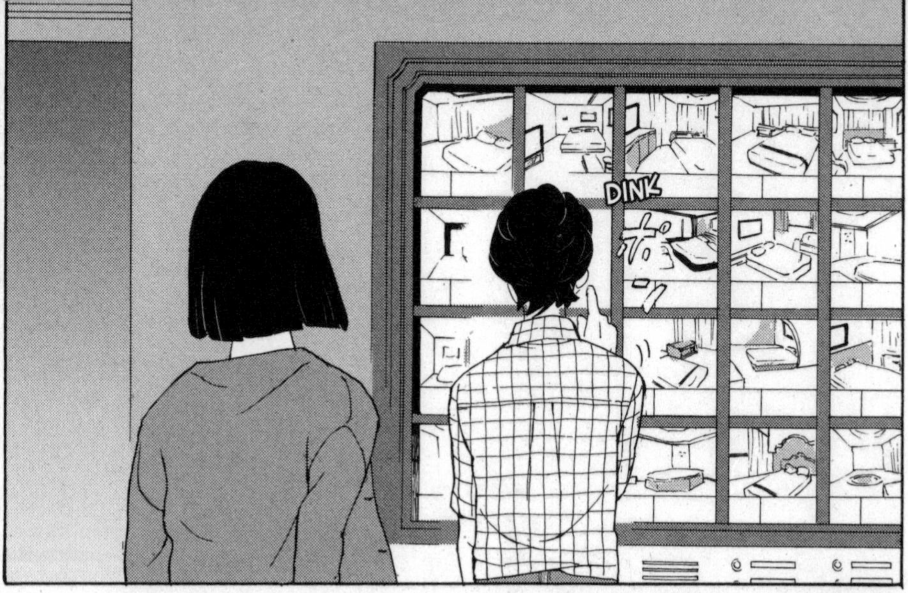
DINK

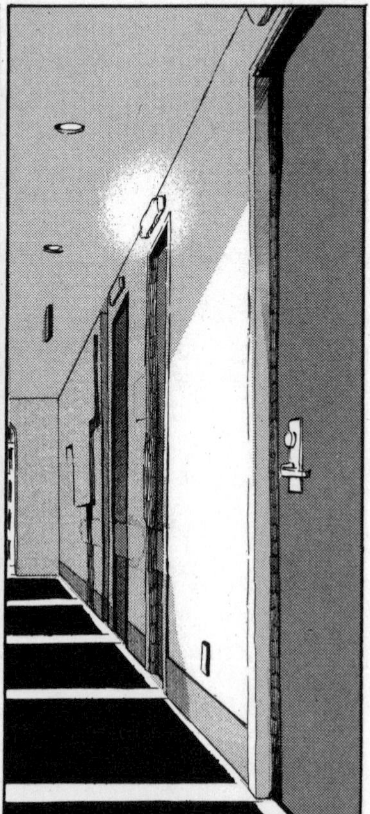

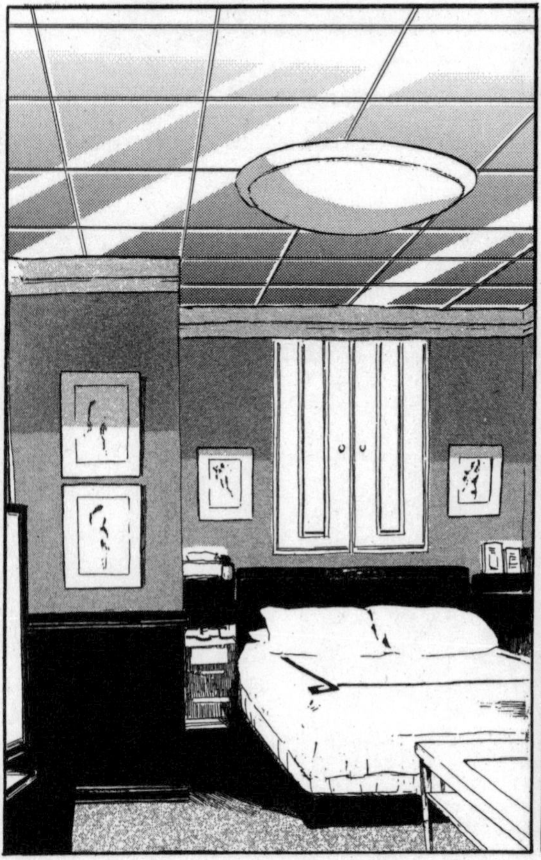

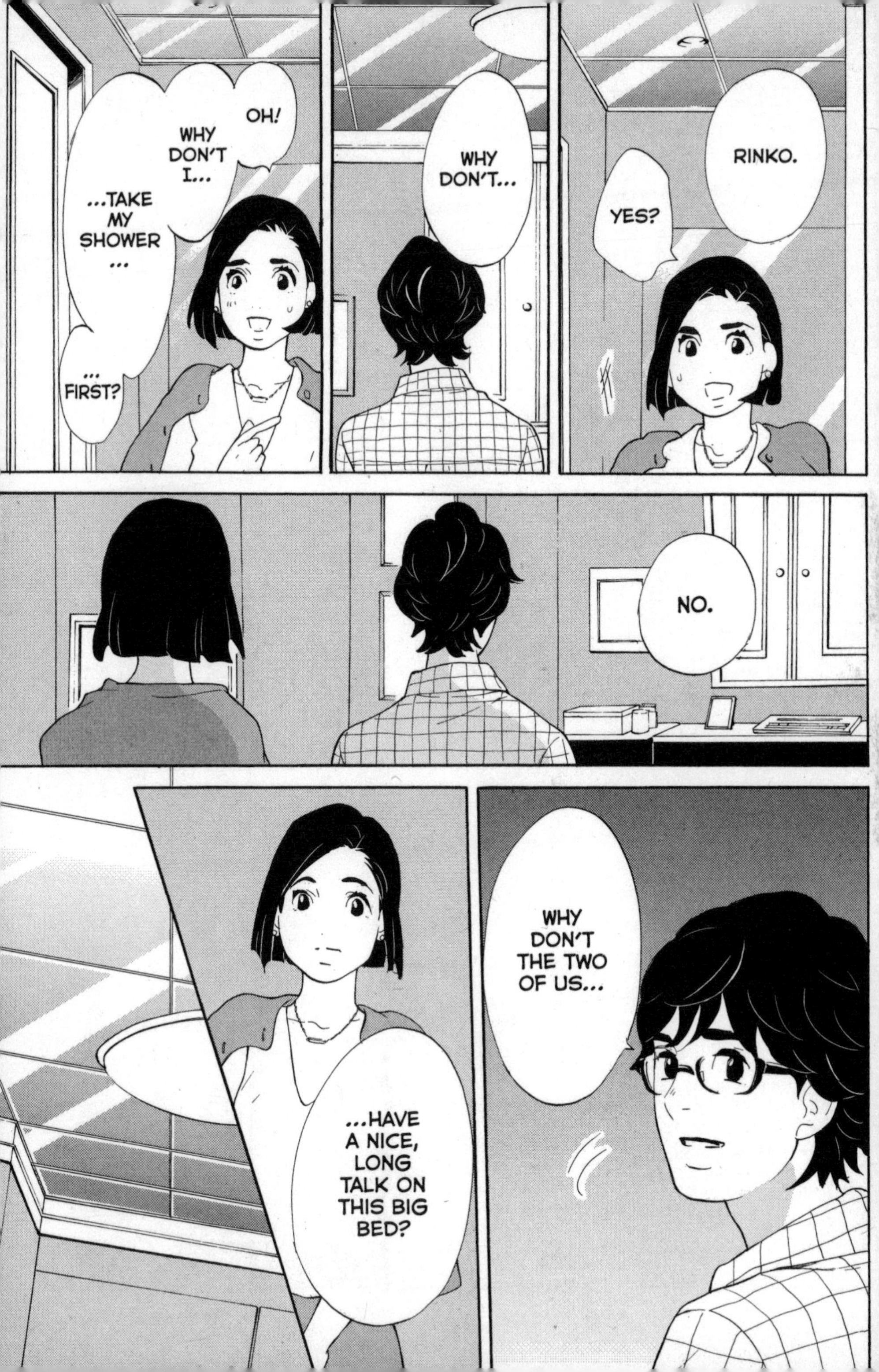
RINKO.
YES?
WHY DON'T...
OH!
WHY DON'T I...
...TAKE MY SHOWER ...
... FIRST?
NO.
WHY DON'T THE TWO OF US...
...HAVE A NICE, LONG TALK ON THIS BIG BED?

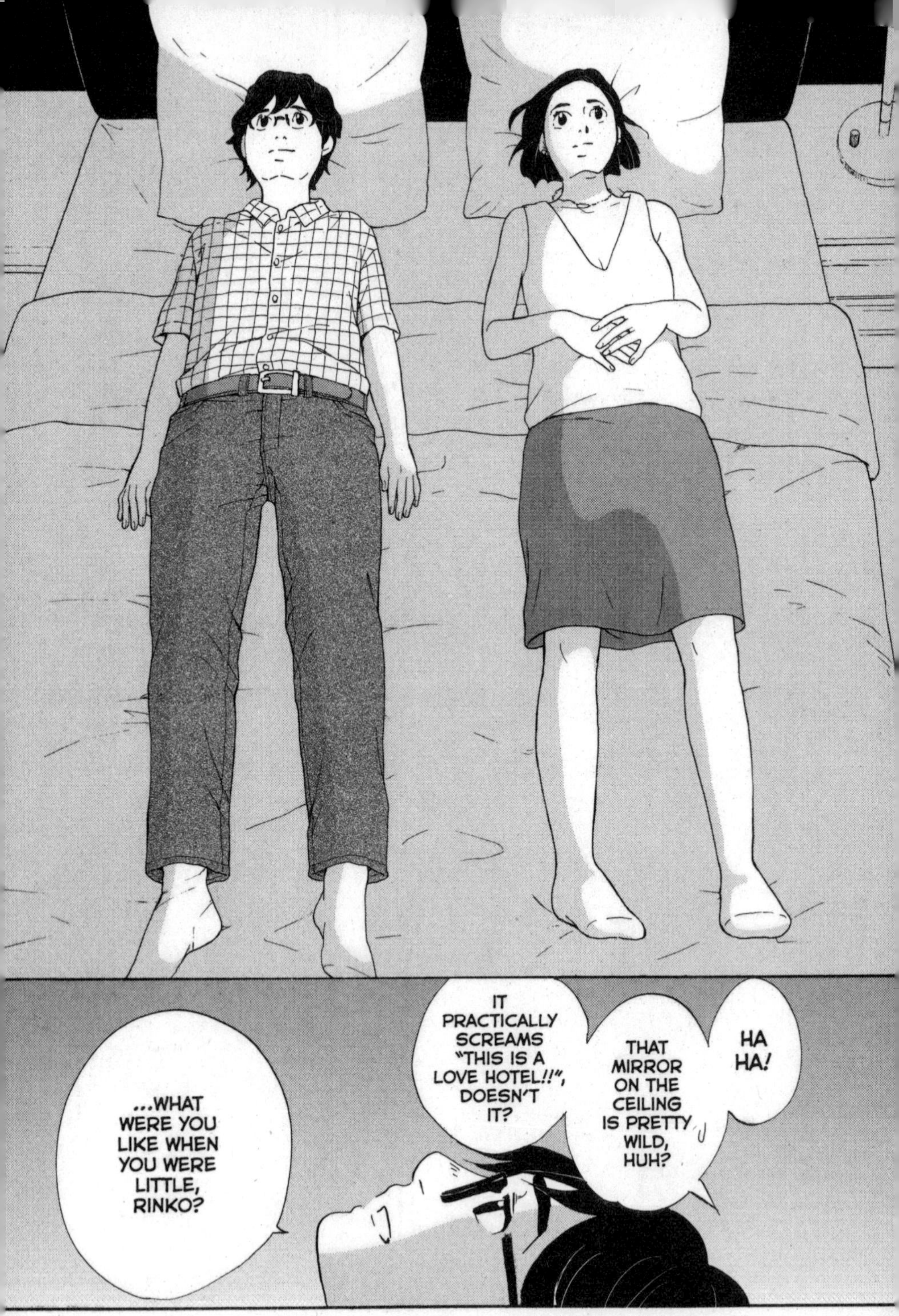
HA HA!
THAT MIRROR ON THE CEILING IS PRETTY WILD, HUH?
IT PRACTICALLY SCREAMS "THIS IS A LOVE HOTEL!!", DOESN'T IT?
...WHAT WERE YOU LIKE WHEN YOU WERE LITTLE, RINKO?

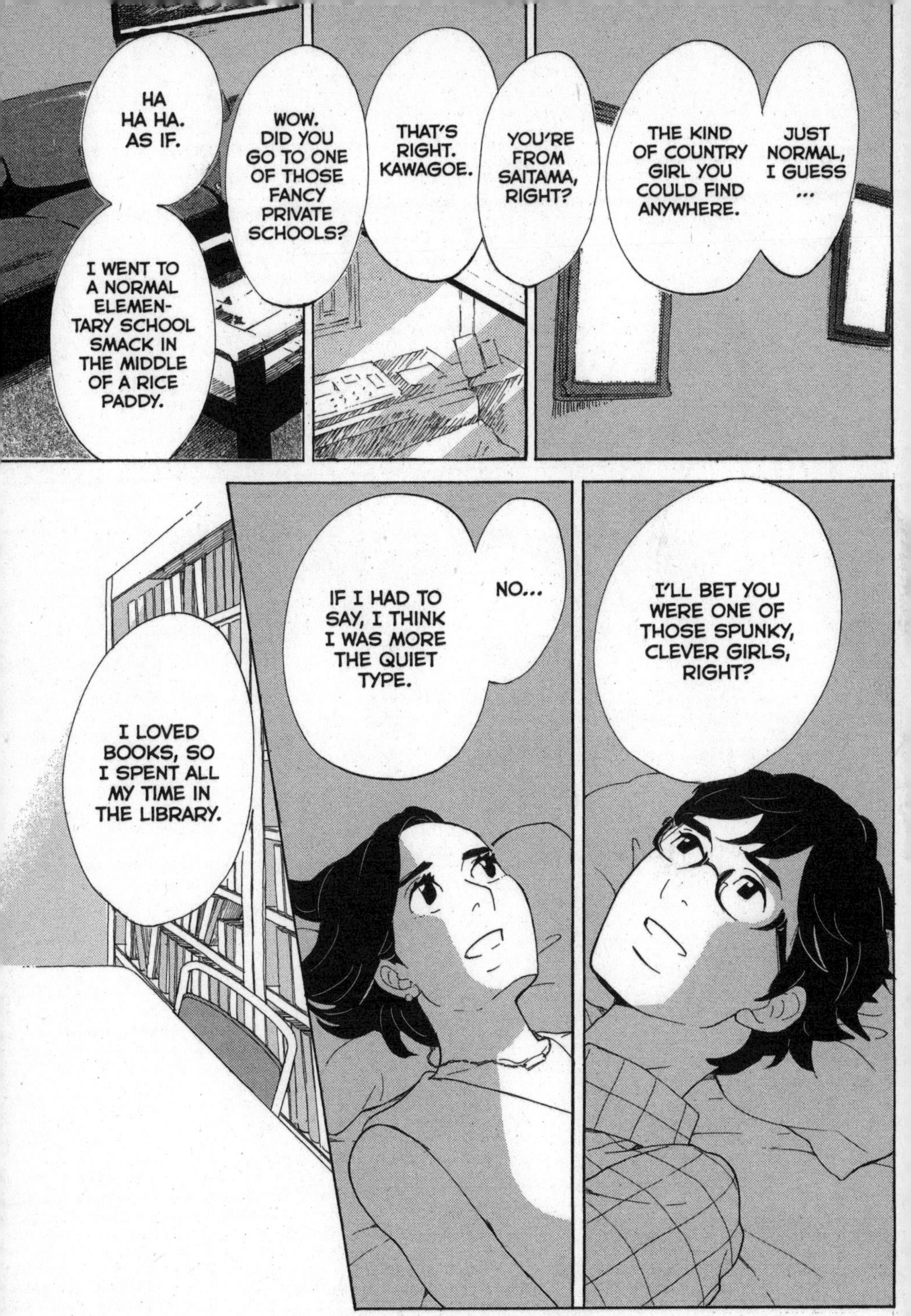
JUST NORMAL, I GUESS ...
THE KIND OF COUNTRY GIRL YOU COULD FIND ANYWHERE.
YOU'RE FROM SAITAMA, RIGHT?
THAT'S RIGHT. KAWAGOE.
WOW. DID YOU GO TO ONE OF THOSE FANCY PRIVATE SCHOOLS?
HA HA HA. AS IF.
I WENT TO A NORMAL ELEMENTARY SCHOOL SMACK IN THE MIDDLE OF A RICE PADDY.
I'LL BET YOU WERE ONE OF THOSE SPUNKY, CLEVER GIRLS, RIGHT?
NO...
IF I HAD TO SAY, I THINK I WAS MORE THE QUIET TYPE.
I LOVED BOOKS, SO I SPENT ALL MY TIME IN THE LIBRARY.

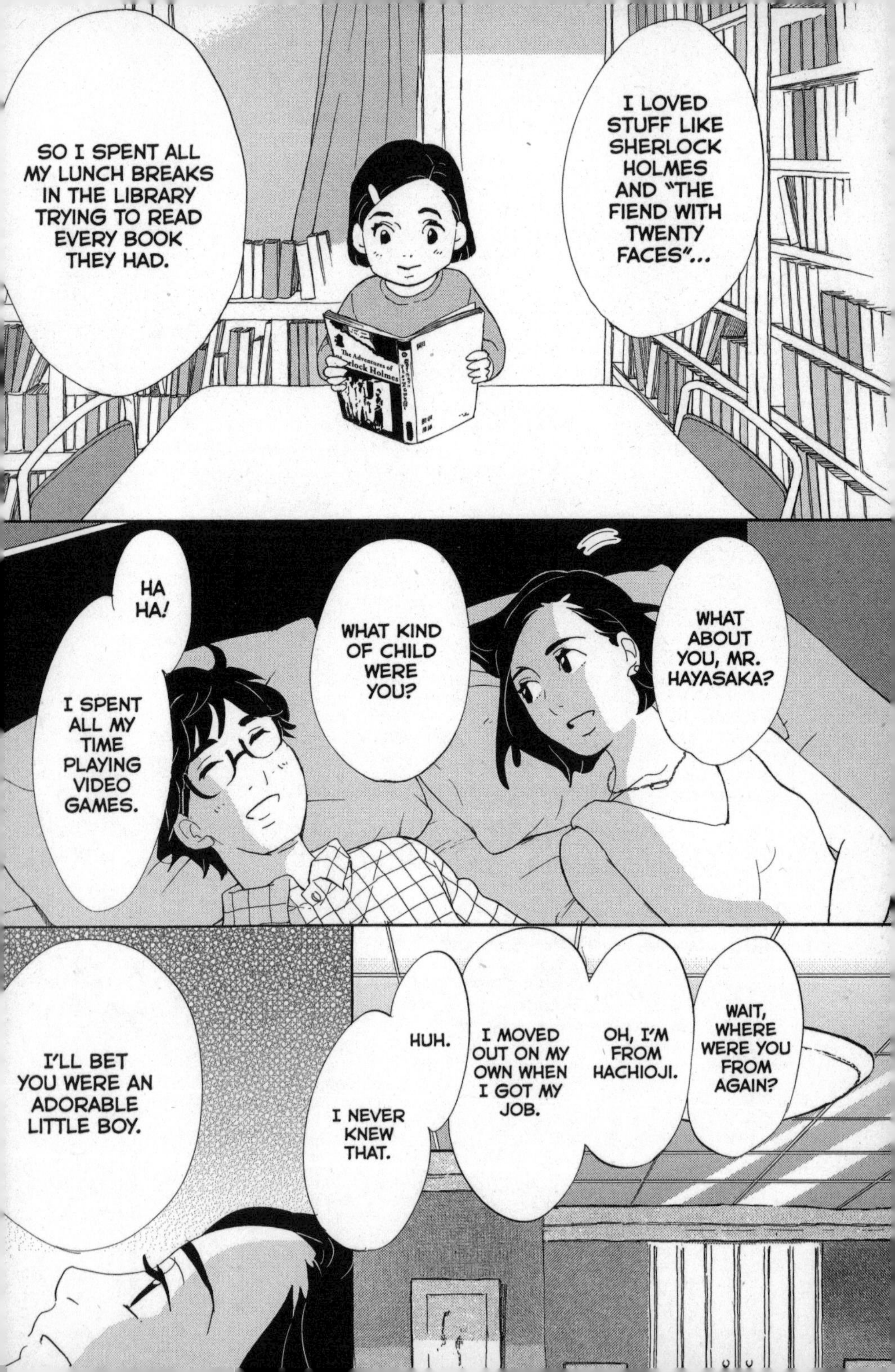
I LOVED STUFF LIKE SHERLOCK HOLMES AND "THE FIEND WITH TWENTY FACES"...
SO I SPENT ALL MY LUNCH BREAKS IN THE LIBRARY TRYING TO READ EVERY BOOK THEY HAD.
WHAT ABOUT YOU, MR. HAYASAKA?
WHAT KIND OF CHILD WERE YOU?
HA HA!
I SPENT ALL MY TIME PLAYING VIDEO GAMES.
WAIT, WHERE WERE YOU FROM AGAIN?
OH, I'M FROM HACHIOJI.
I MOVED OUT ON MY OWN WHEN I GOT MY JOB.
HUH.
I NEVER KNEW THAT.
I'LL BET YOU WERE AN ADORABLE LITTLE BOY.

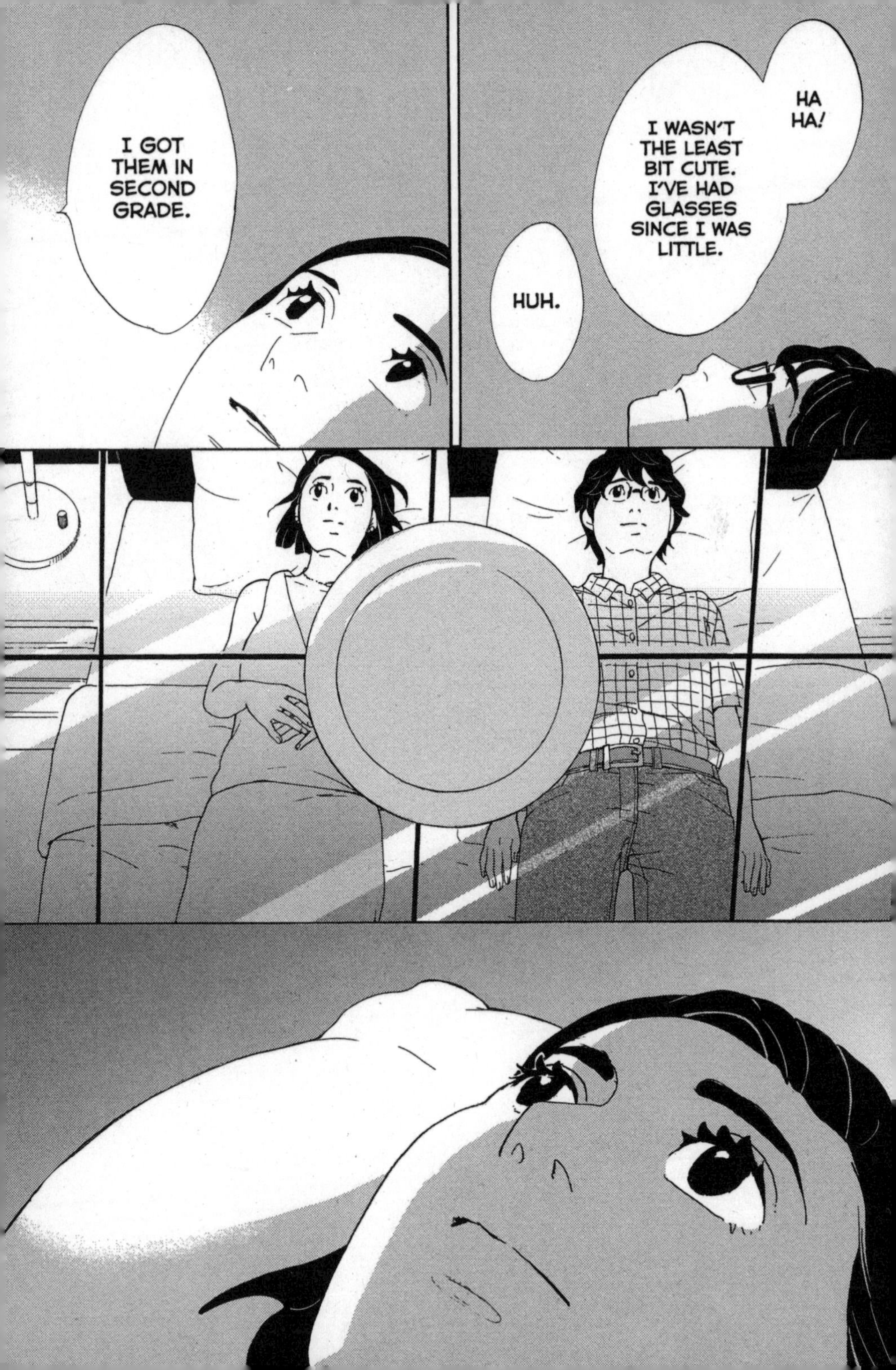
HA HA!
I WASN'T THE LEAST BIT CUTE. I'VE HAD GLASSES SINCE I WAS LITTLE.
HUH.
I GOT THEM IN SECOND GRADE.

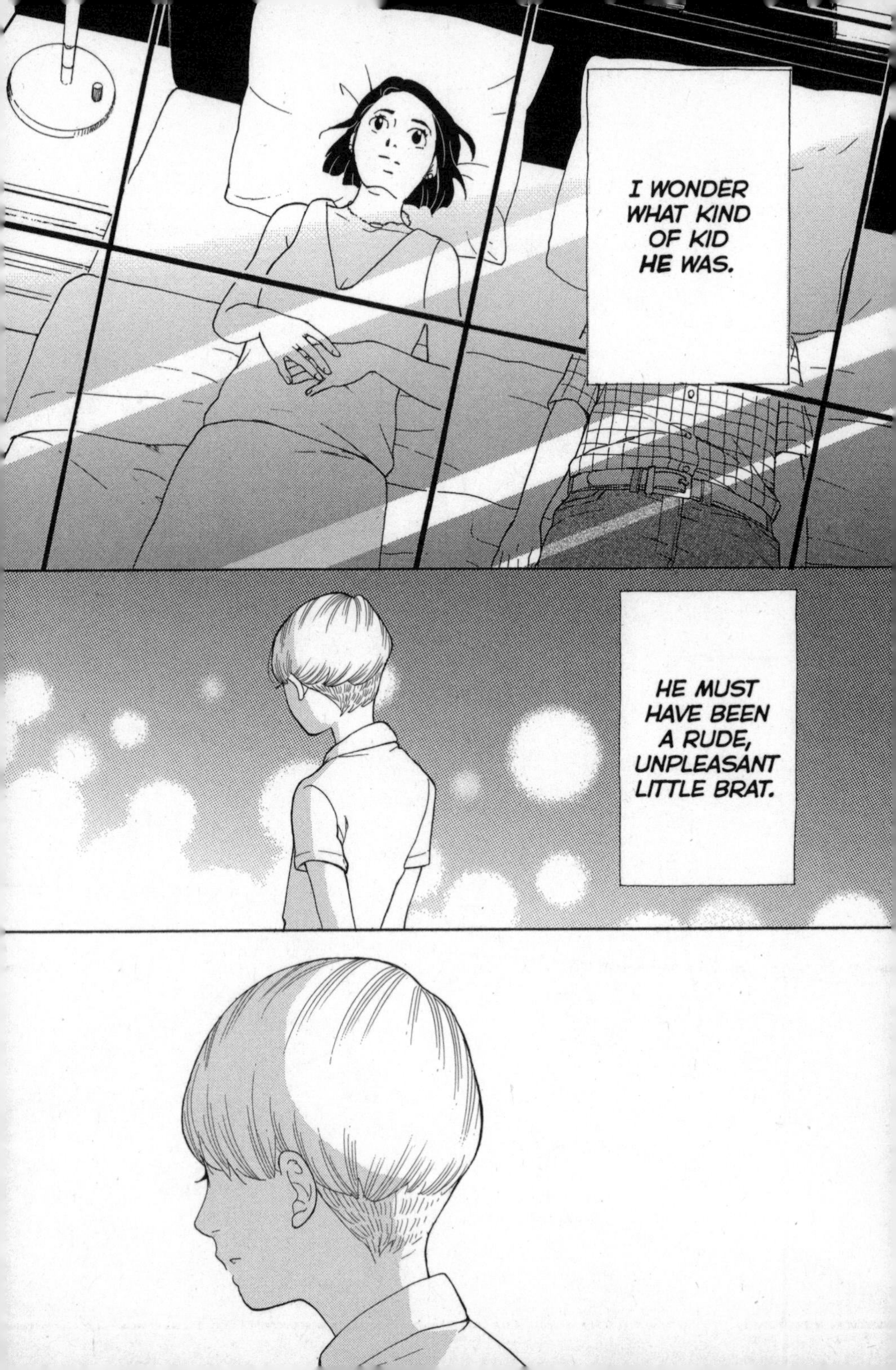
I WONDER WHAT KIND OF KID HE WAS.
HE MUST HAVE BEEN A RUDE, UNPLEASANT LITTLE BRAT.

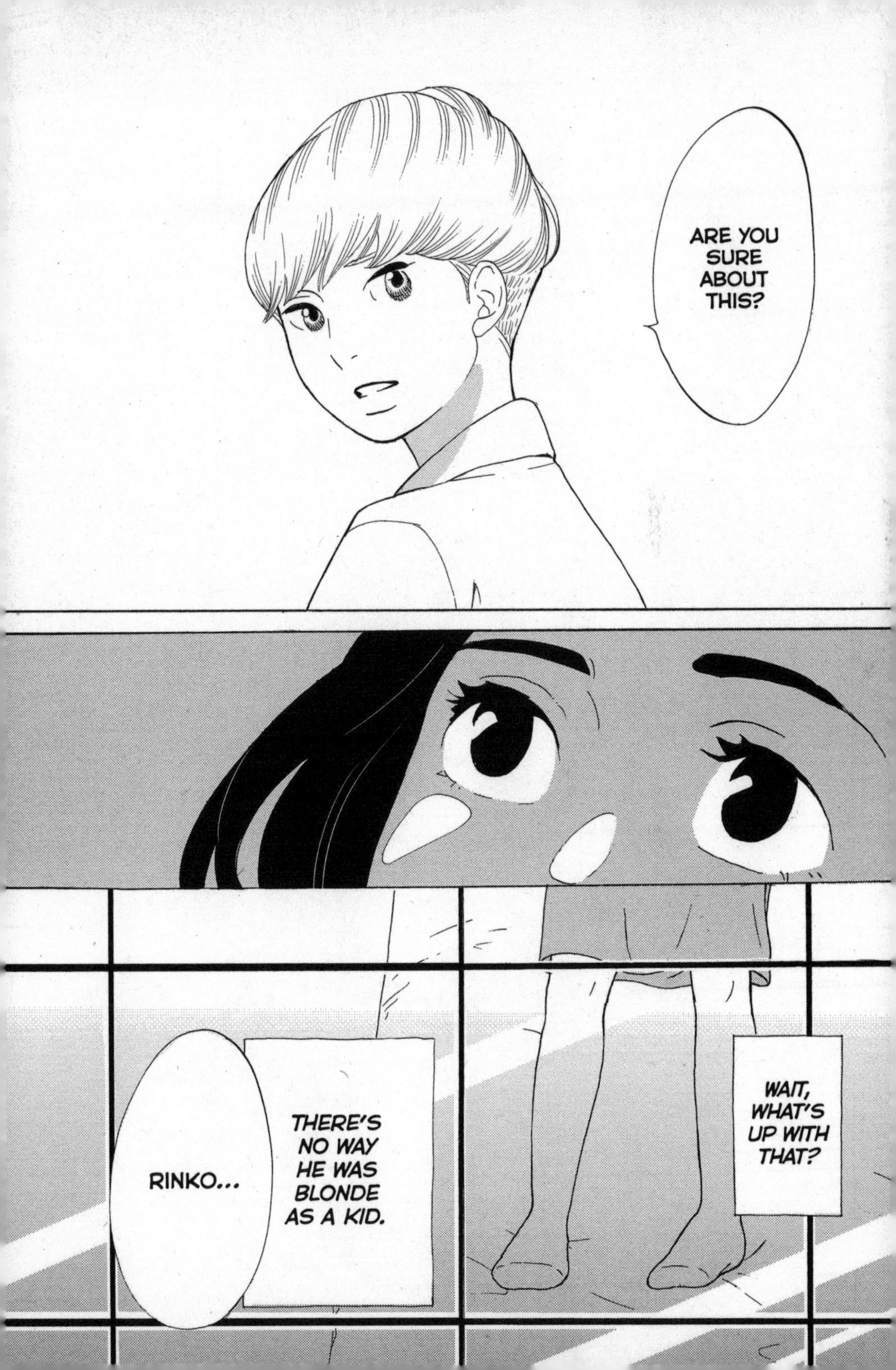
ARE YOU SURE ABOUT THIS?
WAIT, WHAT'S UP WITH THAT?
THERE'S NO WAY HE WAS BLONDE AS A KID.
RINKO...

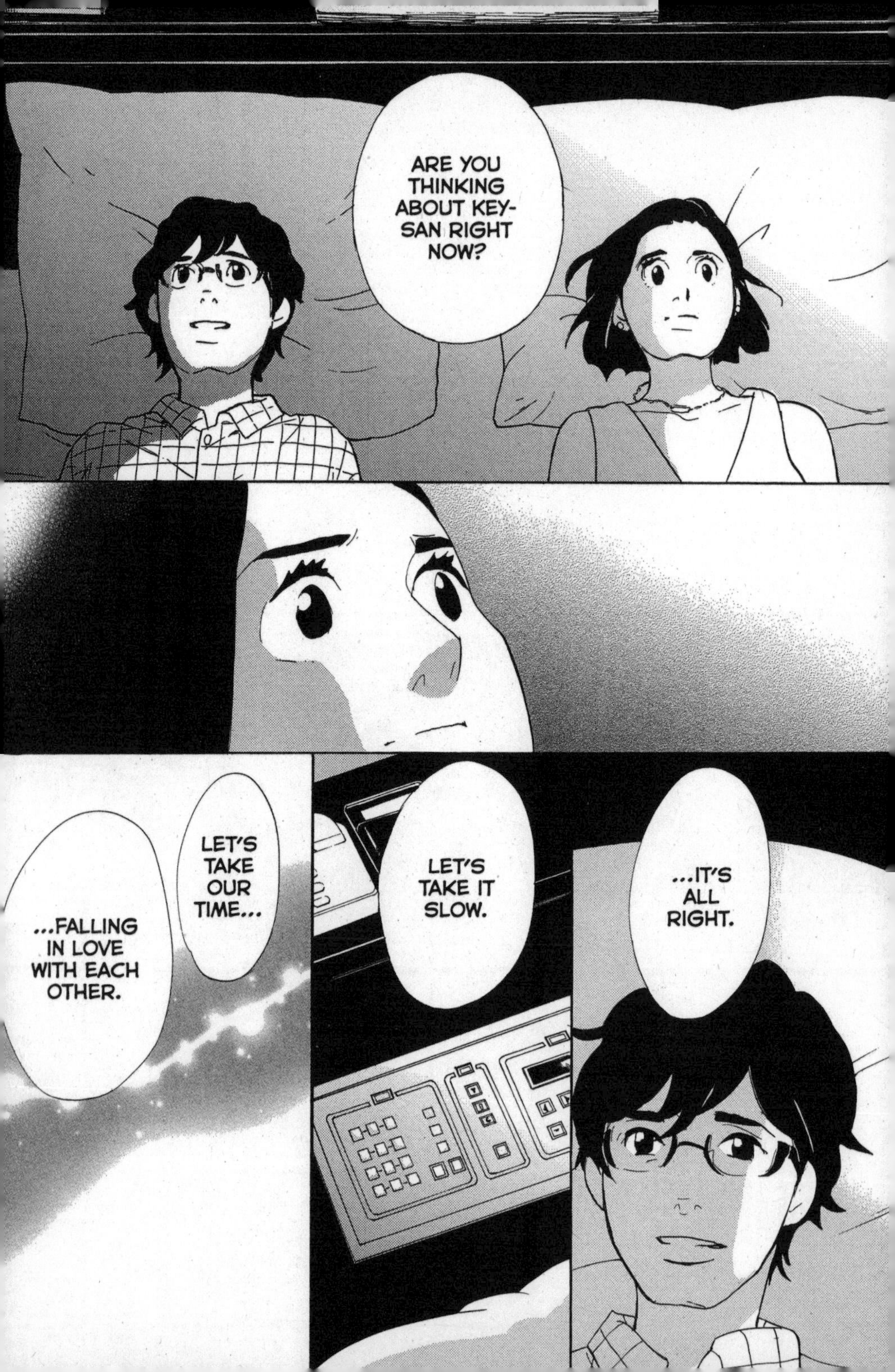
ARE YOU THINKING ABOUT KEY-SAN RIGHT NOW?
...IT'S ALL RIGHT.
LET'S TAKE IT SLOW.
LET'S TAKE OUR TIME...
...FALLING IN LOVE WITH EACH OTHER.

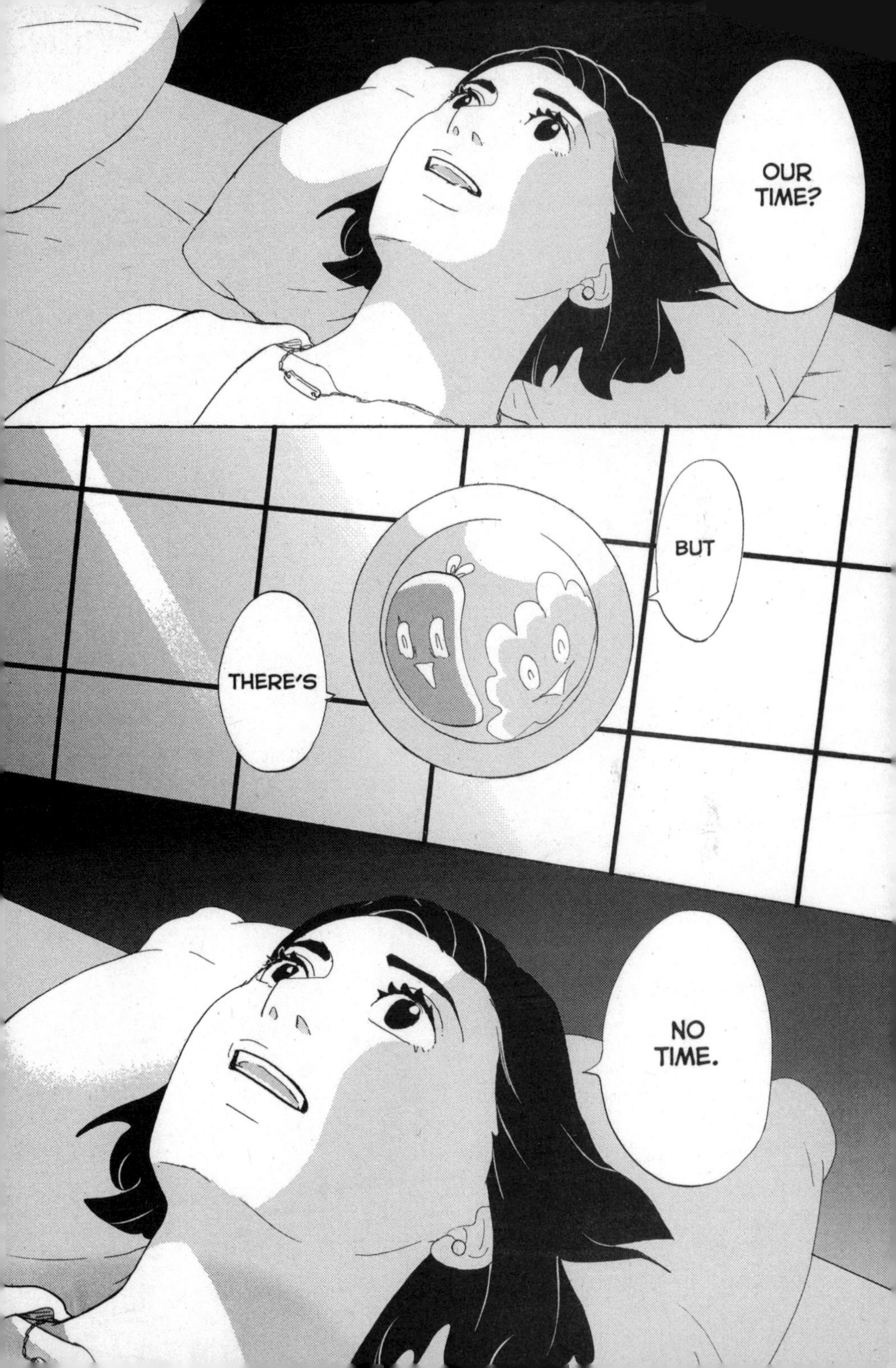
OUR TIME?
BUT
THERE'S
NO TIME.

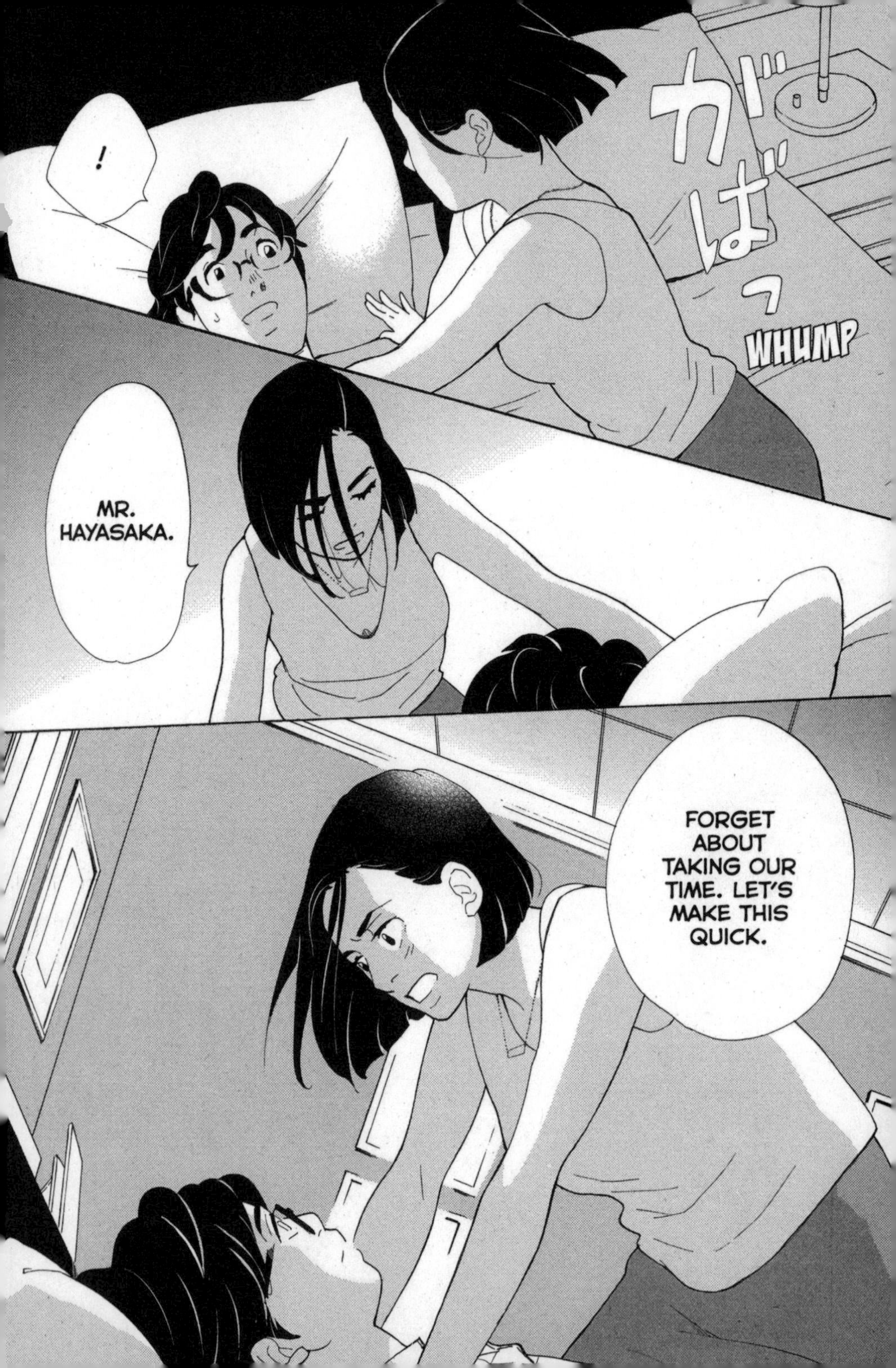
がばっ
WHUMP
!
MR. HAYASAKA.
FORGET ABOUT TAKING OUR TIME. LET'S MAKE THIS QUICK.

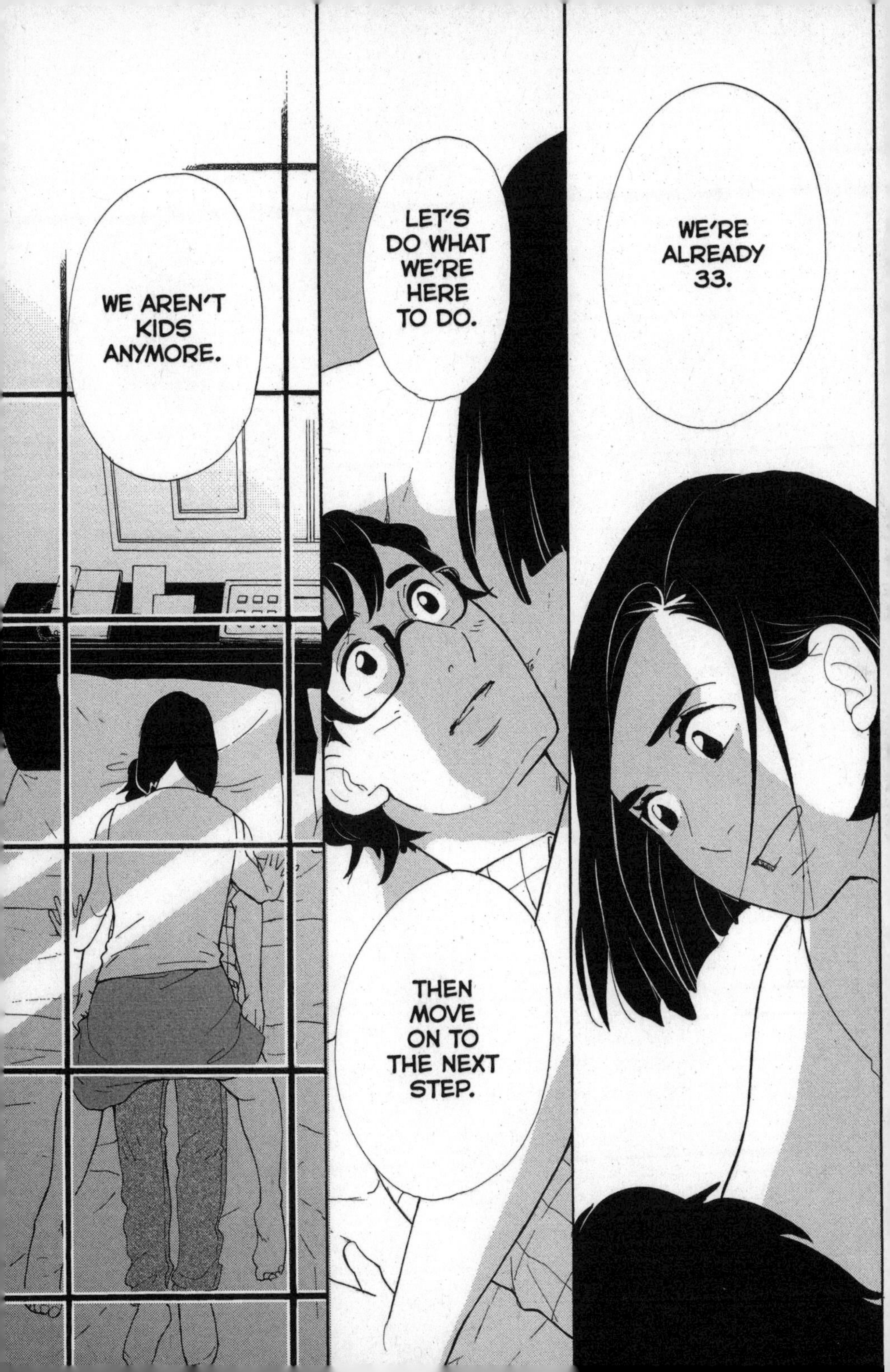
WE'RE ALREADY 33.
LET'S DO WHAT WE'RE HERE TO DO.
THEN MOVE ON TO THE NEXT STEP.
WE AREN'T KIDS ANYMORE.

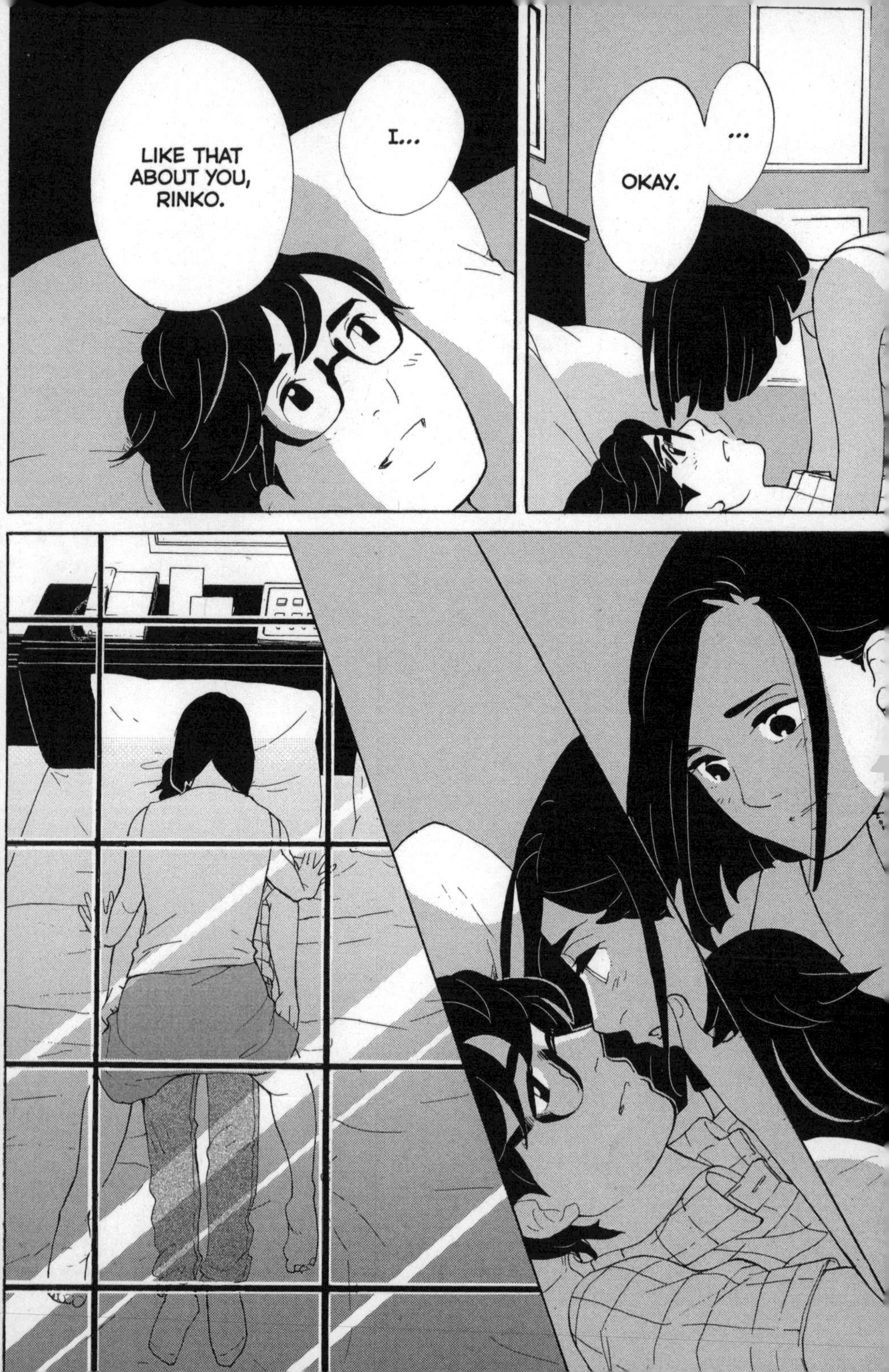
...
OKAY.
I...
LIKE THAT ABOUT YOU, RINKO.

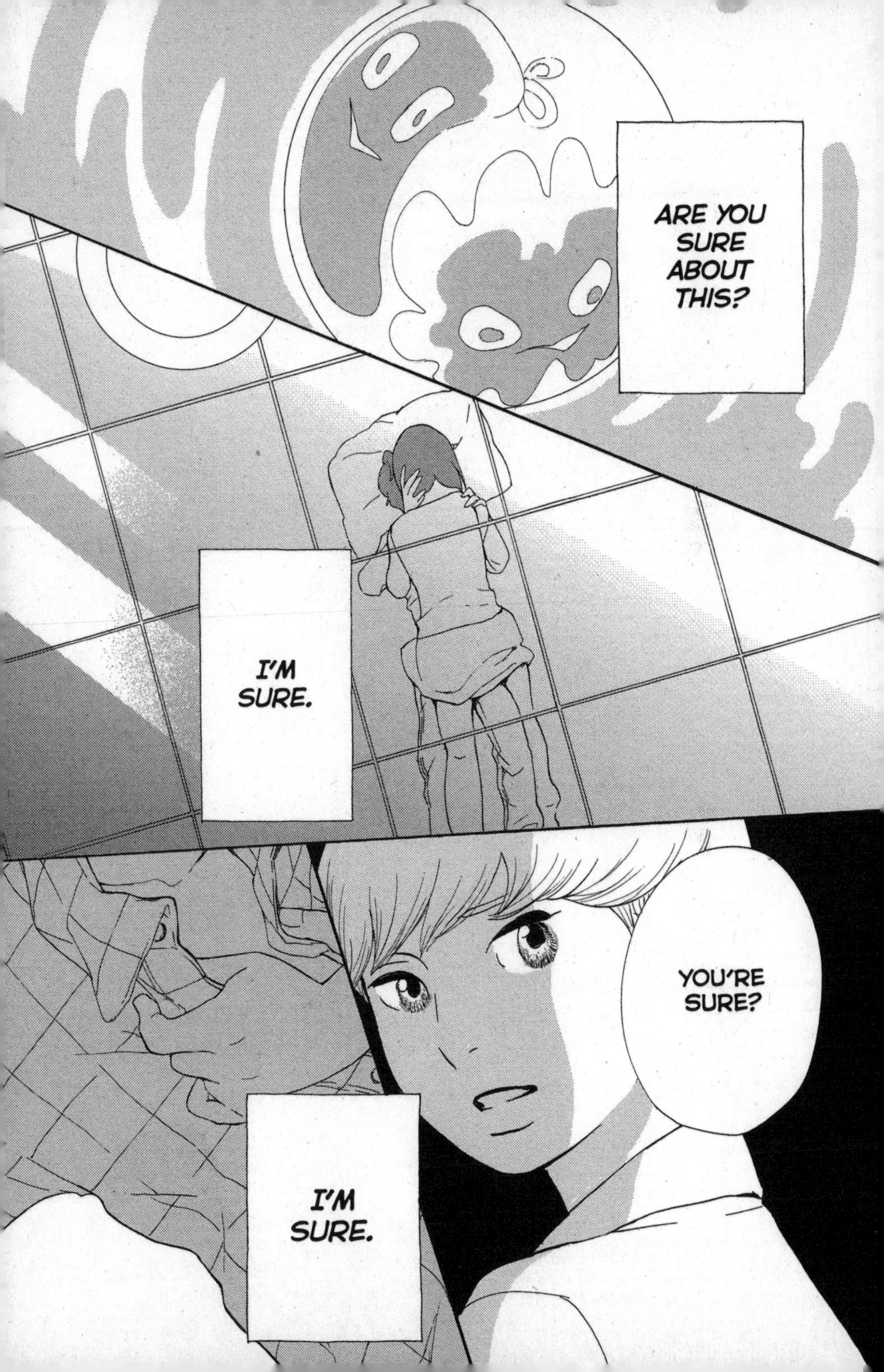
ARE YOU SURE ABOUT THIS?
I'M SURE.
YOU'RE SURE?
I'M SURE.

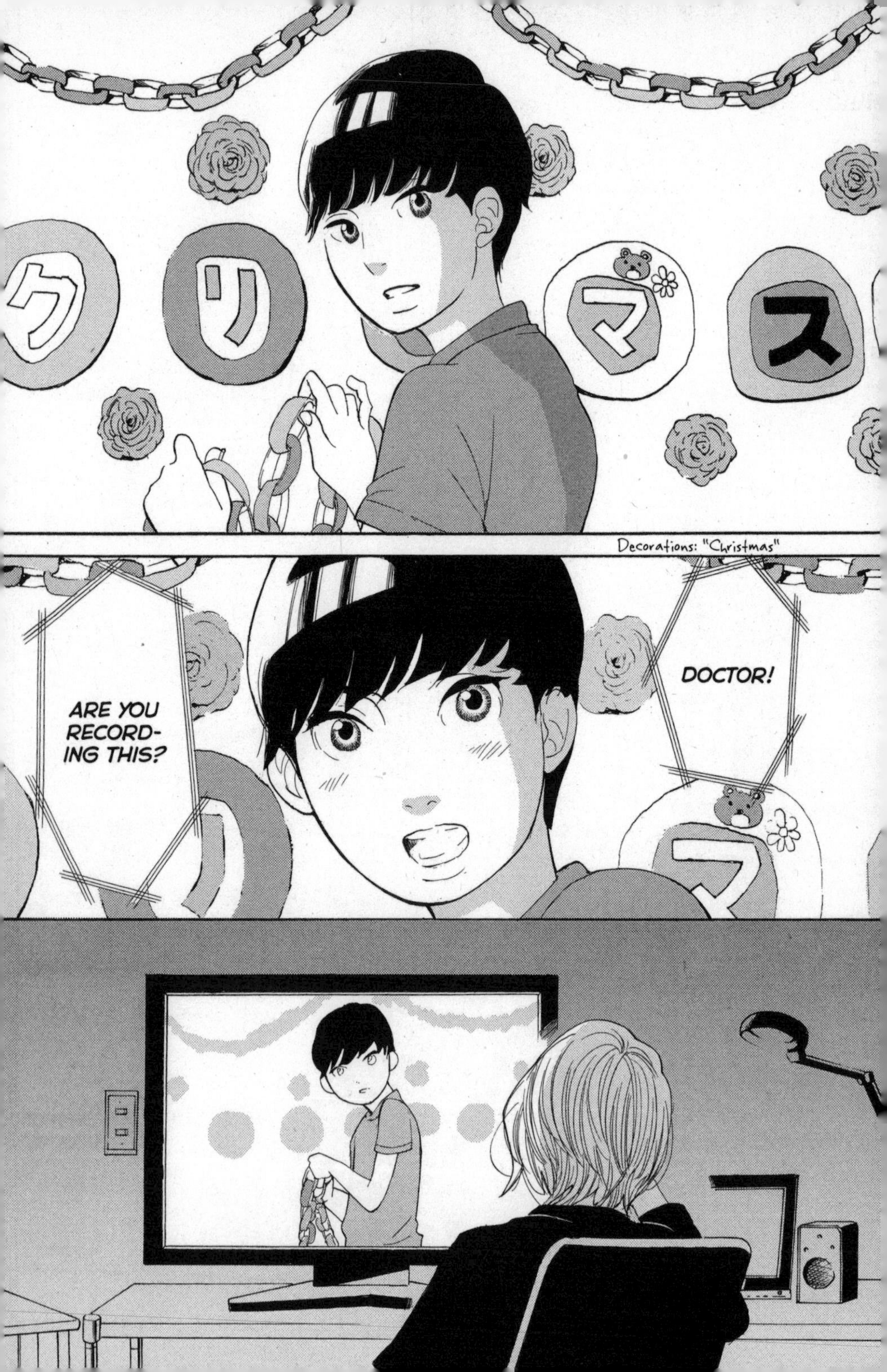
ク リ マ ス
Decorations: "Christmas"
DOCTOR!
ARE YOU RECORD-ING THIS?

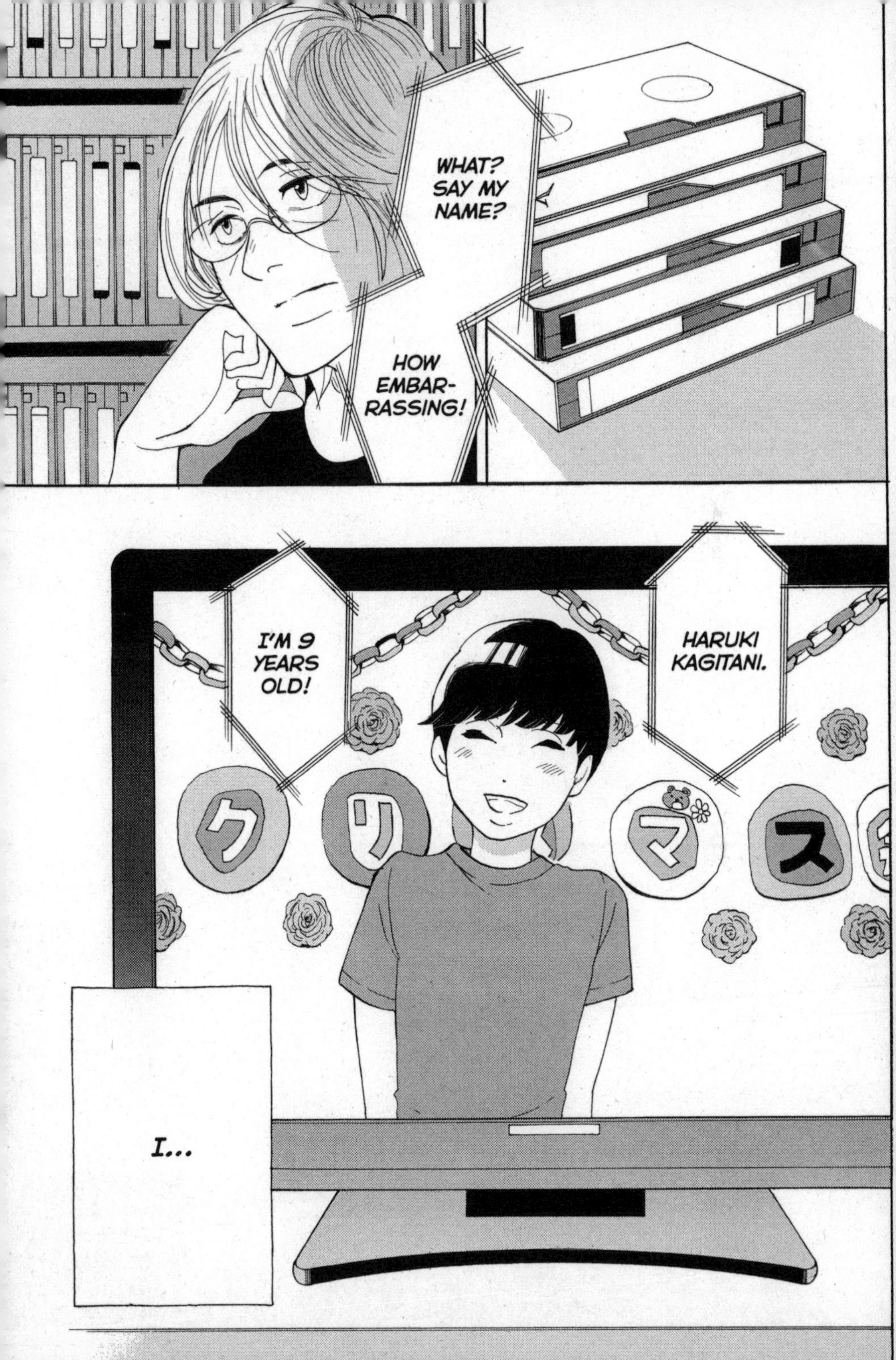
WHAT? SAY MY NAME?
HOW EMBAR-RASSING!
HARUKI KAGITANI.
I'M 9 YEARS OLD!
クリマス
I...

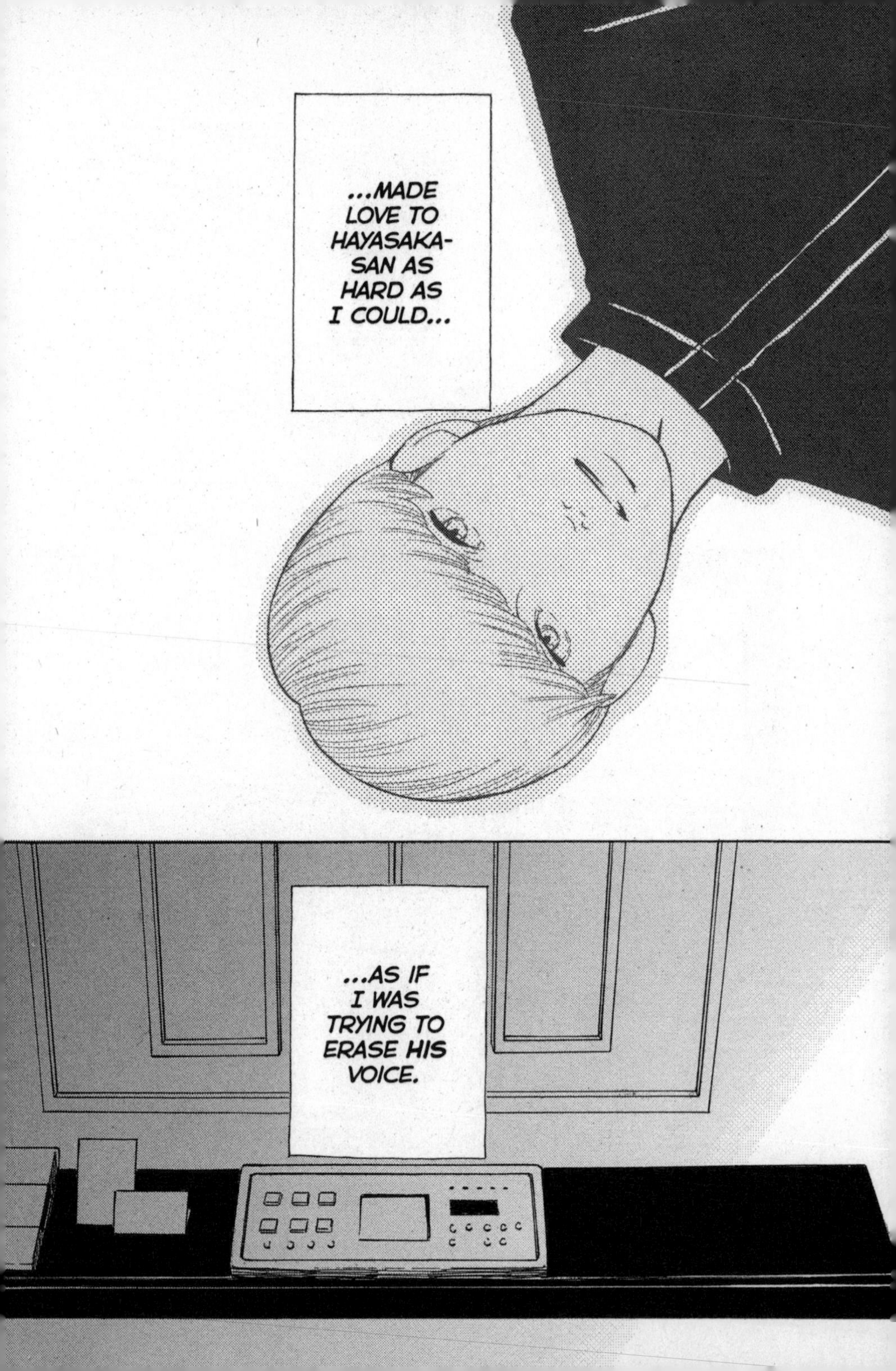
...MADE LOVE TO HAYASAKA-SAN AS HARD AS I COULD...
...AS IF I WAS TRYING TO ERASE HIS VOICE.

ACT 24
THE SETTLER WOMAN

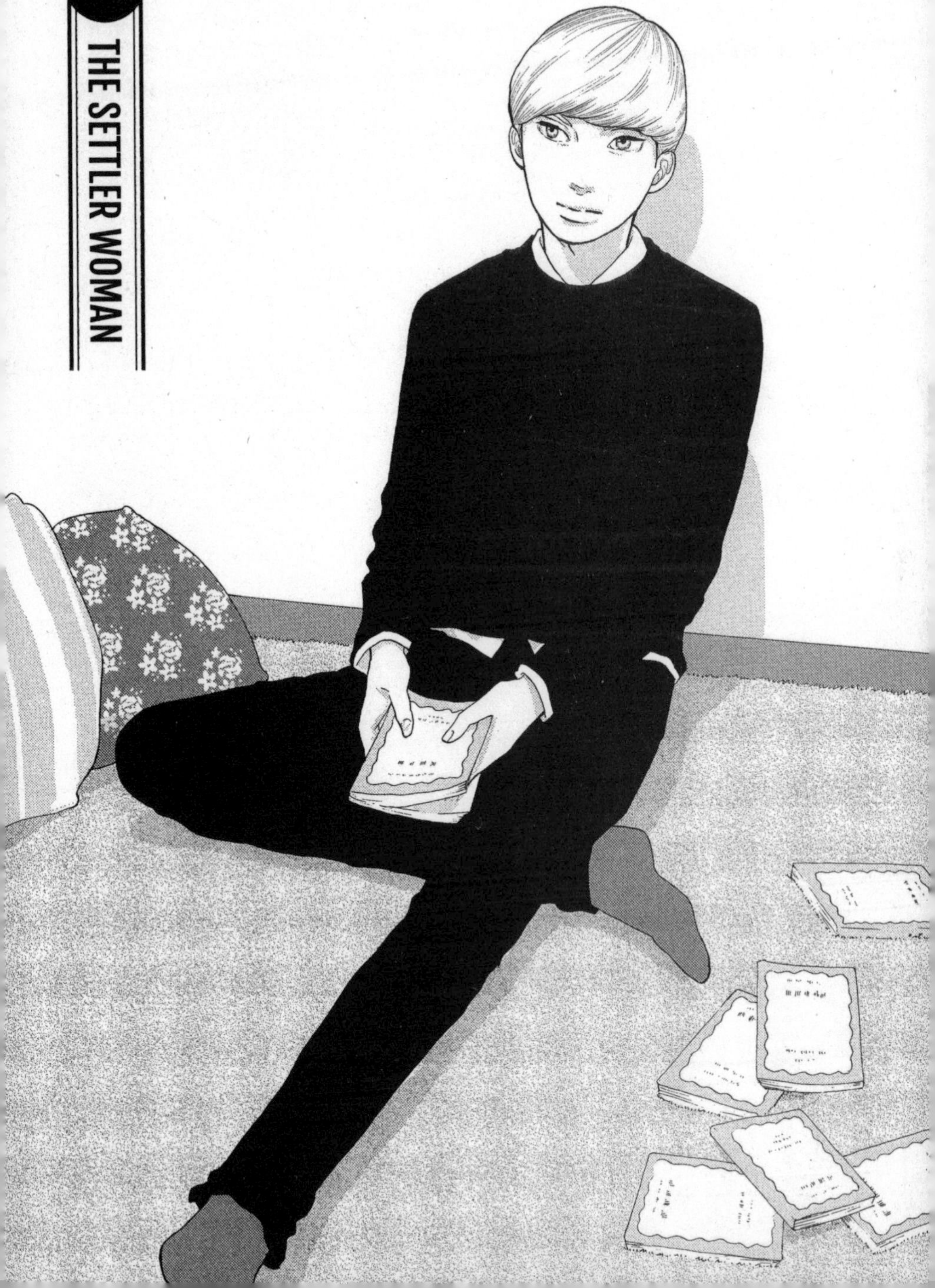

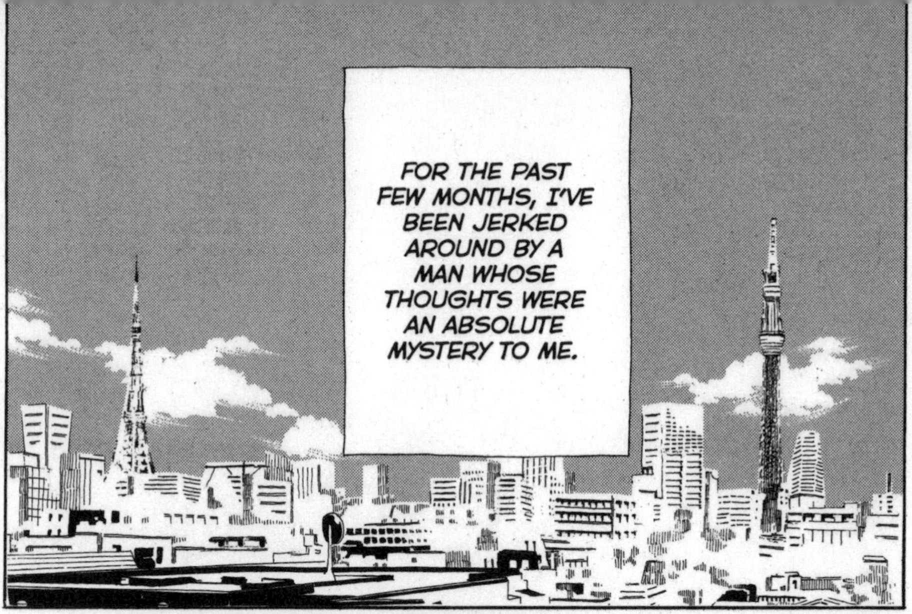
FOR THE PAST FEW MONTHS, I'VE BEEN JERKED AROUND BY A MAN WHOSE THOUGHTS WERE AN ABSOLUTE MYSTERY TO ME.

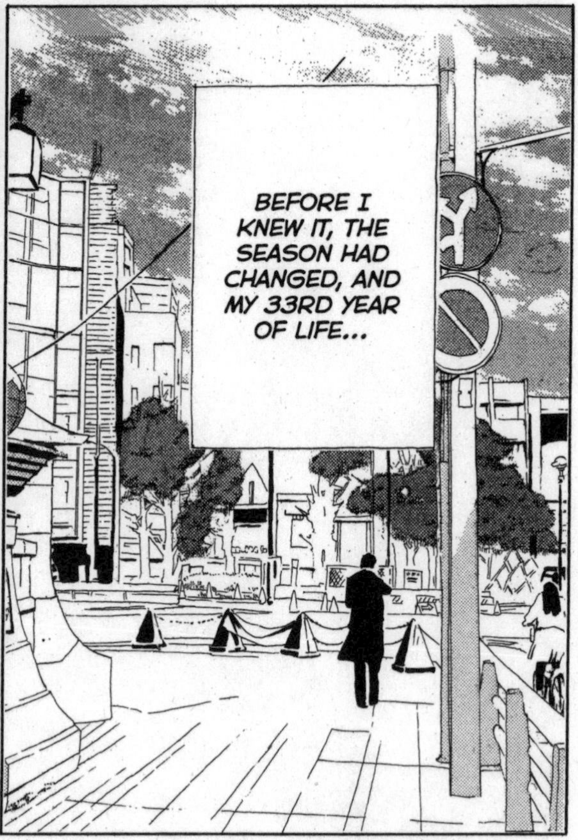
BEFORE I KNEW IT, THE SEASON HAD CHANGED, AND MY 33RD YEAR OF LIFE...

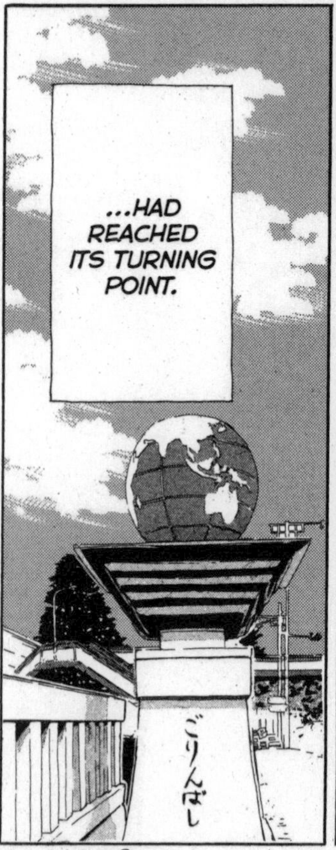
...HAD REACHED ITS TURNING POINT.
ごりんばし

Sign: Five Rings Bridge

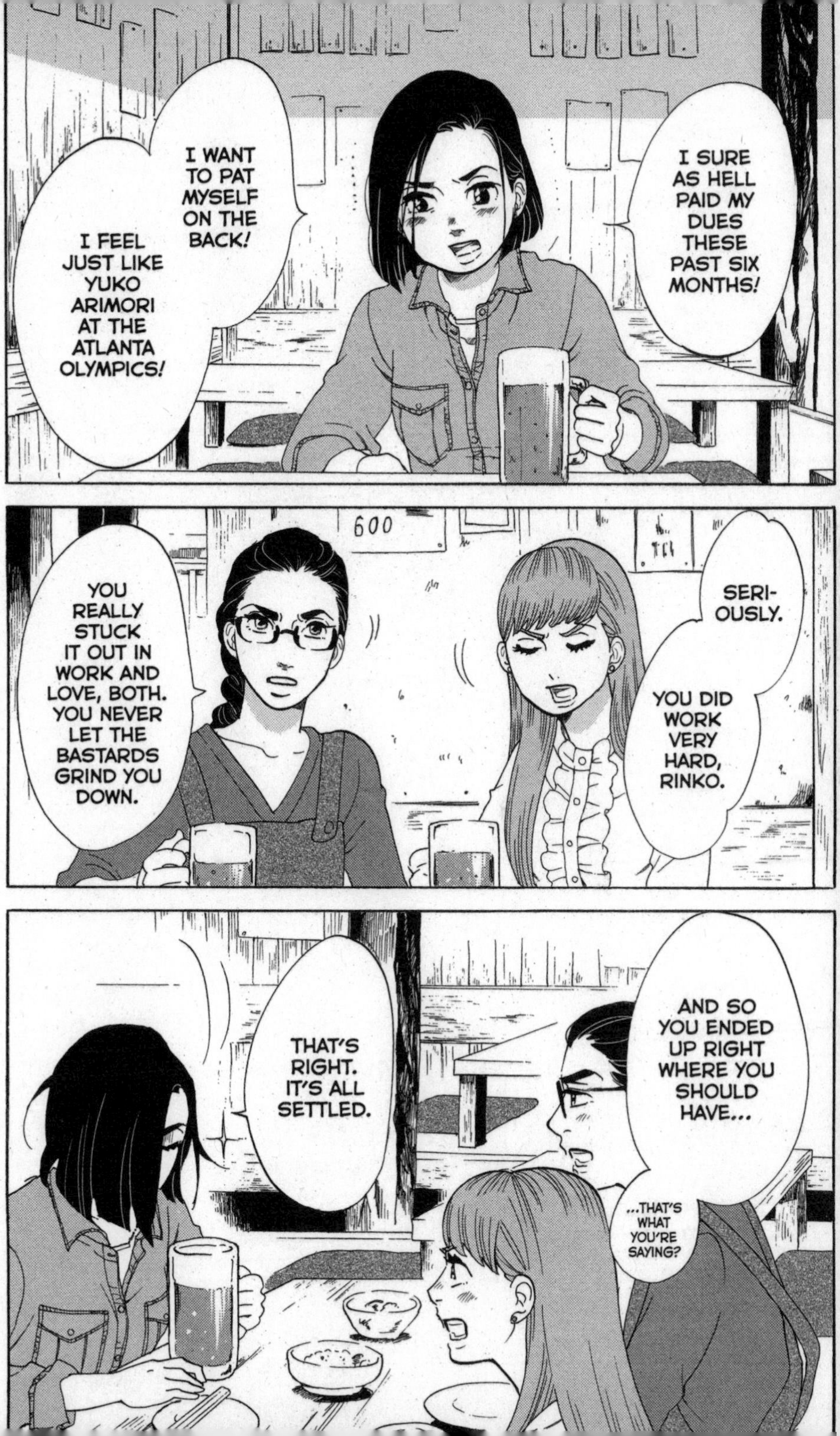
I SURE AS HELL PAID MY DUES THESE PAST SIX MONTHS!
I WANT TO PAT MYSELF ON THE BACK!
I FEEL JUST LIKE YUKO ARIMORI AT THE ATLANTA OLYMPICS!
600
SERI-OUSLY.
YOU DID WORK VERY HARD, RINKO.
YOU REALLY STUCK IT OUT IN WORK AND LOVE, BOTH. YOU NEVER LET THE BASTARDS GRIND YOU DOWN.
AND SO YOU ENDED UP RIGHT WHERE YOU SHOULD HAVE...
...THAT'S WHAT YOU'RE SAYING?
THAT'S RIGHT. IT'S ALL SETTLED.

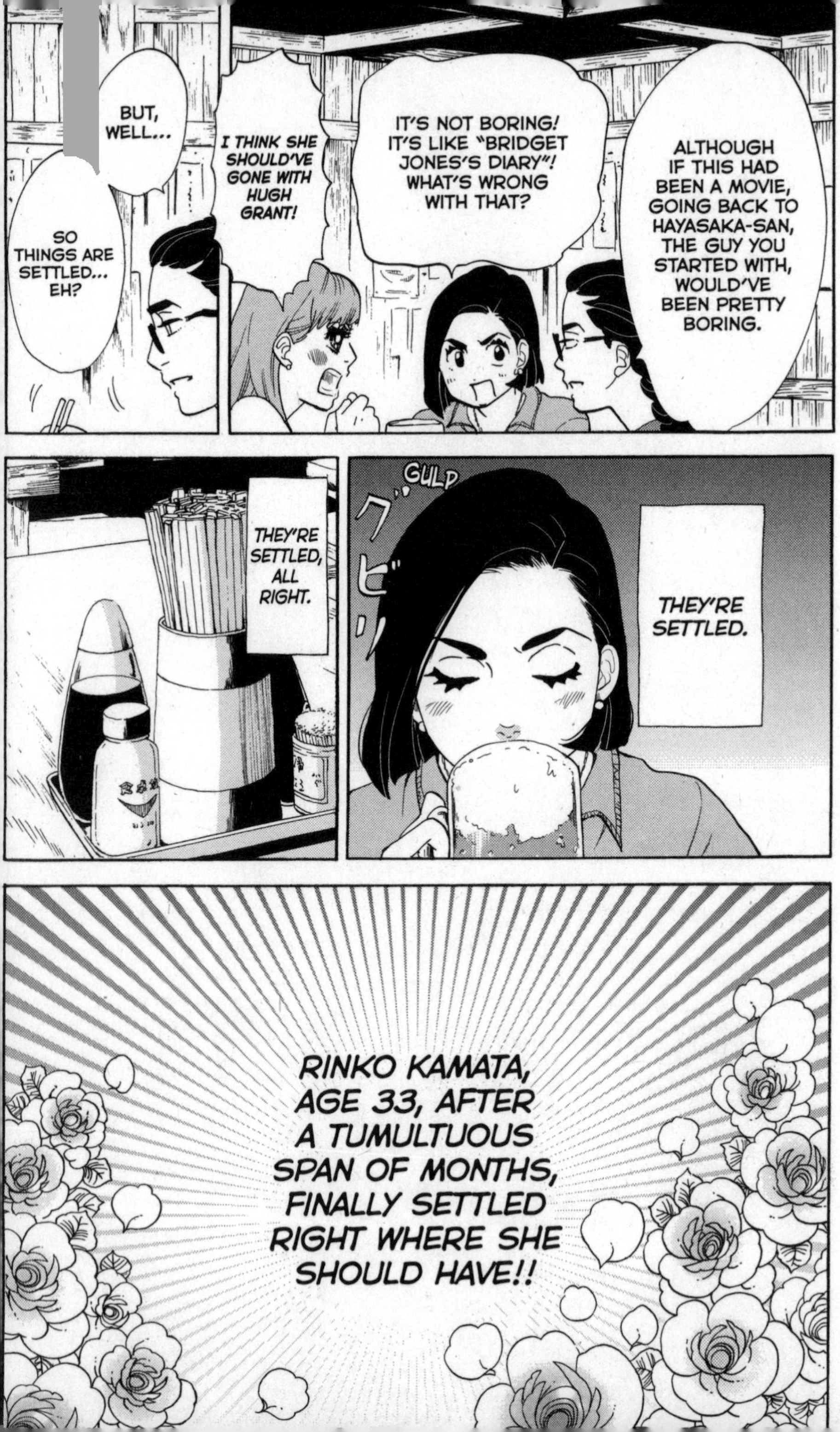
ALTHOUGH IF THIS HAD BEEN A MOVIE, GOING BACK TO HAYASAKA-SAN, THE GUY YOU STARTED WITH, WOULD'VE BEEN PRETTY BORING.
IT'S NOT BORING! IT'S LIKE "BRIDGET JONES'S DIARY"! WHAT'S WRONG WITH THAT?
I THINK SHE SHOULD'VE GONE WITH HUGH GRANT!
BUT, WELL...
SO THINGS ARE SETTLED... EH?
GULP
THEY'RE SETTLED.
THEY'RE SETTLED, ALL RIGHT.
RINKO KAMATA, AGE 33, AFTER A TUMULTUOUS SPAN OF MONTHS, FINALLY SETTLED RIGHT WHERE SHE SHOULD HAVE!!

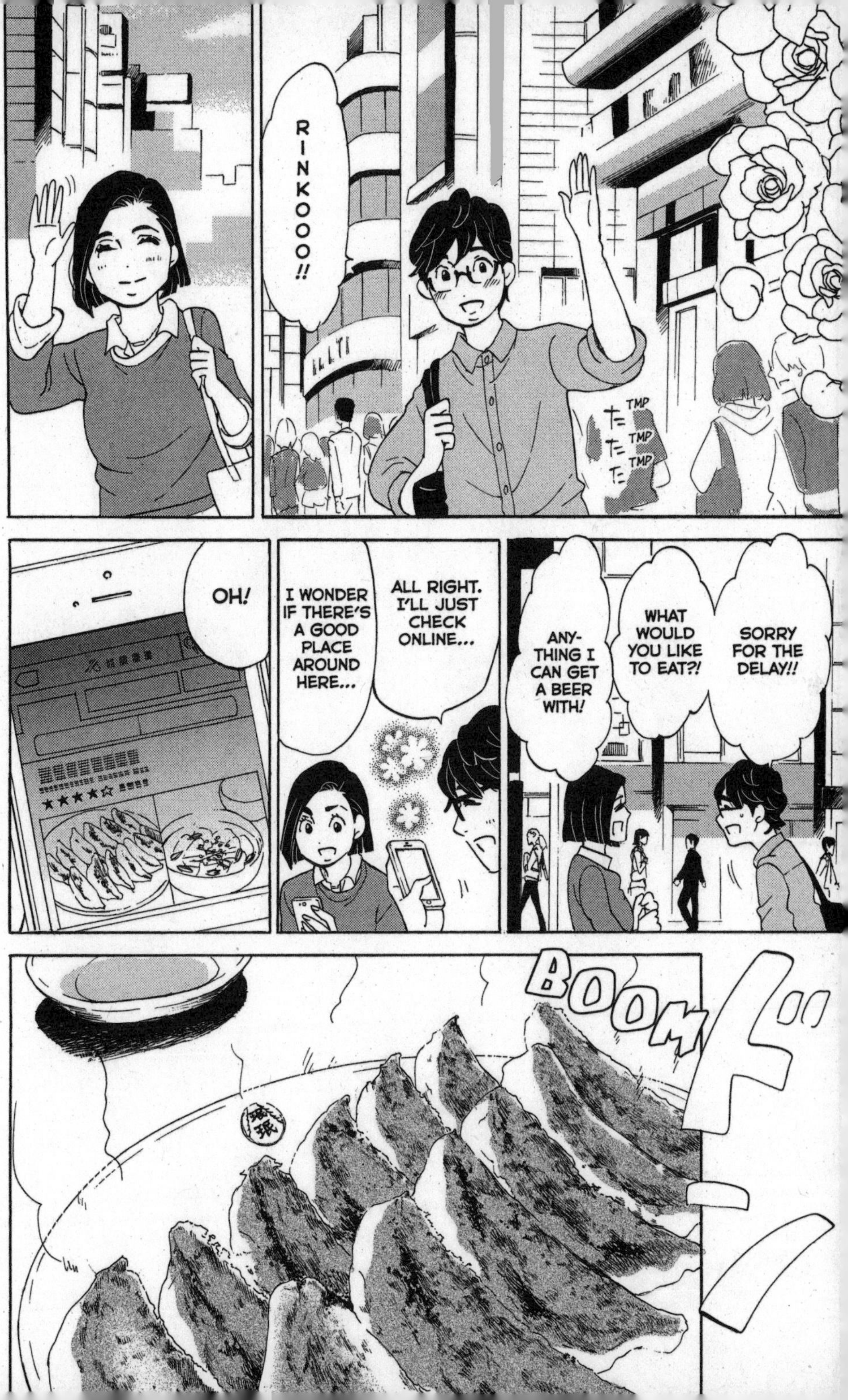

RINKOOOO!!
TMP
TMP
TMP
SORRY FOR THE DELAY!!
WHAT WOULD YOU LIKE TO EAT?!
ANY-THING I CAN GET A BEER WITH!
ALL RIGHT. I'LL JUST CHECK ONLINE...
I WONDER IF THERE'S A GOOD PLACE AROUND HERE...
OH!
BOOM!!

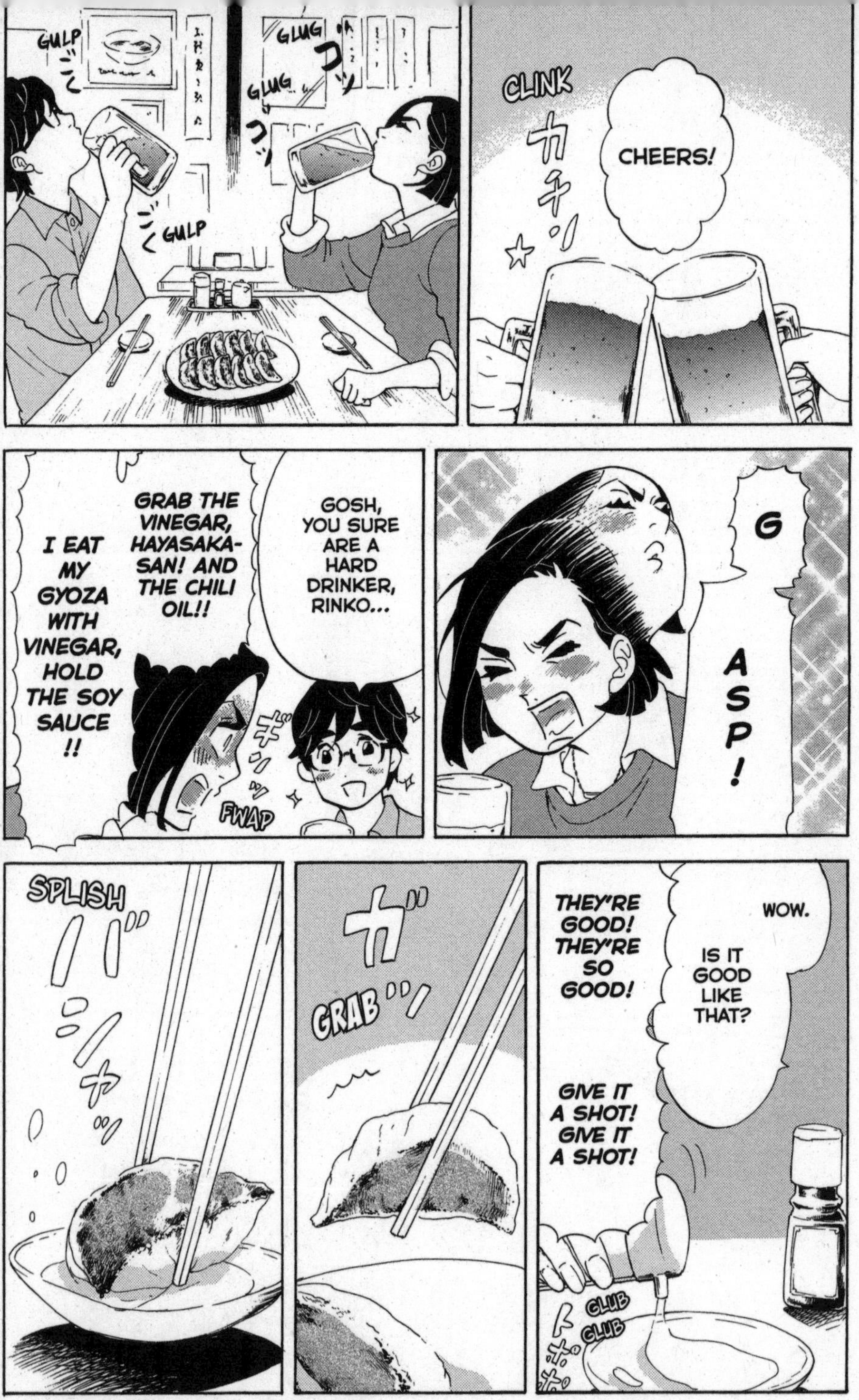
CLINK
CHEERS!
GULP
GLUG
GLUG
GULP
G
ASP!
GOSH, YOU SURE ARE A HARD DRINKER, RINKO...
GRAB THE VINEGAR, HAYASAKA-SAN! AND THE CHILI OIL!!
I EAT MY GYOZA WITH VINEGAR, HOLD THE SOY SAUCE!!
FWAP
WOW.
IS IT GOOD LIKE THAT?
THEY'RE GOOD! THEY'RE SO GOOD!
GIVE IT A SHOT! GIVE IT A SHOT!
GLUB GLUB
GRAB
SPLISH

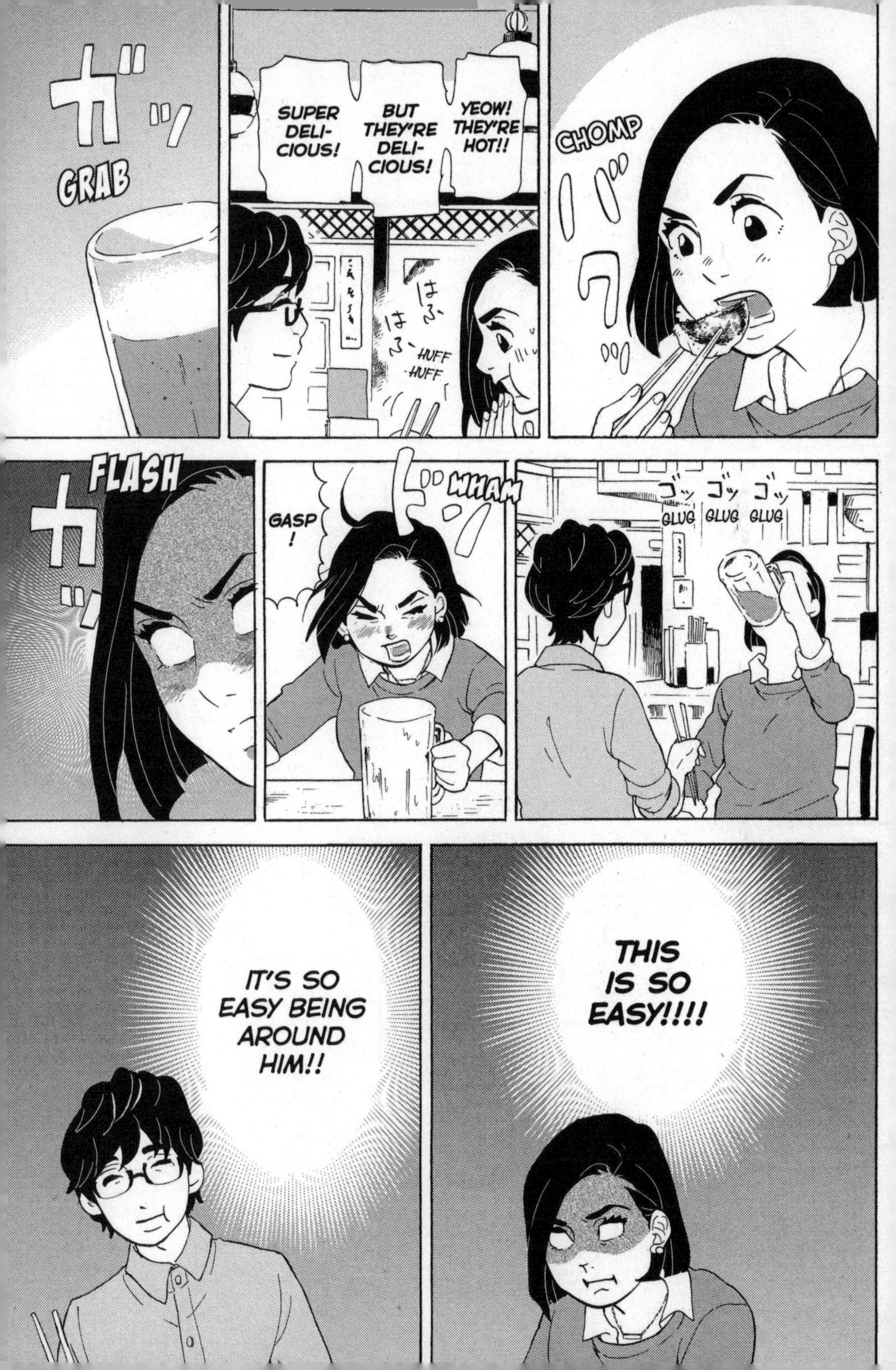
CHOMP
YEOW! THEY'RE HOT!!
BUT THEY'RE DELICIOUS!
SUPER DELICIOUS!
はふはふ
HUFF HUFF
ガッ
GRAB
ゴッゴッゴッ
GLUG GLUG GLUG
WHAM
GASP!
カッ
FLASH
THIS IS SO EASY!!!!
IT'S SO EASY BEING AROUND HIM!!

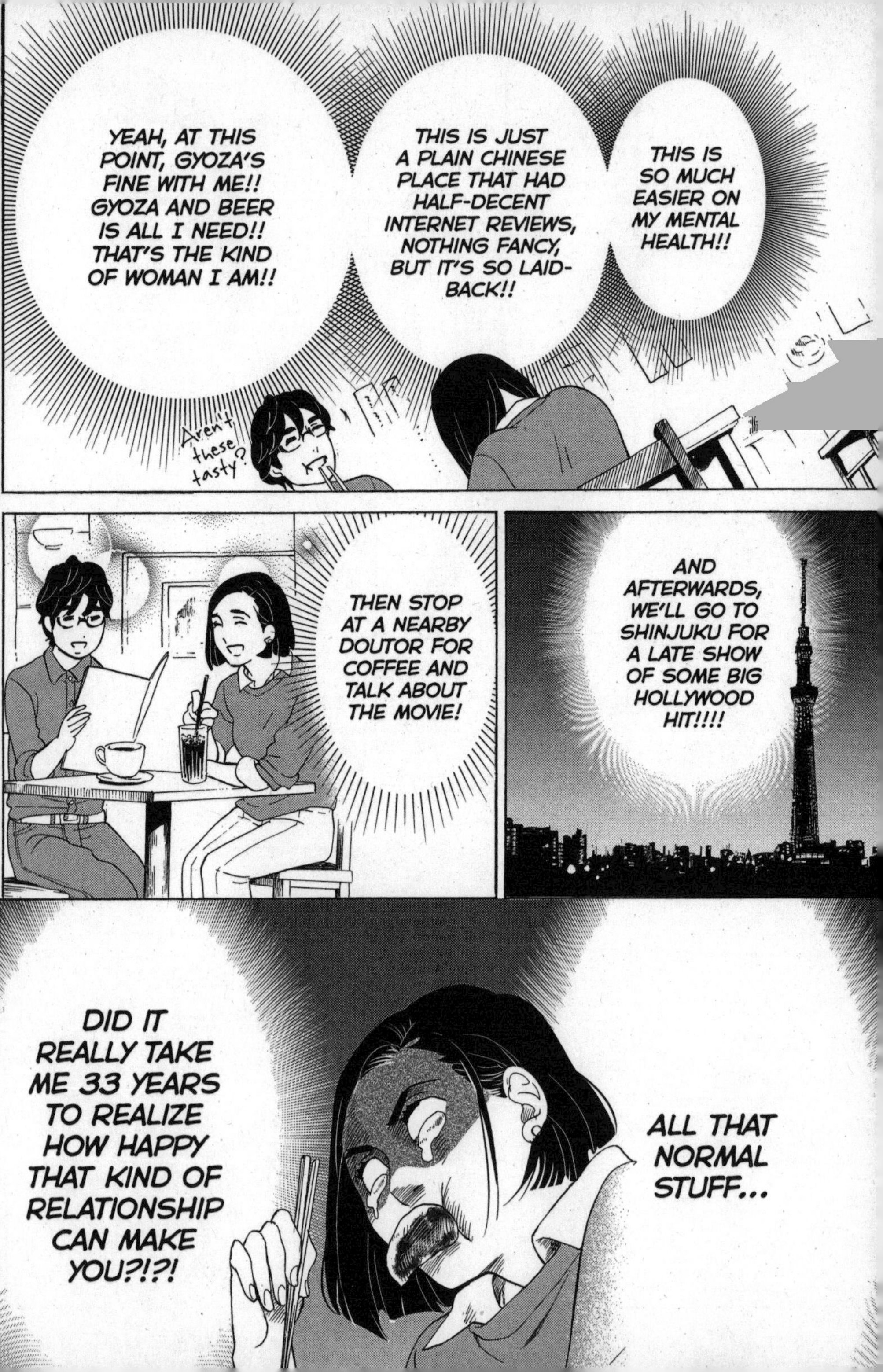
THIS IS SO MUCH EASIER ON MY MENTAL HEALTH!!
THIS IS JUST A PLAIN CHINESE PLACE THAT HAD HALF-DECENT INTERNET REVIEWS, NOTHING FANCY, BUT IT'S SO LAID-BACK!!
YEAH, AT THIS POINT, GYOZA'S FINE WITH ME!! GYOZA AND BEER IS ALL I NEED!! THAT'S THE KIND OF WOMAN I AM!!
Aren't these tasty?
AND AFTERWARDS, WE'LL GO TO SHINJUKU FOR A LATE SHOW OF SOME BIG HOLLYWOOD HIT!!!!
THEN STOP AT A NEARBY DOUTOR FOR COFFEE AND TALK ABOUT THE MOVIE!
ALL THAT NORMAL STUFF...
DID IT REALLY TAKE ME 33 YEARS TO REALIZE HOW HAPPY THAT KIND OF RELATIONSHIP CAN MAKE YOU?!?!

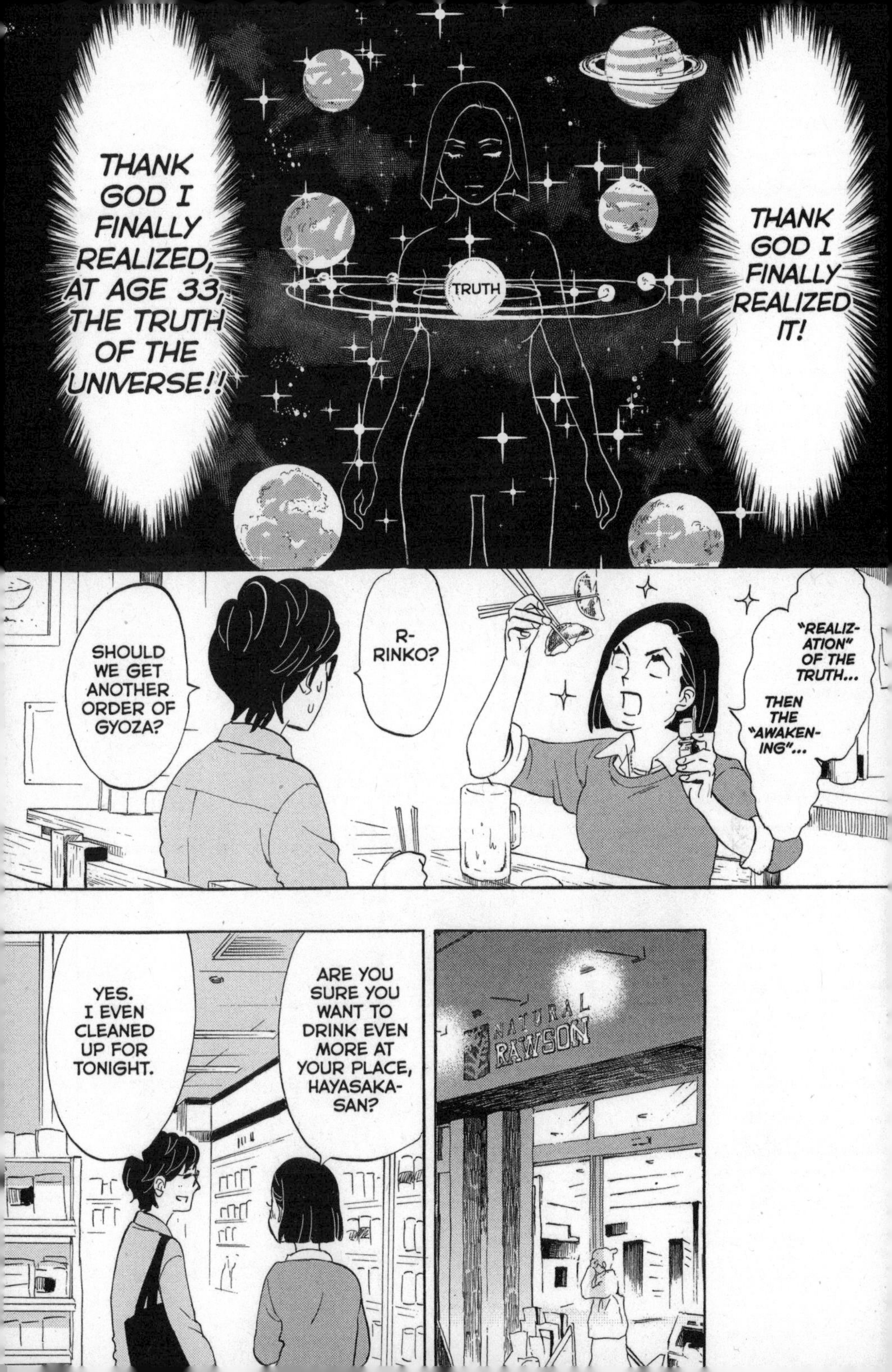
THANK GOD I FINALLY REALIZED IT!
TRUTH
THANK GOD I FINALLY REALIZED, AT AGE 33, THE TRUTH OF THE UNIVERSE!!
"REALIZATION" OF THE TRUTH...
THEN THE "AWAKENING"...
R-RINKO?
SHOULD WE GET ANOTHER ORDER OF GYOZA?
NATURAL RAWSON
ARE YOU SURE YOU WANT TO DRINK EVEN MORE AT YOUR PLACE, HAYASAKA-SAN?
YES. I EVEN CLEANED UP FOR TONIGHT.

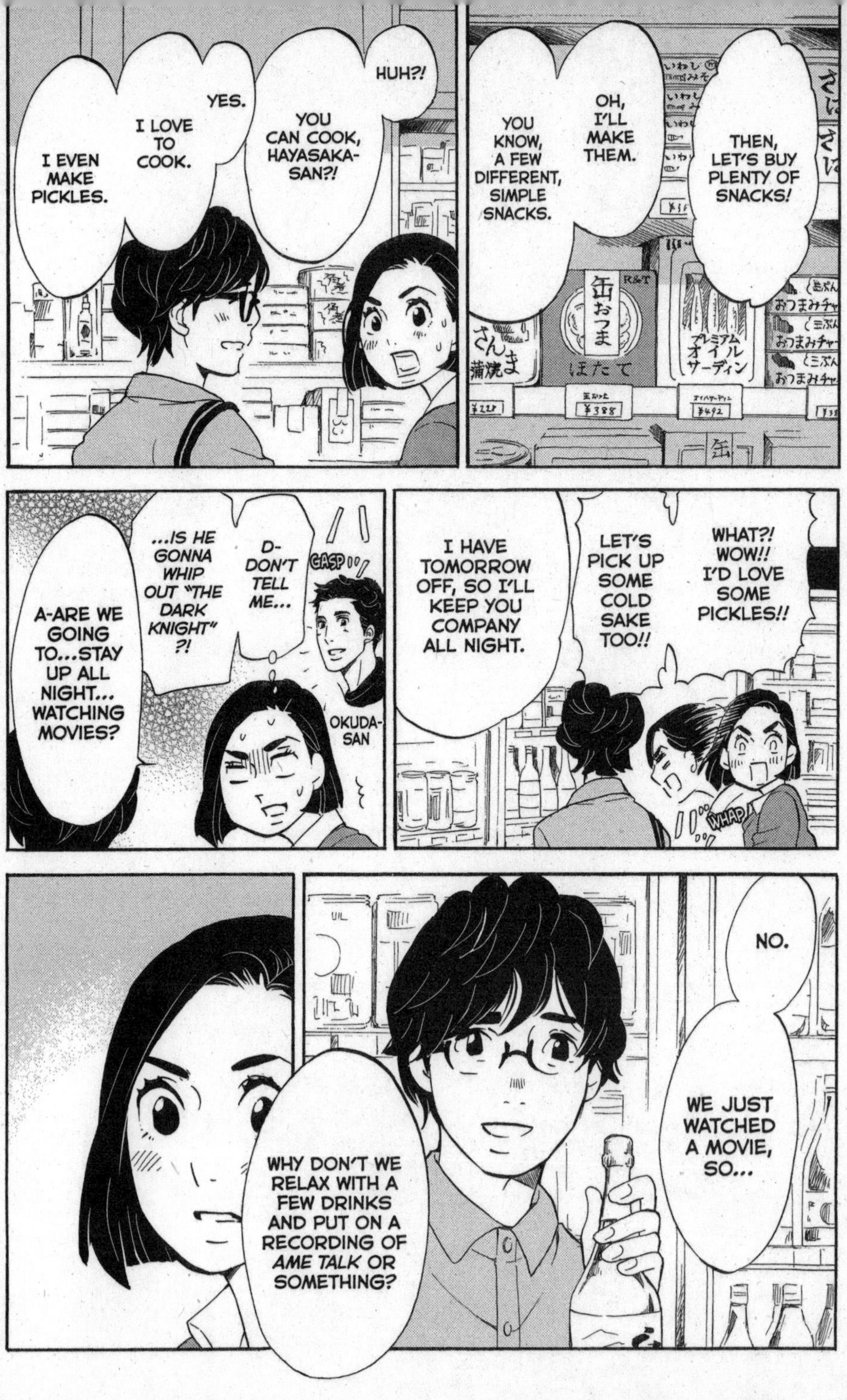
THEN, LET'S BUY PLENTY OF SNACKS!
OH, I'LL MAKE THEM.
YOU KNOW, A FEW DIFFERENT, SIMPLE SNACKS.
缶おつま
ほたて
プレミアム オイル サーディン
さんま 蒲焼き
¥388
¥492
HUH?!
YOU CAN COOK, HAYASAKA-SAN?!
YES.
I LOVE TO COOK.
I EVEN MAKE PICKLES.
WHAT?! WOW!! I'D LOVE SOME PICKLES!!
LET'S PICK UP SOME COLD SAKE TOO!!
WHAP
I HAVE TOMORROW OFF, SO I'LL KEEP YOU COMPANY ALL NIGHT.
GASP
D-DON'T TELL ME...
OKUDA-SAN
...IS HE GONNA WHIP OUT "THE DARK KNIGHT"?!
A-ARE WE GOING TO...STAY UP ALL NIGHT... WATCHING MOVIES?
NO.
WE JUST WATCHED A MOVIE, SO...
WHY DON'T WE RELAX WITH A FEW DRINKS AND PUT ON A RECORDING OF *AME TALK* OR SOMETHING?

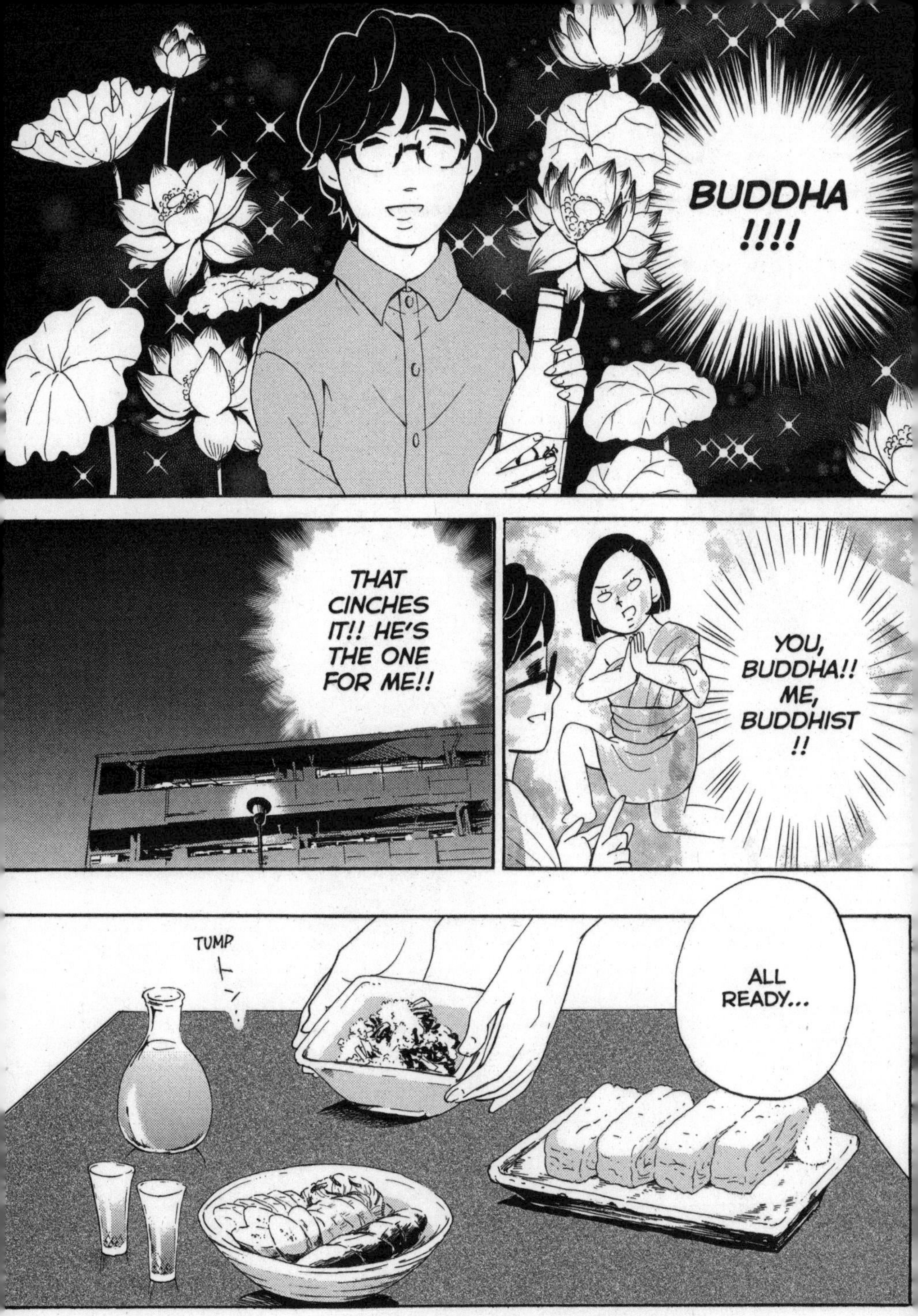
BUDDHA !!!!
YOU, BUDDHA!! ME, BUDDHIST !!
THAT CINCHES IT!! HE'S THE ONE FOR ME!!
ALL READY...
TUMP

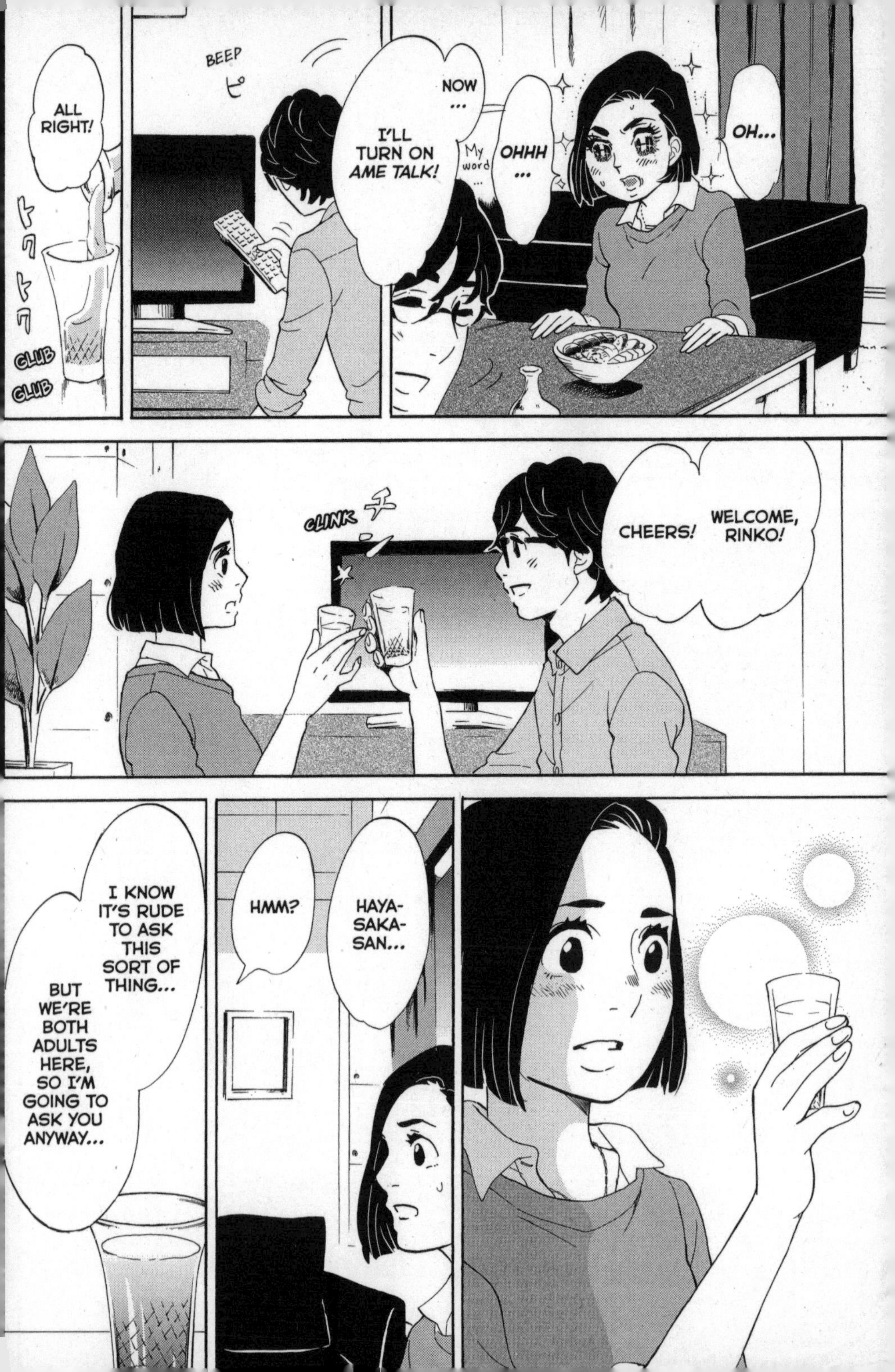
OH...
OHHH...
My word...
NOW...
I'LL TURN ON AME TALK!
BEEP
ピ
ALL RIGHT!
トクトク
GLUB GLUB
WELCOME, RINKO!
CHEERS!
CLINK
チ
HAYA-SAKA-SAN...
HMM?
I KNOW IT'S RUDE TO ASK THIS SORT OF THING...
BUT WE'RE BOTH ADULTS HERE, SO I'M GOING TO ASK YOU ANYWAY...

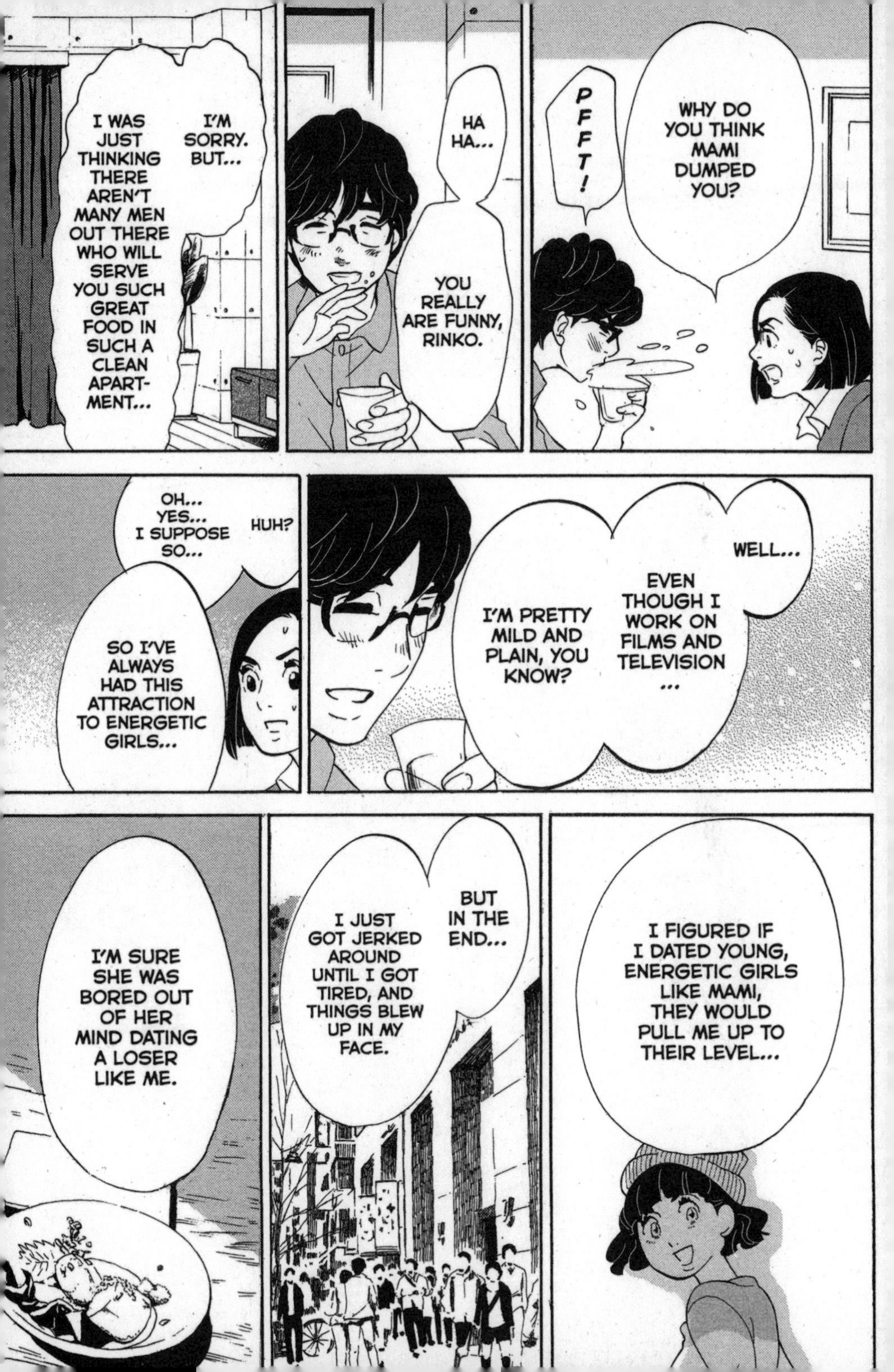
WHY DO YOU THINK MAMI DUMPED YOU?
PFFT!
HA HA...
YOU REALLY ARE FUNNY, RINKO.
I'M SORRY. BUT...
I WAS JUST THINKING THERE AREN'T MANY MEN OUT THERE WHO WILL SERVE YOU SUCH GREAT FOOD IN SUCH A CLEAN APARTMENT...
WELL...
EVEN THOUGH I WORK ON FILMS AND TELEVISION ...
I'M PRETTY MILD AND PLAIN, YOU KNOW?
HUH?
OH... YES... I SUPPOSE SO...
SO I'VE ALWAYS HAD THIS ATTRACTION TO ENERGETIC GIRLS...
I FIGURED IF I DATED YOUNG, ENERGETIC GIRLS LIKE MAMI, THEY WOULD PULL ME UP TO THEIR LEVEL...
BUT IN THE END...
I JUST GOT JERKED AROUND UNTIL I GOT TIRED, AND THINGS BLEW UP IN MY FACE.
I'M SURE SHE WAS BORED OUT OF HER MIND DATING A LOSER LIKE ME.

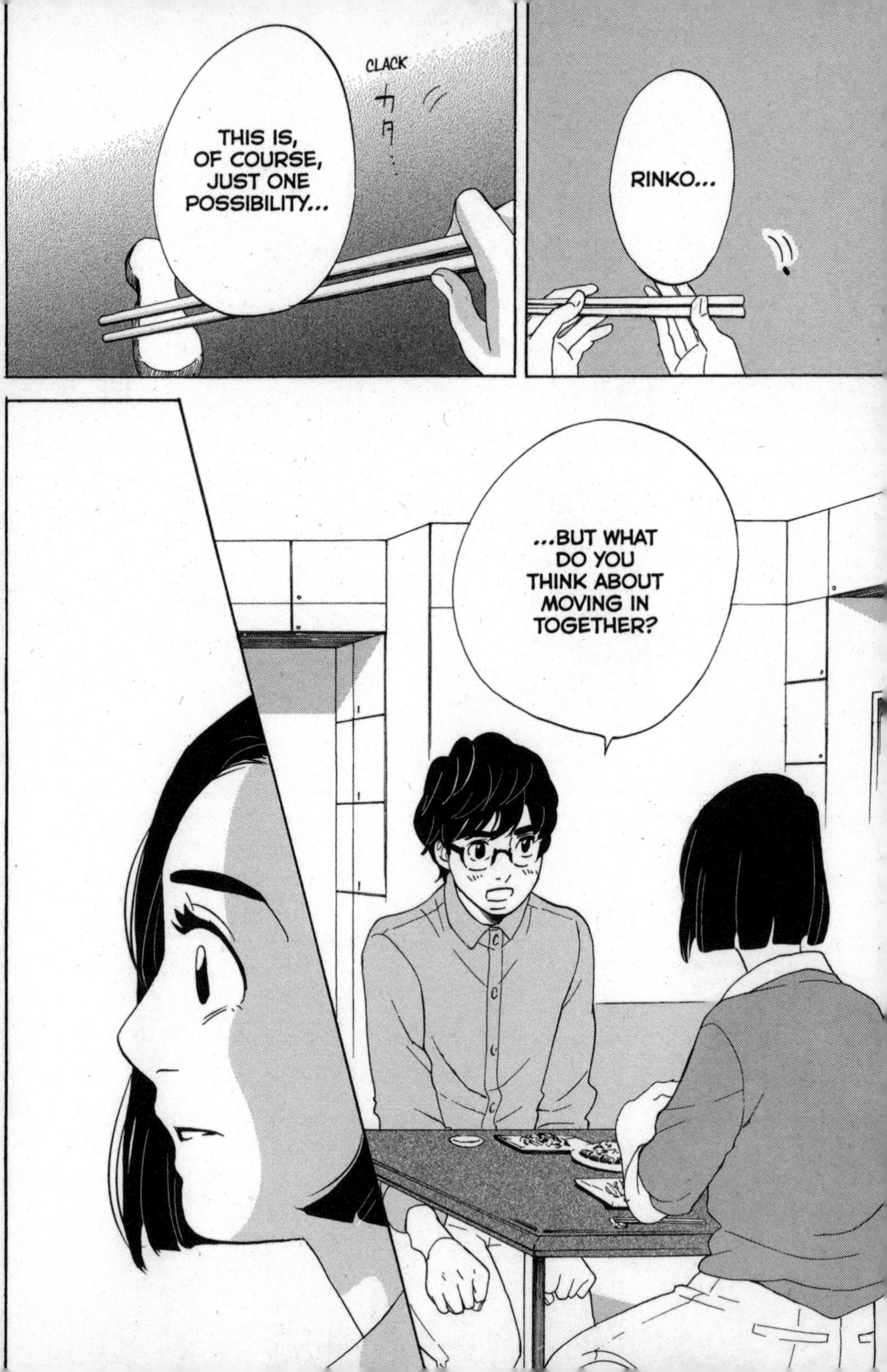
RINKO...
THIS IS, OF COURSE, JUST ONE POSSIBILITY...
CLACK
カタ…
...BUT WHAT DO YOU THINK ABOUT MOVING IN TOGETHER?

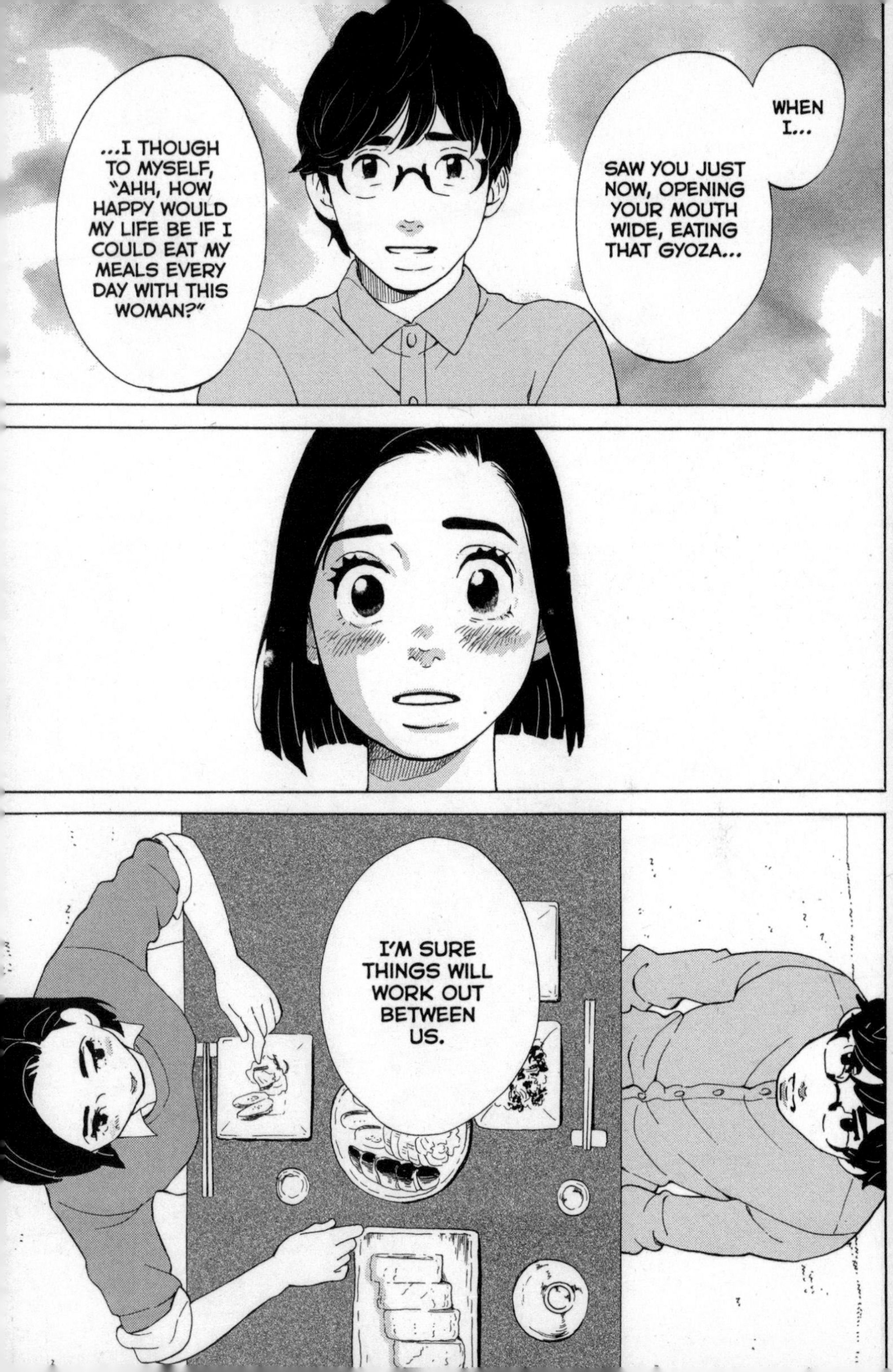
WHEN I...
SAW YOU JUST NOW, OPENING YOUR MOUTH WIDE, EATING THAT GYOZA...
...I THOUGH TO MYSELF, "AHH, HOW HAPPY WOULD MY LIFE BE IF I COULD EAT MY MEALS EVERY DAY WITH THIS WOMAN?"
I'M SURE THINGS WILL WORK OUT BETWEEN US.

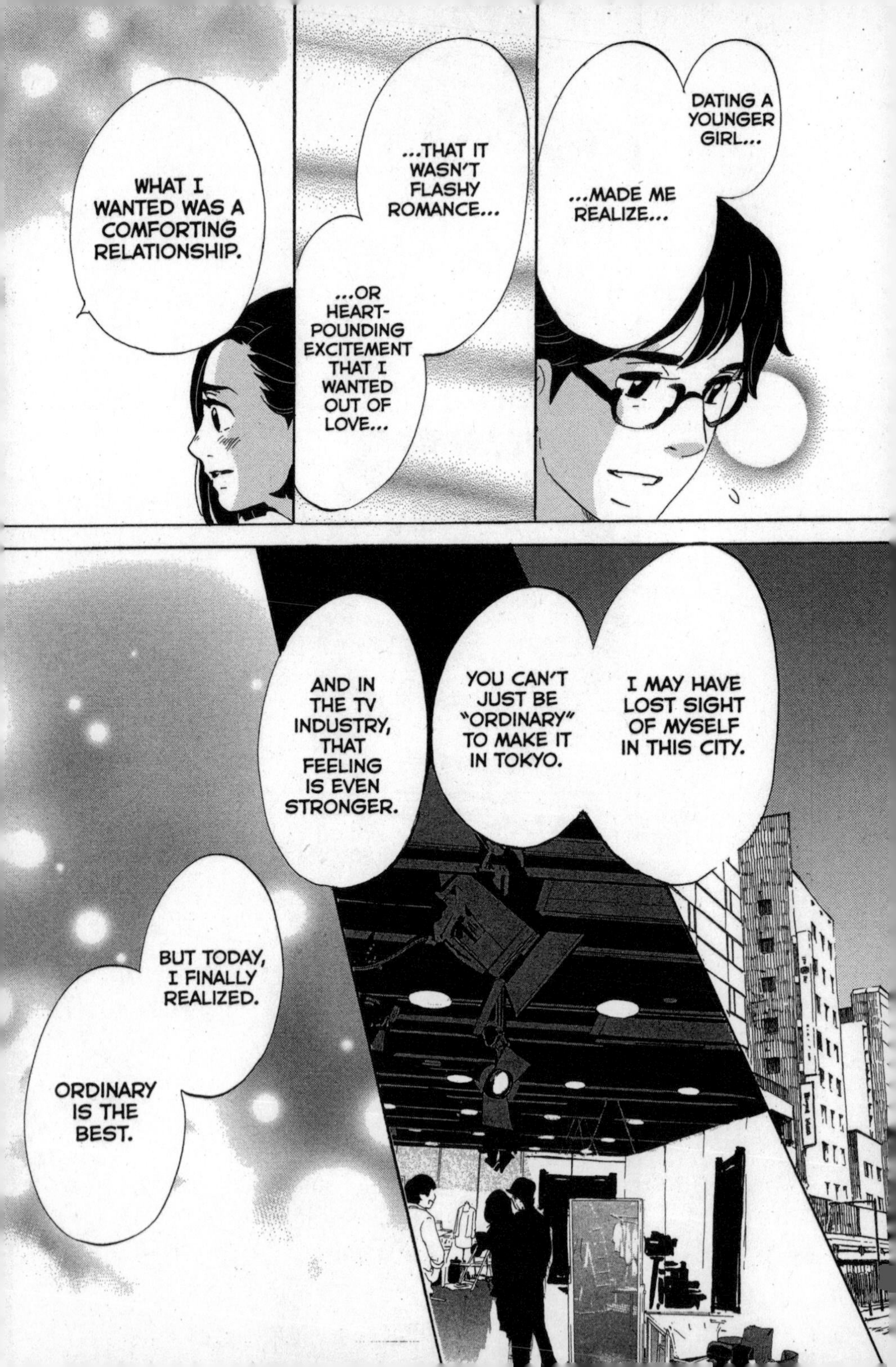
DATING A YOUNGER GIRL...
...MADE ME REALIZE...
...THAT IT WASN'T FLASHY ROMANCE...
...OR HEART-POUNDING EXCITEMENT THAT I WANTED OUT OF LOVE...
WHAT I WANTED WAS A COMFORTING RELATIONSHIP.
I MAY HAVE LOST SIGHT OF MYSELF IN THIS CITY.
YOU CAN'T JUST BE "ORDINARY" TO MAKE IT IN TOKYO.
AND IN THE TV INDUSTRY, THAT FEELING IS EVEN STRONGER.
BUT TODAY, I FINALLY REALIZED.
ORDINARY IS THE BEST.

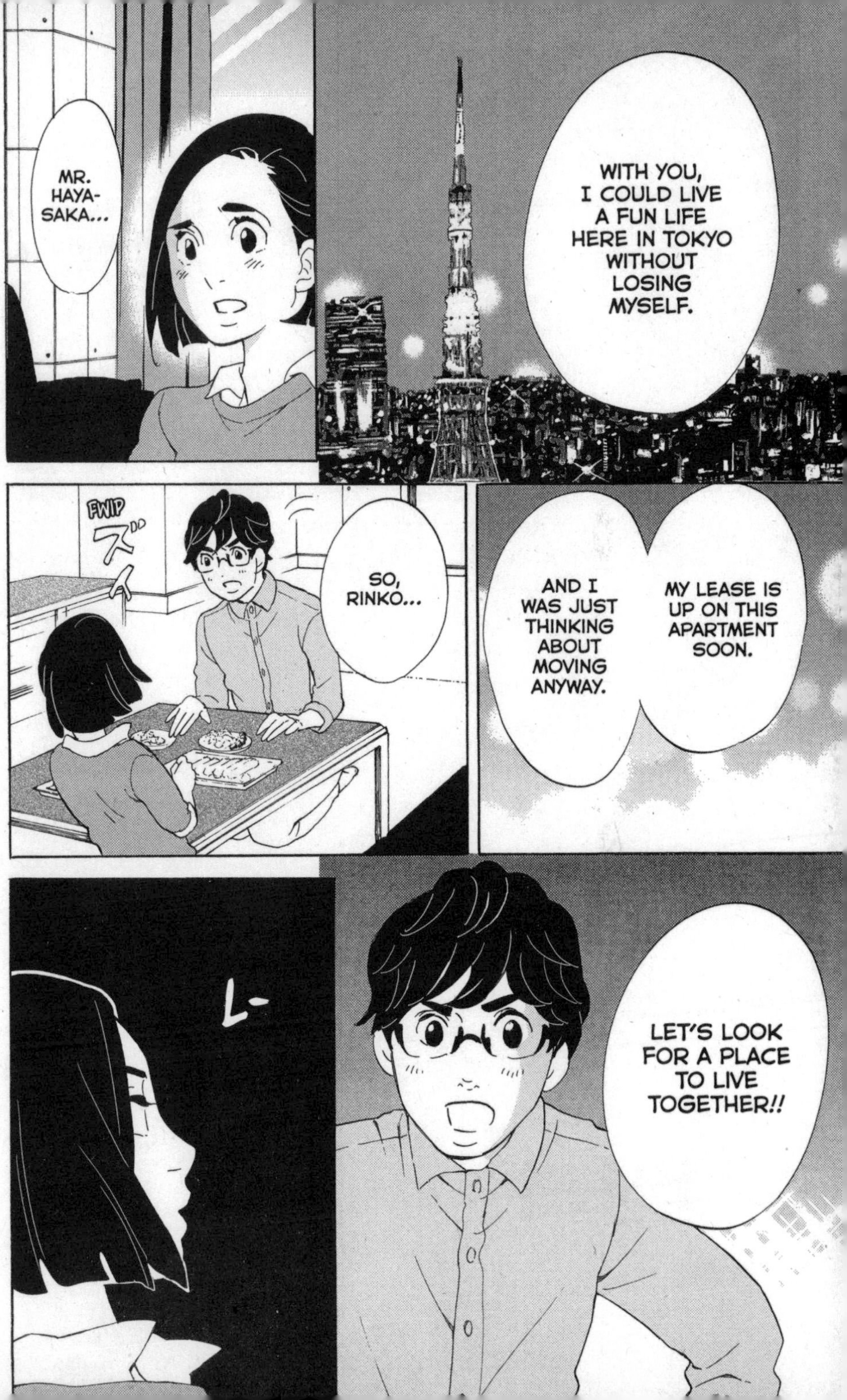
WITH YOU, I COULD LIVE A FUN LIFE HERE IN TOKYO WITHOUT LOSING MYSELF.
MR. HAYA-SAKA...
MY LEASE IS UP ON THIS APARTMENT SOON.
AND I WAS JUST THINKING ABOUT MOVING ANYWAY.
FWIP
SO, RINKO...
LET'S LOOK FOR A PLACE TO LIVE TOGETHER!!

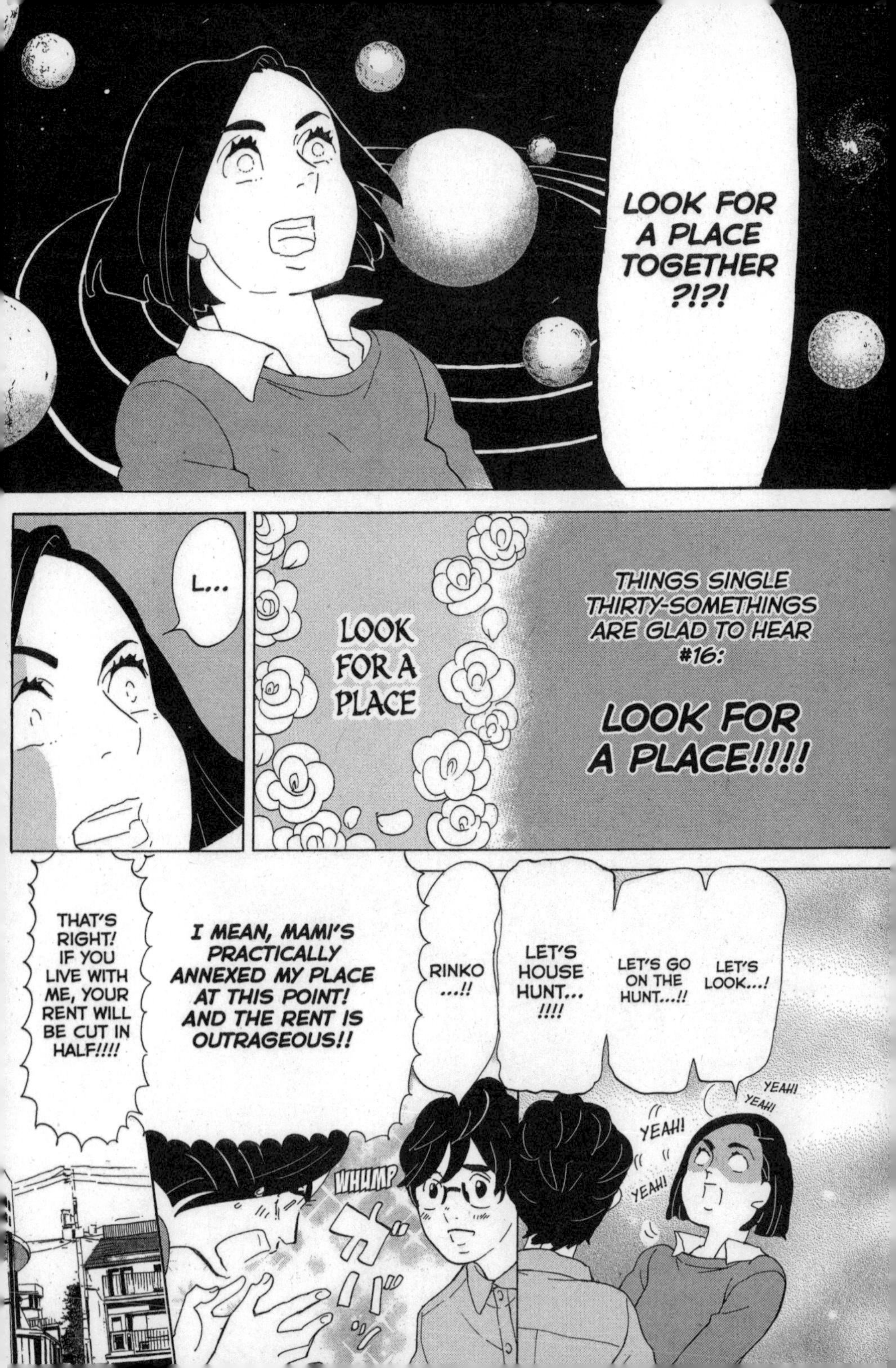
LOOK FOR A PLACE TOGETHER ?!?!
THINGS SINGLE THIRTY-SOMETHINGS ARE GLAD TO HEAR #16:
LOOK FOR A PLACE!!!!
LOOK FOR A PLACE
L...
YEAH! YEAH!
LET'S LOOK...!
LET'S GO ON THE HUNT...!!
LET'S HOUSE HUNT... !!!!
YEAH!
YEAH!
RINKO ...!!
I MEAN, MAMI'S PRACTICALLY ANNEXED MY PLACE AT THIS POINT! AND THE RENT IS OUTRAGEOUS!!
WHHMP
THAT'S RIGHT! IF YOU LIVE WITH ME, YOUR RENT WILL BE CUT IN HALF!!!!

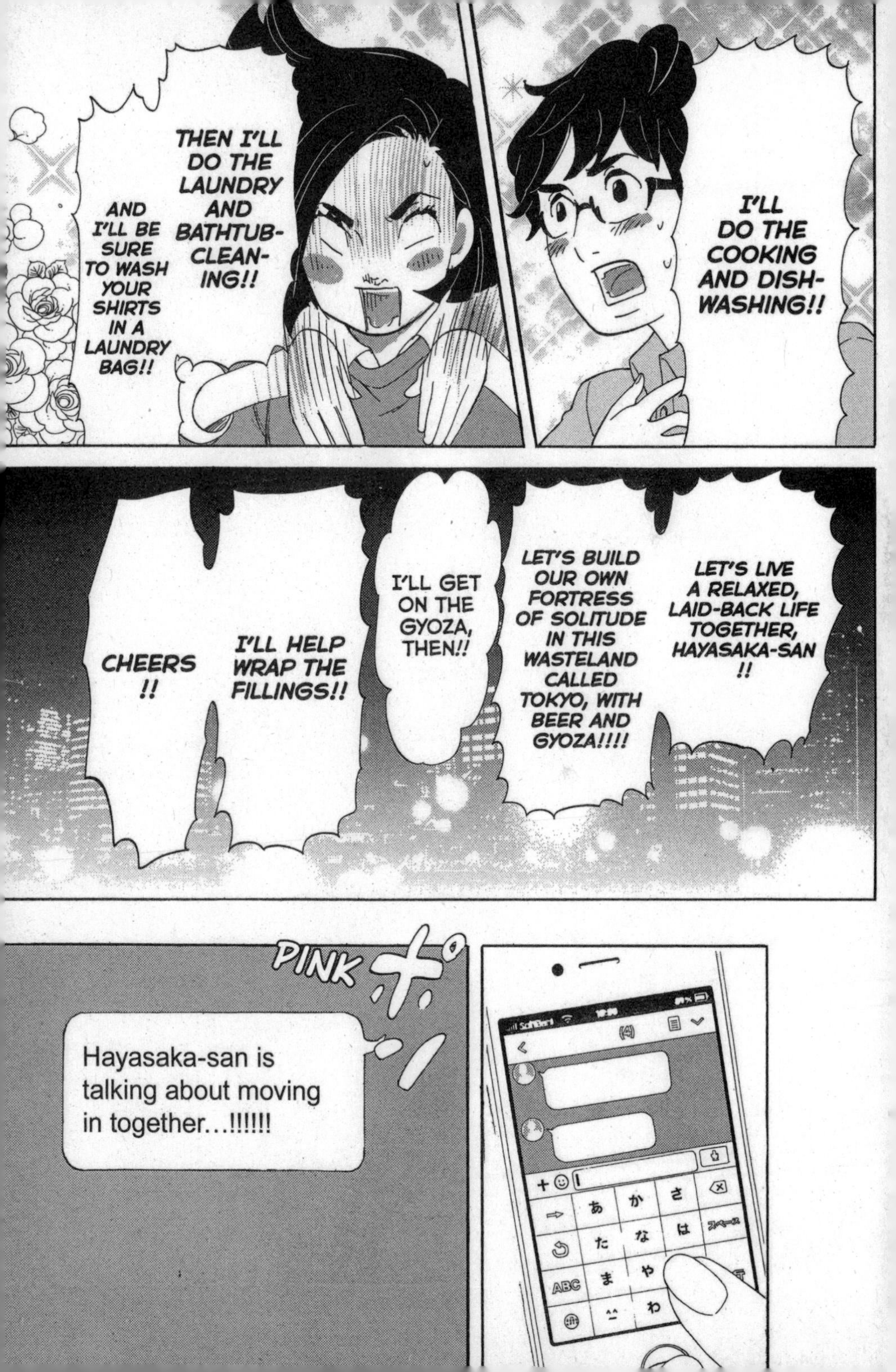
I'LL DO THE COOKING AND DISH-WASHING!!
THEN I'LL DO THE LAUNDRY AND BATHTUB-CLEANING!!
AND I'LL BE SURE TO WASH YOUR SHIRTS IN A LAUNDRY BAG!!
LET'S LIVE A RELAXED, LAID-BACK LIFE TOGETHER, HAYASAKA-SAN!!
LET'S BUILD OUR OWN FORTRESS OF SOLITUDE IN THIS WASTELAND CALLED TOKYO, WITH BEER AND GYOZA!!!!
I'LL GET ON THE GYOZA, THEN!!
I'LL HELP WRAP THE FILLINGS!!
CHEERS!!
PINK
Hayasaka-san is talking about moving in together…!!!!!!

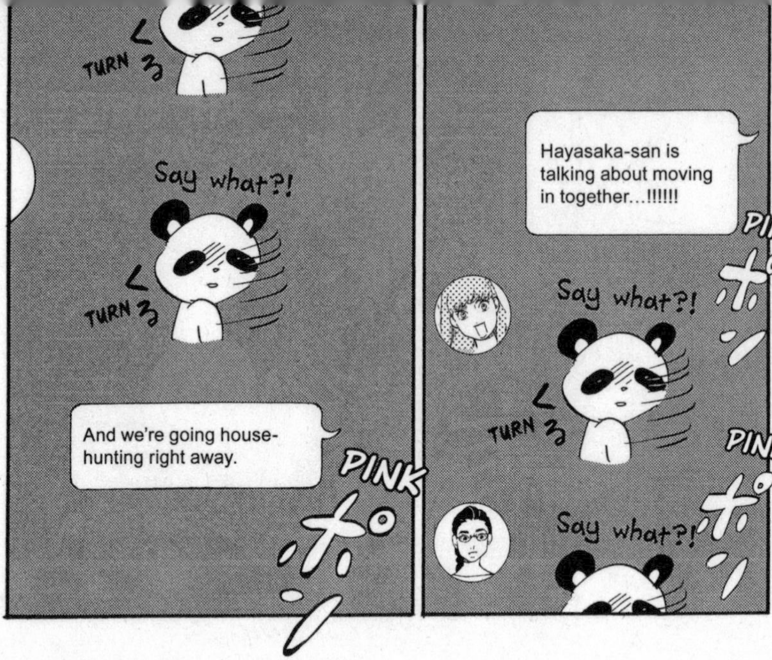
Hayasaka-san is talking about moving in together...!!!!!!
PINK
Say what?!
TURN
PINK
Say what?!
TURN
Say what?!
TURN
And we're going house-hunting right away.
PINK

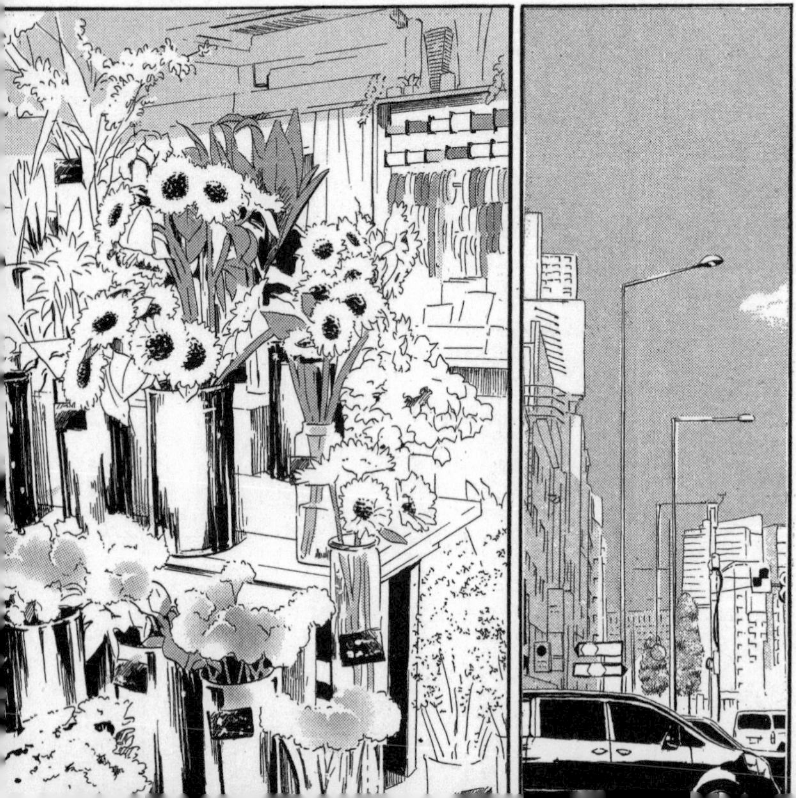

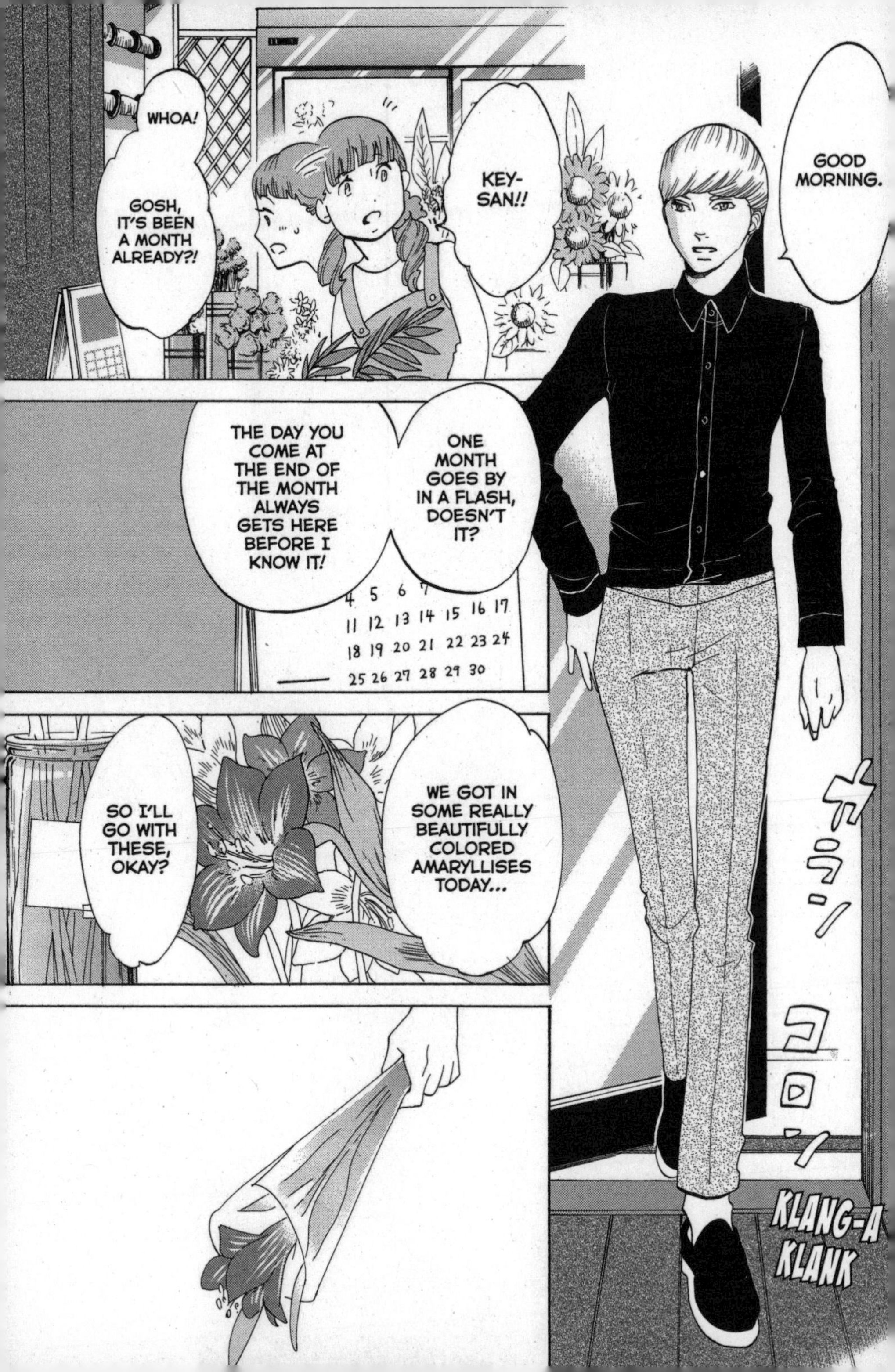
GOOD MORNING.
カラン
コロン
KLANG-A KLANK
KEY-SAN!!
WHOA!
GOSH, IT'S BEEN A MONTH ALREADY?!
ONE MONTH GOES BY IN A FLASH, DOESN'T IT?
THE DAY YOU COME AT THE END OF THE MONTH ALWAYS GETS HERE BEFORE I KNOW IT!
4 5 6 7
11 12 13 14 15 16 17
18 19 20 21 22 23 24
25 26 27 28 29 30
WE GOT IN SOME REALLY BEAUTIFULLY COLORED AMARYLLISES TODAY...
SO I'LL GO WITH THESE, OKAY?

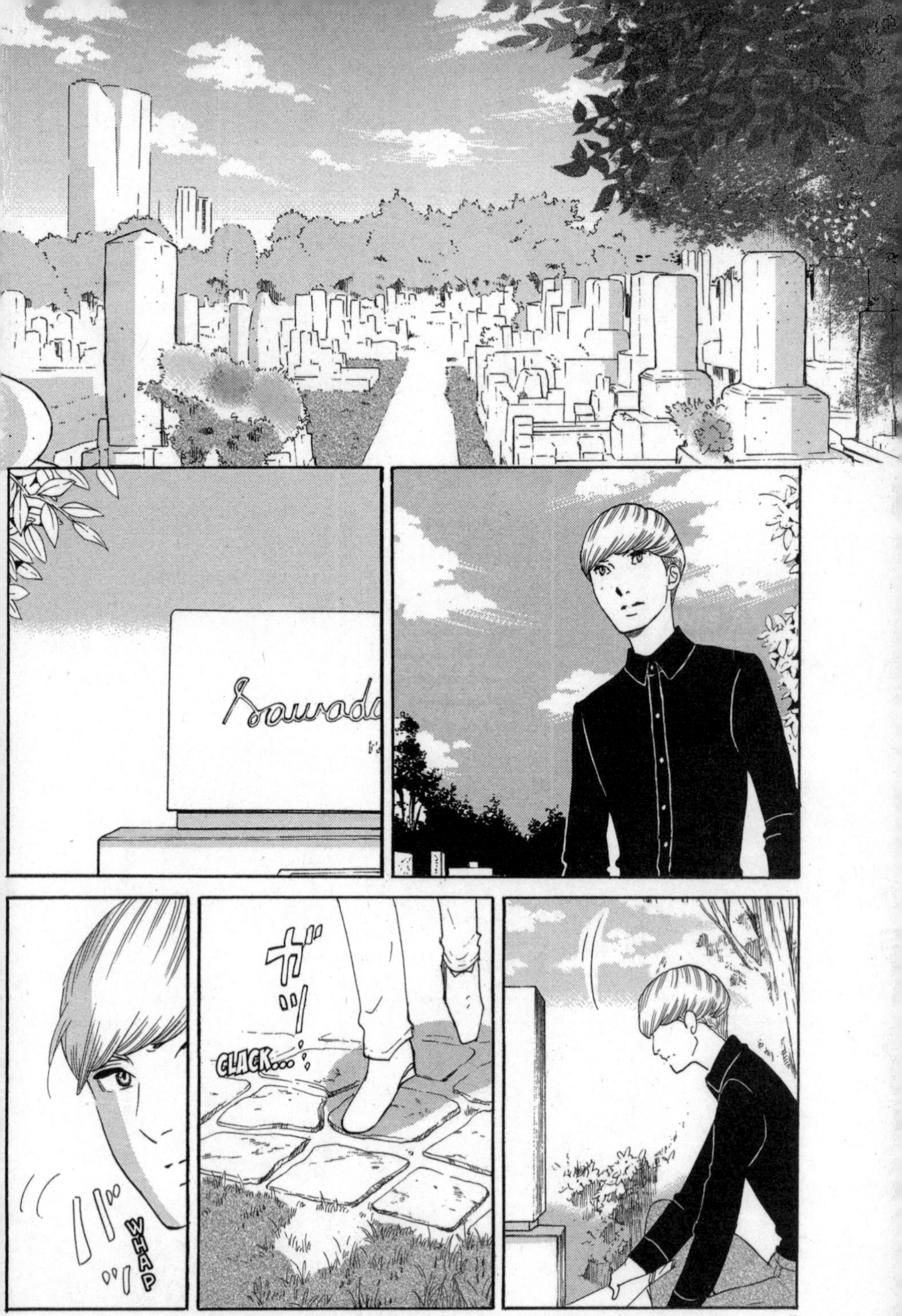
Sawada
ガッ
CLACK...
WHAP

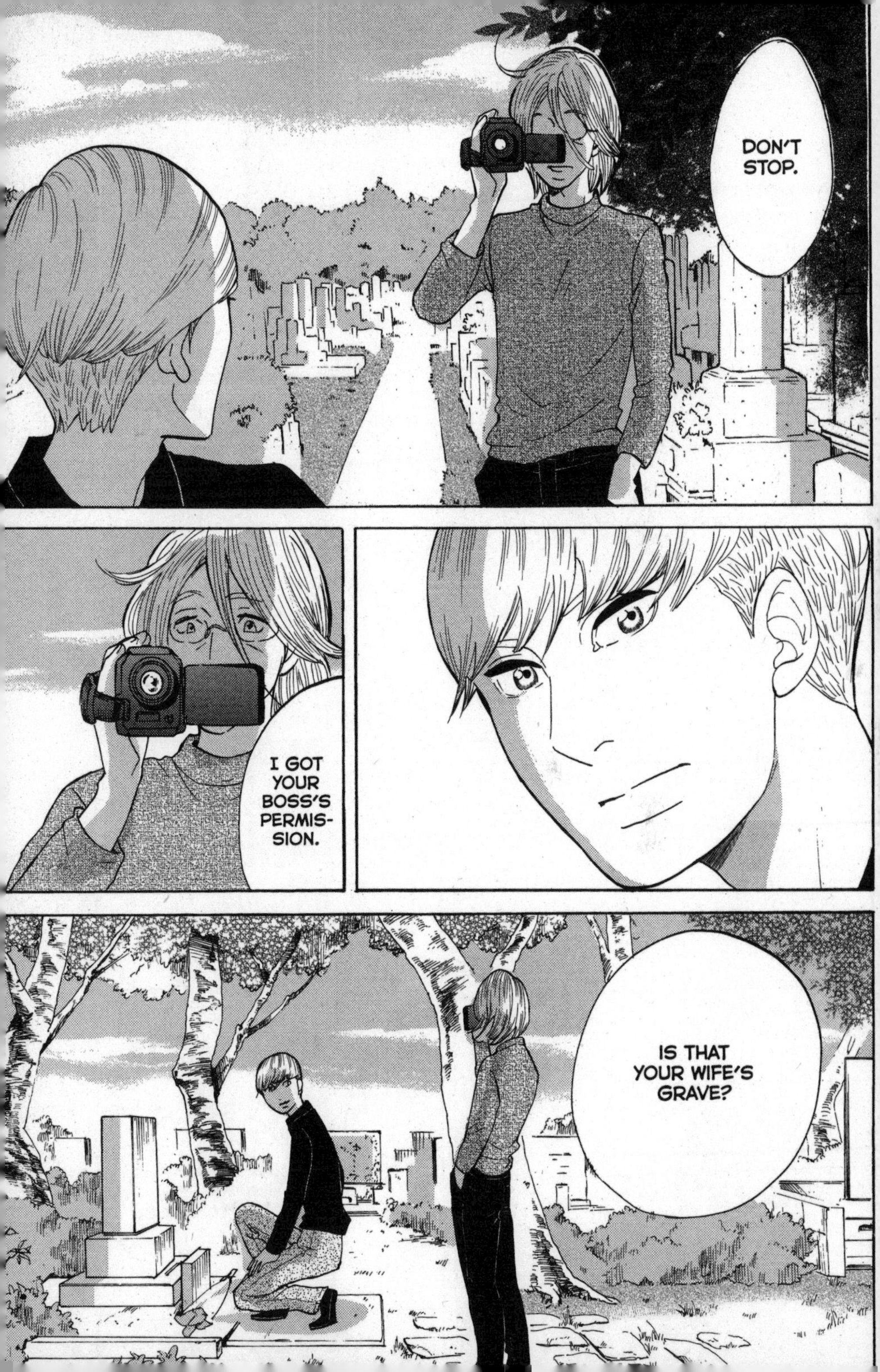
DON'T STOP.
I GOT YOUR BOSS'S PERMIS- SION.
IS THAT YOUR WIFE'S GRAVE?

WHY DON'T WE CHAT A LITTLE ON THAT BENCH?

ザ" SHHH...

ア ..

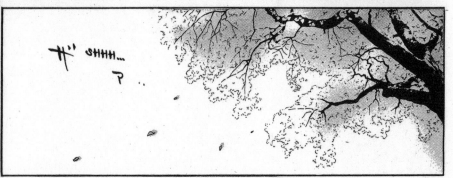

I'LL BET YOUR FANS WOULD SURE BE SURPRISED IF THEY FOUND OUT YOU WERE MARRIED, KEY.

BOY...

...OH, I DON'T KNOW.

ウィ... WHRRRR...

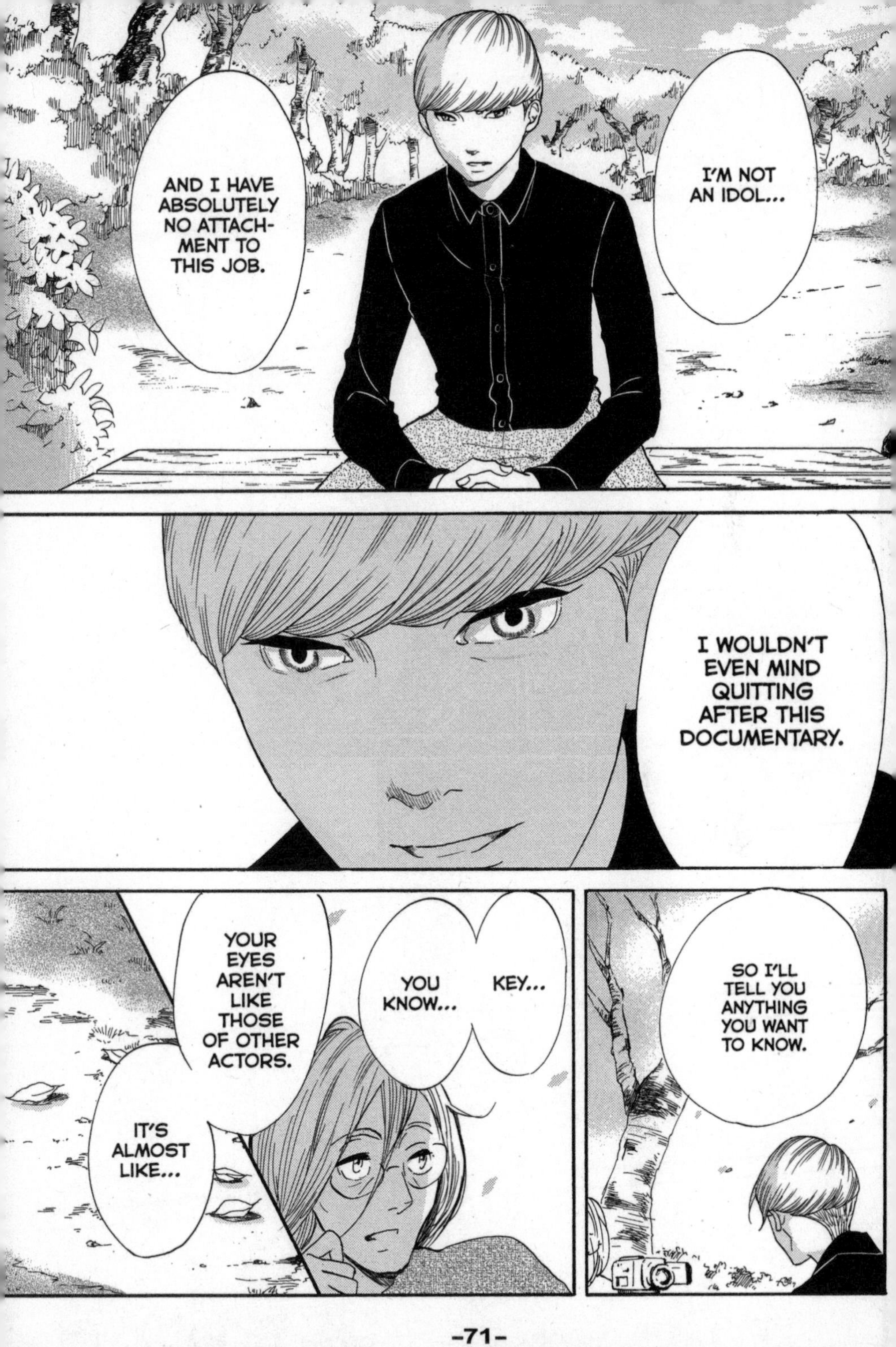
I'M NOT AN IDOL...
AND I HAVE ABSOLUTELY NO ATTACHMENT TO THIS JOB.
I WOULDN'T EVEN MIND QUITTING AFTER THIS DOCUMENTARY.
SO I'LL TELL YOU ANYTHING YOU WANT TO KNOW.
KEY...
YOU KNOW...
YOUR EYES AREN'T LIKE THOSE OF OTHER ACTORS.
IT'S ALMOST LIKE...

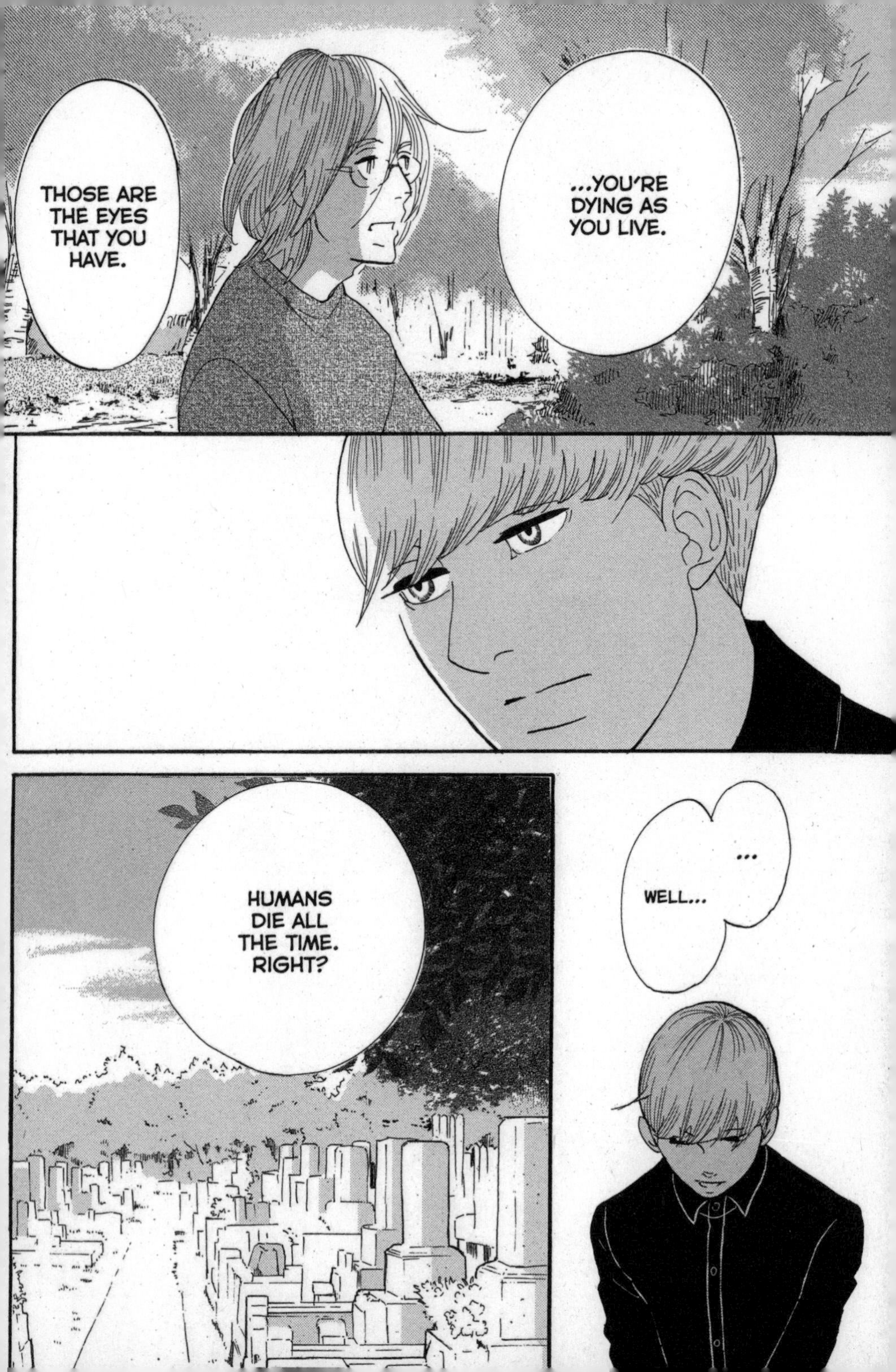
...YOU'RE DYING AS YOU LIVE.
THOSE ARE THE EYES THAT YOU HAVE.
... WELL...
HUMANS DIE ALL THE TIME. RIGHT?

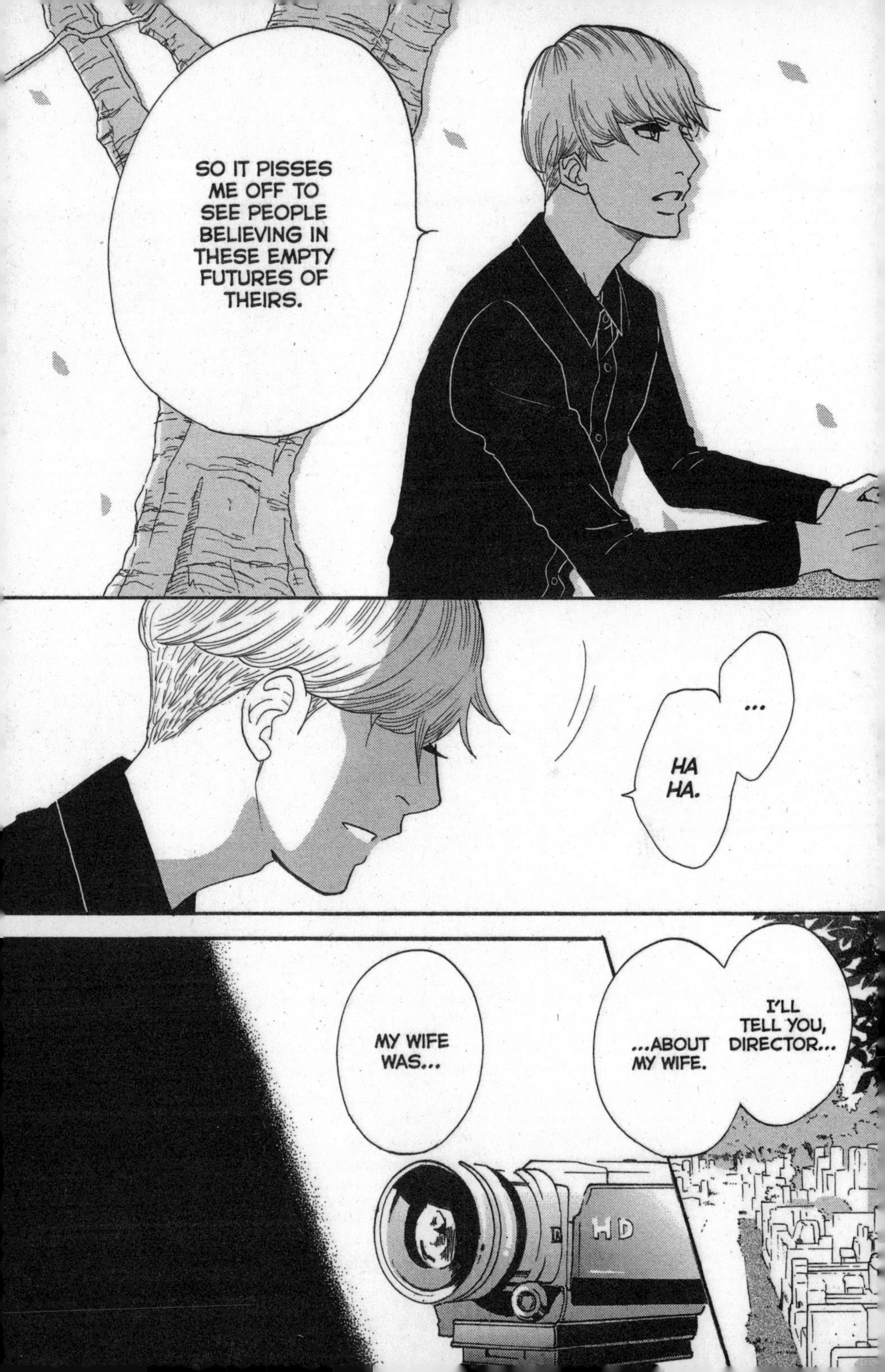
SO IT PISSES ME OFF TO SEE PEOPLE BELIEVING IN THESE EMPTY FUTURES OF THEIRS.
... HA HA.
I'LL TELL YOU, DIRECTOR...
...ABOUT MY WIFE.
MY WIFE WAS...

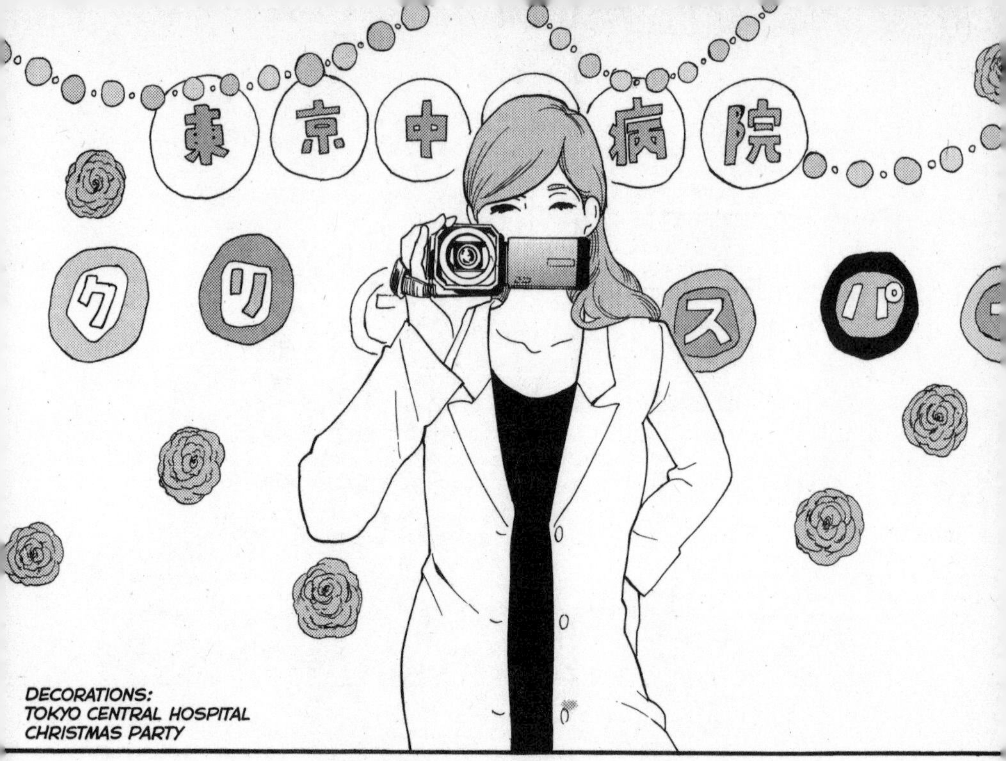
東京中病院
クリ ス パ
DECORATIONS:
TOKYO CENTRAL HOSPITAL
CHRISTMAS PARTY

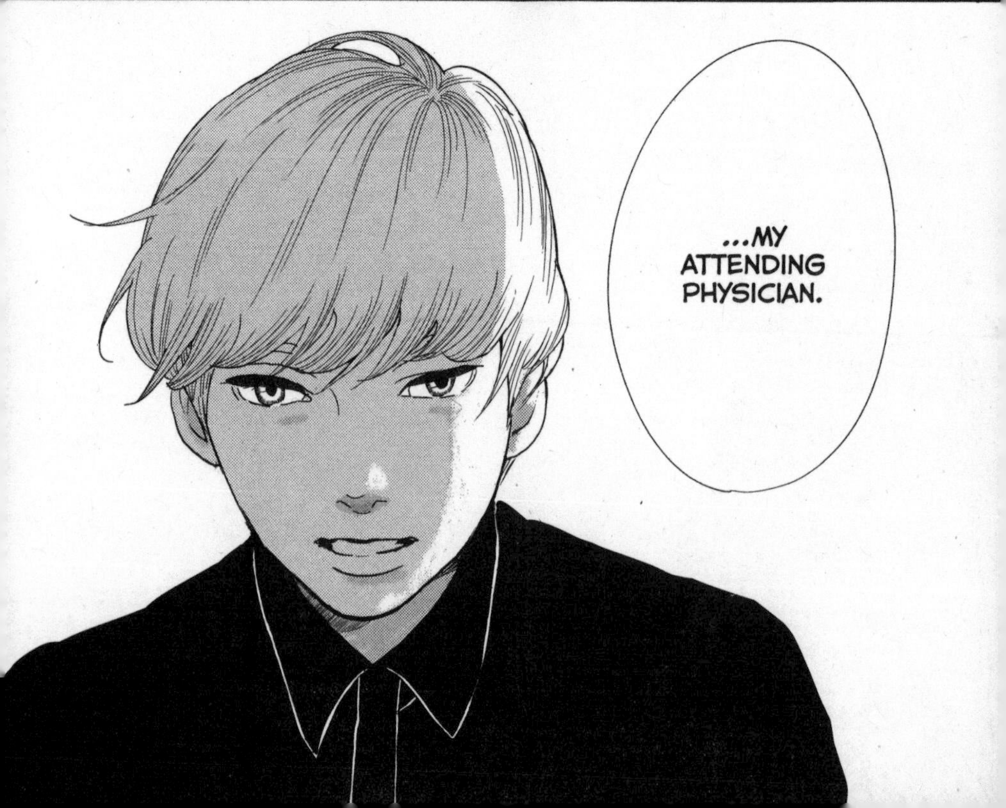
...MY ATTENDING PHYSICIAN.

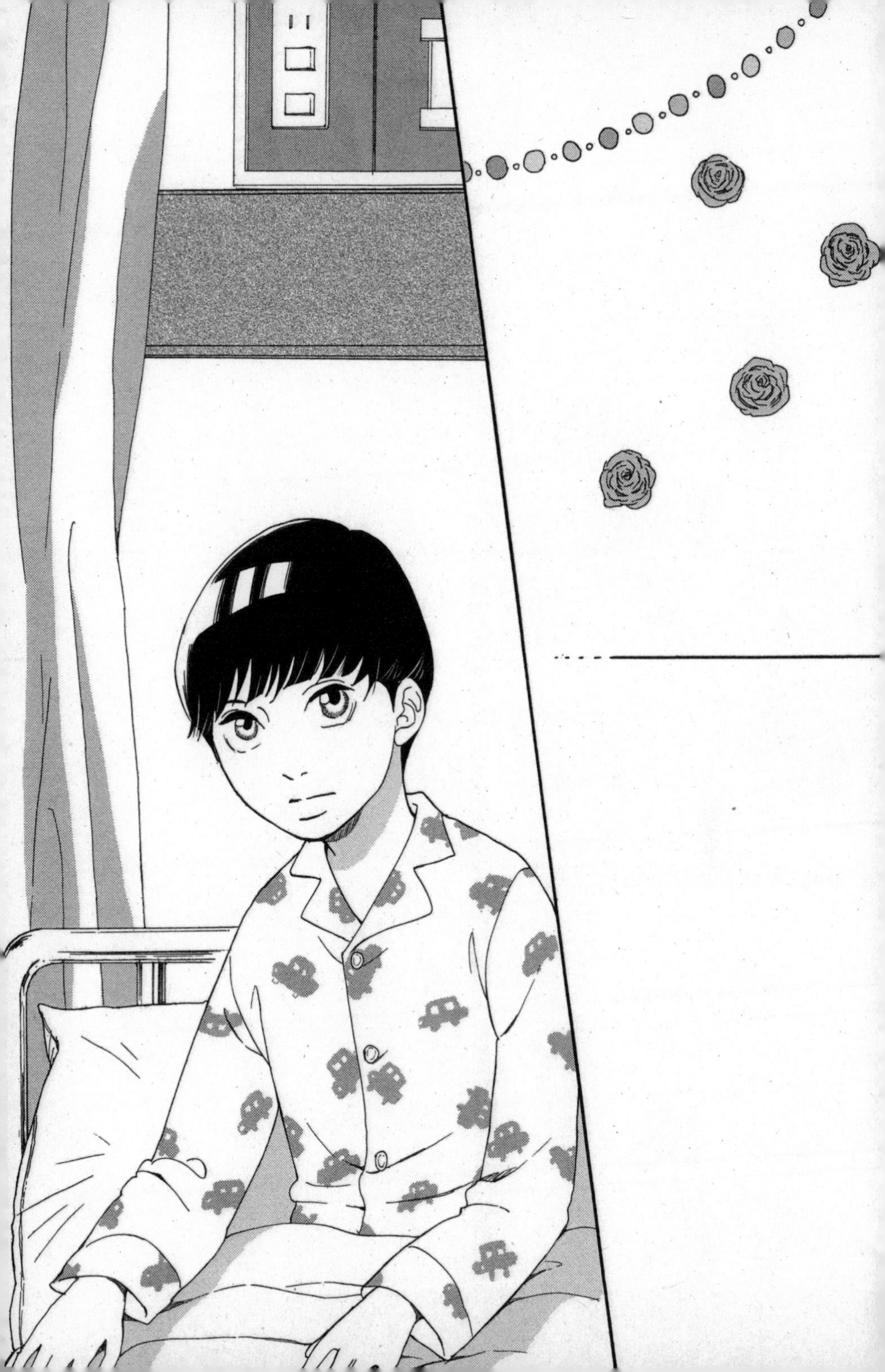

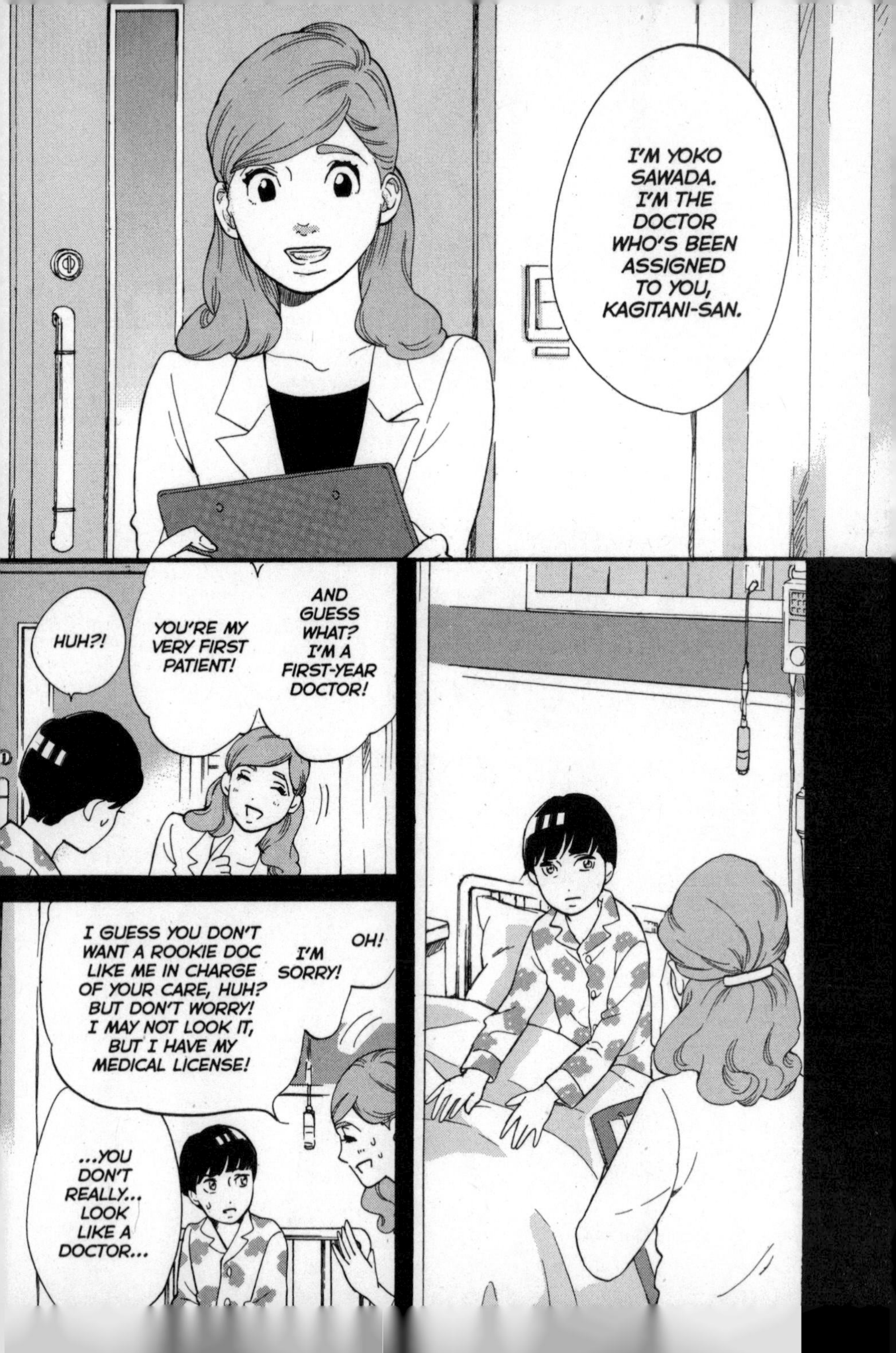
I'M YOKO SAWADA. I'M THE DOCTOR WHO'S BEEN ASSIGNED TO YOU, KAGITANI-SAN.
YOU'RE MY VERY FIRST PATIENT!
AND GUESS WHAT? I'M A FIRST-YEAR DOCTOR!
HUH?!
OH!
I'M SORRY!
I GUESS YOU DON'T WANT A ROOKIE DOC LIKE ME IN CHARGE OF YOUR CARE, HUH? BUT DON'T WORRY! I MAY NOT LOOK IT, BUT I HAVE MY MEDICAL LICENSE!
...YOU DON'T REALLY... LOOK LIKE A DOCTOR...

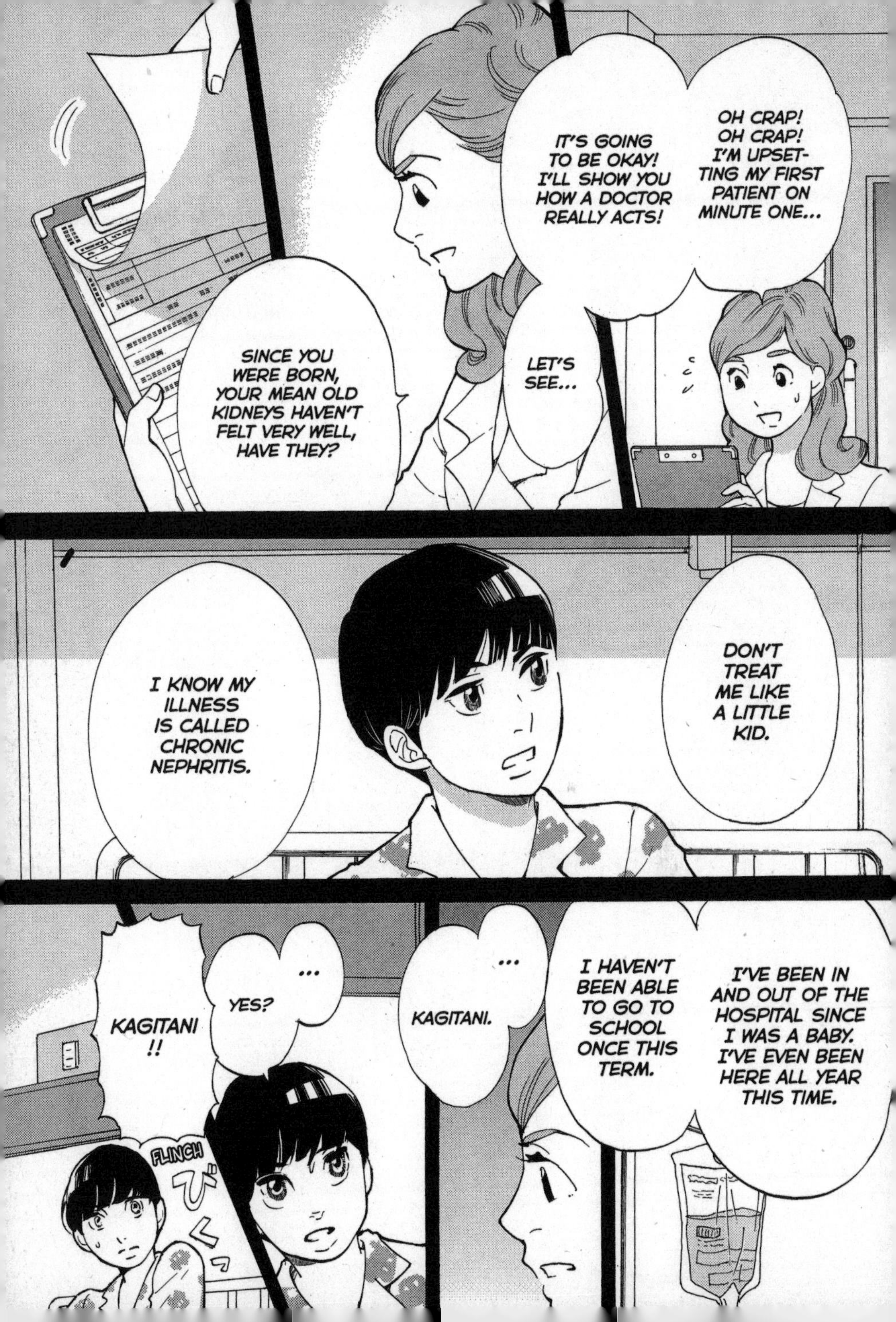
OH CRAP! OH CRAP! I'M UPSET-TING MY FIRST PATIENT ON MINUTE ONE...
IT'S GOING TO BE OKAY! I'LL SHOW YOU HOW A DOCTOR REALLY ACTS!
LET'S SEE...
SINCE YOU WERE BORN, YOUR MEAN OLD KIDNEYS HAVEN'T FELT VERY WELL, HAVE THEY?
DON'T TREAT ME LIKE A LITTLE KID.
I KNOW MY ILLNESS IS CALLED CHRONIC NEPHRITIS.
I'VE BEEN IN AND OUT OF THE HOSPITAL SINCE I WAS A BABY. I'VE EVEN BEEN HERE ALL YEAR THIS TIME.
I HAVEN'T BEEN ABLE TO GO TO SCHOOL ONCE THIS TERM.
...
KAGITANI.
...
YES?
KAGITANI !!
FLINCH

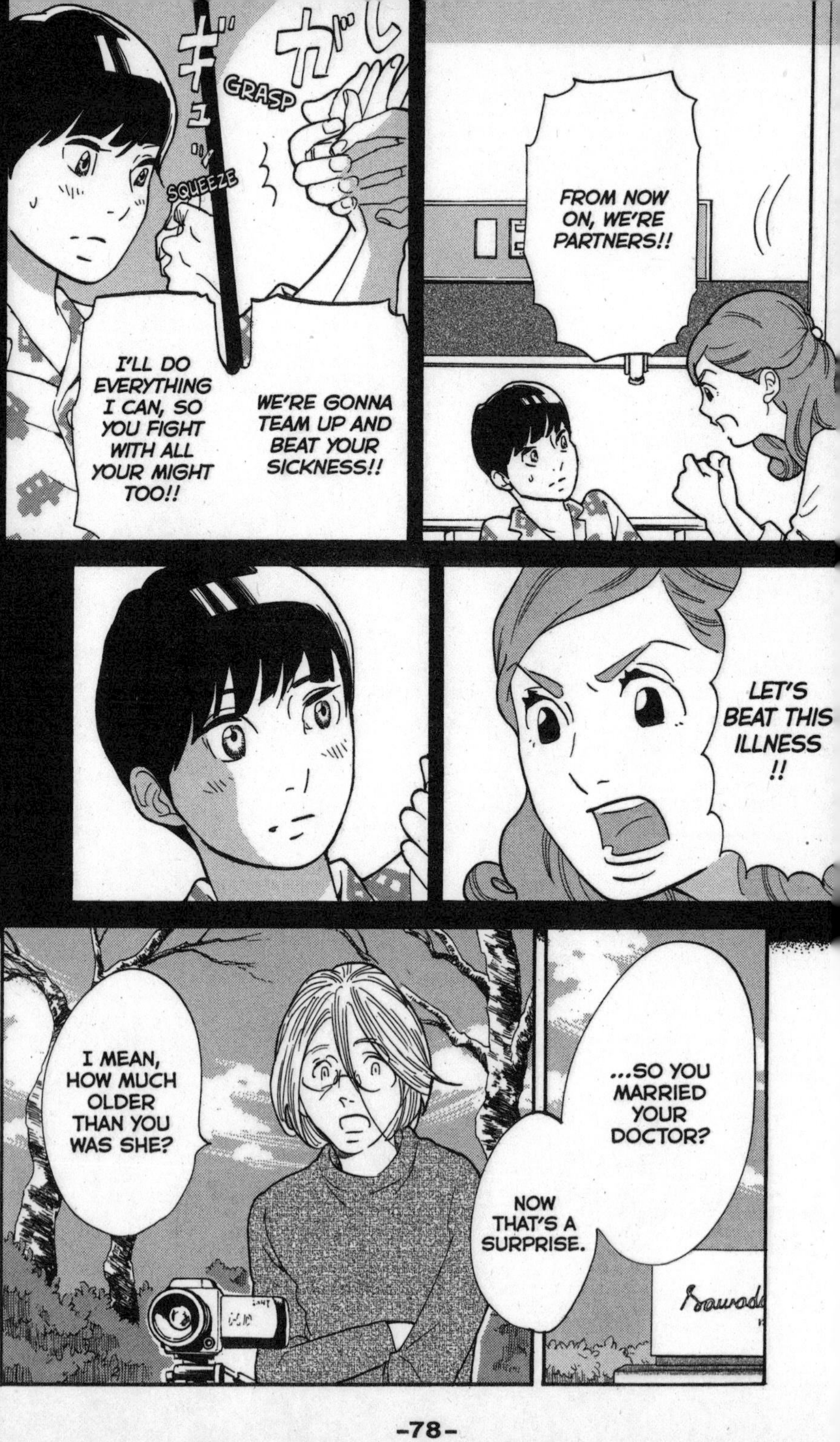
FROM NOW ON, WE'RE PARTNERS!!
ガし
GRASP
ギュ
SQUEEZE
WE'RE GONNA TEAM UP AND BEAT YOUR SICKNESS!!
I'LL DO EVERYTHING I CAN, SO YOU FIGHT WITH ALL YOUR MIGHT TOO!!
LET'S BEAT THIS ILLNESS !!
...SO YOU MARRIED YOUR DOCTOR?
NOW THAT'S A SURPRISE.
Sawada
I MEAN, HOW MUCH OLDER THAN YOU WAS SHE?

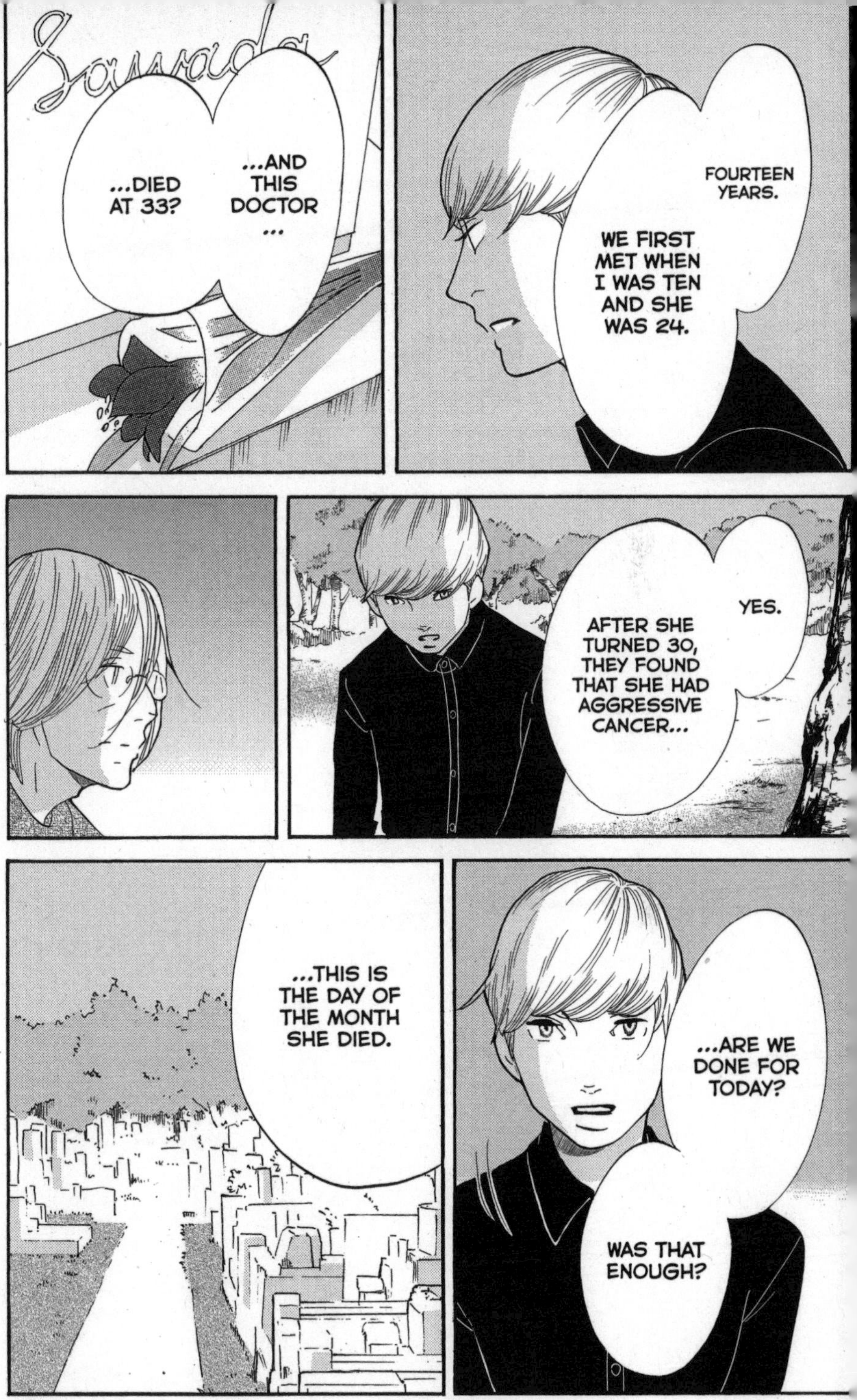
FOURTEEN YEARS.
WE FIRST MET WHEN I WAS TEN AND SHE WAS 24.
Sawada
...AND THIS DOCTOR ...
...DIED AT 33?
YES.
AFTER SHE TURNED 30, THEY FOUND THAT SHE HAD AGGRESSIVE CANCER...
...ARE WE DONE FOR TODAY?
WAS THAT ENOUGH?
...THIS IS THE DAY OF THE MONTH SHE DIED.

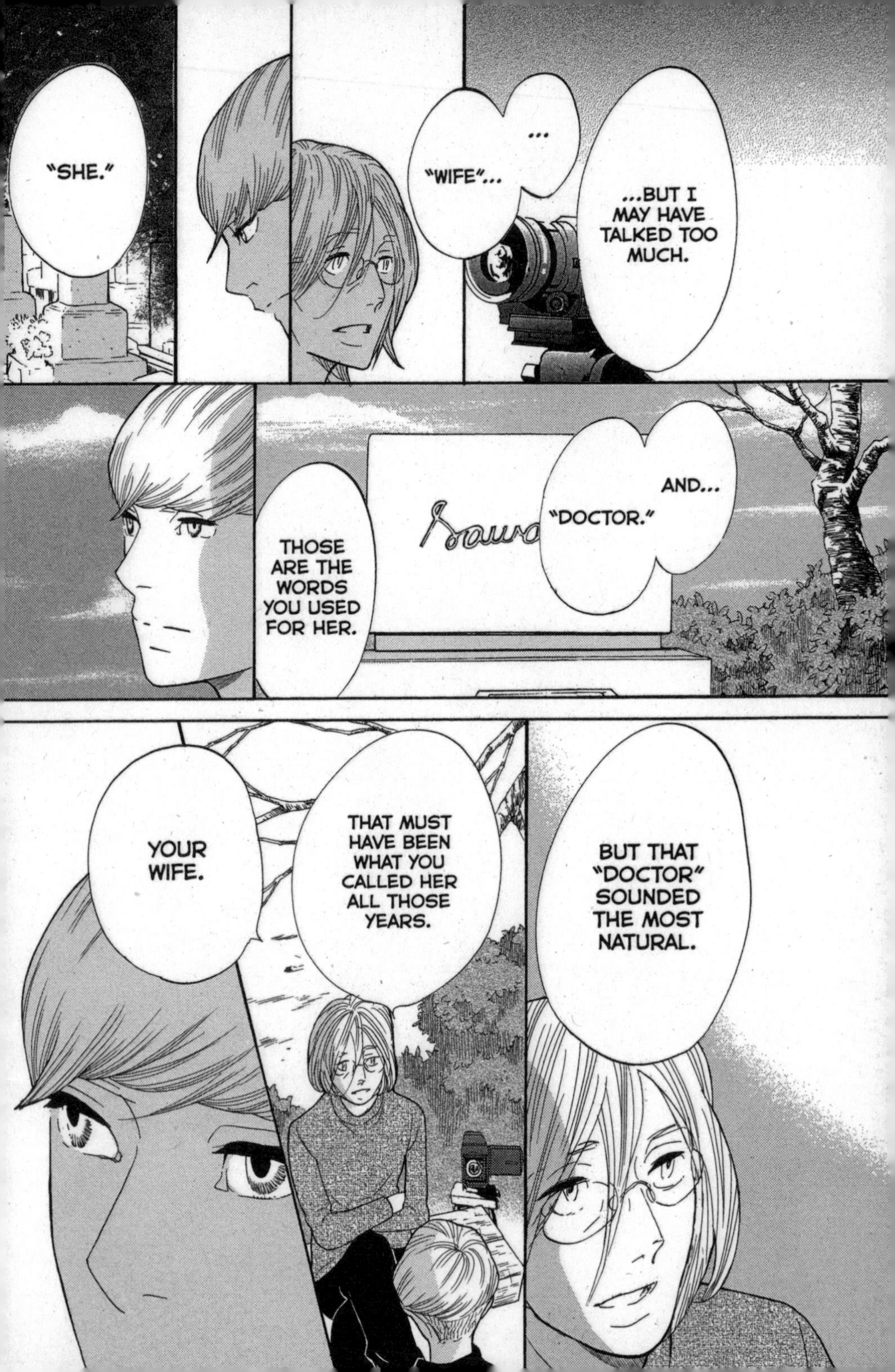
...BUT I MAY HAVE TALKED TOO MUCH.
...
"WIFE"...
"SHE."
AND... "DOCTOR."
THOSE ARE THE WORDS YOU USED FOR HER.
BUT THAT "DOCTOR" SOUNDED THE MOST NATURAL.
THAT MUST HAVE BEEN WHAT YOU CALLED HER ALL THOSE YEARS.
YOUR WIFE.

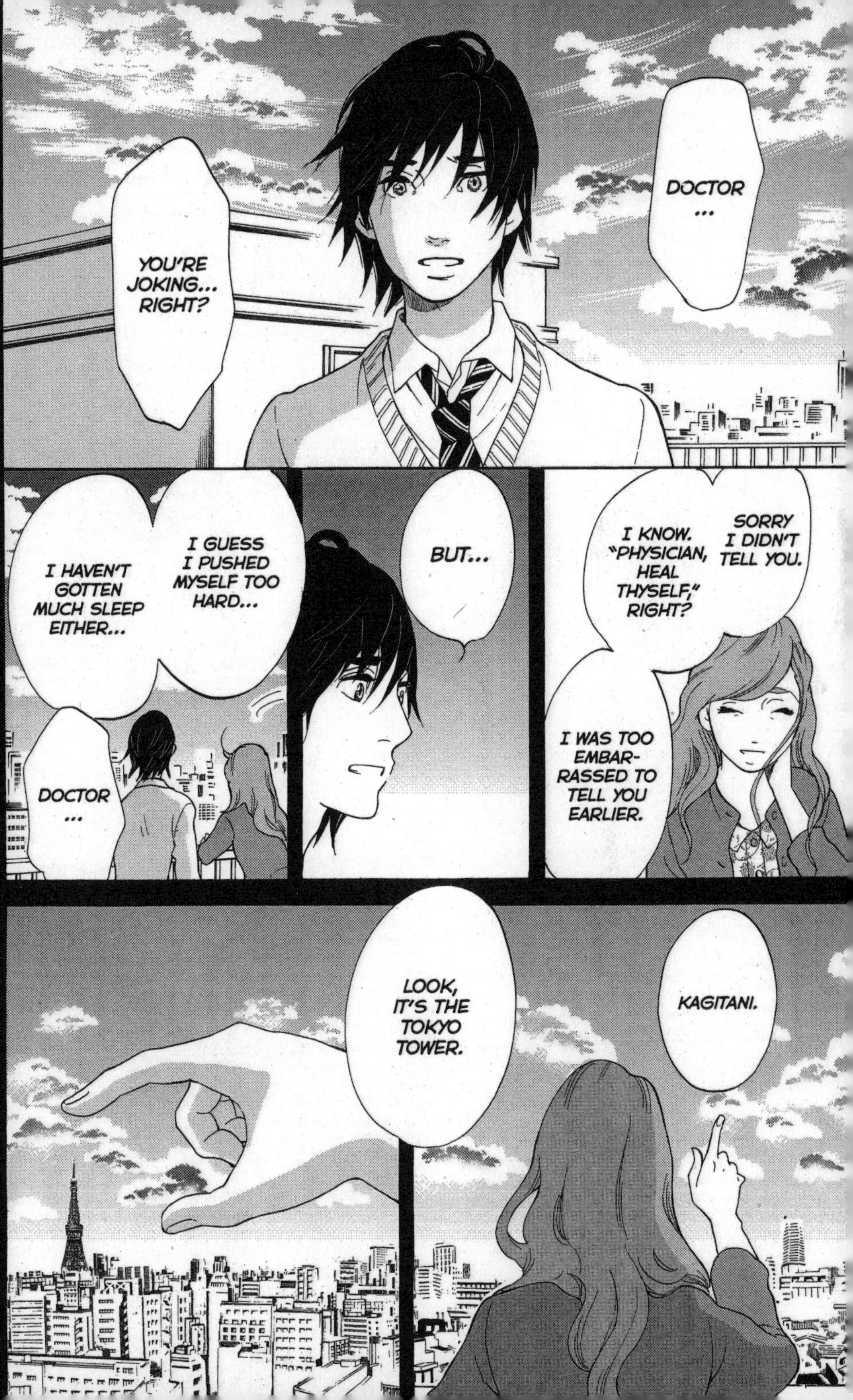
DOCTOR ...
YOU'RE JOKING... RIGHT?
SORRY I DIDN'T TELL YOU.
I KNOW. "PHYSICIAN, HEAL THYSELF," RIGHT?
I WAS TOO EMBAR-RASSED TO TELL YOU EARLIER.
BUT...
I GUESS I PUSHED MYSELF TOO HARD...
I HAVEN'T GOTTEN MUCH SLEEP EITHER...
DOCTOR ...
KAGITANI.
LOOK, IT'S THE TOKYO TOWER.

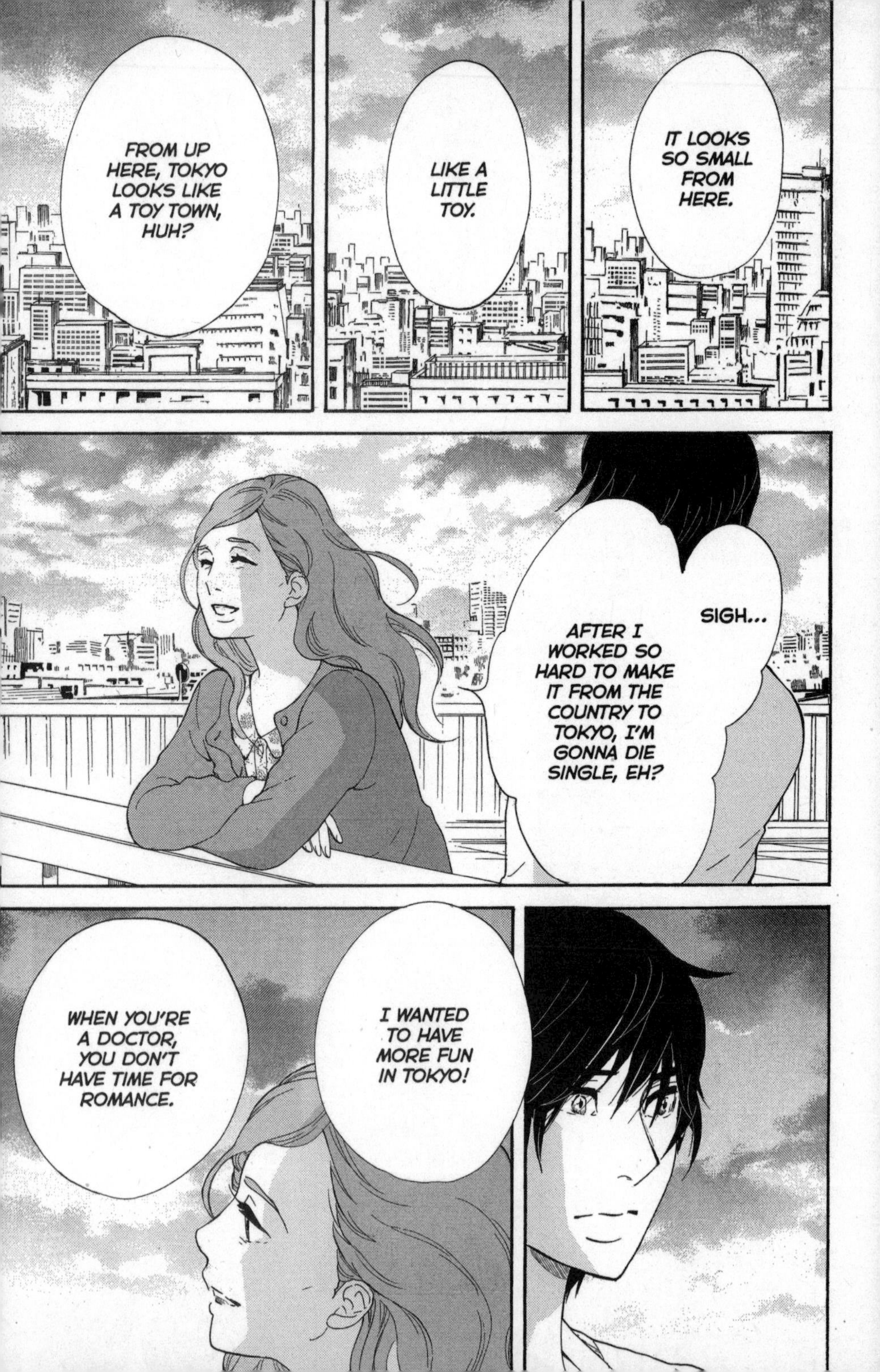
IT LOOKS SO SMALL FROM HERE.
LIKE A LITTLE TOY.
FROM UP HERE, TOKYO LOOKS LIKE A TOY TOWN, HUH?
SIGH...
AFTER I WORKED SO HARD TO MAKE IT FROM THE COUNTRY TO TOKYO, I'M GONNA DIE SINGLE, EH?
I WANTED TO HAVE MORE FUN IN TOKYO!
WHEN YOU'RE A DOCTOR, YOU DON'T HAVE TIME FOR ROMANCE.

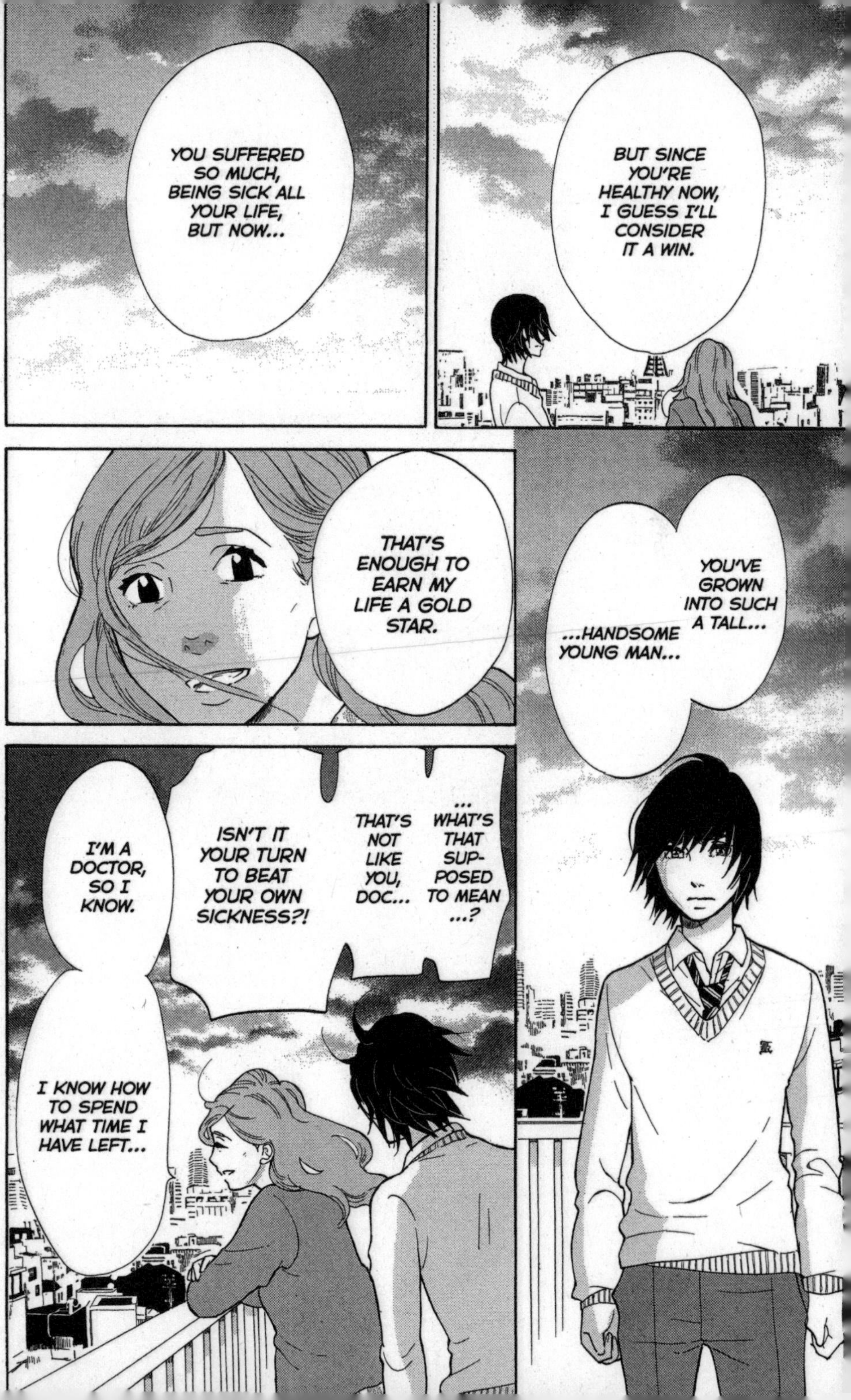
BUT SINCE YOU'RE HEALTHY NOW, I GUESS I'LL CONSIDER IT A WIN.
YOU SUFFERED SO MUCH, BEING SICK ALL YOUR LIFE, BUT NOW...
YOU'VE GROWN INTO SUCH A TALL...
...HANDSOME YOUNG MAN...
THAT'S ENOUGH TO EARN MY LIFE A GOLD STAR.
...WHAT'S THAT SUP-POSED TO MEAN ...?
THAT'S NOT LIKE YOU, DOC...
ISN'T IT YOUR TURN TO BEAT YOUR OWN SICKNESS?!
I'M A DOCTOR, SO I KNOW.
I KNOW HOW TO SPEND WHAT TIME I HAVE LEFT...

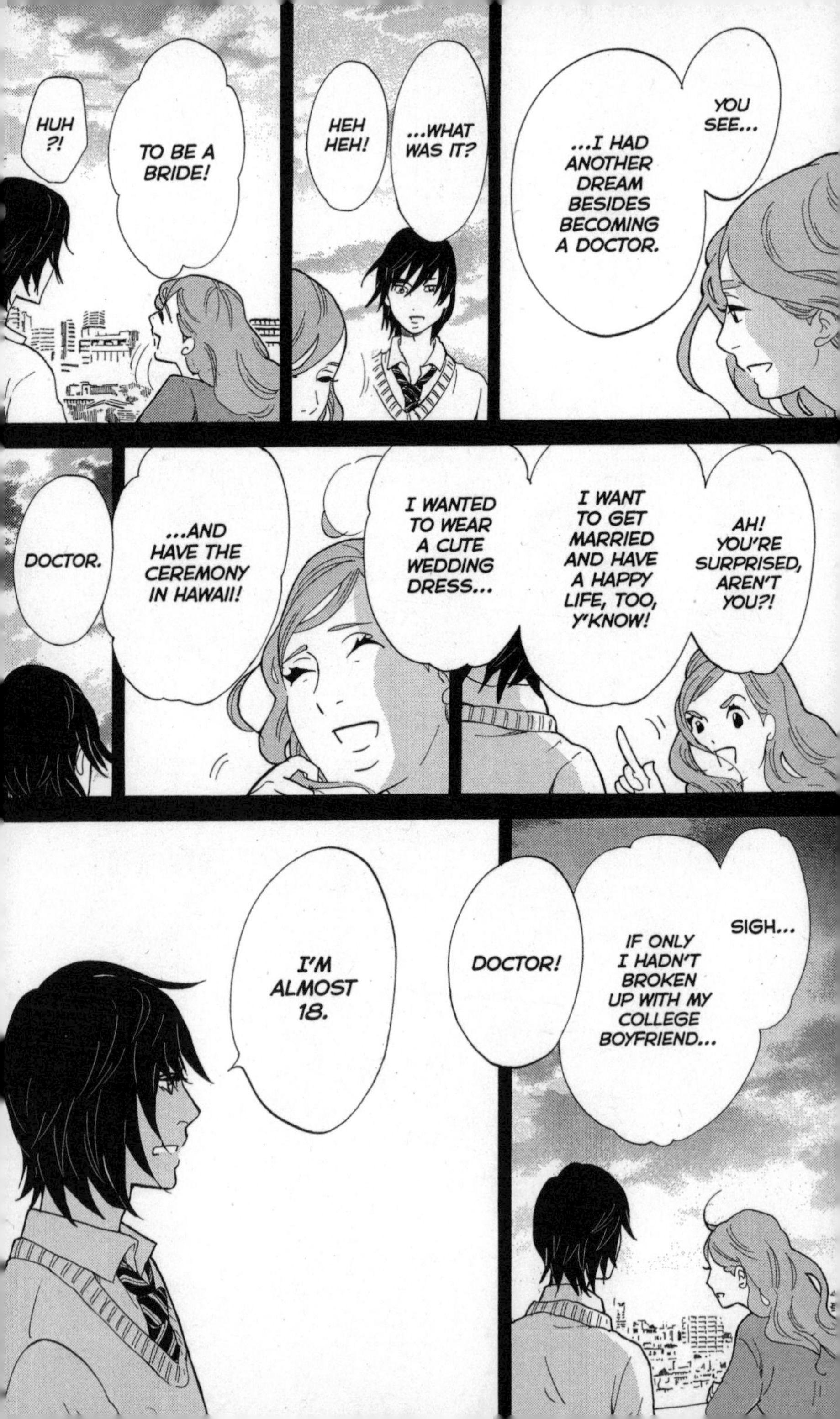
YOU SEE...
...I HAD ANOTHER DREAM BESIDES BECOMING A DOCTOR.
...WHAT WAS IT?
HEH HEH!
TO BE A BRIDE!
HUH ?!
AH! YOU'RE SURPRISED, AREN'T YOU?!
I WANT TO GET MARRIED AND HAVE A HAPPY LIFE, TOO, Y'KNOW!
I WANTED TO WEAR A CUTE WEDDING DRESS...
...AND HAVE THE CEREMONY IN HAWAII!
DOCTOR.
SIGH...
IF ONLY I HADN'T BROKEN UP WITH MY COLLEGE BOYFRIEND...
DOCTOR!
I'M ALMOST 18.

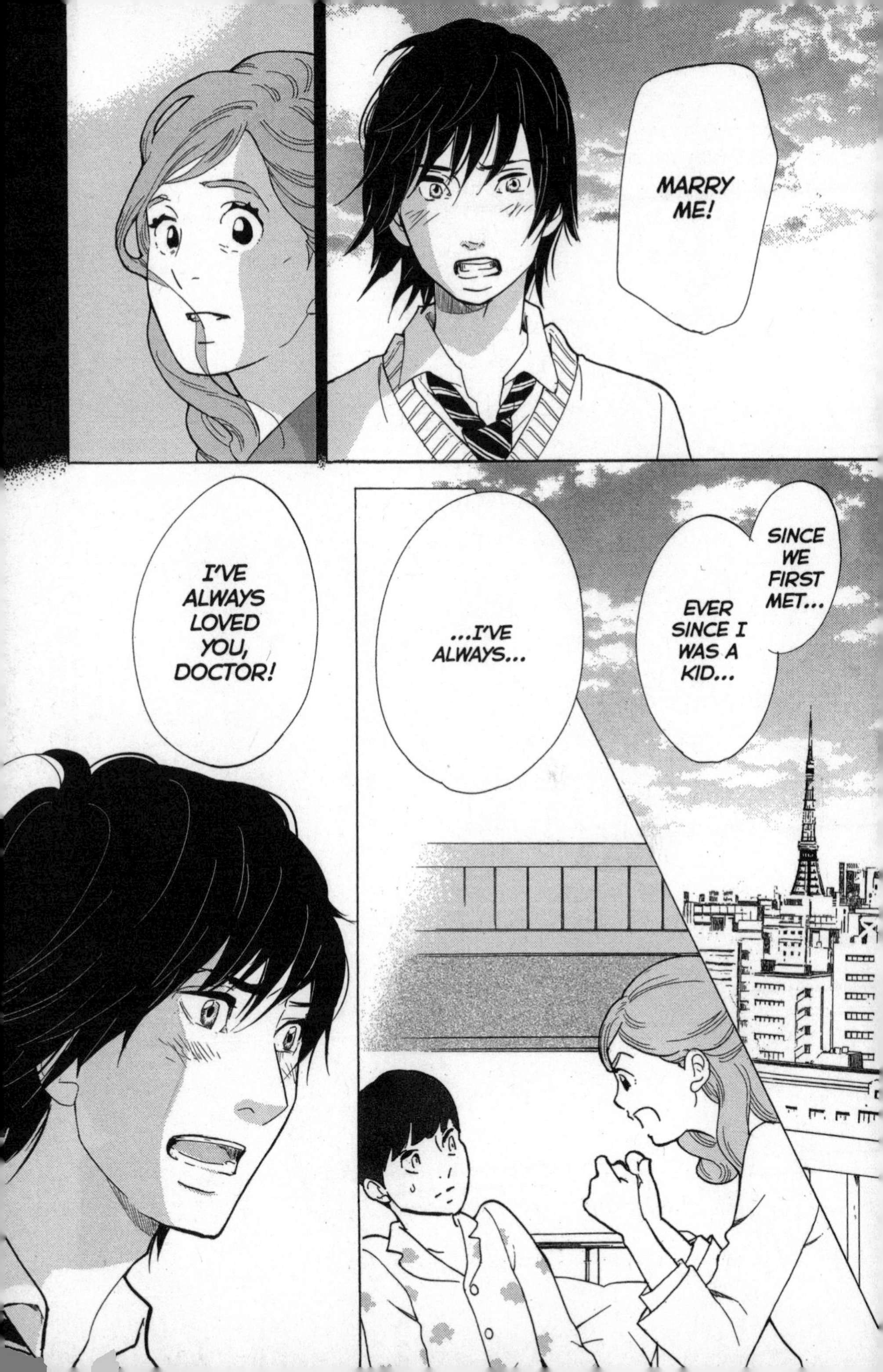
MARRY ME!
SINCE WE FIRST MET...
EVER SINCE I WAS A KID...
...I'VE ALWAYS...
I'VE ALWAYS LOVED YOU, DOCTOR!

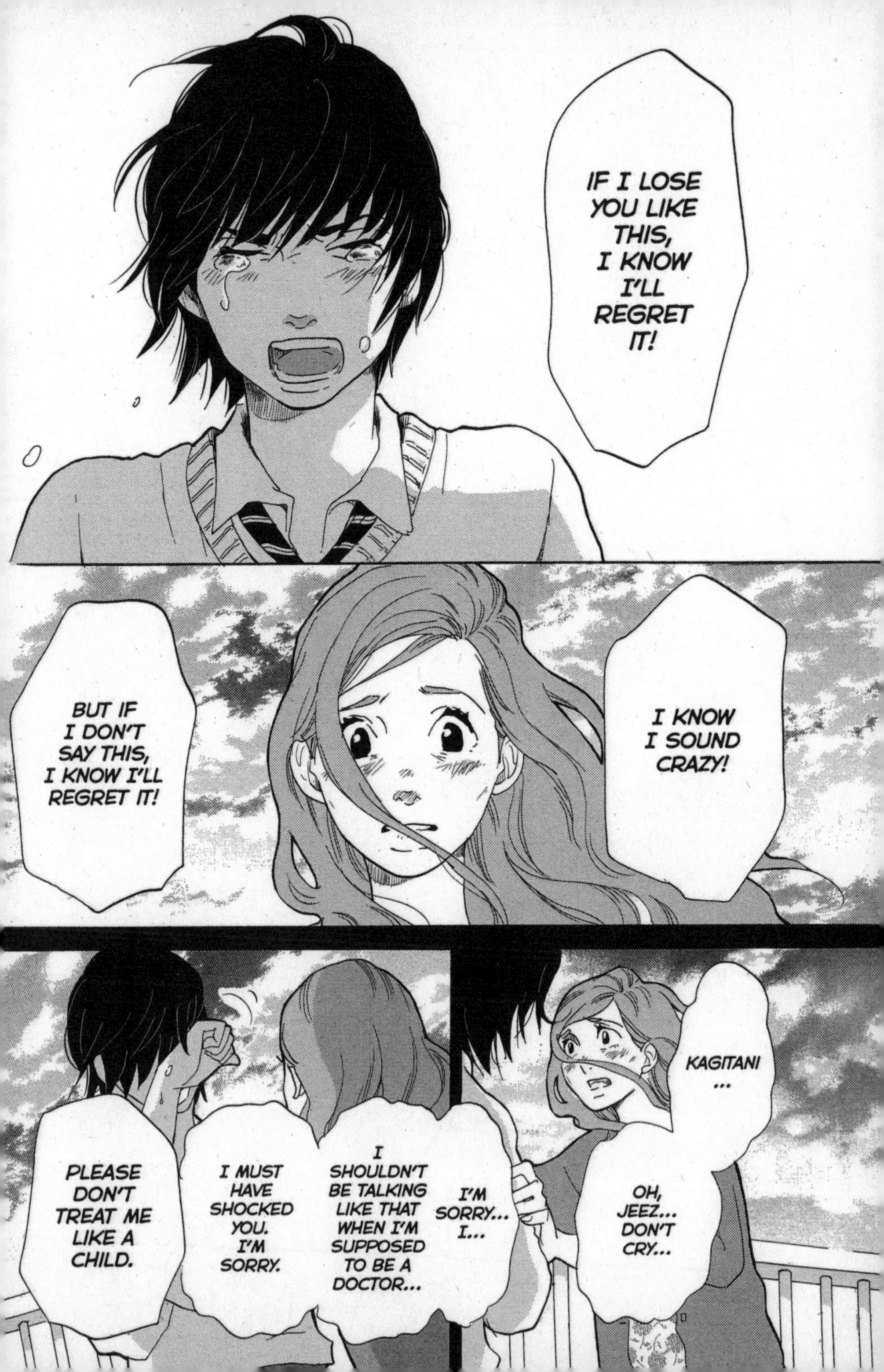
IF I LOSE YOU LIKE THIS, I KNOW I'LL REGRET IT!
I KNOW I SOUND CRAZY!
BUT IF I DON'T SAY THIS, I KNOW I'LL REGRET IT!
KAGITANI ...
OH, JEEZ... DON'T CRY...
I'M SORRY... I...
I SHOULDN'T BE TALKING LIKE THAT WHEN I'M SUPPOSED TO BE A DOCTOR...
I MUST HAVE SHOCKED YOU. I'M SORRY.
PLEASE DON'T TREAT ME LIKE A CHILD.

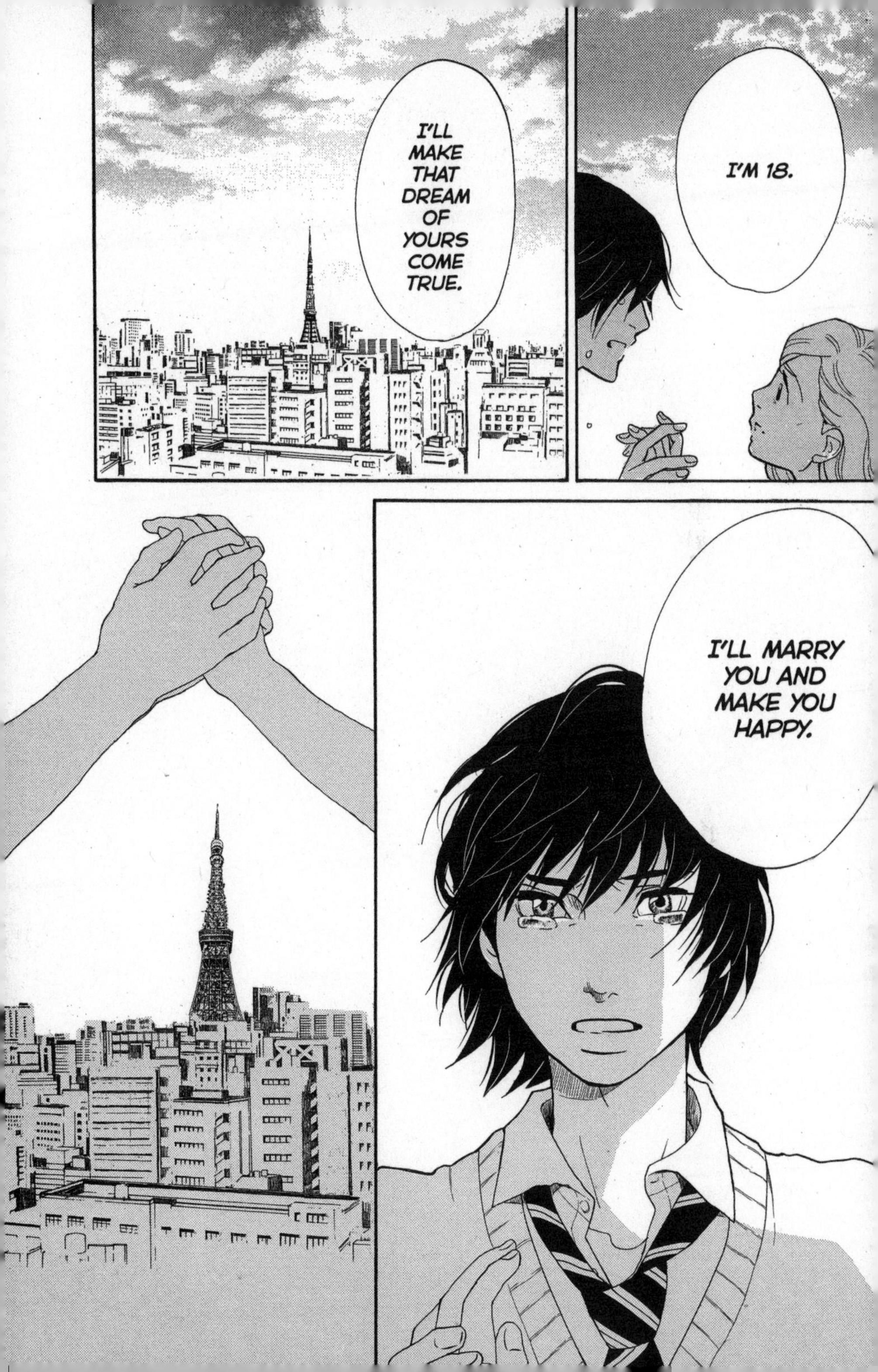
I'M 18.
I'LL MAKE THAT DREAM OF YOURS COME TRUE.
I'LL MARRY YOU AND MAKE YOU HAPPY.

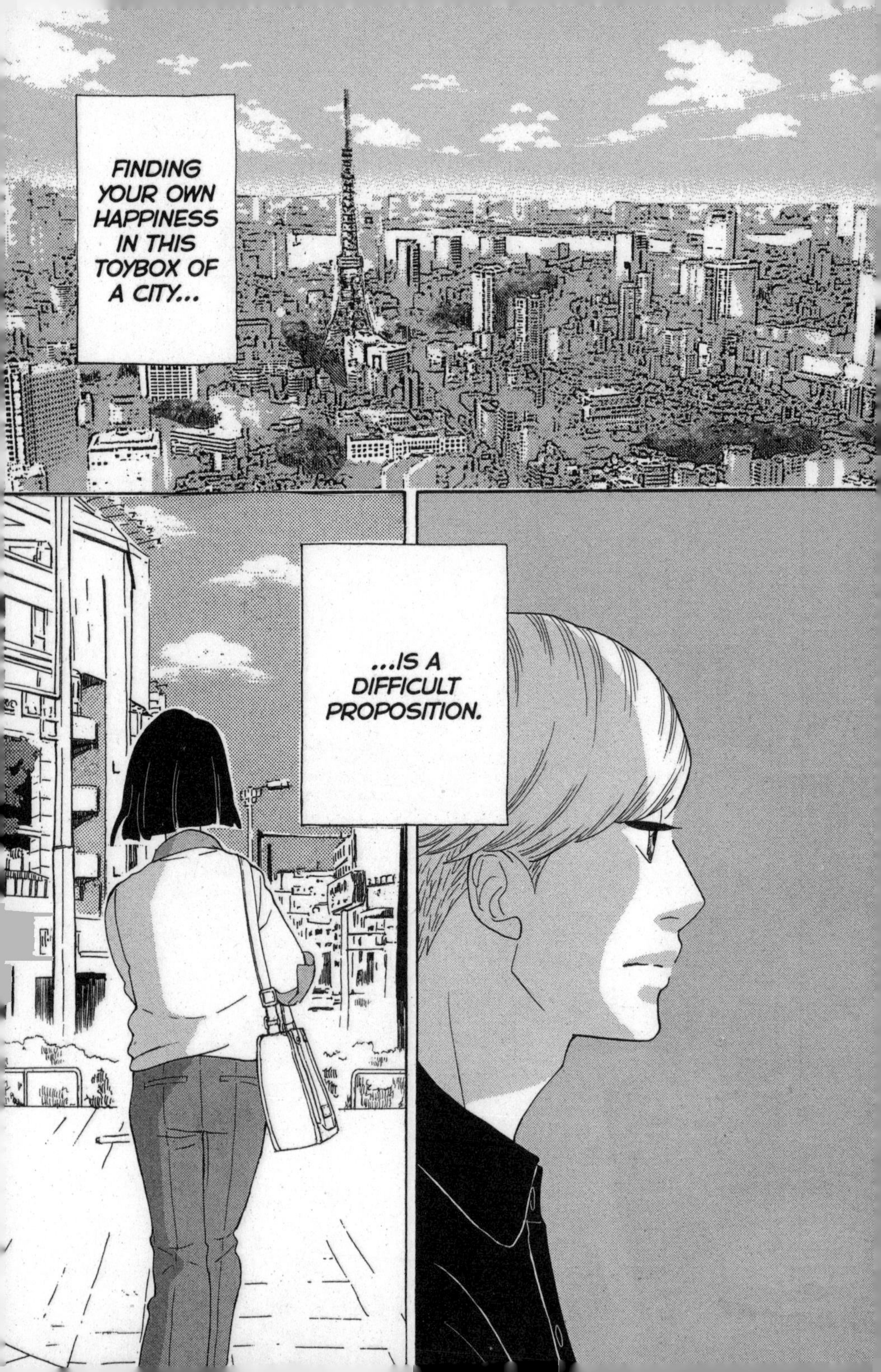
FINDING YOUR OWN HAPPINESS IN THIS TOYBOX OF A CITY...
...IS A DIFFICULT PROPOSITION.

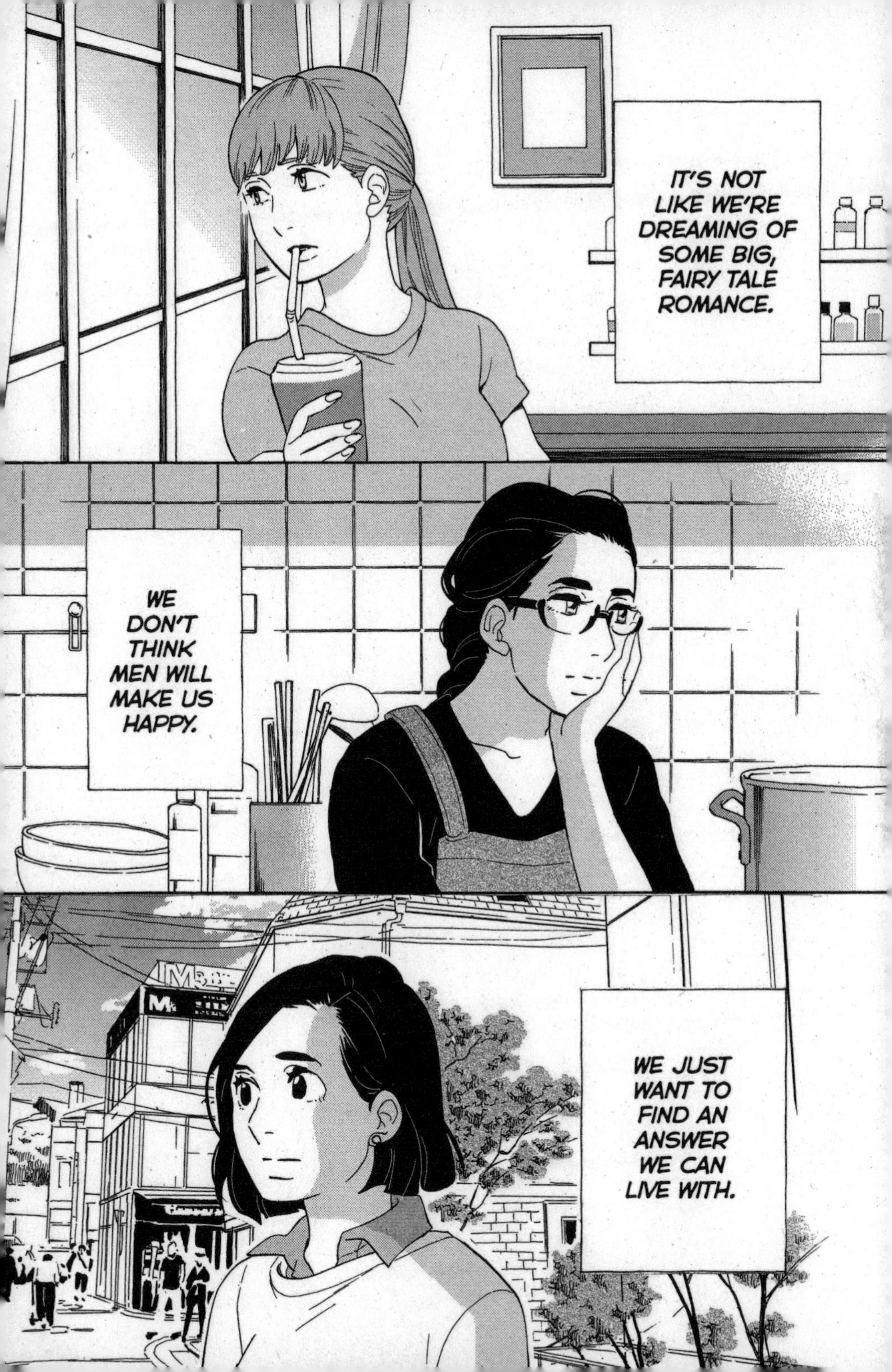
IT'S NOT LIKE WE'RE DREAMING OF SOME BIG, FAIRY TALE ROMANCE.
WE DON'T THINK MEN WILL MAKE US HAPPY.
WE JUST WANT TO FIND AN ANSWER WE CAN LIVE WITH.

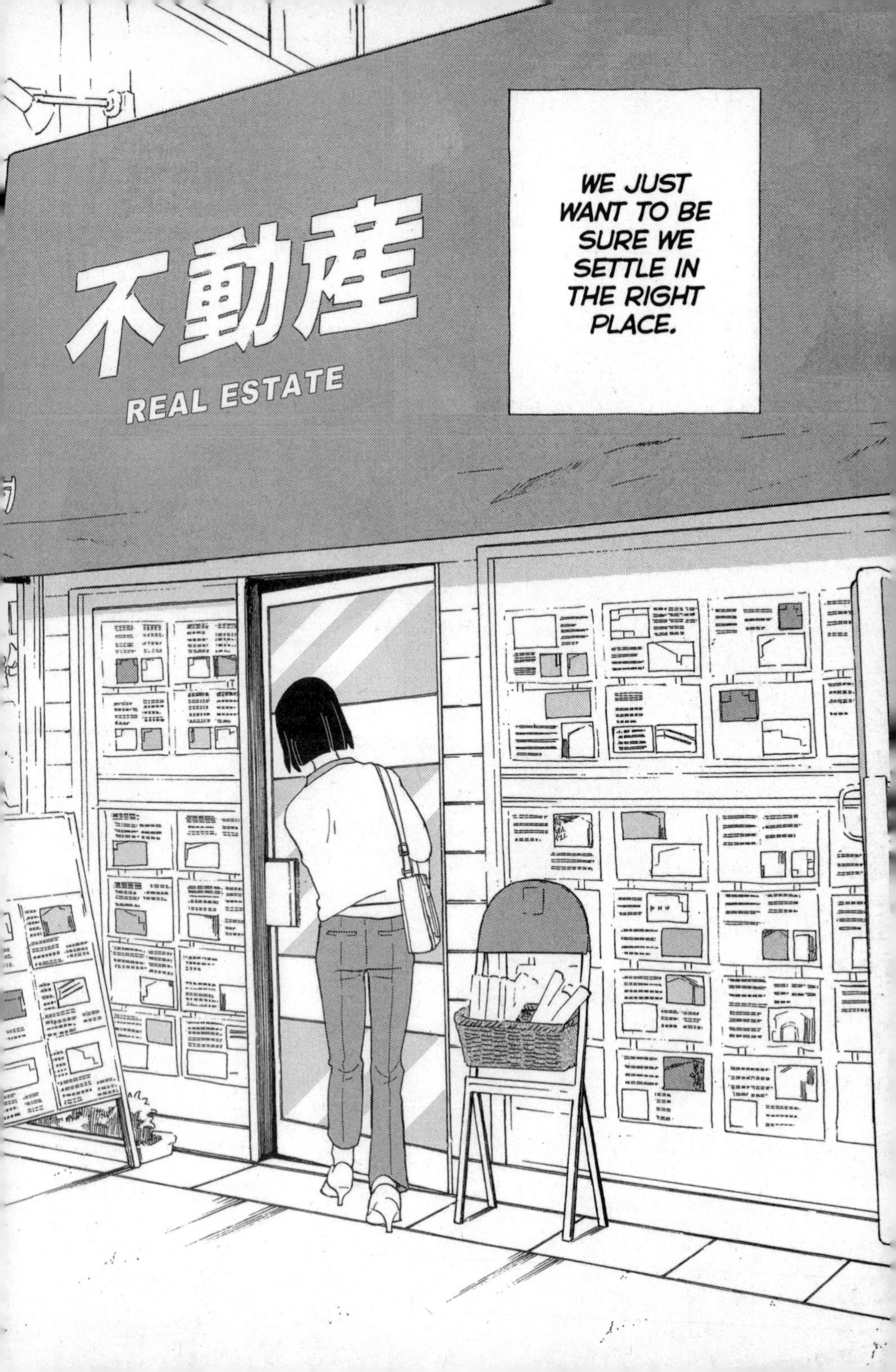
WE JUST WANT TO BE SURE WE SETTLE IN THE RIGHT PLACE.
不動産
REAL ESTATE

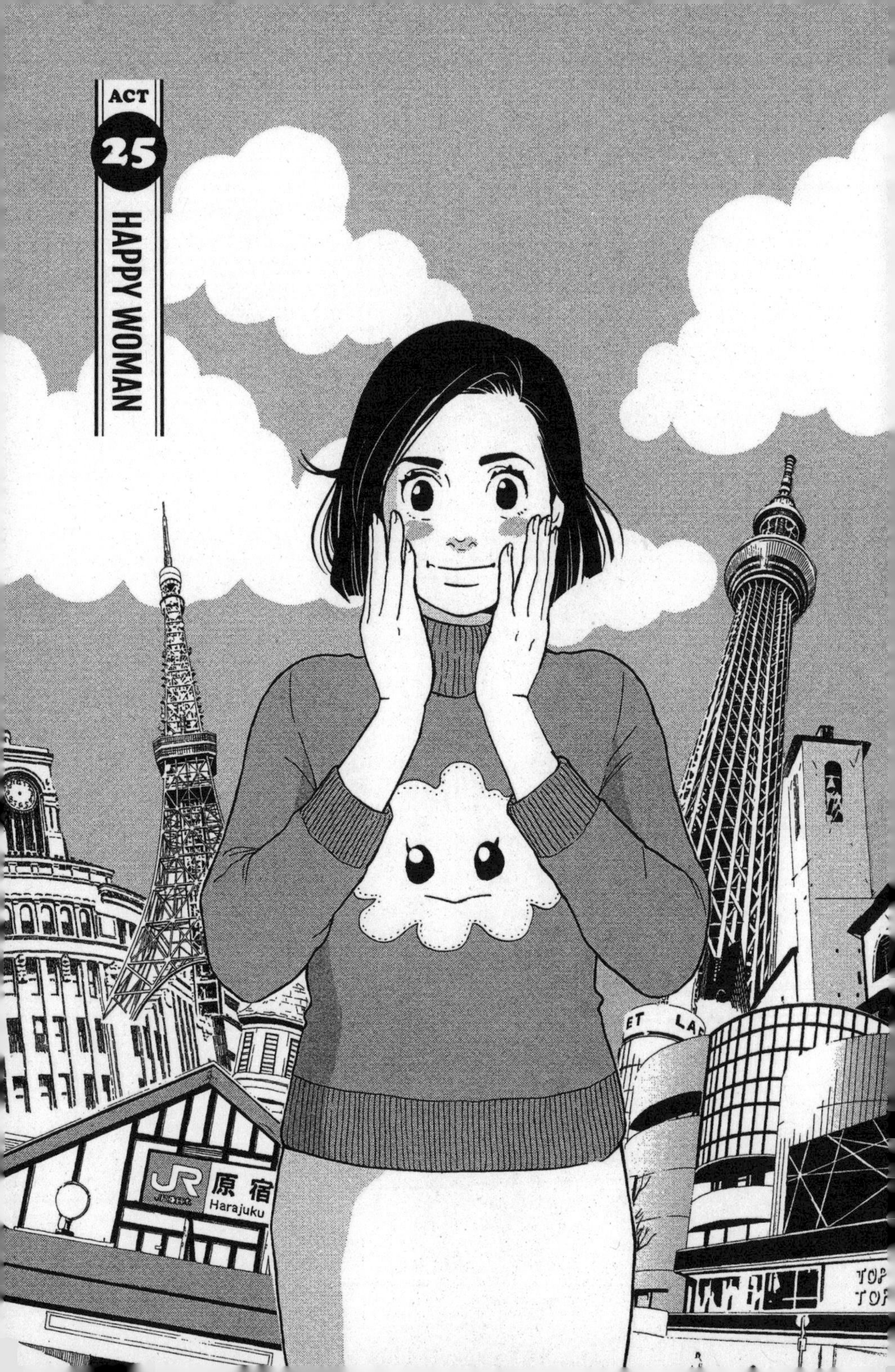
ACT
25
HAPPY WOMAN
JR
原宿
Harajuku

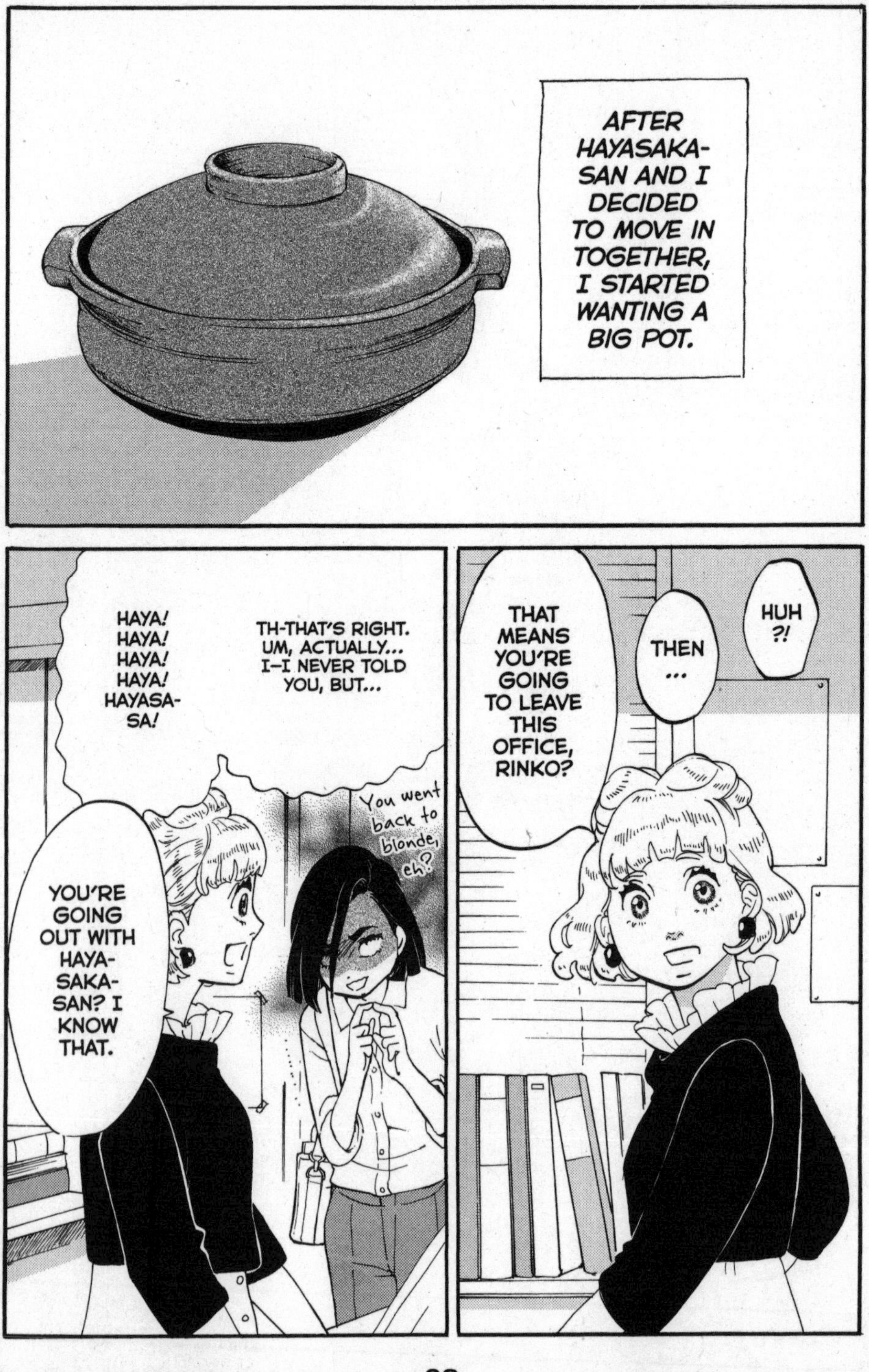
AFTER HAYASAKA-SAN AND I DECIDED TO MOVE IN TOGETHER, I STARTED WANTING A BIG POT.
HUH ?!
THEN ...
THAT MEANS YOU'RE GOING TO LEAVE THIS OFFICE, RINKO?
TH-THAT'S RIGHT. UM, ACTUALLY... I-I NEVER TOLD YOU, BUT...
HAYA! HAYA! HAYA! HAYA! HAYASA-SA!
You went back to blonde, eh?
YOU'RE GOING OUT WITH HAYA-SAKA-SAN? I KNOW THAT.

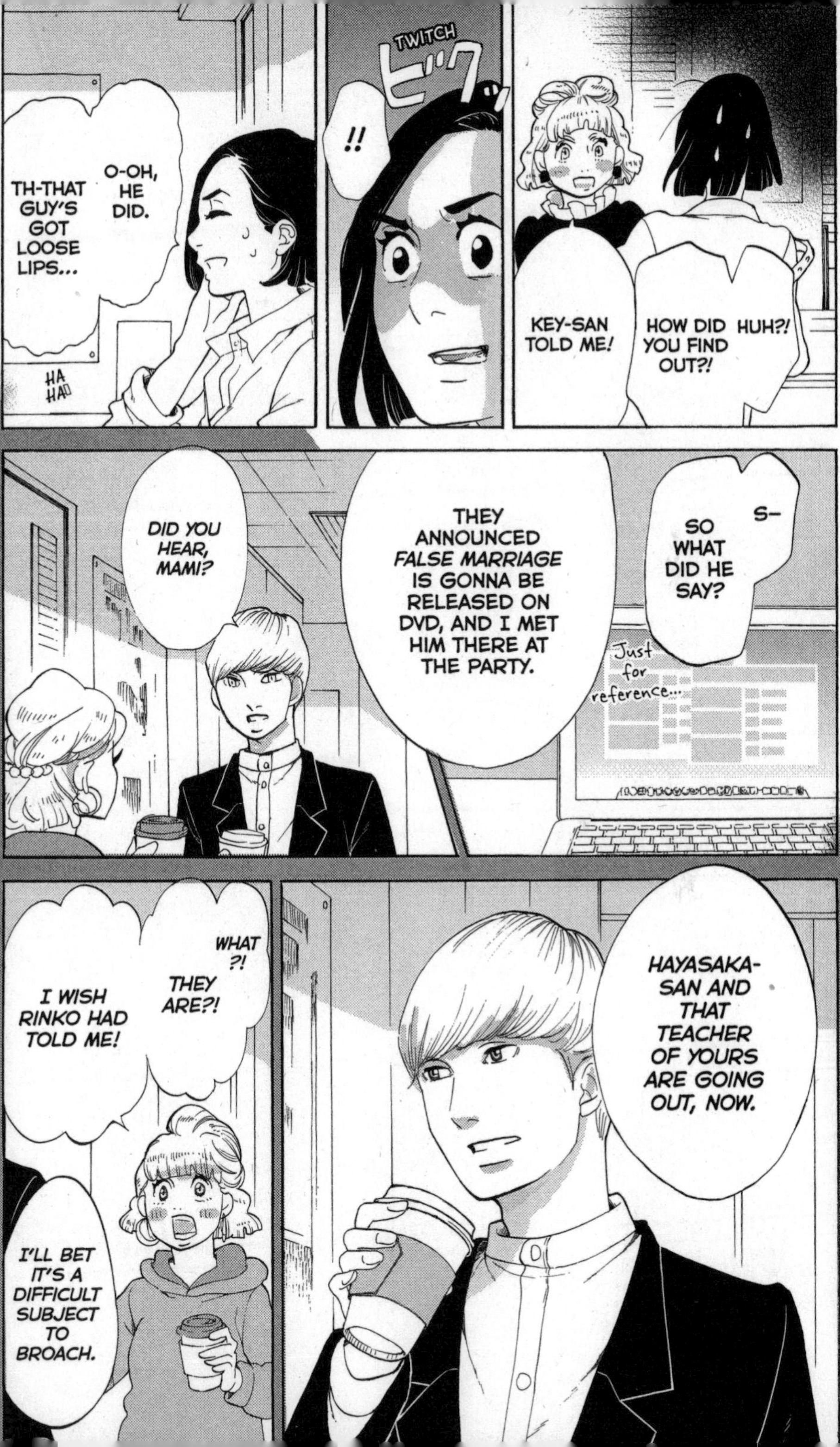
HUH?! HOW DID YOU FIND OUT?!
KEY-SAN TOLD ME!
TWITCH
!!
O-OH, HE DID.
TH-THAT GUY'S GOT LOOSE LIPS...
HA HA
S— SO WHAT DID HE SAY?
THEY ANNOUNCED FALSE MARRIAGE IS GONNA BE RELEASED ON DVD, AND I MET HIM THERE AT THE PARTY.
DID YOU HEAR, MAMI?
Just for reference...
HAYASAKA-SAN AND THAT TEACHER OF YOURS ARE GOING OUT, NOW.
WHAT?! THEY ARE?!
I WISH RINKO HAD TOLD ME!
I'LL BET IT'S A DIFFICULT SUBJECT TO BROACH.

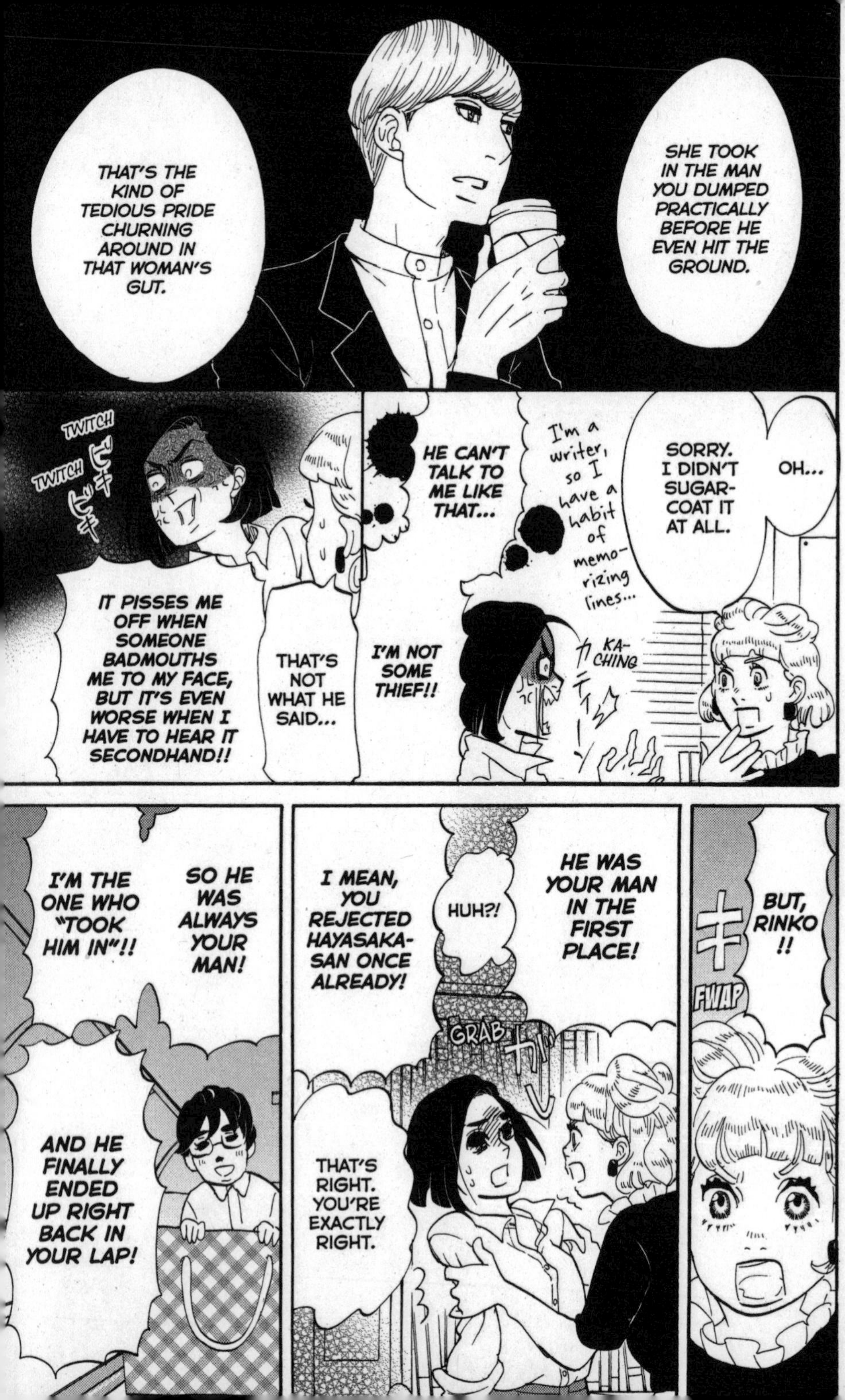
SHE TOOK IN THE MAN YOU DUMPED PRACTICALLY BEFORE HE EVEN HIT THE GROUND.
THAT'S THE KIND OF TEDIOUS PRIDE CHURNING AROUND IN THAT WOMAN'S GUT.
OH...
SORRY. I DIDN'T SUGAR-COAT IT AT ALL.
I'm a writer, so I have a habit of memo-rizing lines...
HE CAN'T TALK TO ME LIKE THAT...
I'M NOT SOME THIEF!!
KA-CHING
TWITCH TWITCH
THAT'S NOT WHAT HE SAID...
IT PISSES ME OFF WHEN SOMEONE BADMOUTHS ME TO MY FACE, BUT IT'S EVEN WORSE WHEN I HAVE TO HEAR IT SECONDHAND!!
FWAP
BUT, RINKO!!
HE WAS YOUR MAN IN THE FIRST PLACE!
HUH?!
I MEAN, YOU REJECTED HAYASAKA-SAN ONCE ALREADY!
GRAB
THAT'S RIGHT. YOU'RE EXACTLY RIGHT.
SO HE WAS ALWAYS YOUR MAN!
I'M THE ONE WHO "TOOK HIM IN"!!
AND HE FINALLY ENDED UP RIGHT BACK IN YOUR LAP!

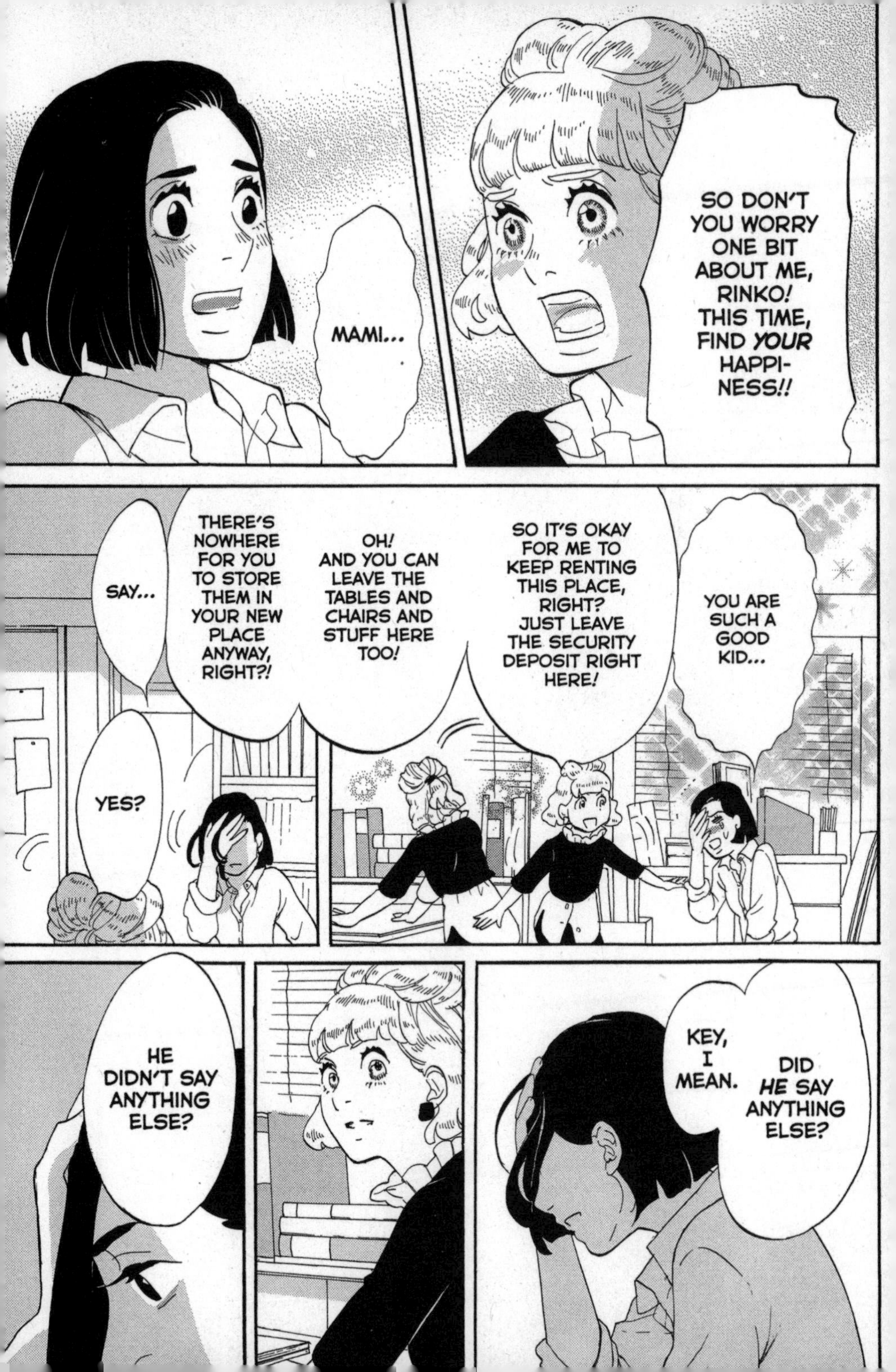
SO DON'T YOU WORRY ONE BIT ABOUT ME, RINKO! THIS TIME, FIND *YOUR* HAPPINESS!!
MAMI...
YOU ARE SUCH A GOOD KID...
SO IT'S OKAY FOR ME TO KEEP RENTING THIS PLACE, RIGHT? JUST LEAVE THE SECURITY DEPOSIT RIGHT HERE!
OH! AND YOU CAN LEAVE THE TABLES AND CHAIRS AND STUFF HERE TOO!
THERE'S NOWHERE FOR YOU TO STORE THEM IN YOUR NEW PLACE ANYWAY, RIGHT?!
SAY...
YES?
DID *HE* SAY ANYTHING ELSE?
KEY, I MEAN.
HE DIDN'T SAY ANYTHING ELSE?

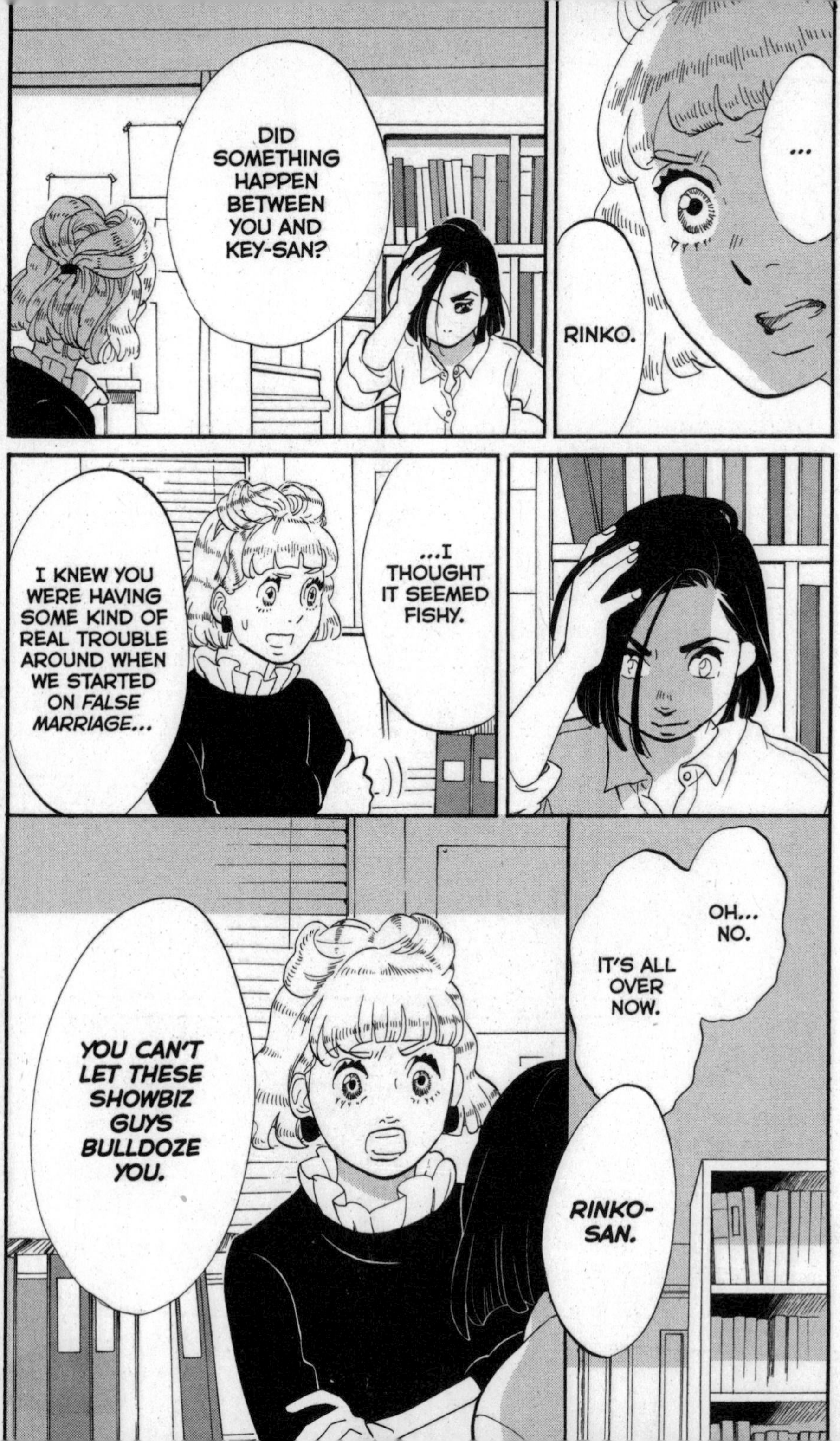
...
RINKO.
DID SOMETHING HAPPEN BETWEEN YOU AND KEY-SAN?
...I THOUGHT IT SEEMED FISHY.
I KNEW YOU WERE HAVING SOME KIND OF REAL TROUBLE AROUND WHEN WE STARTED ON *FALSE MARRIAGE*...
OH... NO. IT'S ALL OVER NOW.
RINKO-SAN.
YOU CAN'T LET THESE SHOWBIZ GUYS BULLDOZE YOU.

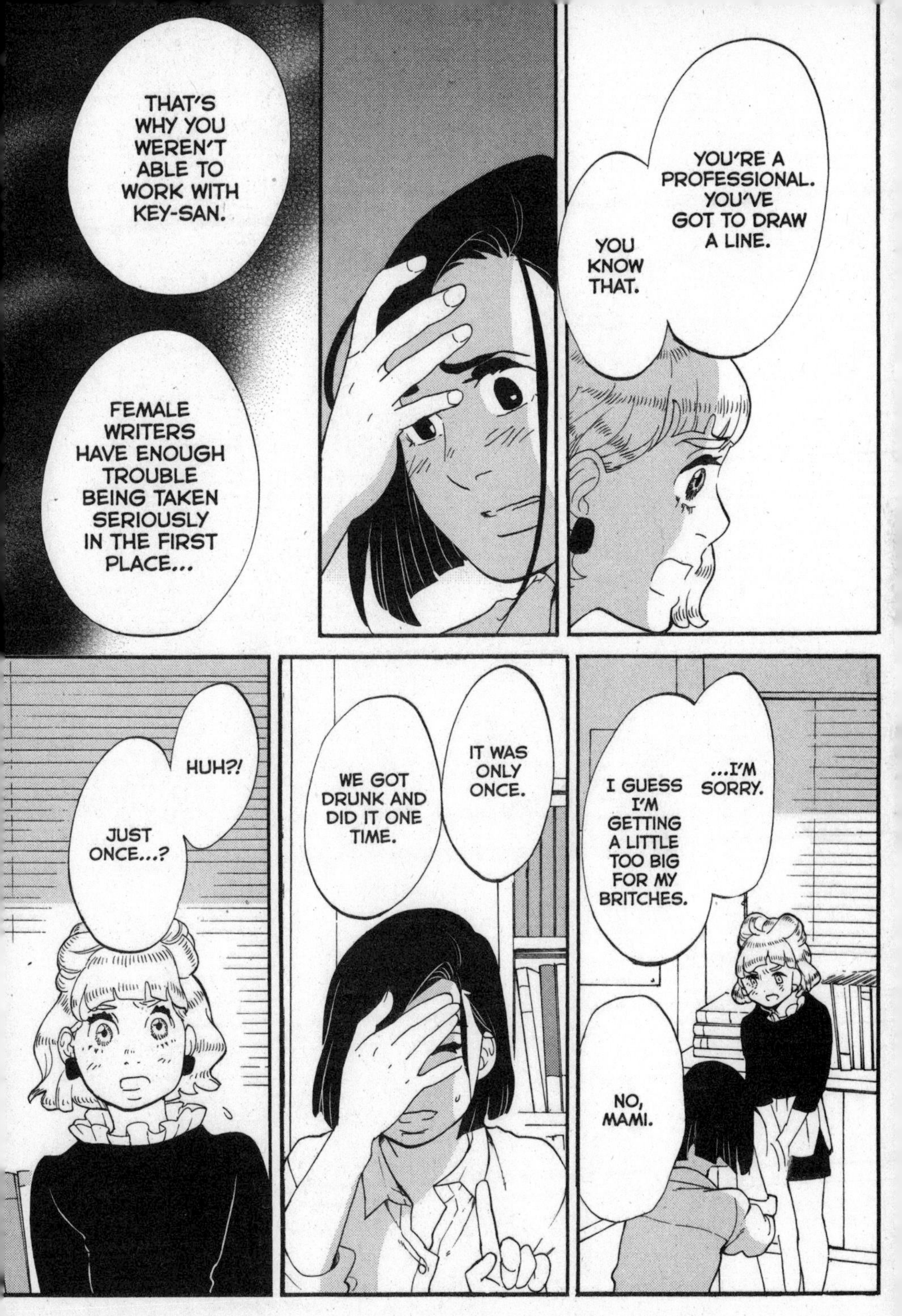
YOU'RE A PROFESSIONAL. YOU'VE GOT TO DRAW A LINE.
YOU KNOW THAT.
THAT'S WHY YOU WEREN'T ABLE TO WORK WITH KEY-SAN.
FEMALE WRITERS HAVE ENOUGH TROUBLE BEING TAKEN SERIOUSLY IN THE FIRST PLACE...
...I'M SORRY.
I GUESS I'M GETTING A LITTLE TOO BIG FOR MY BRITCHES.
NO, MAMI.
IT WAS ONLY ONCE.
WE GOT DRUNK AND DID IT ONE TIME.
HUH?!
JUST ONCE...?

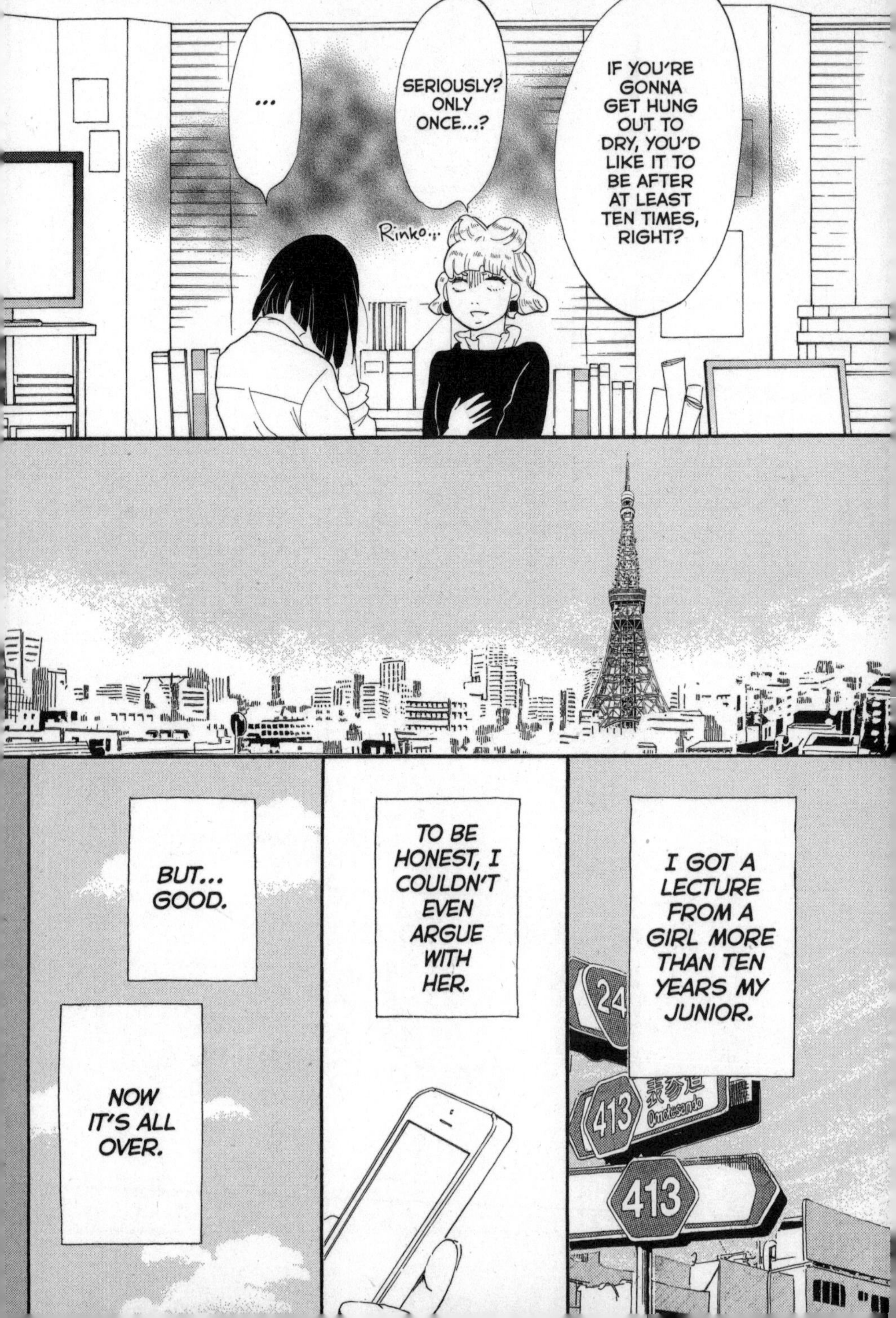
IF YOU'RE GONNA GET HUNG OUT TO DRY, YOU'D LIKE IT TO BE AFTER AT LEAST TEN TIMES, RIGHT?
SERIOUSLY? ONLY ONCE...?
Rinko...
...
I GOT A LECTURE FROM A GIRL MORE THAN TEN YEARS MY JUNIOR.
24
表参道
Omotesando
413
413
TO BE HONEST, I COULDN'T EVEN ARGUE WITH HER.
BUT... GOOD.
NOW IT'S ALL OVER.

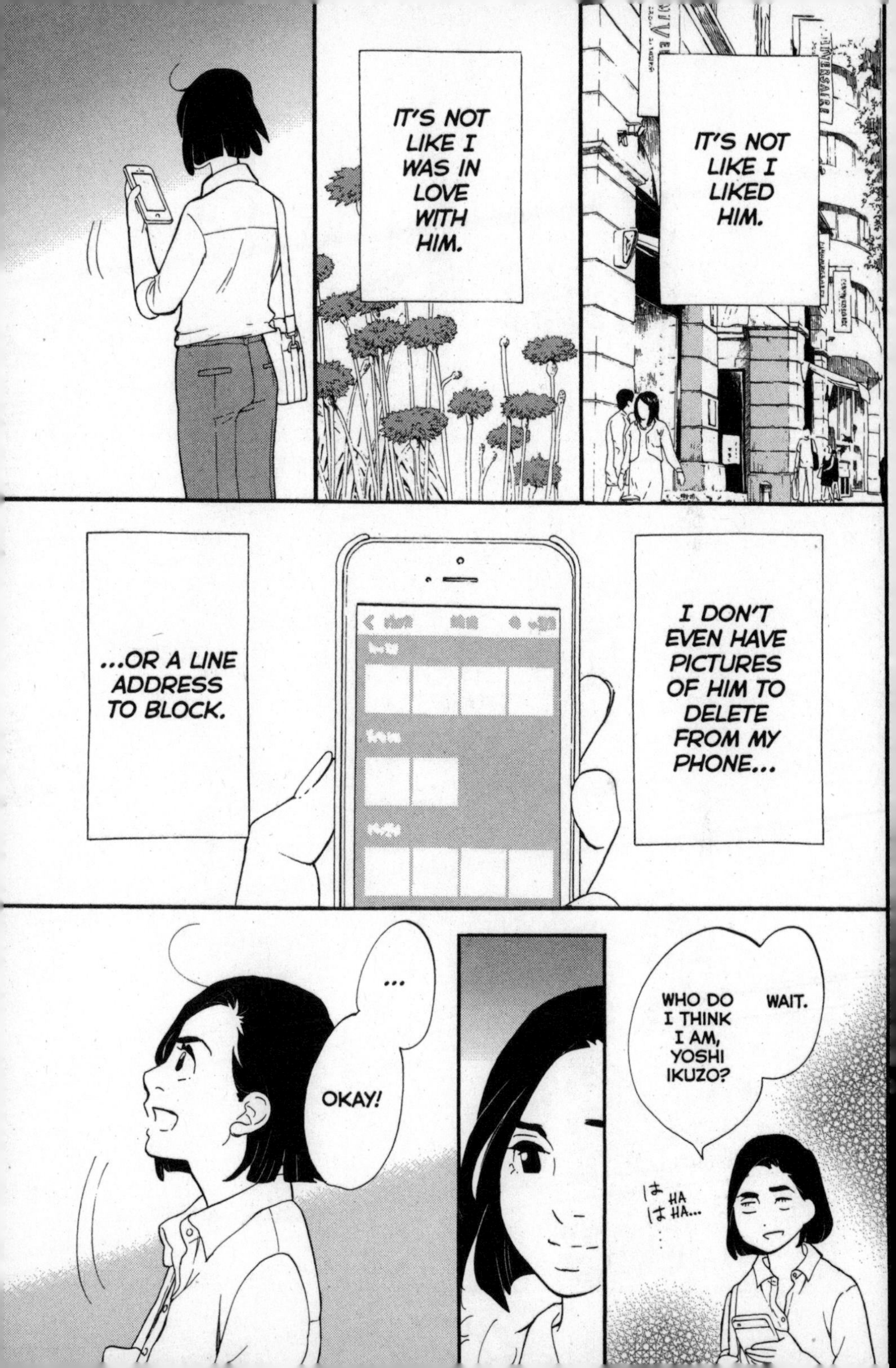
IT'S NOT LIKE I LIKED HIM.
IT'S NOT LIKE I WAS IN LOVE WITH HIM.
I DON'T EVEN HAVE PICTURES OF HIM TO DELETE FROM MY PHONE...
...OR A LINE ADDRESS TO BLOCK.
WAIT.
WHO DO I THINK I AM, YOSHI IKUZO?
はは HA HA...
...
OKAY!

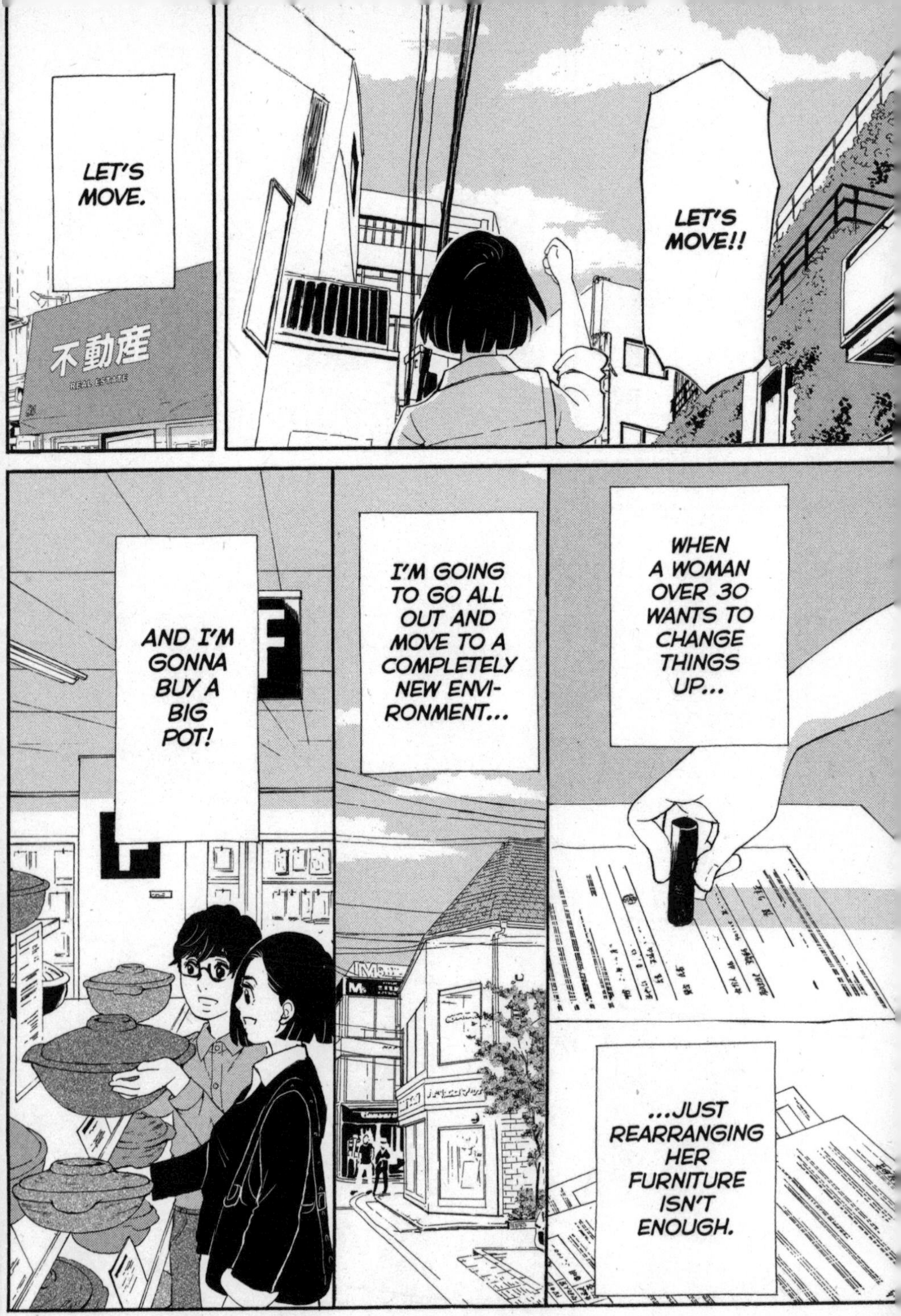
LET'S MOVE!!
LET'S MOVE.
不動産
REAL ESTATE
WHEN A WOMAN OVER 30 WANTS TO CHANGE THINGS UP...
...JUST REARRANGING HER FURNITURE ISN'T ENOUGH.
I'M GOING TO GO ALL OUT AND MOVE TO A COMPLETELY NEW ENVI-RONMENT...
AND I'M GONNA BUY A BIG POT!

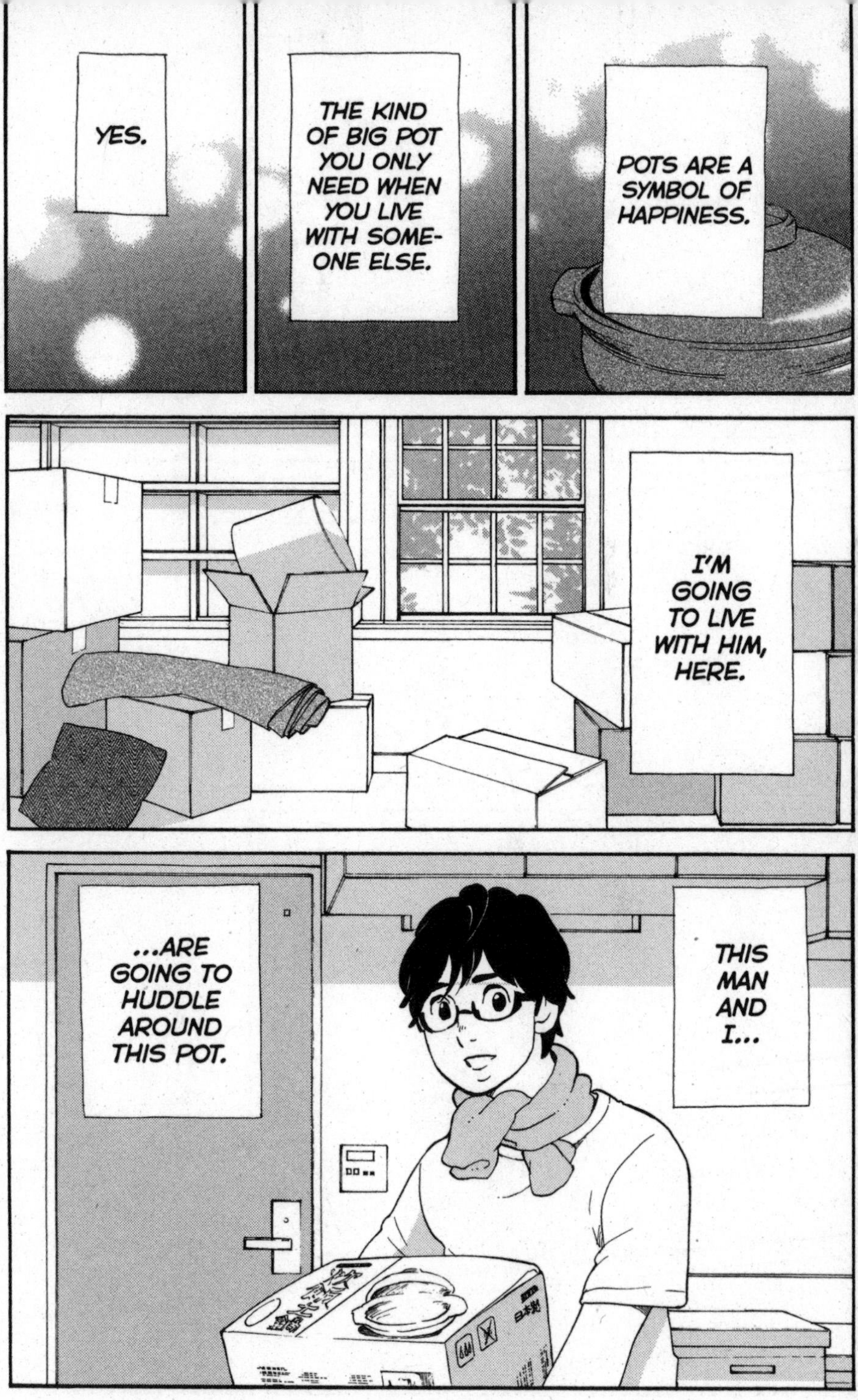
POTS ARE A SYMBOL OF HAPPINESS.
THE KIND OF BIG POT YOU ONLY NEED WHEN YOU LIVE WITH SOME-ONE ELSE.
YES.
I'M GOING TO LIVE WITH HIM, HERE.
THIS MAN AND I...
...ARE GOING TO HUDDLE AROUND THIS POT.

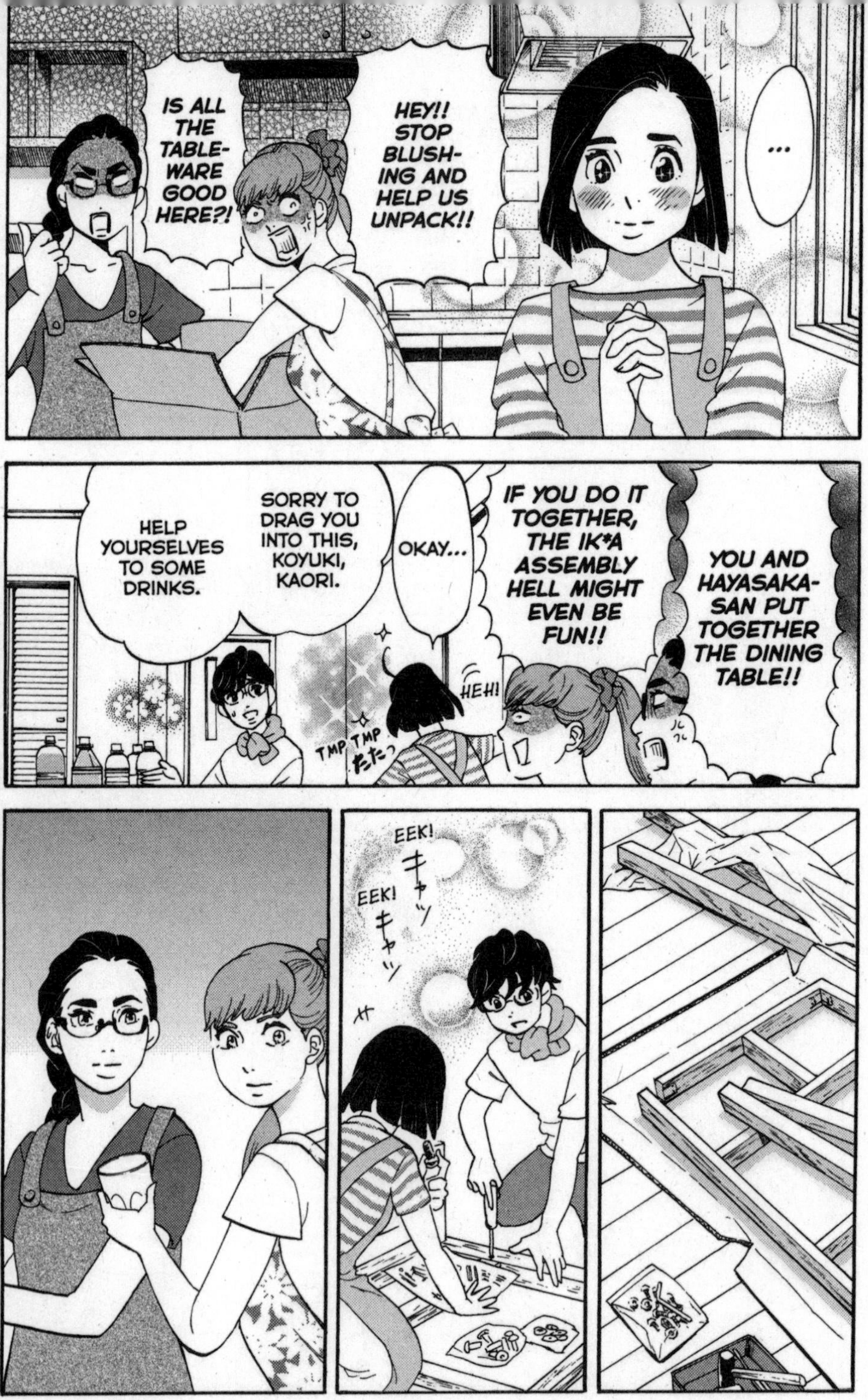
...
HEY!! STOP BLUSHING AND HELP US UNPACK!!
IS ALL THE TABLEWARE GOOD HERE?!
YOU AND HAYASAKA-SAN PUT TOGETHER THE DINING TABLE!!
IF YOU DO IT TOGETHER, THE IK*A ASSEMBLY HELL MIGHT EVEN BE FUN!!
HEH!
OKAY...
TMP TMP たたっ
SORRY TO DRAG YOU INTO THIS, KOYUKI, KAORI.
HELP YOURSELVES TO SOME DRINKS.
EEK! キャッ
EEK! キャッ

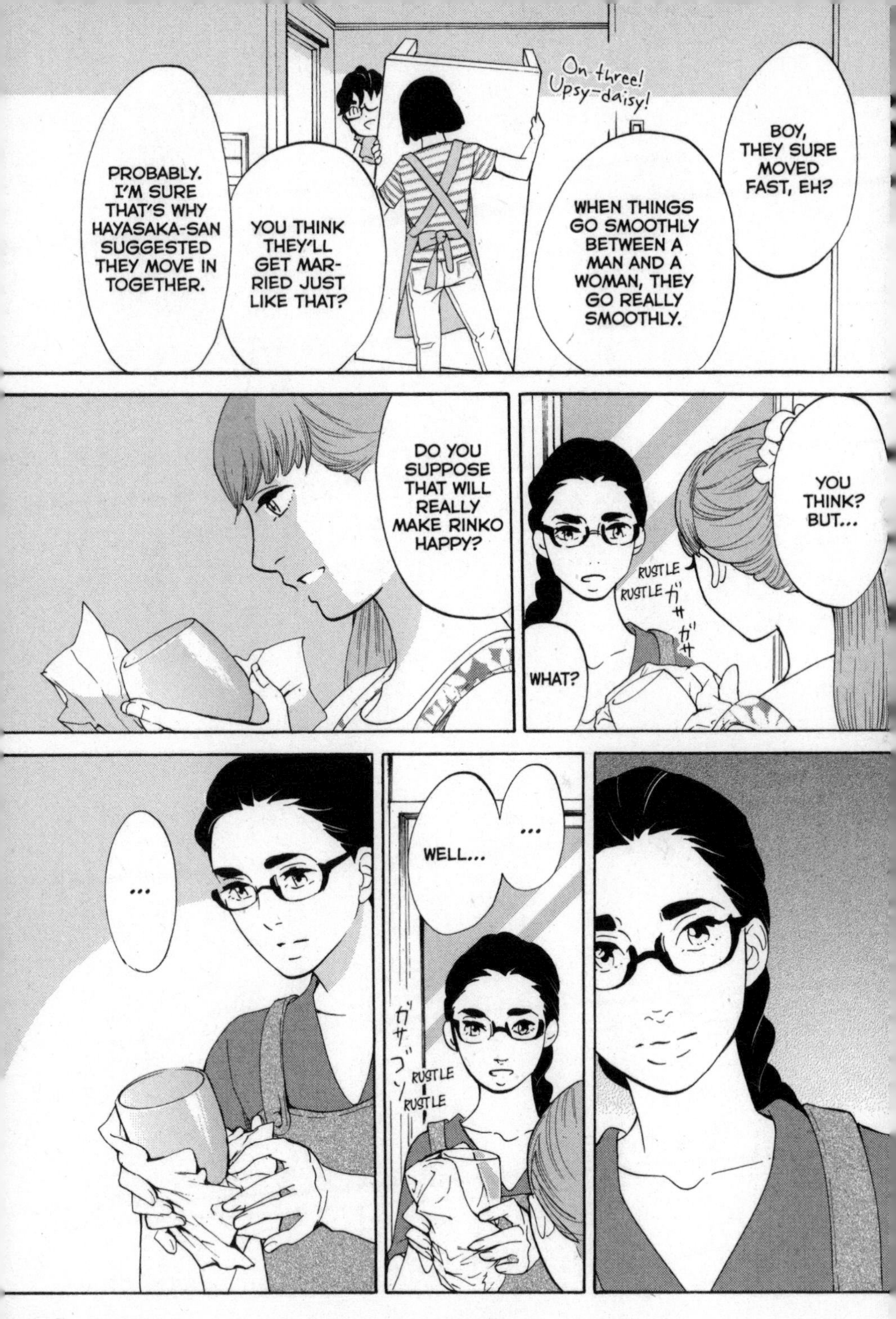
BOY, THEY SURE MOVED FAST, EH?
On three! Upsy-daisy!
WHEN THINGS GO SMOOTHLY BETWEEN A MAN AND A WOMAN, THEY GO REALLY SMOOTHLY.
YOU THINK THEY'LL GET MAR-RIED JUST LIKE THAT?
PROBABLY. I'M SURE THAT'S WHY HAYASAKA-SAN SUGGESTED THEY MOVE IN TOGETHER.
YOU THINK? BUT...
RUSTLE RUSTLE
ガサガサ
WHAT?
DO YOU SUPPOSE THAT WILL REALLY MAKE RINKO HAPPY?
...
WELL...
ガサゴソ
RUSTLE RUSTLE
...

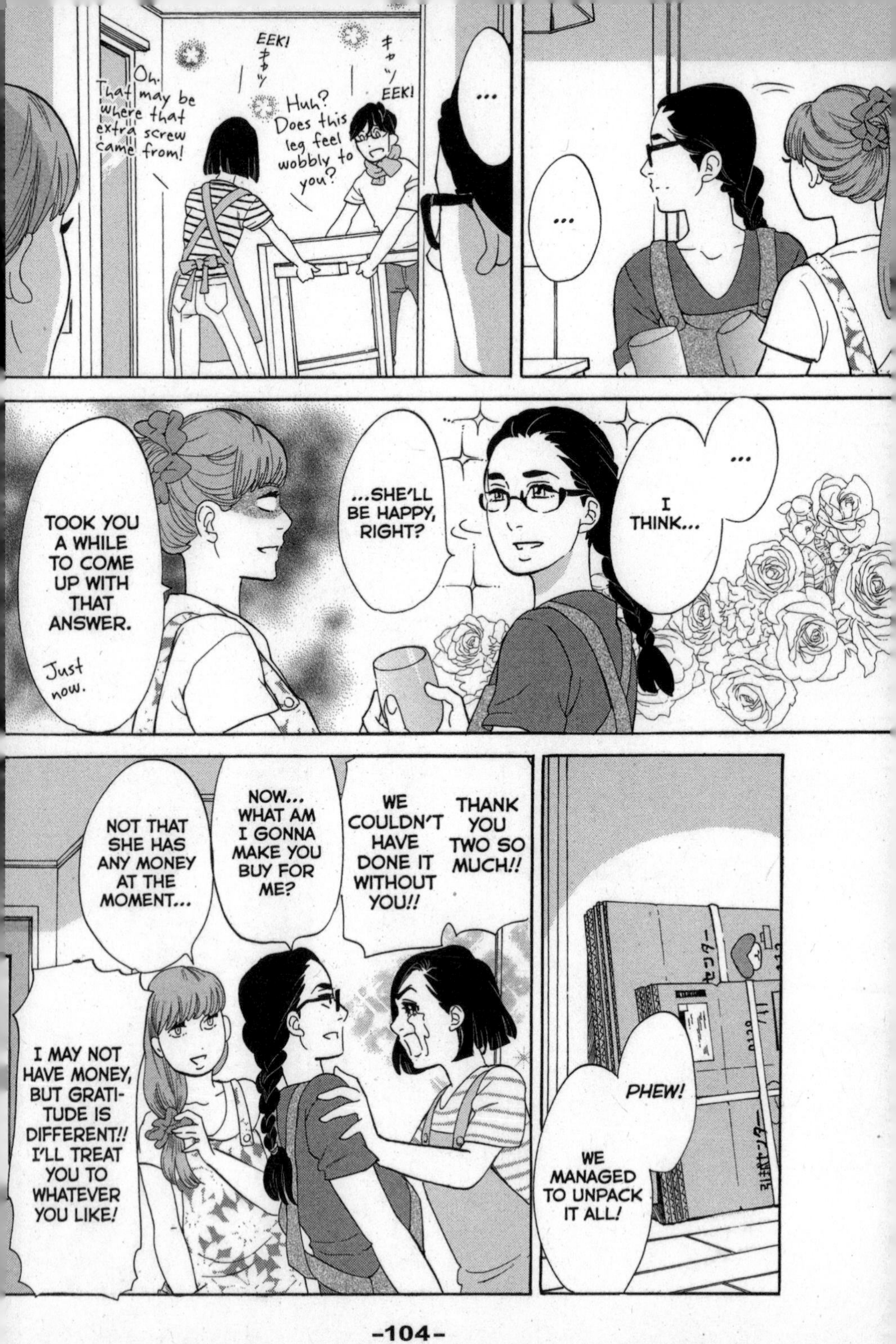
...
...
キャッ EEK!
EEK! キャッ
Huh? Does this leg feel wobbly to you?
Oh. That may be where that extra screw came from!
... I THINK...
...SHE'LL BE HAPPY, RIGHT?
TOOK YOU A WHILE TO COME UP WITH THAT ANSWER.
Just now.
PHEW!
WE MANAGED TO UNPACK IT ALL!
THANK YOU TWO SO MUCH!!
WE COULDN'T HAVE DONE IT WITHOUT YOU!!
NOW... WHAT AM I GONNA MAKE YOU BUY FOR ME?
NOT THAT SHE HAS ANY MONEY AT THE MOMENT...
I MAY NOT HAVE MONEY, BUT GRATITUDE IS DIFFERENT!! I'LL TREAT YOU TO WHATEVER YOU LIKE!

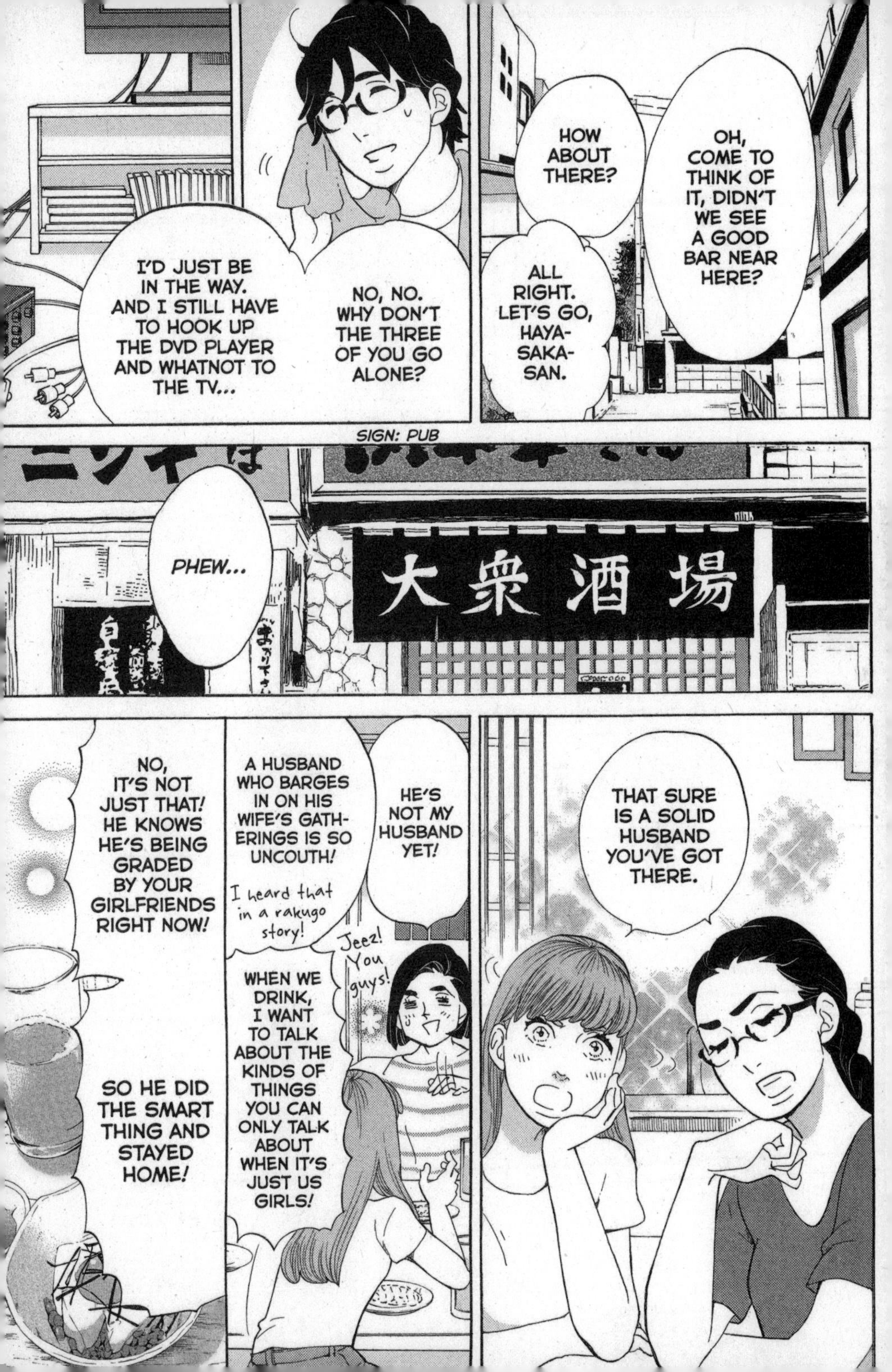
OH, COME TO THINK OF IT, DIDN'T WE SEE A GOOD BAR NEAR HERE?
HOW ABOUT THERE?
ALL RIGHT. LET'S GO, HAYA-SAKA-SAN.
NO, NO. WHY DON'T THE THREE OF YOU GO ALONE?
I'D JUST BE IN THE WAY. AND I STILL HAVE TO HOOK UP THE DVD PLAYER AND WHATNOT TO THE TV...
SIGN: PUB
大衆酒場
PHEW...
THAT SURE IS A SOLID HUSBAND YOU'VE GOT THERE.
HE'S NOT MY HUSBAND YET!
A HUSBAND WHO BARGES IN ON HIS WIFE'S GATH-ERINGS IS SO UNCOUTH!
I heard that in a rakugo story!
Jeez! You guys!
WHEN WE DRINK, I WANT TO TALK ABOUT THE KINDS OF THINGS YOU CAN ONLY TALK ABOUT WHEN IT'S JUST US GIRLS!
NO, IT'S NOT JUST THAT! HE KNOWS HE'S BEING GRADED BY YOUR GIRLFRIENDS RIGHT NOW!
SO HE DID THE SMART THING AND STAYED HOME!

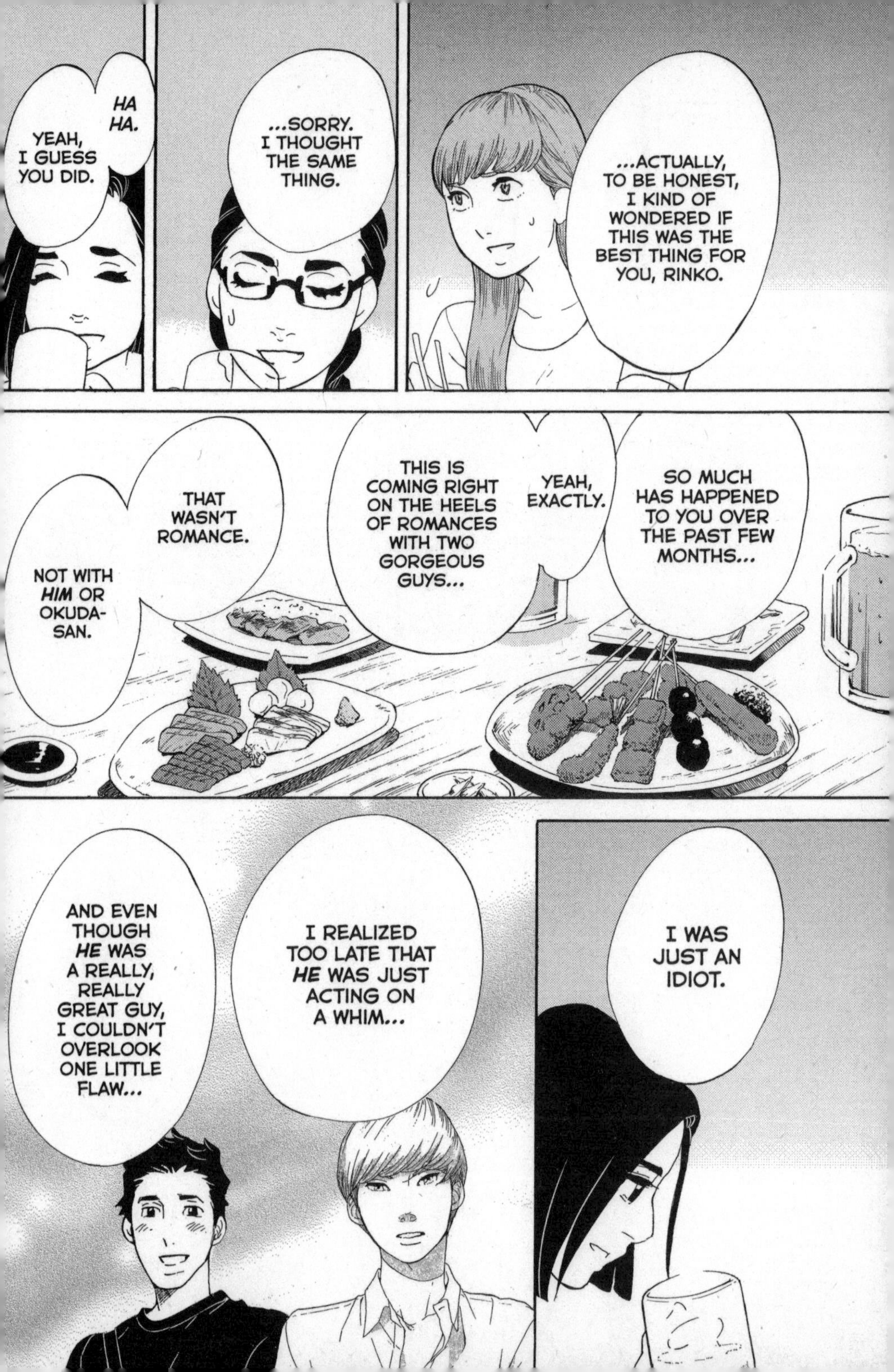
...ACTUALLY, TO BE HONEST, I KIND OF WONDERED IF THIS WAS THE BEST THING FOR YOU, RINKO.
...SORRY. I THOUGHT THE SAME THING.
HA HA.
YEAH, I GUESS YOU DID.
SO MUCH HAS HAPPENED TO YOU OVER THE PAST FEW MONTHS...
YEAH, EXACTLY.
THIS IS COMING RIGHT ON THE HEELS OF ROMANCES WITH TWO GORGEOUS GUYS...
THAT WASN'T ROMANCE.
NOT WITH *HIM* OR OKUDA-SAN.
I WAS JUST AN IDIOT.
I REALIZED TOO LATE THAT *HE* WAS JUST ACTING ON A WHIM...
AND EVEN THOUGH *HE* WAS A REALLY, REALLY GREAT GUY, I COULDN'T OVERLOOK ONE LITTLE FLAW...

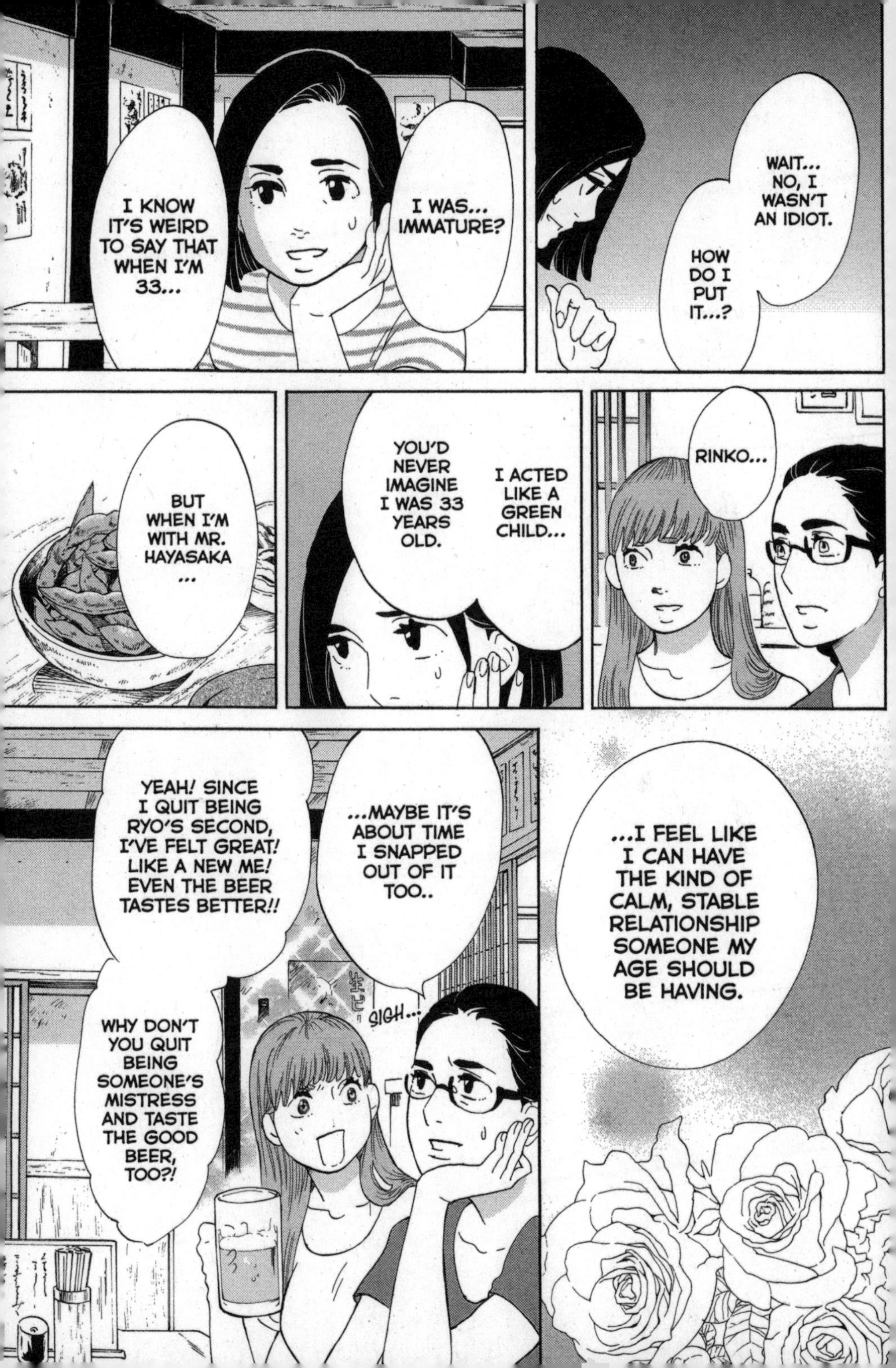
WAIT... NO, I WASN'T AN IDIOT.
HOW DO I PUT IT...?
I WAS... IMMATURE?
I KNOW IT'S WEIRD TO SAY THAT WHEN I'M 33...
RINKO...
I ACTED LIKE A GREEN CHILD...
YOU'D NEVER IMAGINE I WAS 33 YEARS OLD.
BUT WHEN I'M WITH MR. HAYASAKA ...
...I FEEL LIKE I CAN HAVE THE KIND OF CALM, STABLE RELATIONSHIP SOMEONE MY AGE SHOULD BE HAVING.
...MAYBE IT'S ABOUT TIME I SNAPPED OUT OF IT TOO..
SIGH...
YEAH! SINCE I QUIT BEING RYO'S SECOND, I'VE FELT GREAT! LIKE A NEW ME! EVEN THE BEER TASTES BETTER!!
WHY DON'T YOU QUIT BEING SOMEONE'S MISTRESS AND TASTE THE GOOD BEER, TOO?!

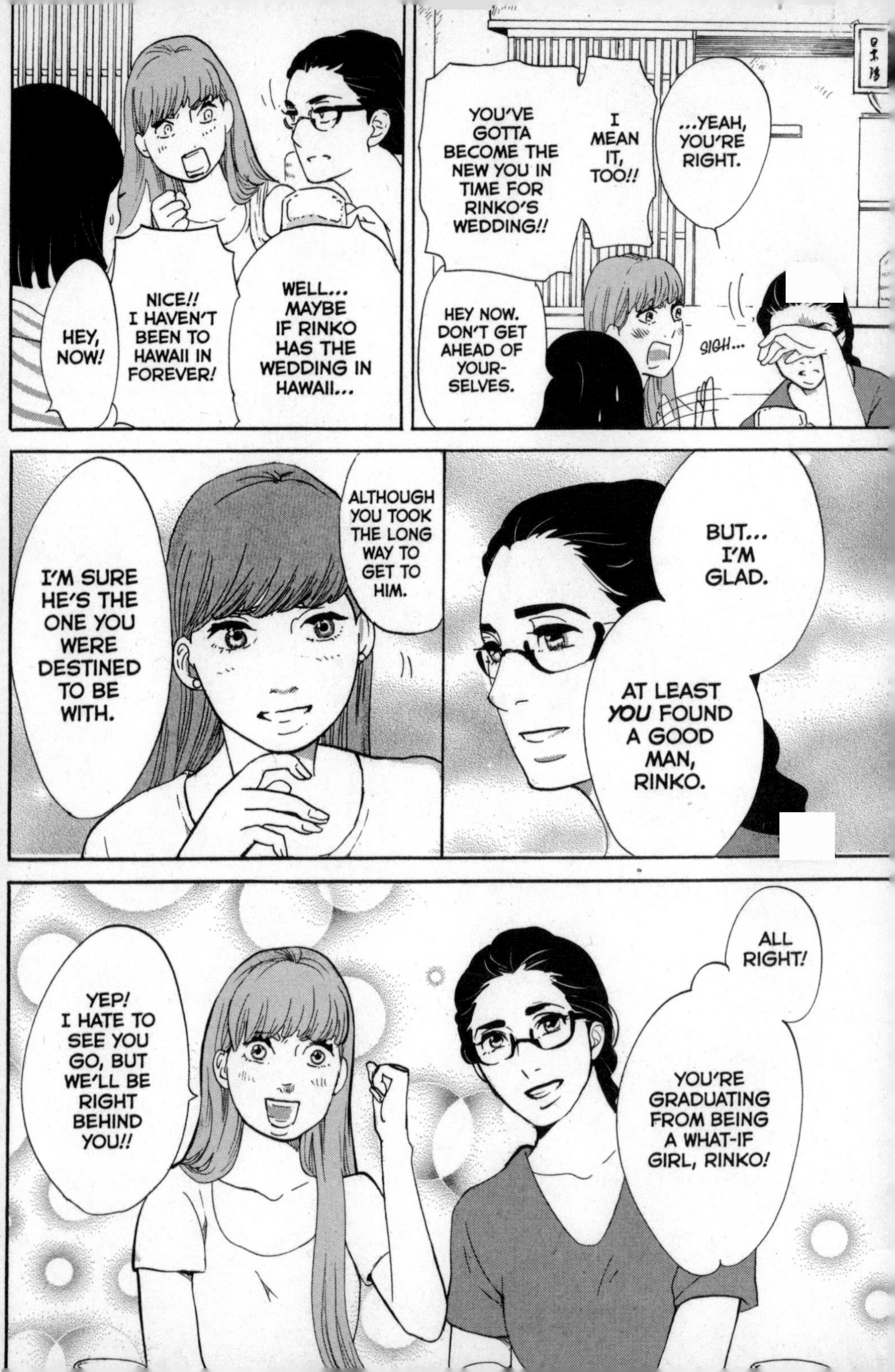
...YEAH, YOU'RE RIGHT.
I MEAN IT, TOO!!
YOU'VE GOTTA BECOME THE NEW YOU IN TIME FOR RINKO'S WEDDING!!
SIGH...
HEY NOW. DON'T GET AHEAD OF YOUR-SELVES.
WELL... MAYBE IF RINKO HAS THE WEDDING IN HAWAII...
NICE!! I HAVEN'T BEEN TO HAWAII IN FOREVER!
HEY, NOW!
BUT... I'M GLAD.
AT LEAST *YOU* FOUND A GOOD MAN, RINKO.
ALTHOUGH YOU TOOK THE LONG WAY TO GET TO HIM.
I'M SURE HE'S THE ONE YOU WERE DESTINED TO BE WITH.
ALL RIGHT!
YOU'RE GRADUATING FROM BEING A WHAT-IF GIRL, RINKO!
YEP! I HATE TO SEE YOU GO, BUT WE'LL BE RIGHT BEHIND YOU!!

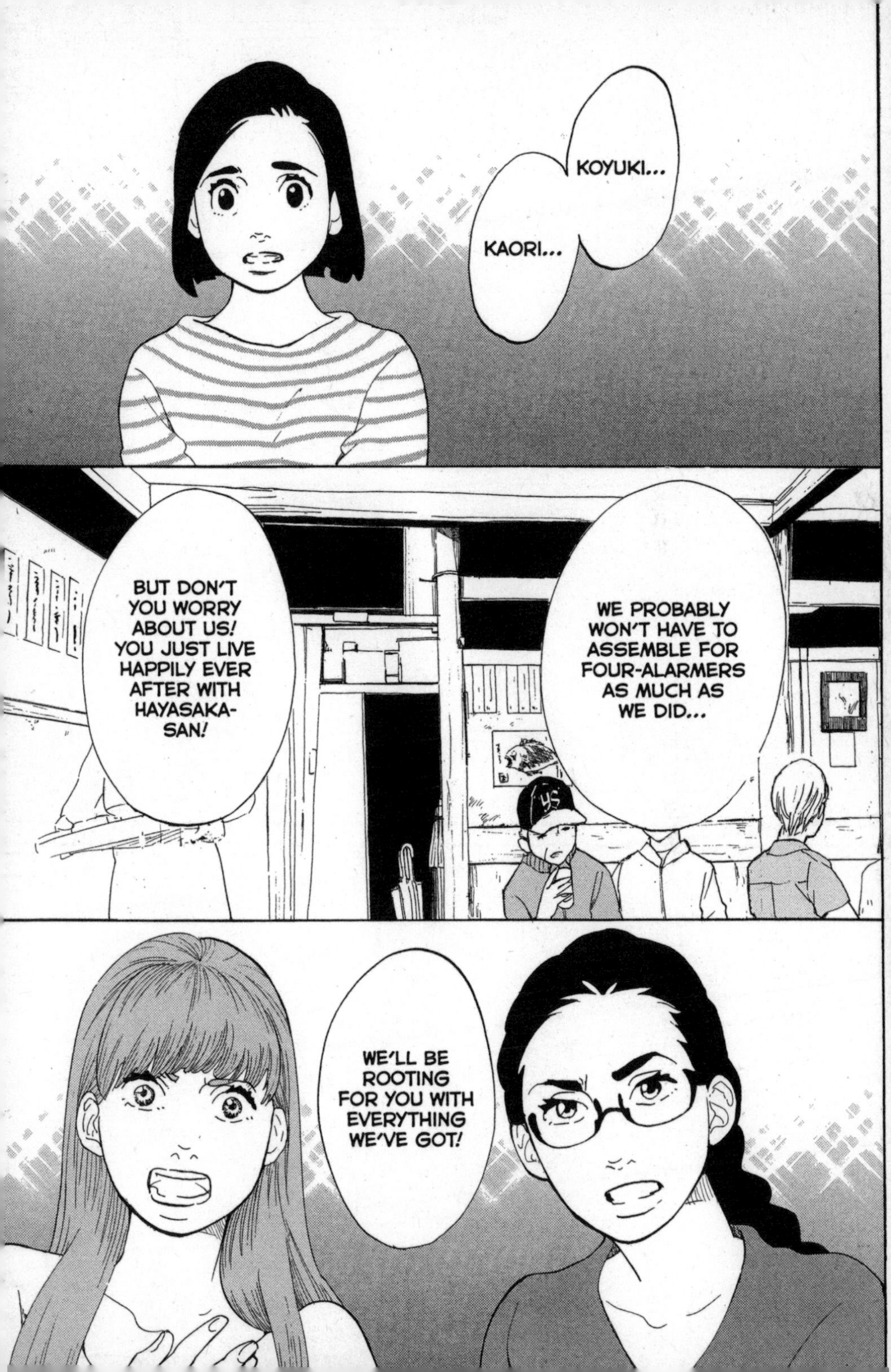
KOYUKI...
KAORI...
WE PROBABLY WON'T HAVE TO ASSEMBLE FOR FOUR-ALARMERS AS MUCH AS WE DID...
BUT DON'T YOU WORRY ABOUT US! YOU JUST LIVE HAPPILY EVER AFTER WITH HAYASAKA-SAN!
WE'LL BE ROOTING FOR YOU WITH EVERYTHING WE'VE GOT!

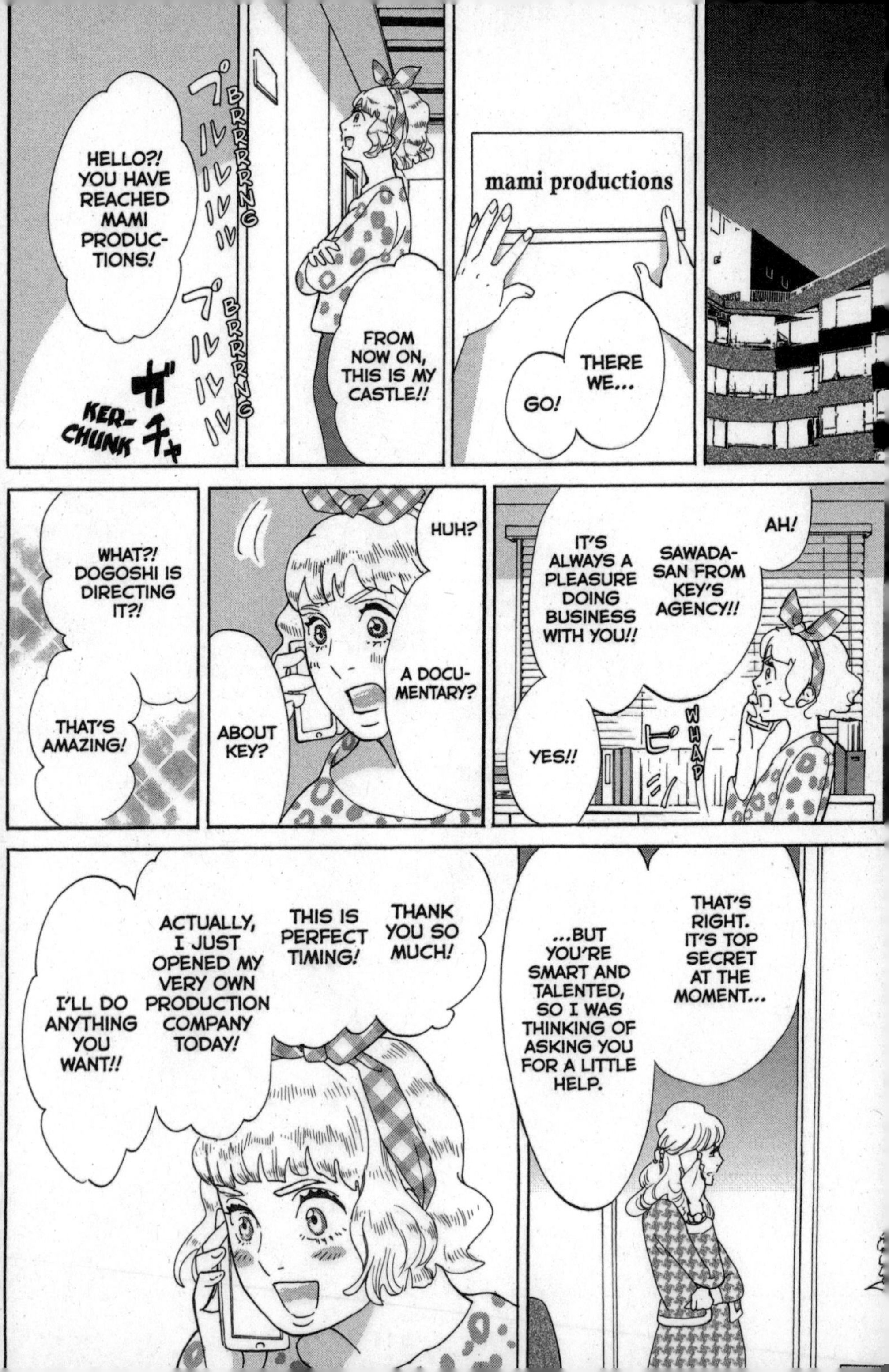
mami productions
THERE WE...
GO!
FROM NOW ON, THIS IS MY CASTLE!!
BRRRRRNG
BRRRRRNG
HELLO?! YOU HAVE REACHED MAMI PRODUCTIONS!
KER-CHUNK
AH!
SAWADA-SAN FROM KEY'S AGENCY!!
IT'S ALWAYS A PLEASURE DOING BUSINESS WITH YOU!!
YES!!
WHAP
HUH?
A DOCUMENTARY?
ABOUT KEY?
WHAT?! DOGOSHI IS DIRECTING IT?!
THAT'S AMAZING!
THAT'S RIGHT. IT'S TOP SECRET AT THE MOMENT...
...BUT YOU'RE SMART AND TALENTED, SO I WAS THINKING OF ASKING YOU FOR A LITTLE HELP.
THANK YOU SO MUCH!
THIS IS PERFECT TIMING!
ACTUALLY, I JUST OPENED MY VERY OWN PRODUCTION COMPANY TODAY!
I'LL DO ANYTHING YOU WANT!!

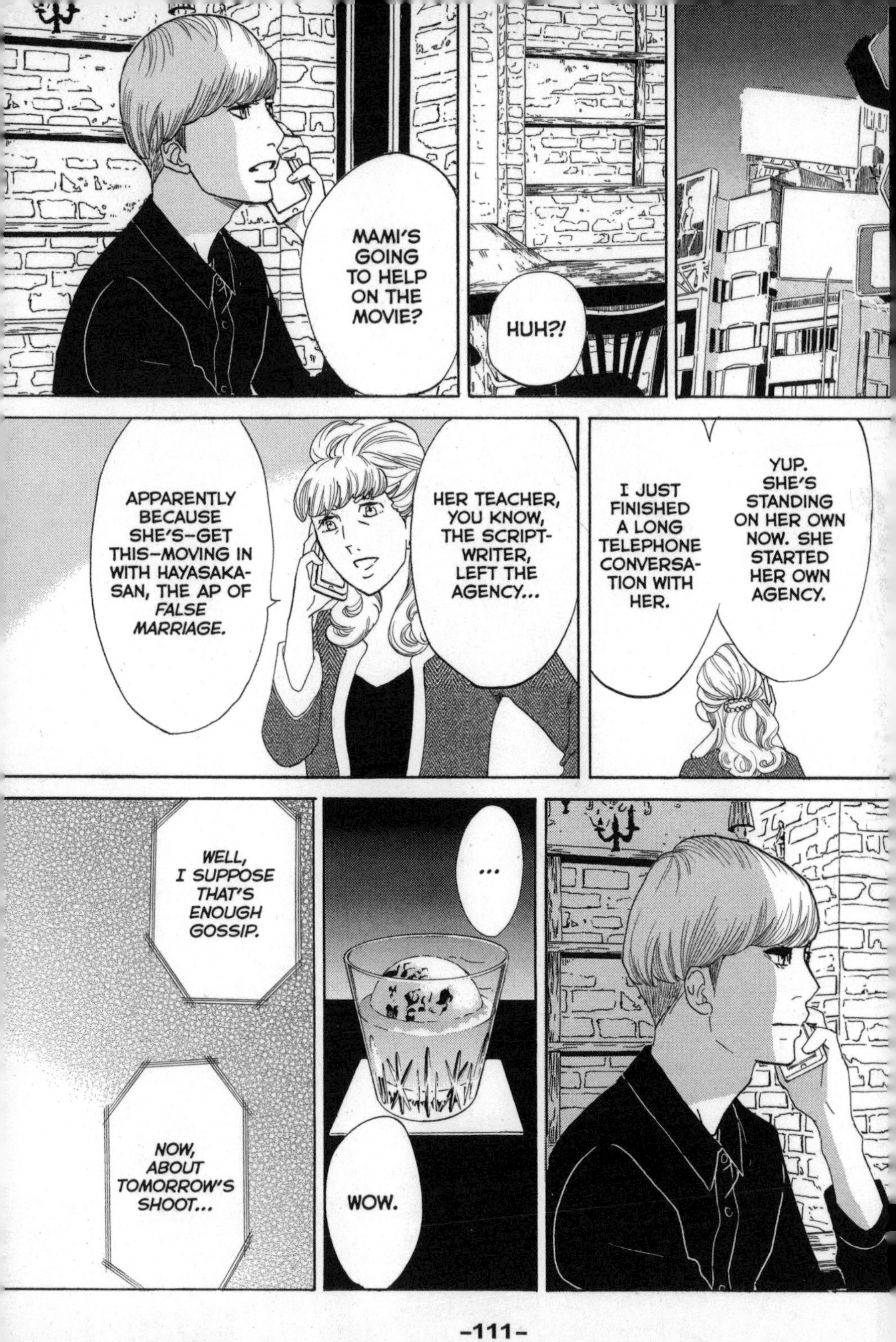
HUH?!
MAMI'S GOING TO HELP ON THE MOVIE?
YUP. SHE'S STANDING ON HER OWN NOW. SHE STARTED HER OWN AGENCY.
I JUST FINISHED A LONG TELEPHONE CONVERSATION WITH HER.
HER TEACHER, YOU KNOW, THE SCRIPT-WRITER, LEFT THE AGENCY...
APPARENTLY BECAUSE SHE'S—GET THIS—MOVING IN WITH HAYASAKA-SAN, THE AP OF *FALSE MARRIAGE*.
...
WOW.
WELL, I SUPPOSE THAT'S ENOUGH GOSSIP.
NOW, ABOUT TOMORROW'S SHOOT...

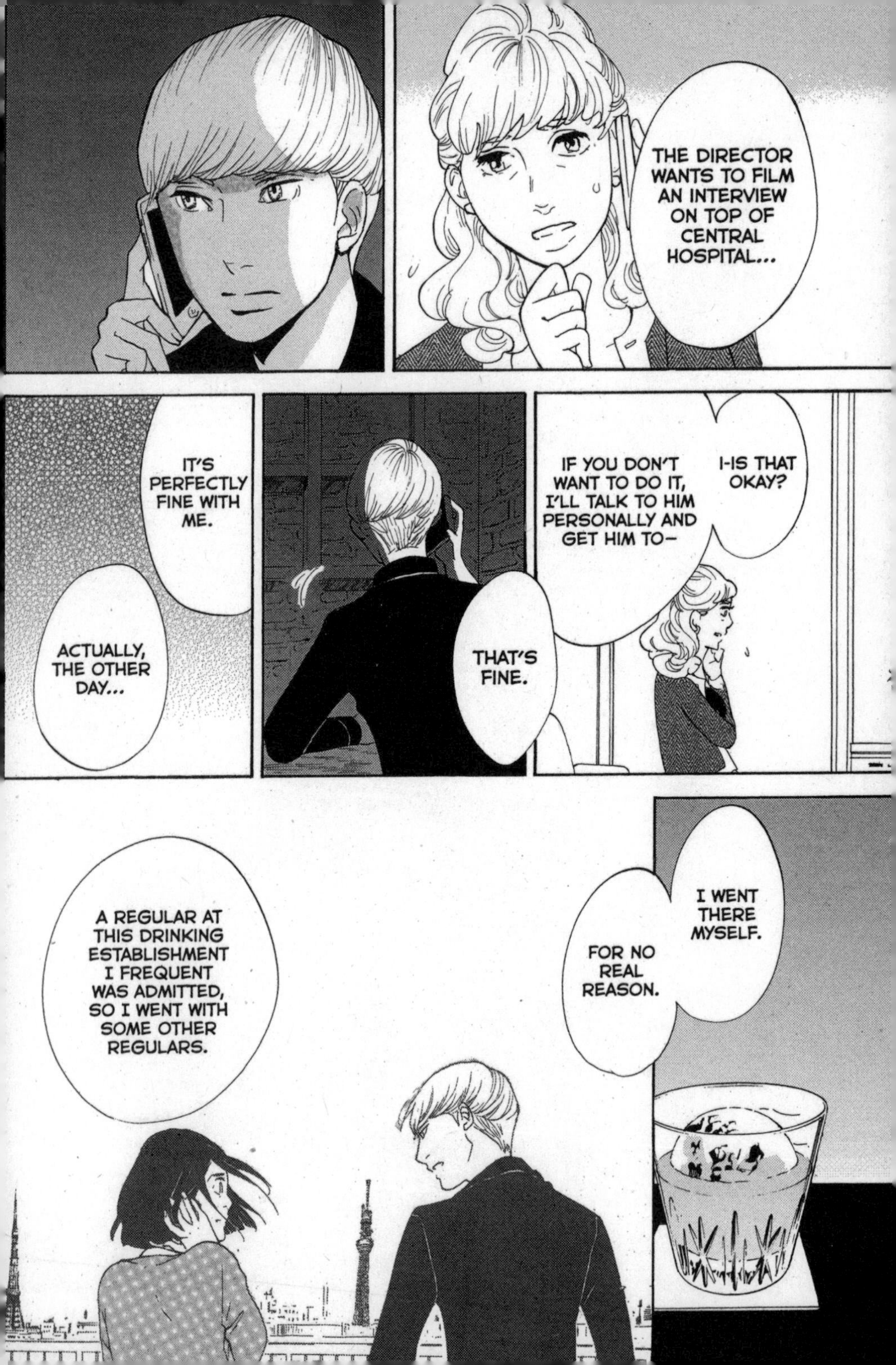
THE DIRECTOR WANTS TO FILM AN INTERVIEW ON TOP OF CENTRAL HOSPITAL...
I-IS THAT OKAY?
IF YOU DON'T WANT TO DO IT, I'LL TALK TO HIM PERSONALLY AND GET HIM TO—
THAT'S FINE.
IT'S PERFECTLY FINE WITH ME.
ACTUALLY, THE OTHER DAY...
I WENT THERE MYSELF.
FOR NO REAL REASON.
A REGULAR AT THIS DRINKING ESTABLISHMENT I FREQUENT WAS ADMITTED, SO I WENT WITH SOME OTHER REGULARS.

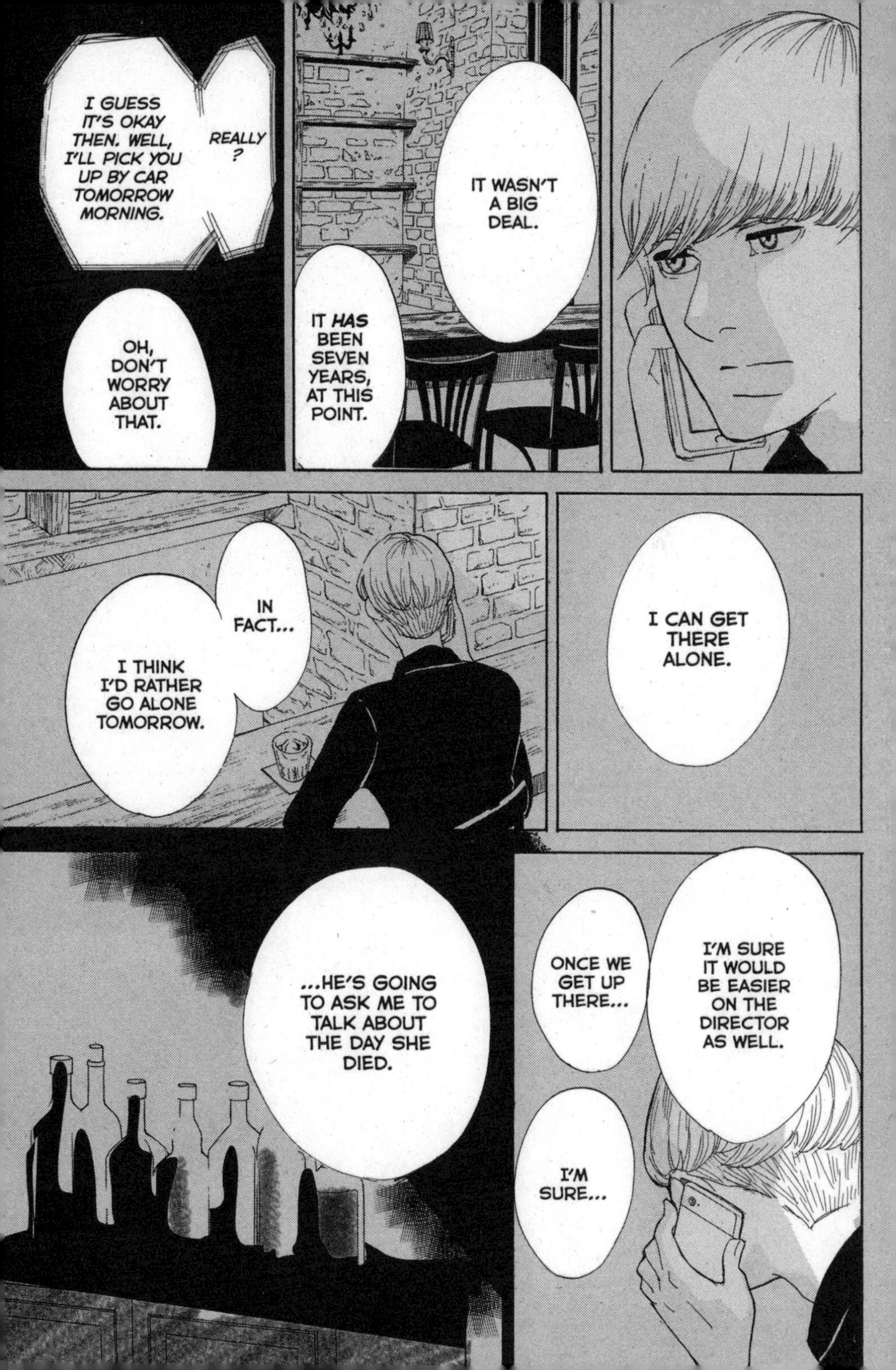
IT WASN'T A BIG DEAL.
IT *HAS* BEEN SEVEN YEARS, AT THIS POINT.
REALLY?
I GUESS IT'S OKAY THEN. WELL, I'LL PICK YOU UP BY CAR TOMORROW MORNING.
OH, DON'T WORRY ABOUT THAT.
I CAN GET THERE ALONE.
IN FACT...
I THINK I'D RATHER GO ALONE TOMORROW.
I'M SURE IT WOULD BE EASIER ON THE DIRECTOR AS WELL.
ONCE WE GET UP THERE...
I'M SURE...
...HE'S GOING TO ASK ME TO TALK ABOUT THE DAY SHE DIED.

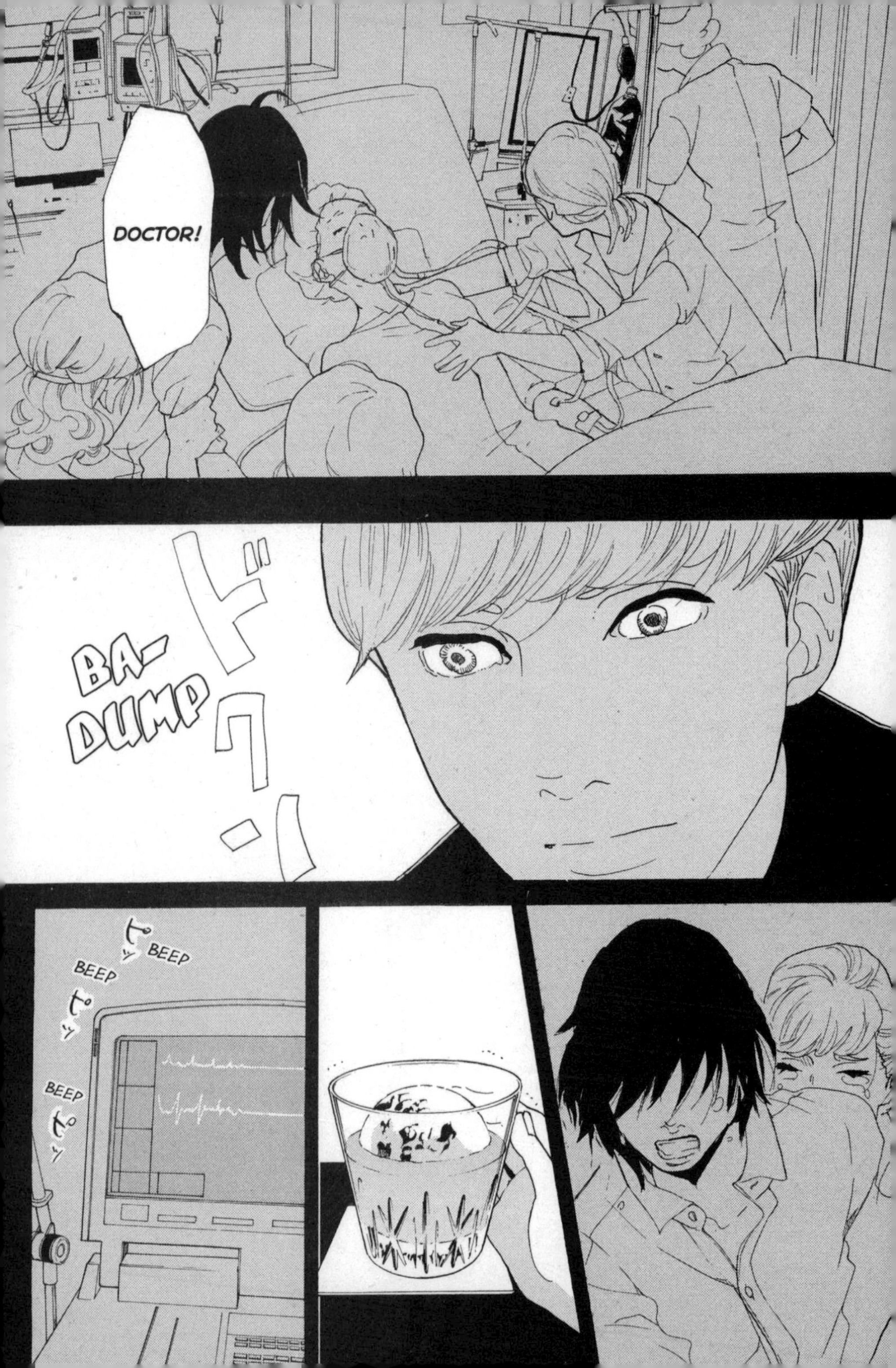
DOCTOR!
BA-DUMP
ピッ BEEP
BEEP ピッ
BEEP ピッ

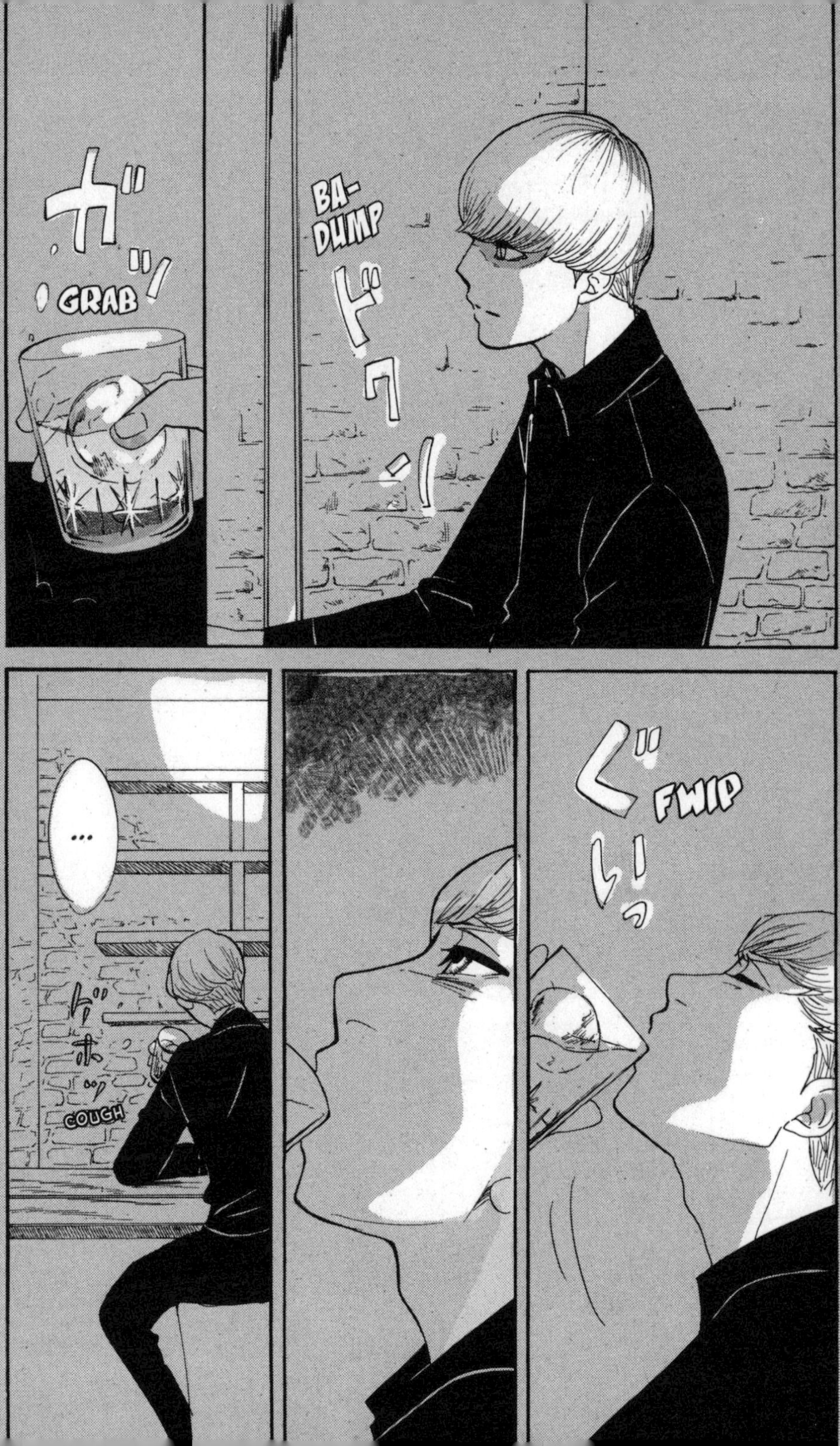
BA-DUMP
ドクッ
ガッ
GRAB
ぐいっ
FWIP
...
ゴホッ
COUGH

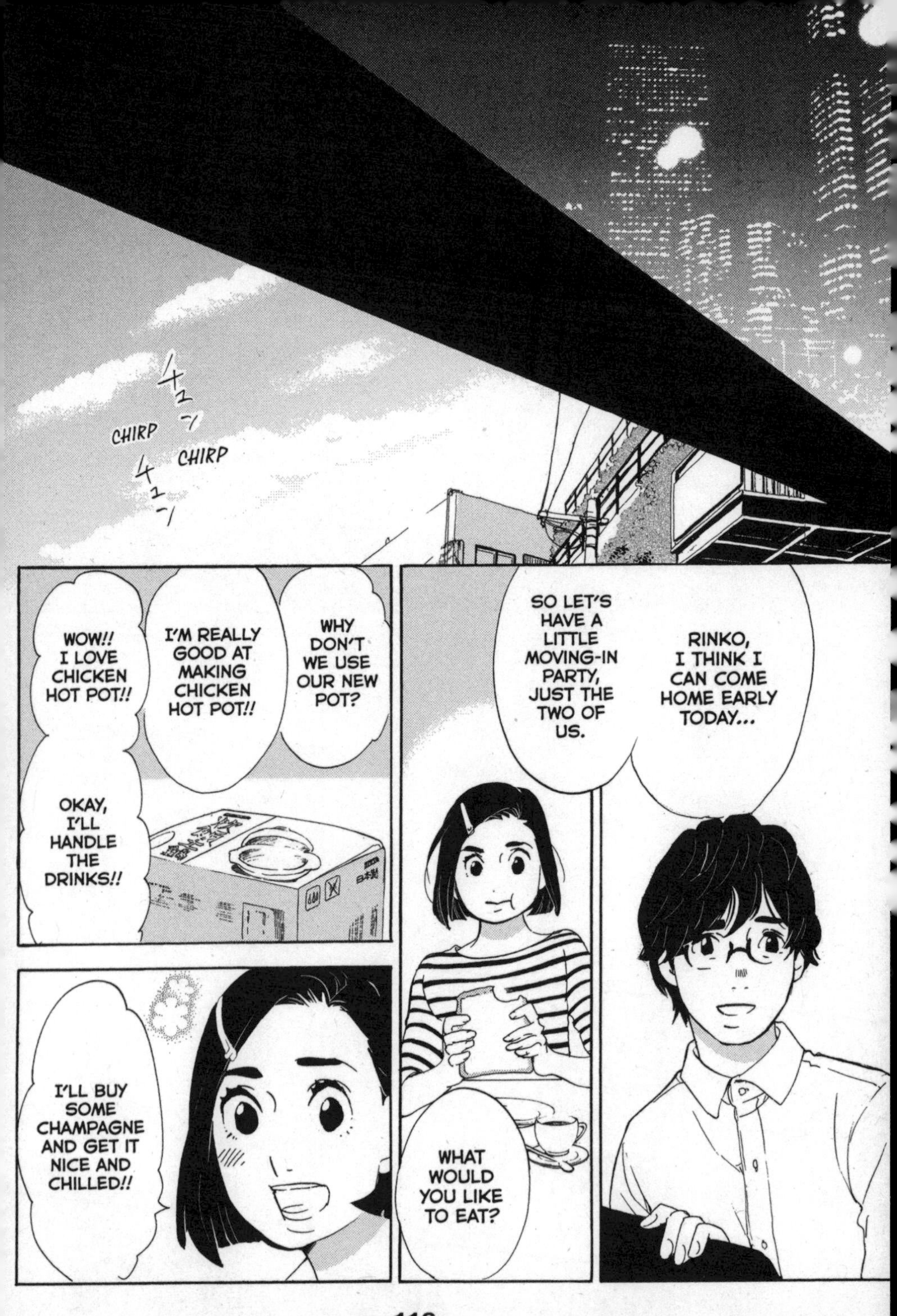
CHIRP
CHIRP
RINKO, I THINK I CAN COME HOME EARLY TODAY...
SO LET'S HAVE A LITTLE MOVING-IN PARTY, JUST THE TWO OF US.
WHAT WOULD YOU LIKE TO EAT?
WHY DON'T WE USE OUR NEW POT?
I'M REALLY GOOD AT MAKING CHICKEN HOT POT!!
WOW!! I LOVE CHICKEN HOT POT!!
OKAY, I'LL HANDLE THE DRINKS!!
I'LL BUY SOME CHAMPAGNE AND GET IT NICE AND CHILLED!!

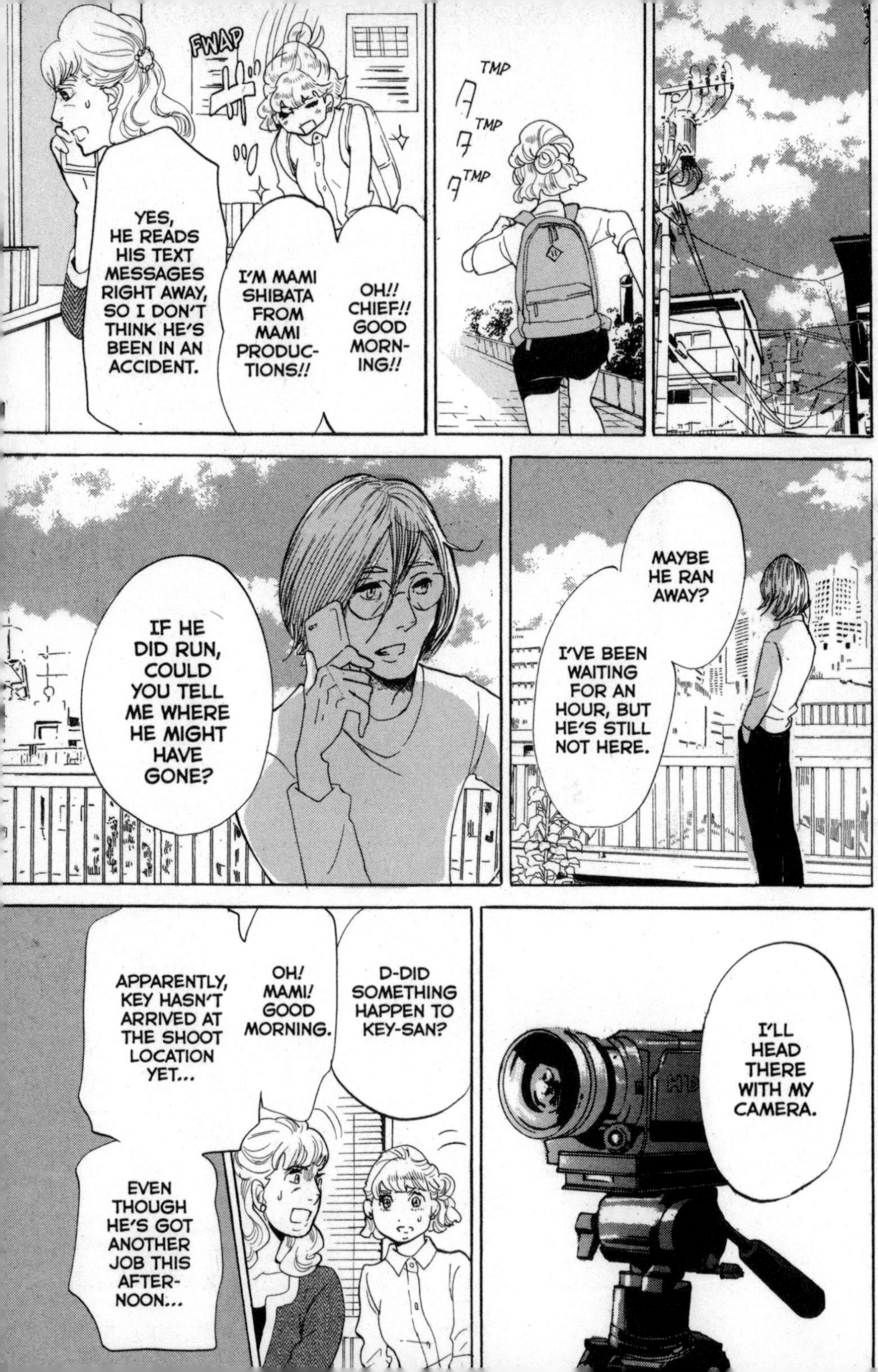
TMP
TMP
TMP
FWAP
OH!! CHIEF!! GOOD MORNING!!
I'M MAMI SHIBATA FROM MAMI PRODUCTIONS!!
YES, HE READS HIS TEXT MESSAGES RIGHT AWAY, SO I DON'T THINK HE'S BEEN IN AN ACCIDENT.
MAYBE HE RAN AWAY?
I'VE BEEN WAITING FOR AN HOUR, BUT HE'S STILL NOT HERE.
IF HE DID RUN, COULD YOU TELL ME WHERE HE MIGHT HAVE GONE?
I'LL HEAD THERE WITH MY CAMERA.
D-DID SOMETHING HAPPEN TO KEY-SAN?
OH! MAMI! GOOD MORNING.
APPARENTLY, KEY HASN'T ARRIVED AT THE SHOOT LOCATION YET...
EVEN THOUGH HE'S GOT ANOTHER JOB THIS AFTERNOON...

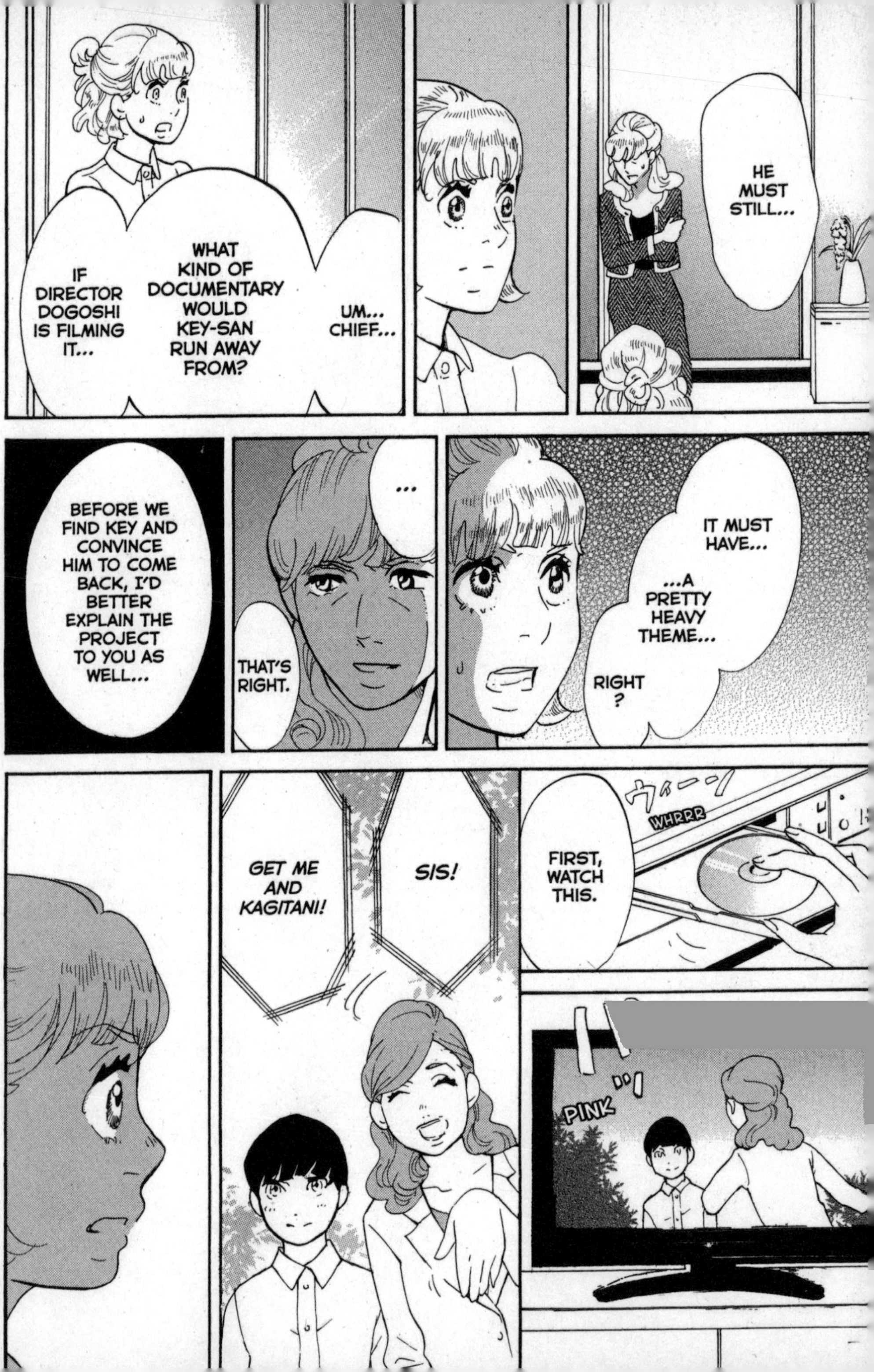
HE MUST STILL...
UM... CHIEF...
WHAT KIND OF DOCUMENTARY WOULD KEY-SAN RUN AWAY FROM?
IF DIRECTOR DOGOSHI IS FILMING IT...
IT MUST HAVE...
...A PRETTY HEAVY THEME...
RIGHT?
...
THAT'S RIGHT.
BEFORE WE FIND KEY AND CONVINCE HIM TO COME BACK, I'D BETTER EXPLAIN THE PROJECT TO YOU AS WELL...
WHRRR
FIRST, WATCH THIS.
PINK
SIS!
GET ME AND KAGITANI!

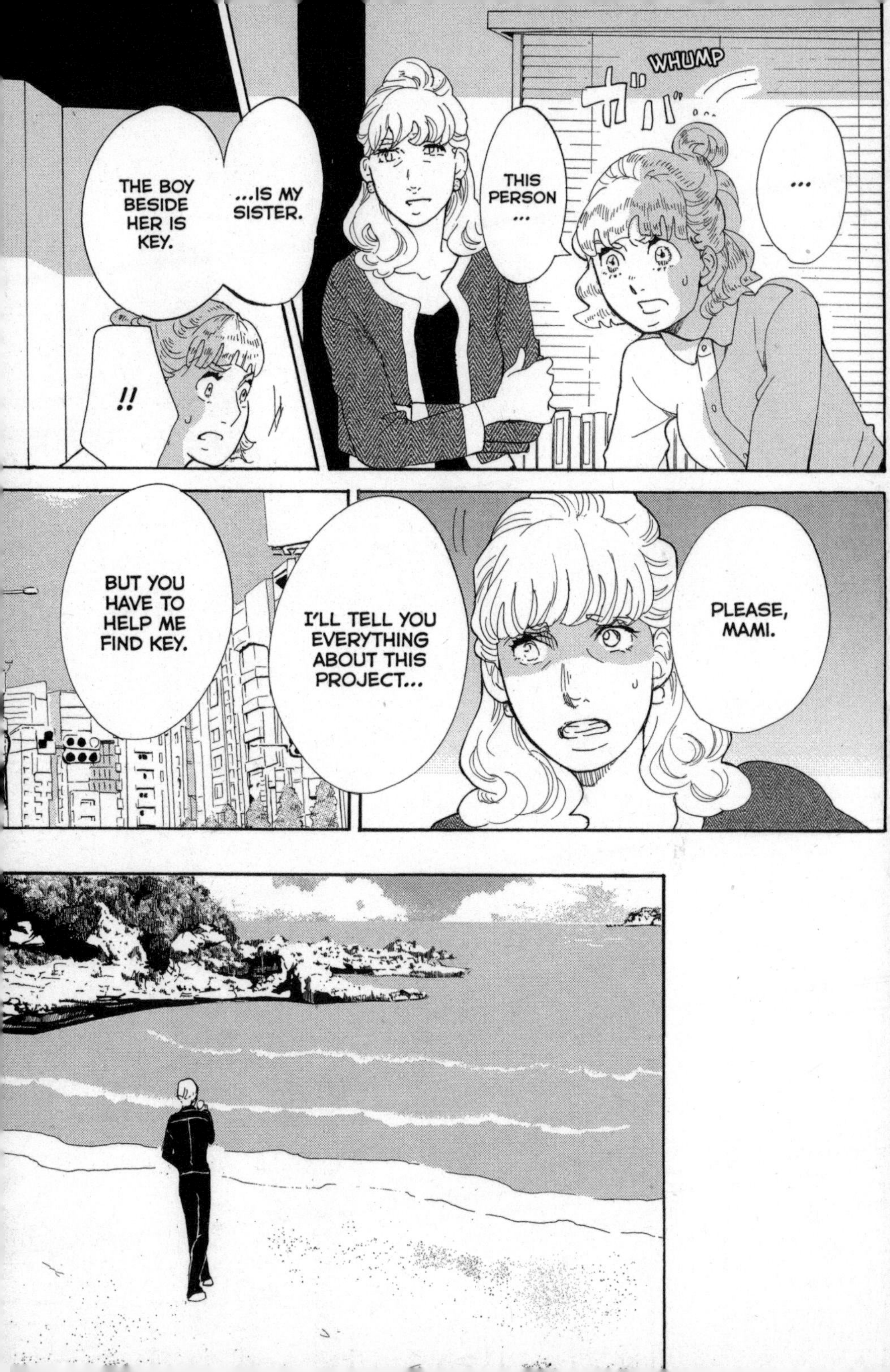
WHUMP
...
THIS PERSON ...
...IS MY SISTER.
THE BOY BESIDE HER IS KEY.
!!
PLEASE, MAMI.
I'LL TELL YOU EVERYTHING ABOUT THIS PROJECT...
BUT YOU HAVE TO HELP ME FIND KEY.

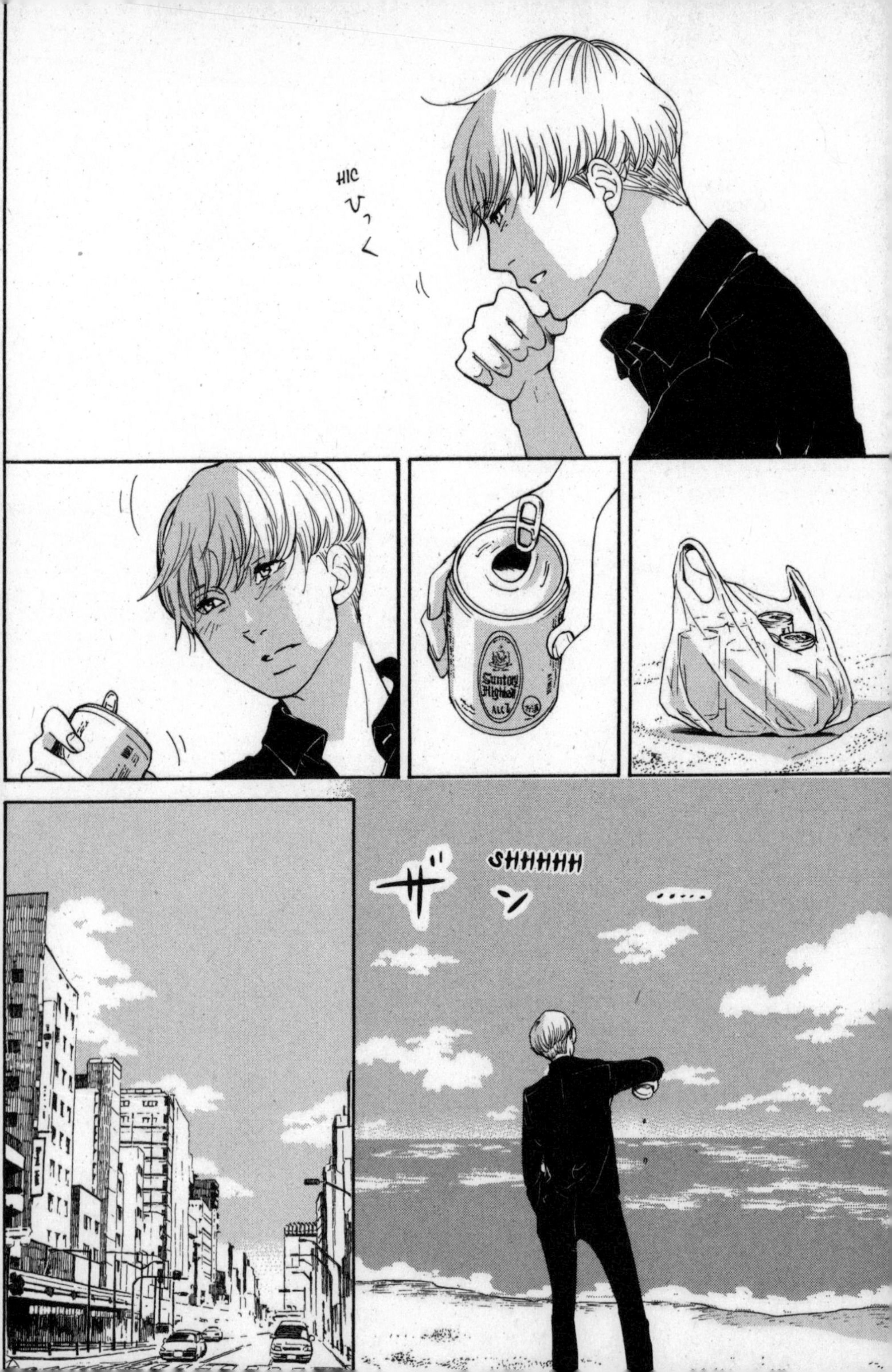
HIC
ひっく
SHHHHH
ザン
.....

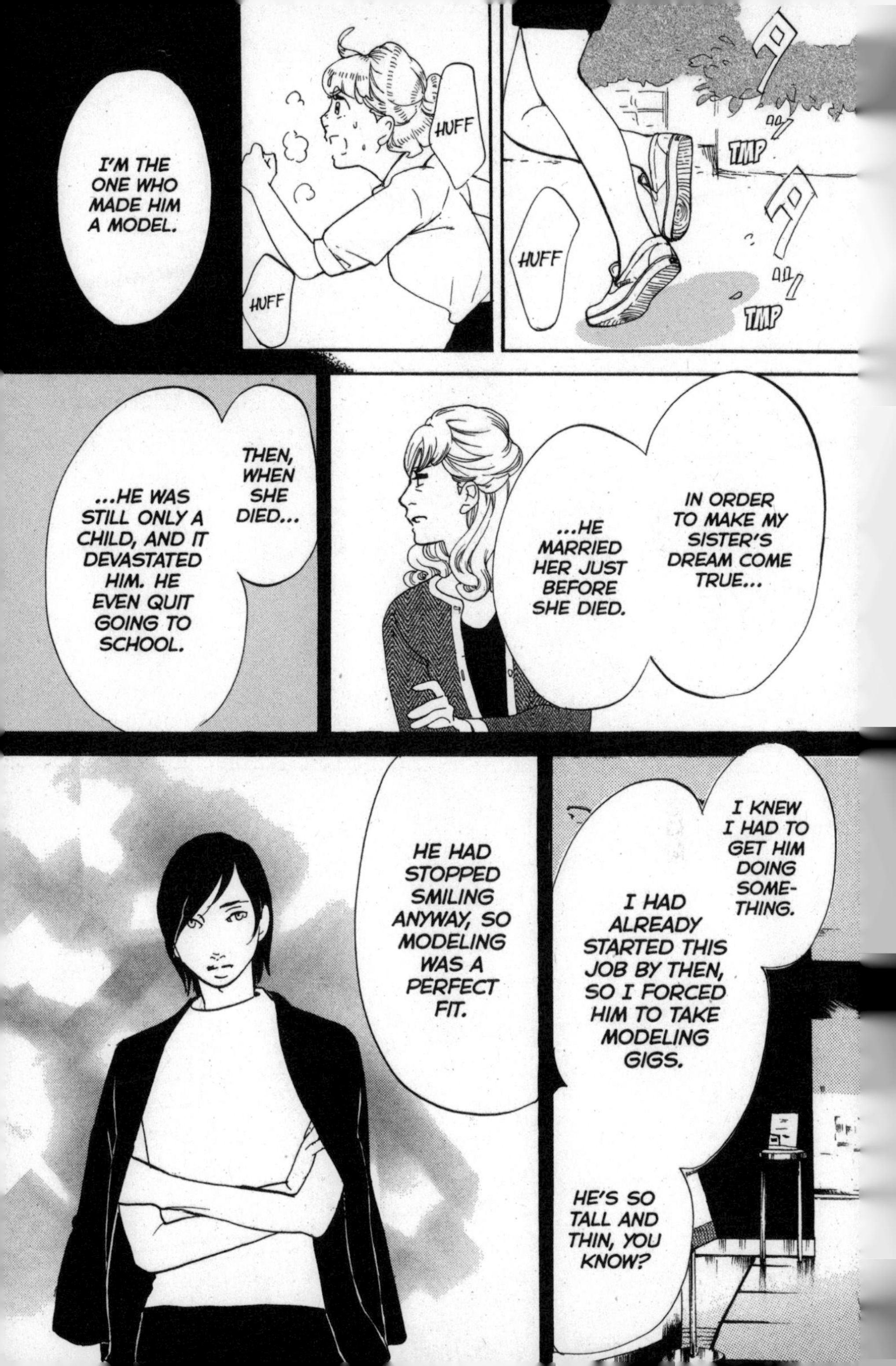
HUFF
TMP
TMP
HUFF
HUFF
I'M THE ONE WHO MADE HIM A MODEL.
IN ORDER TO MAKE MY SISTER'S DREAM COME TRUE...
...HE MARRIED HER JUST BEFORE SHE DIED.
THEN, WHEN SHE DIED...
...HE WAS STILL ONLY A CHILD, AND IT DEVASTATED HIM. HE EVEN QUIT GOING TO SCHOOL.
I KNEW I HAD TO GET HIM DOING SOME-THING.
I HAD ALREADY STARTED THIS JOB BY THEN, SO I FORCED HIM TO TAKE MODELING GIGS.
HE'S SO TALL AND THIN, YOU KNOW?
HE HAD STOPPED SMILING ANYWAY, SO MODELING WAS A PERFECT FIT.

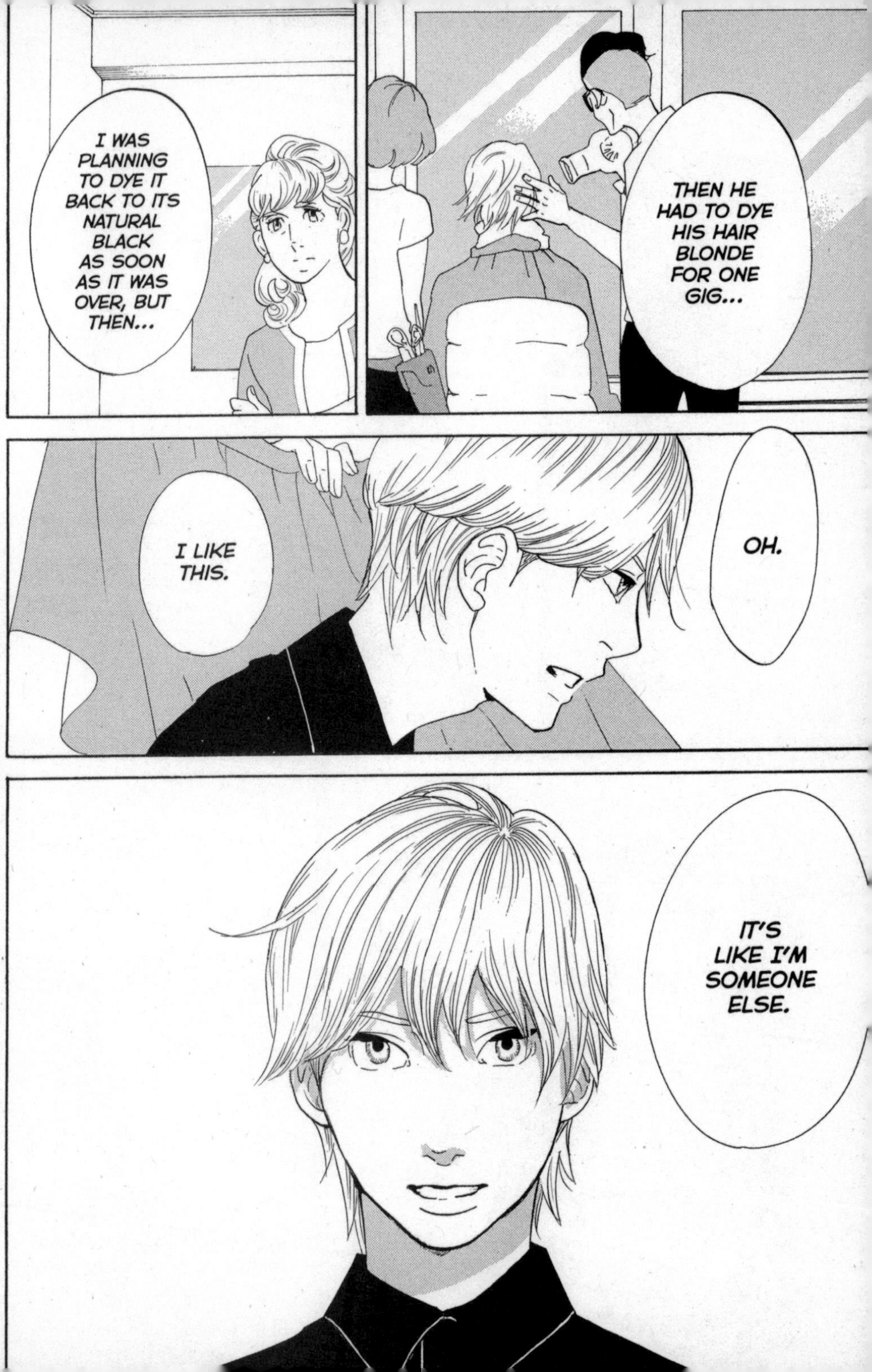
THEN HE HAD TO DYE HIS HAIR BLONDE FOR ONE GIG...
I WAS PLANNING TO DYE IT BACK TO ITS NATURAL BLACK AS SOON AS IT WAS OVER, BUT THEN...
OH.
I LIKE THIS.
IT'S LIKE I'M SOMEONE ELSE.

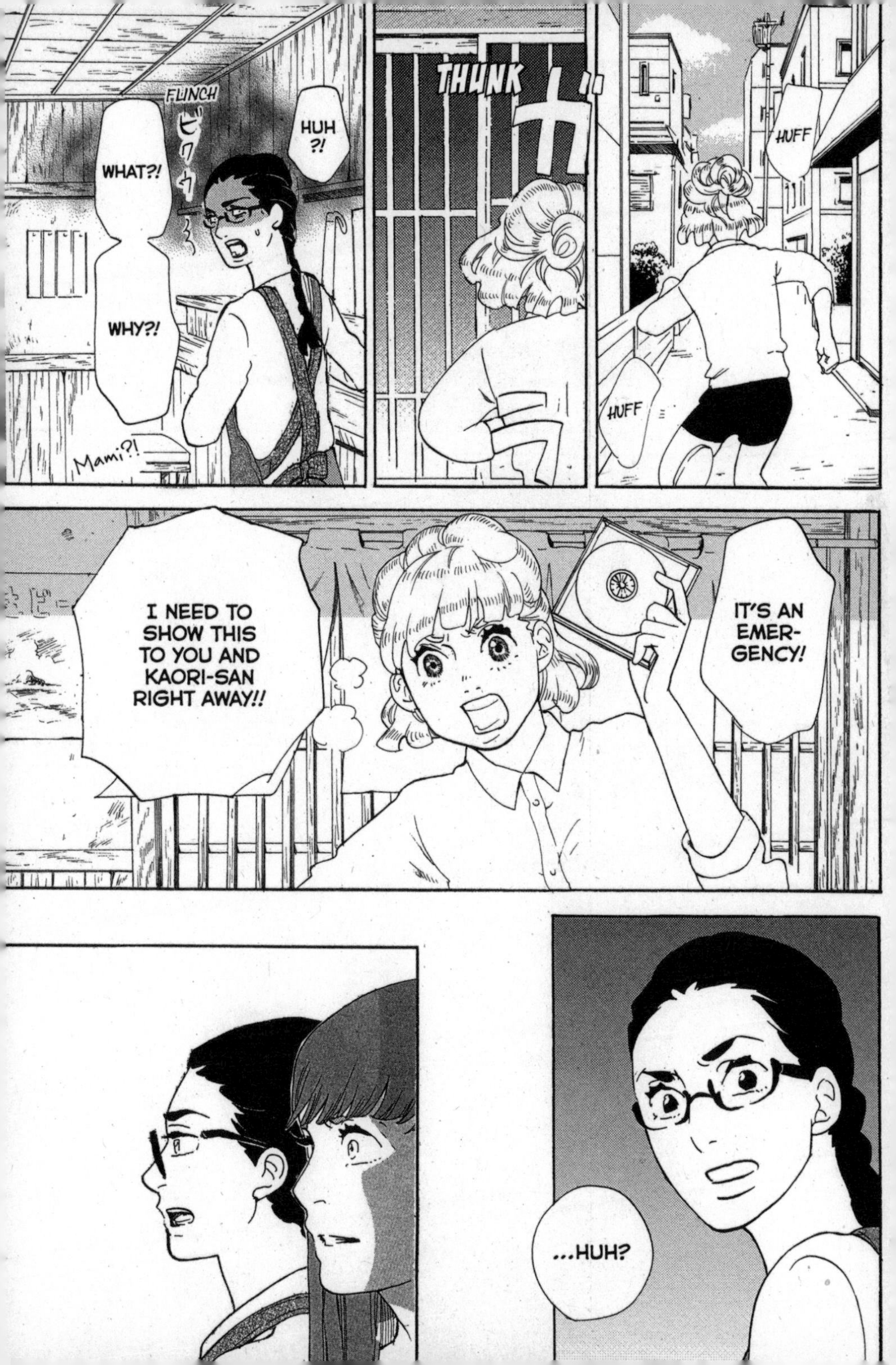
HUFF
HUFF
THUNK
ガ
HUH ?!
FLINCH
ビクゥ
WHAT?! WHY?!
Mami?!
IT'S AN EMERGENCY!
I NEED TO SHOW THIS TO YOU AND KAORI-SAN RIGHT AWAY!!
...HUH?

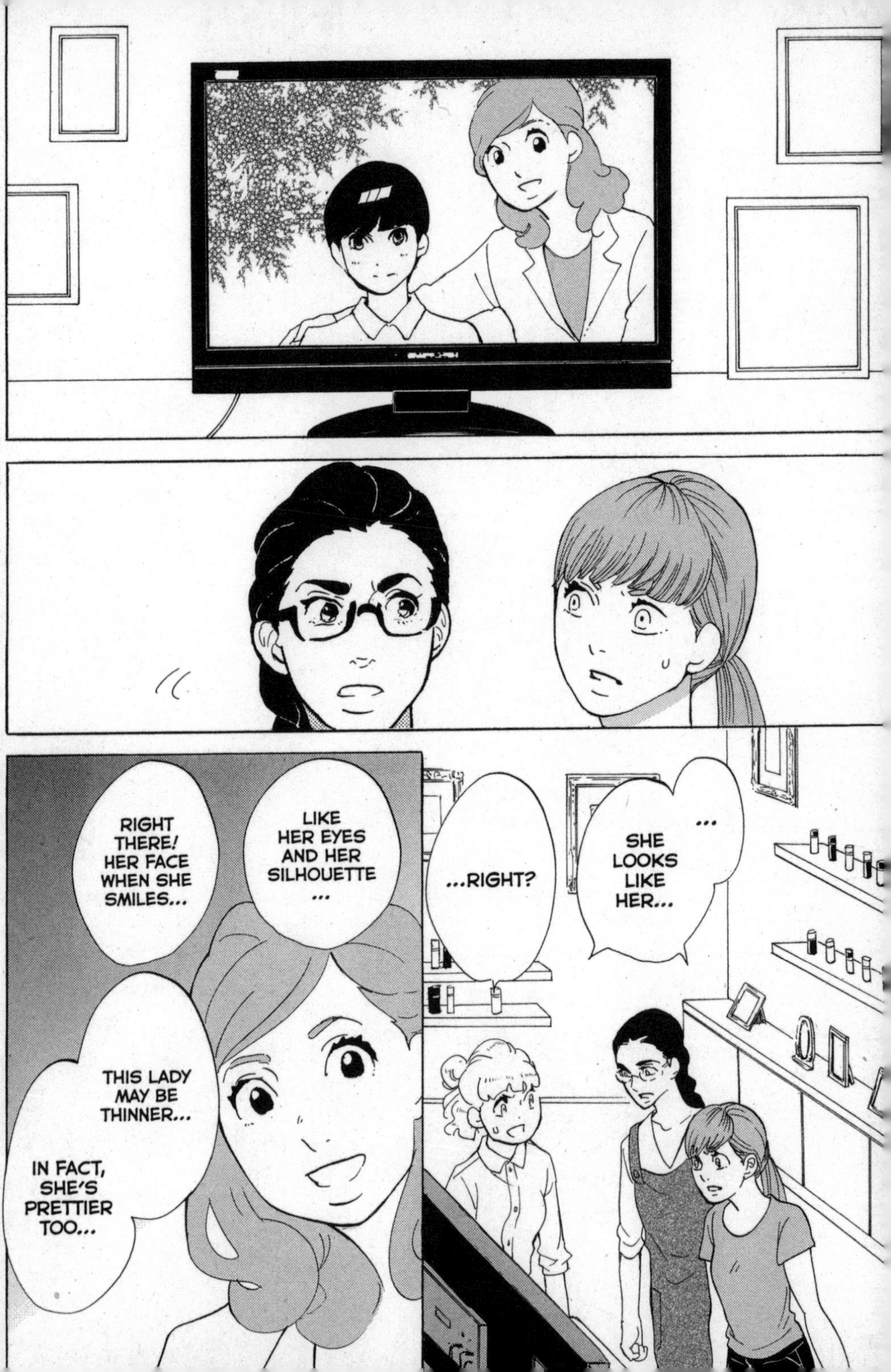
...
SHE LOOKS LIKE HER...
...RIGHT?
LIKE HER EYES AND HER SILHOUETTE ...
RIGHT THERE! HER FACE WHEN SHE SMILES...
THIS LADY MAY BE THINNER...
IN FACT, SHE'S PRETTIER TOO...

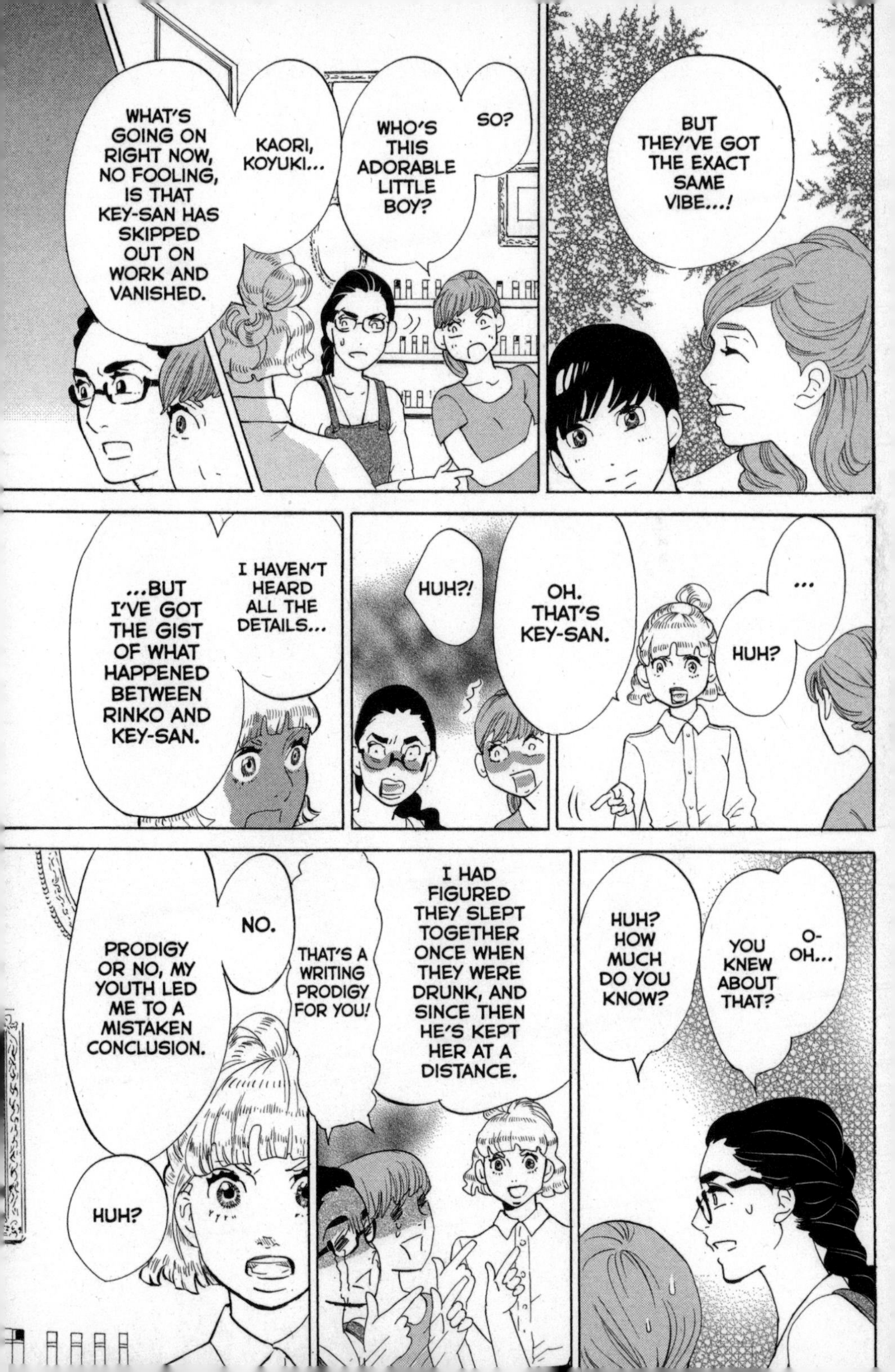
BUT THEY'VE GOT THE EXACT SAME VIBE...!
SO?
WHO'S THIS ADORABLE LITTLE BOY?
KAORI, KOYUKI...
WHAT'S GOING ON RIGHT NOW, NO FOOLING, IS THAT KEY-SAN HAS SKIPPED OUT ON WORK AND VANISHED.
...
HUH?
OH. THAT'S KEY-SAN.
HUH?!
I HAVEN'T HEARD ALL THE DETAILS...
...BUT I'VE GOT THE GIST OF WHAT HAPPENED BETWEEN RINKO AND KEY-SAN.
O-OH...
YOU KNEW ABOUT THAT?
HUH? HOW MUCH DO YOU KNOW?
I HAD FIGURED THEY SLEPT TOGETHER ONCE WHEN THEY WERE DRUNK, AND SINCE THEN HE'S KEPT HER AT A DISTANCE.
THAT'S A WRITING PRODIGY FOR YOU!
NO.
PRODIGY OR NO, MY YOUTH LED ME TO A MISTAKEN CONCLUSION.
HUH?

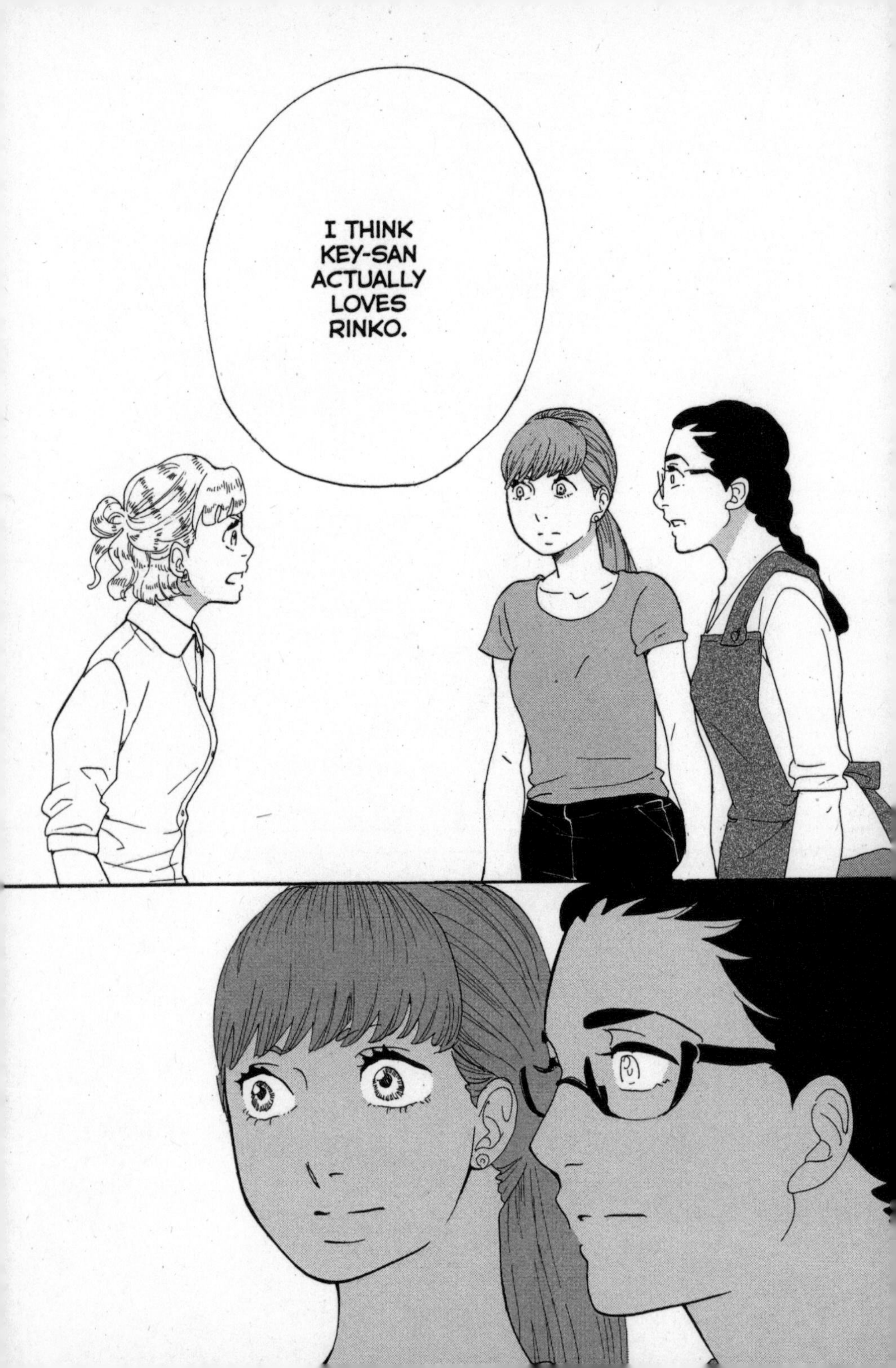
I THINK KEY-SAN ACTUALLY LOVES RINKO.

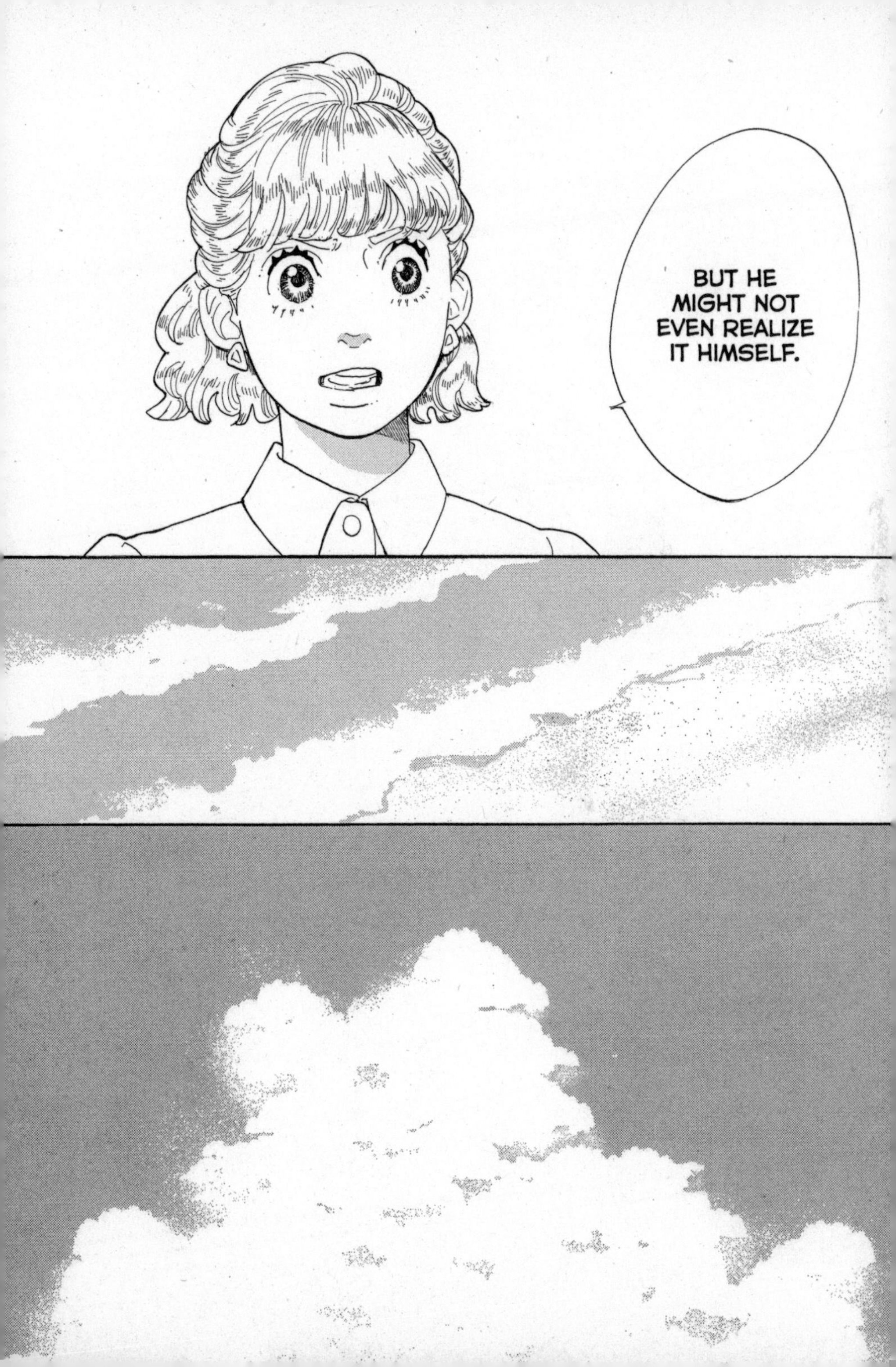
BUT HE MIGHT NOT EVEN REALIZE IT HIMSELF.

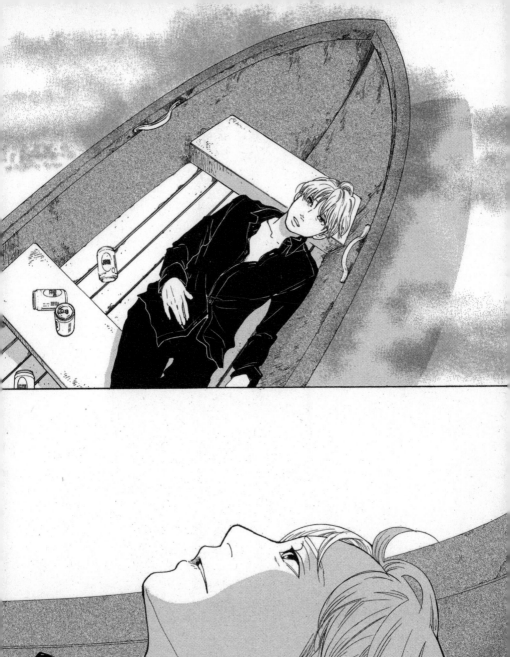

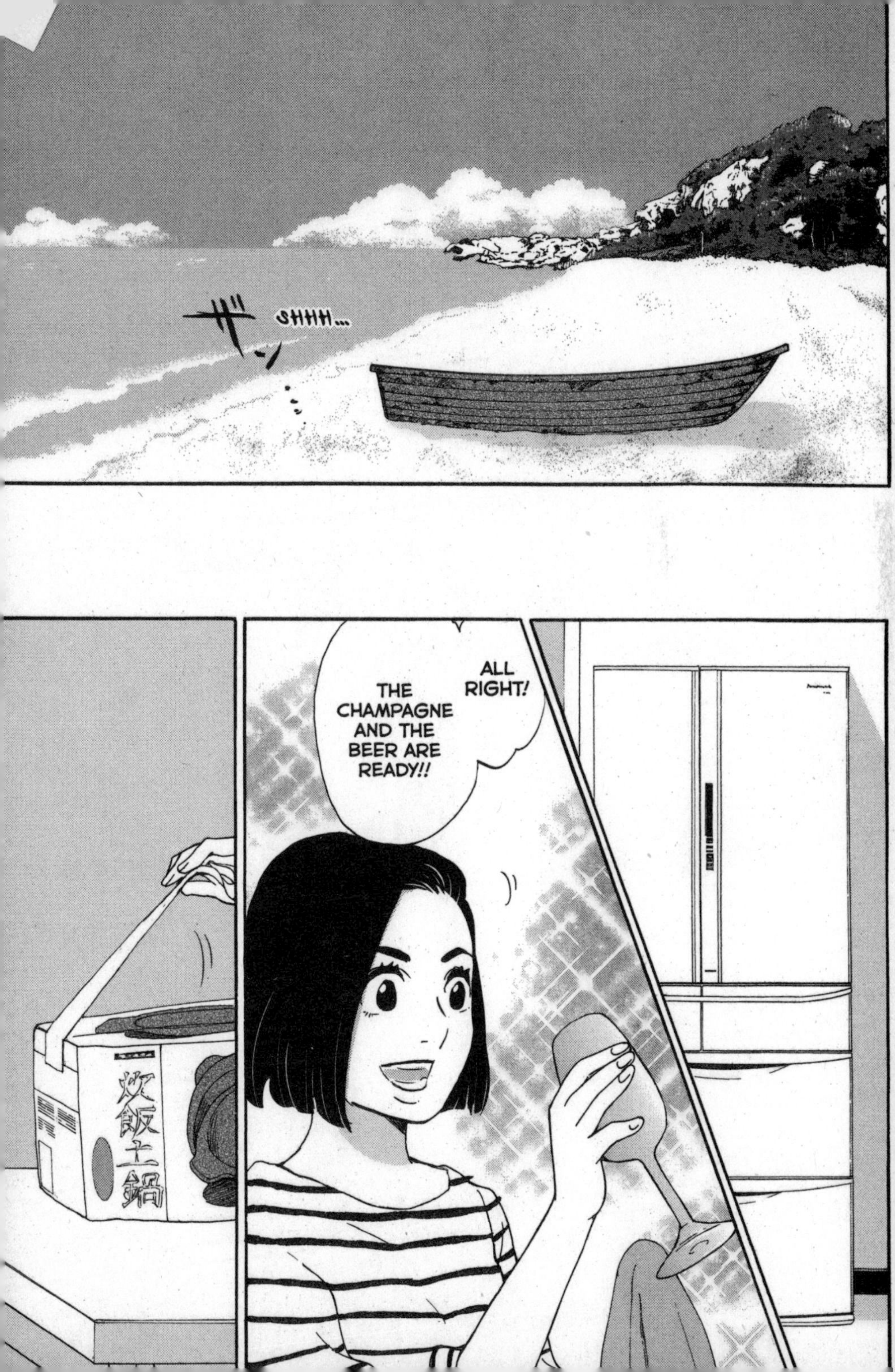
SHHH...
ALL RIGHT!
THE CHAMPAGNE AND THE BEER ARE READY!!

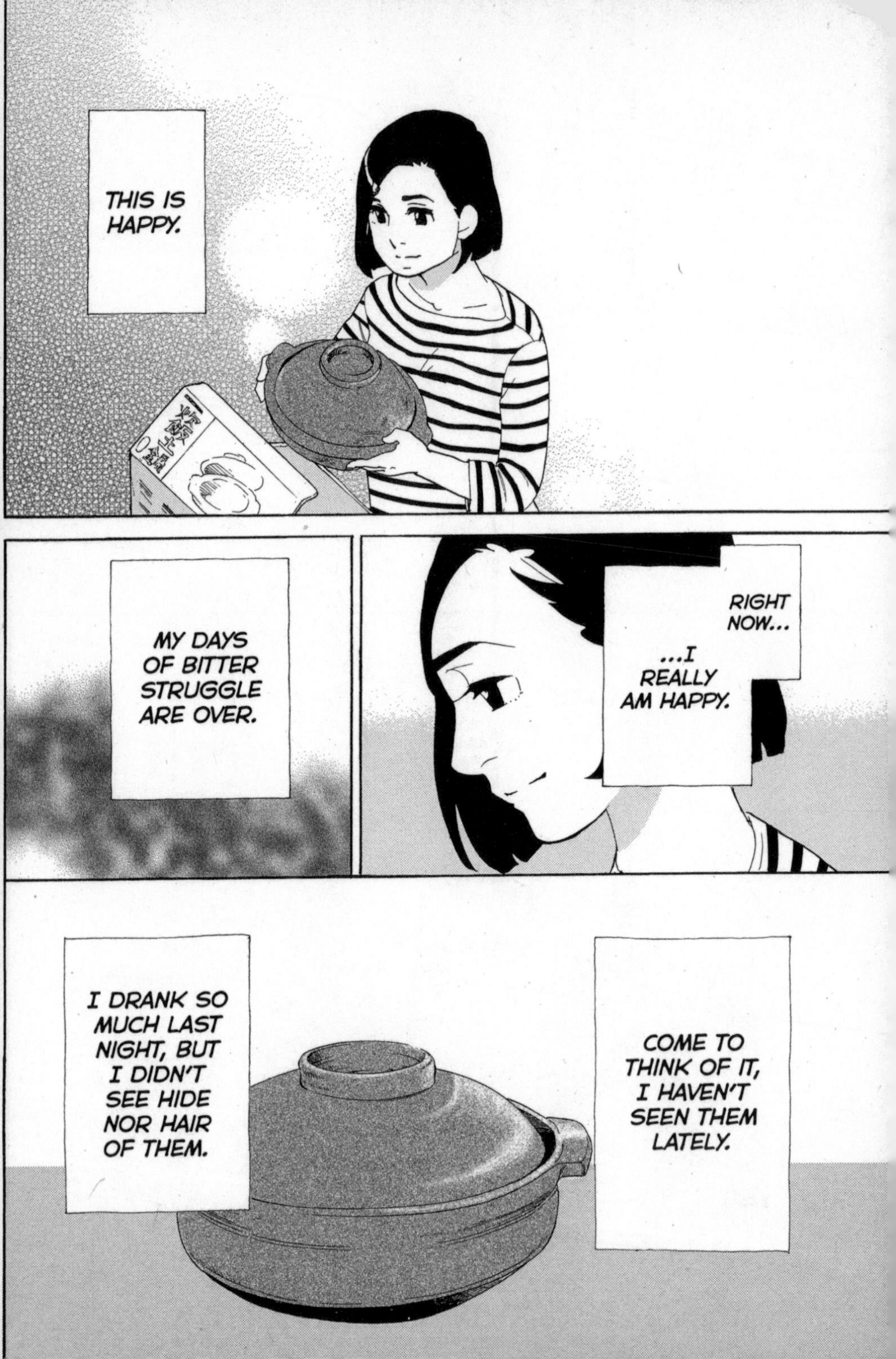
THIS IS HAPPY.
RIGHT NOW...
...I REALLY AM HAPPY.
MY DAYS OF BITTER STRUGGLE ARE OVER.
COME TO THINK OF IT, I HAVEN'T SEEN THEM LATELY.
I DRANK SO MUCH LAST NIGHT, BUT I DIDN'T SEE HIDE NOR HAIR OF THEM.

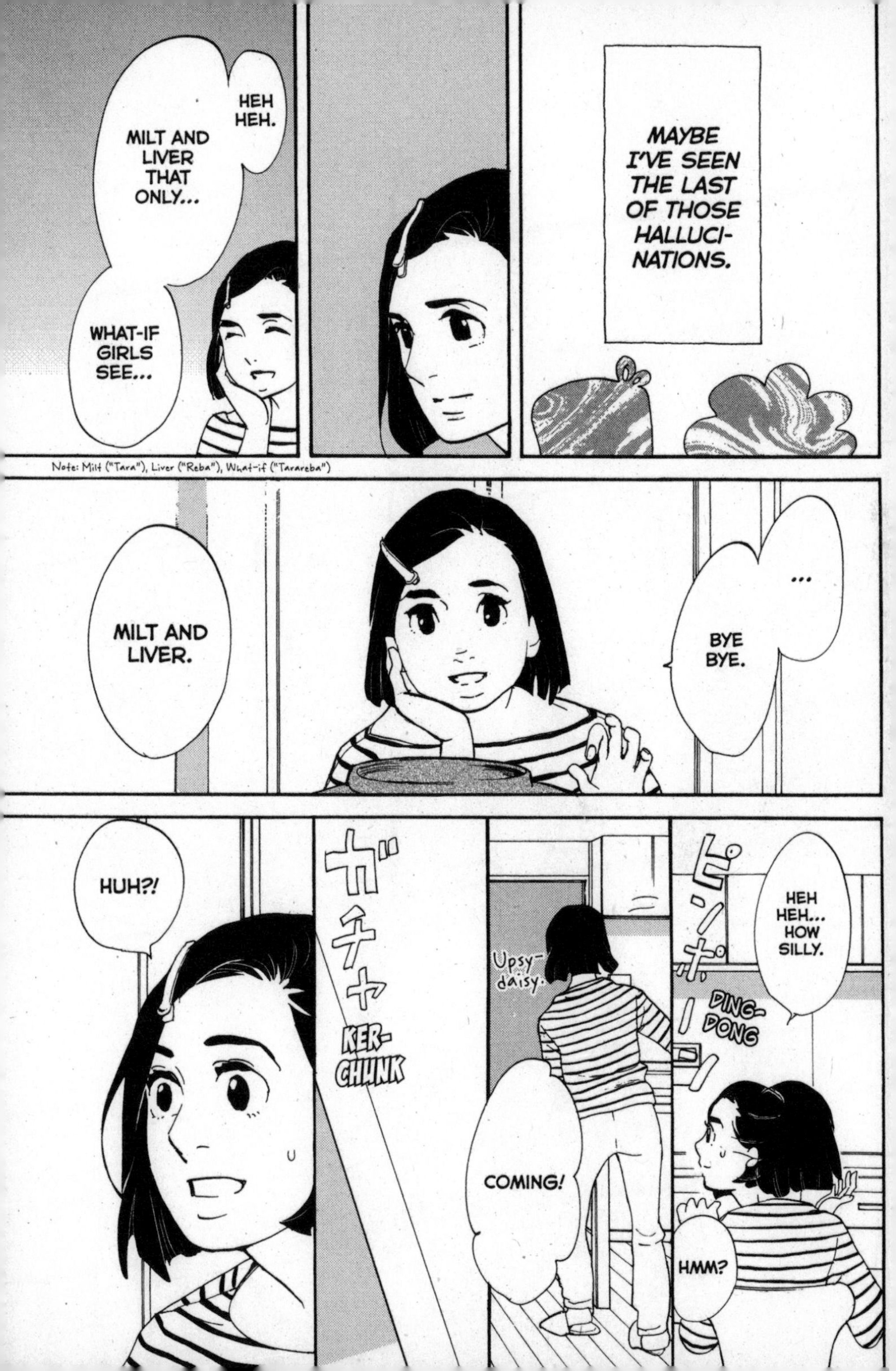
MAYBE I'VE SEEN THE LAST OF THOSE HALLUCI-NATIONS.
HEH HEH.
MILT AND LIVER THAT ONLY...
WHAT-IF GIRLS SEE...
Note: Milt ("Tara"), Liver ("Reba"), What-if ("Tarareba")
...
BYE BYE.
MILT AND LIVER.
ピンポーン
DING-DONG
HEH HEH... HOW SILLY.
HMM?
Upsy-daisy.
COMING!
ガチャ
KER-CHUNK
HUH?!

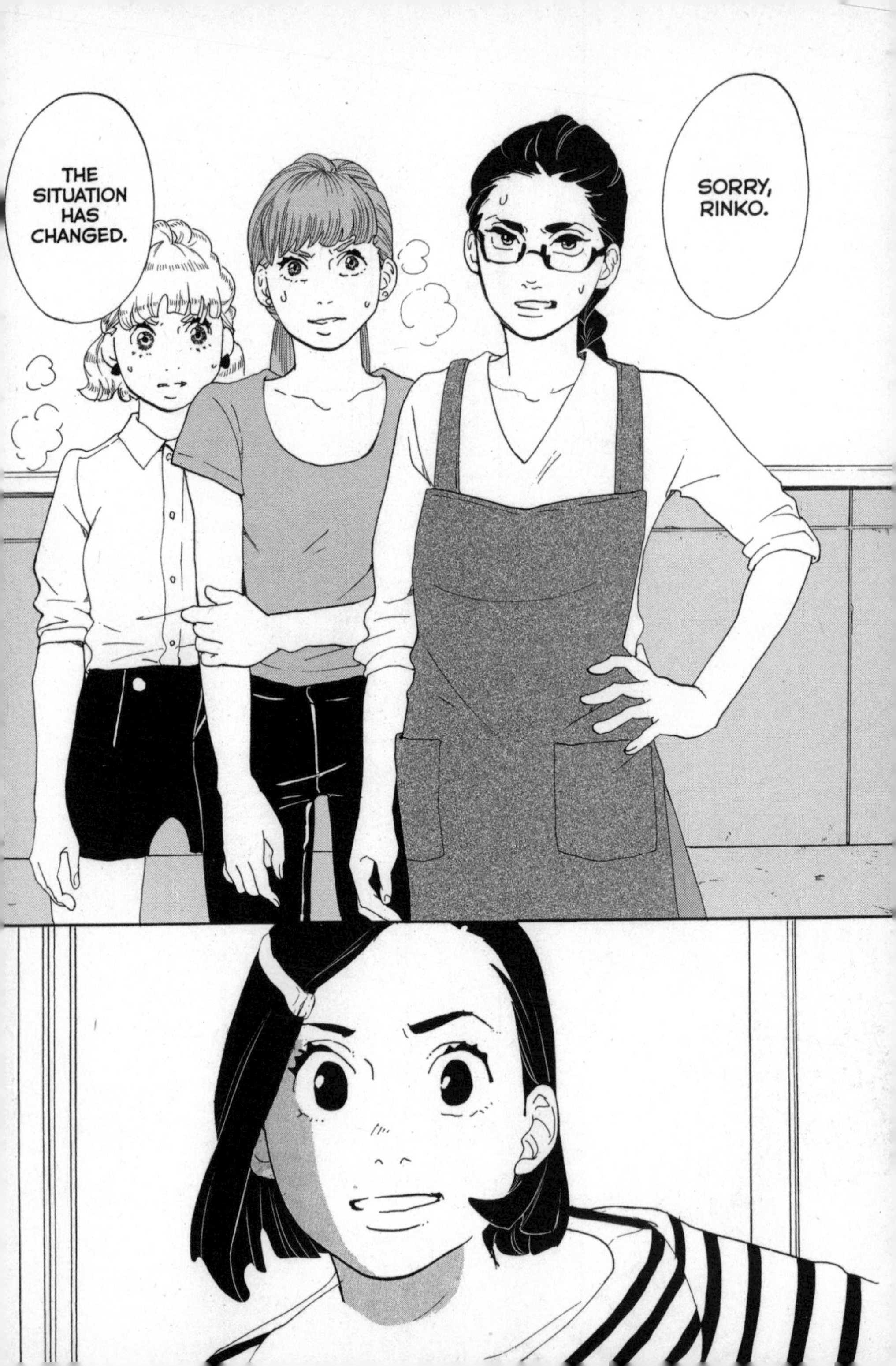
SORRY, RINKO.
THE SITUATION HAS CHANGED.

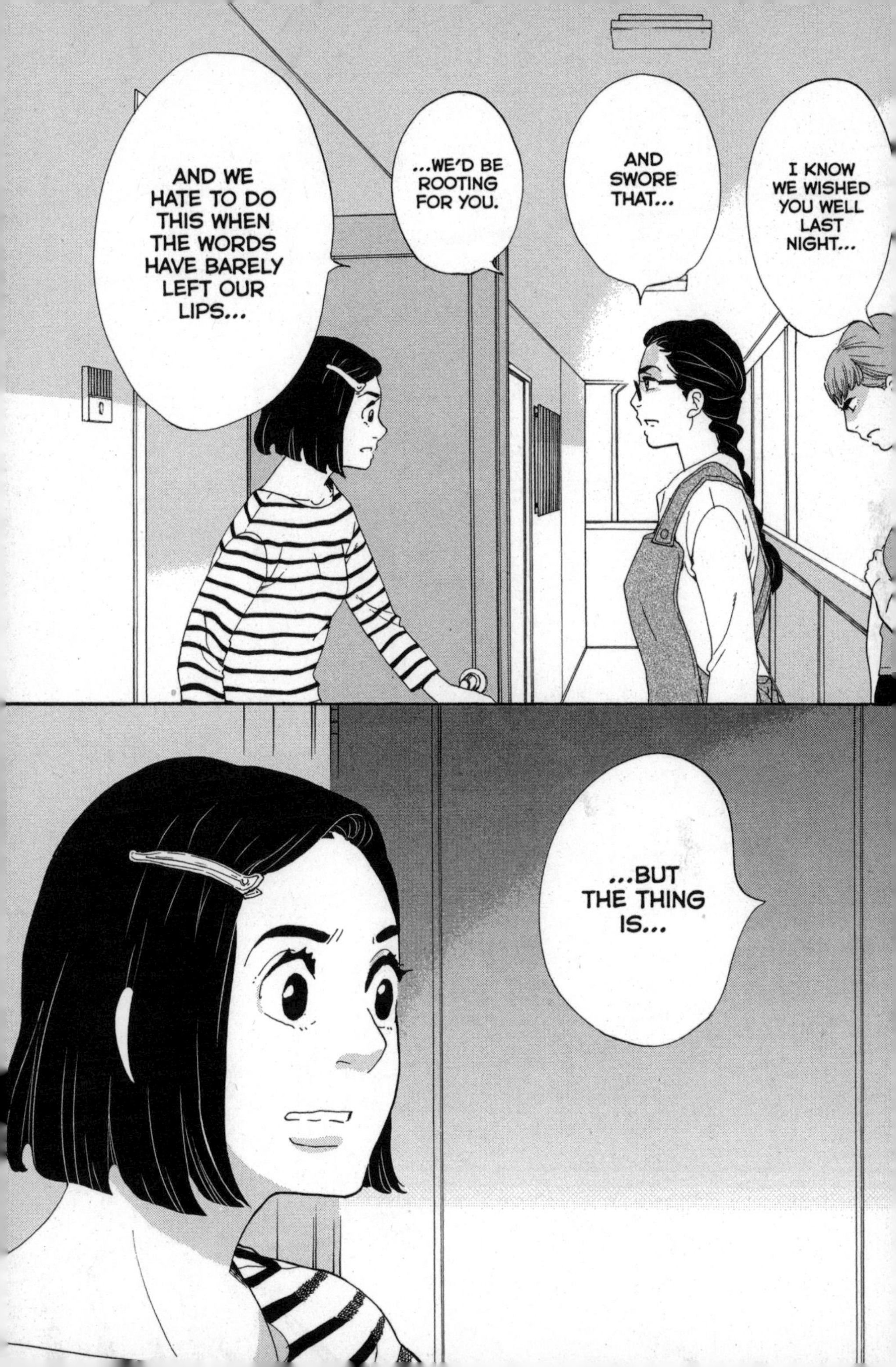
I KNOW WE WISHED YOU WELL LAST NIGHT...
AND SWORE THAT...
...WE'D BE ROOTING FOR YOU.
AND WE HATE TO DO THIS WHEN THE WORDS HAVE BARELY LEFT OUR LIPS...
...BUT THE THING IS...

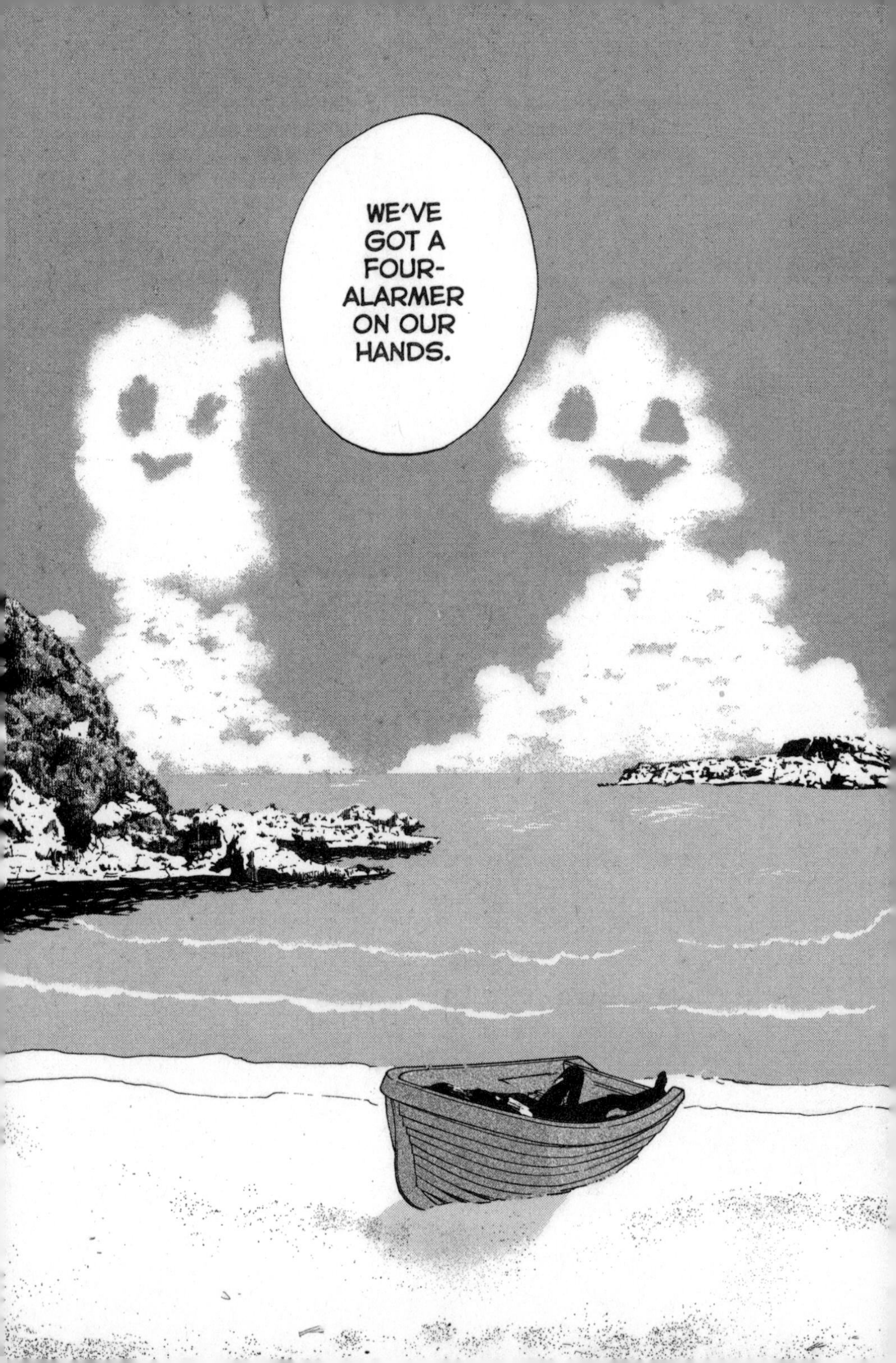
WE'VE GOT A FOUR-ALARMER ON OUR HANDS.

TOKYO

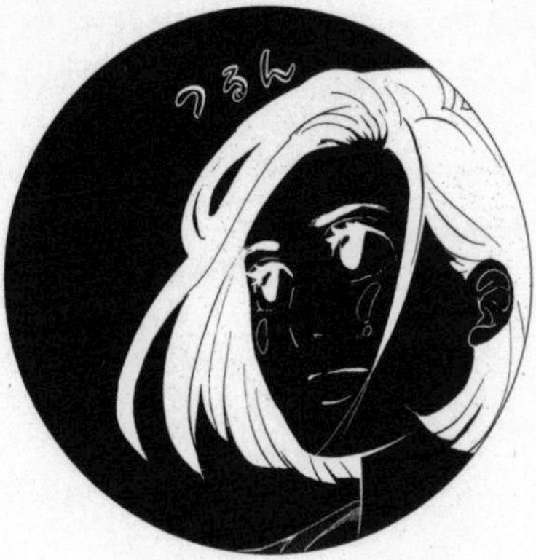
つるん

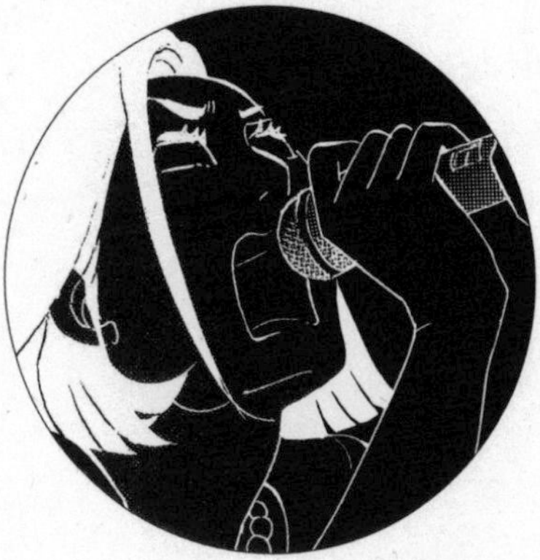

TARAREBA

GIRLS

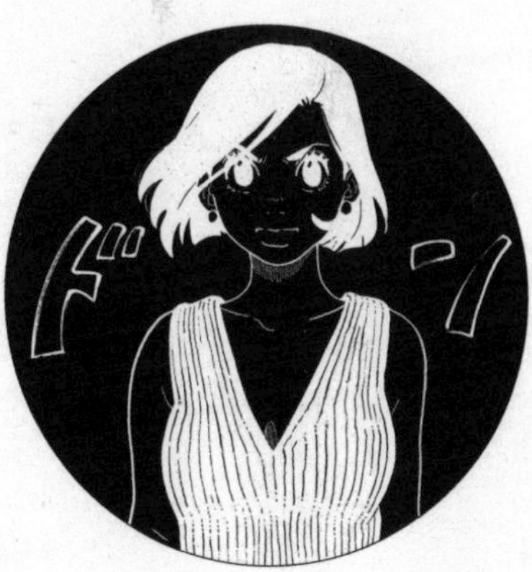
ドーン

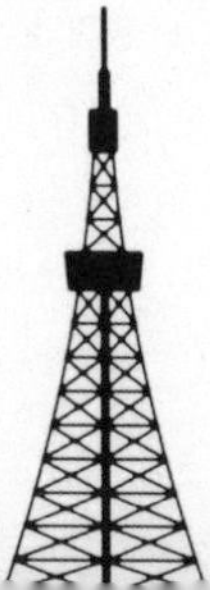

TOKYO TARAREBA GIRLS
(SIDE STORY)

Tarare-Bar

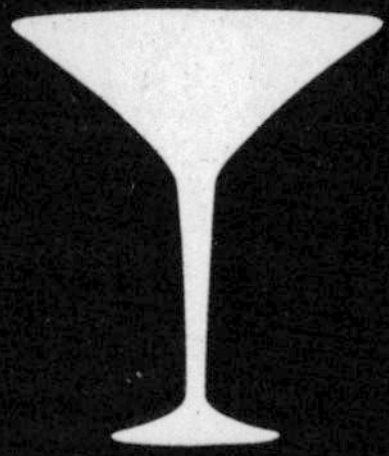

IN THE FOLLOWING SIDE STORY, "TARARE-BAR," WE PUBLISH PROBLEMS SUBMITTED BY READERS FROM ACROSS THE COUNTRY.

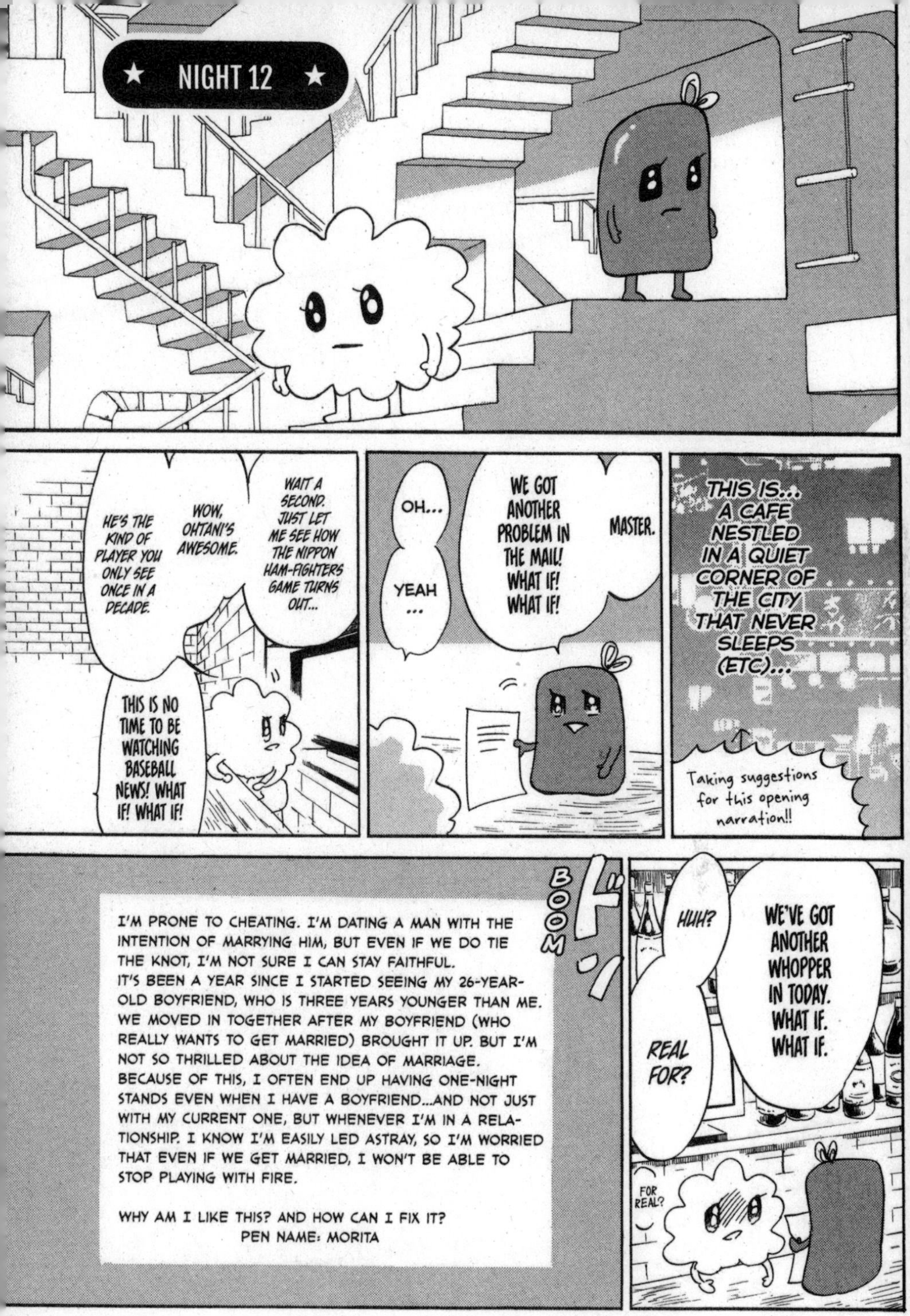

NIGHT 12
THIS IS... A CAFE NESTLED IN A QUIET CORNER OF THE CITY THAT NEVER SLEEPS (ETC)...
Taking suggestions for this opening narration!!
MASTER.
WE GOT ANOTHER PROBLEM IN THE MAIL! WHAT IF! WHAT IF!
OH...
YEAH...
WAIT A SECOND. JUST LET ME SEE HOW THE NIPPON HAM-FIGHTERS GAME TURNS OUT...
WOW, OHTANI'S AWESOME.
HE'S THE KIND OF PLAYER YOU ONLY SEE ONCE IN A DECADE.
THIS IS NO TIME TO BE WATCHING BASEBALL NEWS! WHAT IF! WHAT IF!
WE'VE GOT ANOTHER WHOPPER IN TODAY. WHAT IF. WHAT IF.
HUH?
REAL FOR?
FOR REAL?
BOOM
I'M PRONE TO CHEATING. I'M DATING A MAN WITH THE INTENTION OF MARRYING HIM, BUT EVEN IF WE DO TIE THE KNOT, I'M NOT SURE I CAN STAY FAITHFUL.
IT'S BEEN A YEAR SINCE I STARTED SEEING MY 26-YEAR-OLD BOYFRIEND, WHO IS THREE YEARS YOUNGER THAN ME. WE MOVED IN TOGETHER AFTER MY BOYFRIEND (WHO REALLY WANTS TO GET MARRIED) BROUGHT IT UP. BUT I'M NOT SO THRILLED ABOUT THE IDEA OF MARRIAGE. BECAUSE OF THIS, I OFTEN END UP HAVING ONE-NIGHT STANDS EVEN WHEN I HAVE A BOYFRIEND...AND NOT JUST WITH MY CURRENT ONE, BUT WHENEVER I'M IN A RELATIONSHIP. I KNOW I'M EASILY LED ASTRAY, SO I'M WORRIED THAT EVEN IF WE GET MARRIED, I WON'T BE ABLE TO STOP PLAYING WITH FIRE.
WHY AM I LIKE THIS? AND HOW CAN I FIX IT?
PEN NAME: MORITA

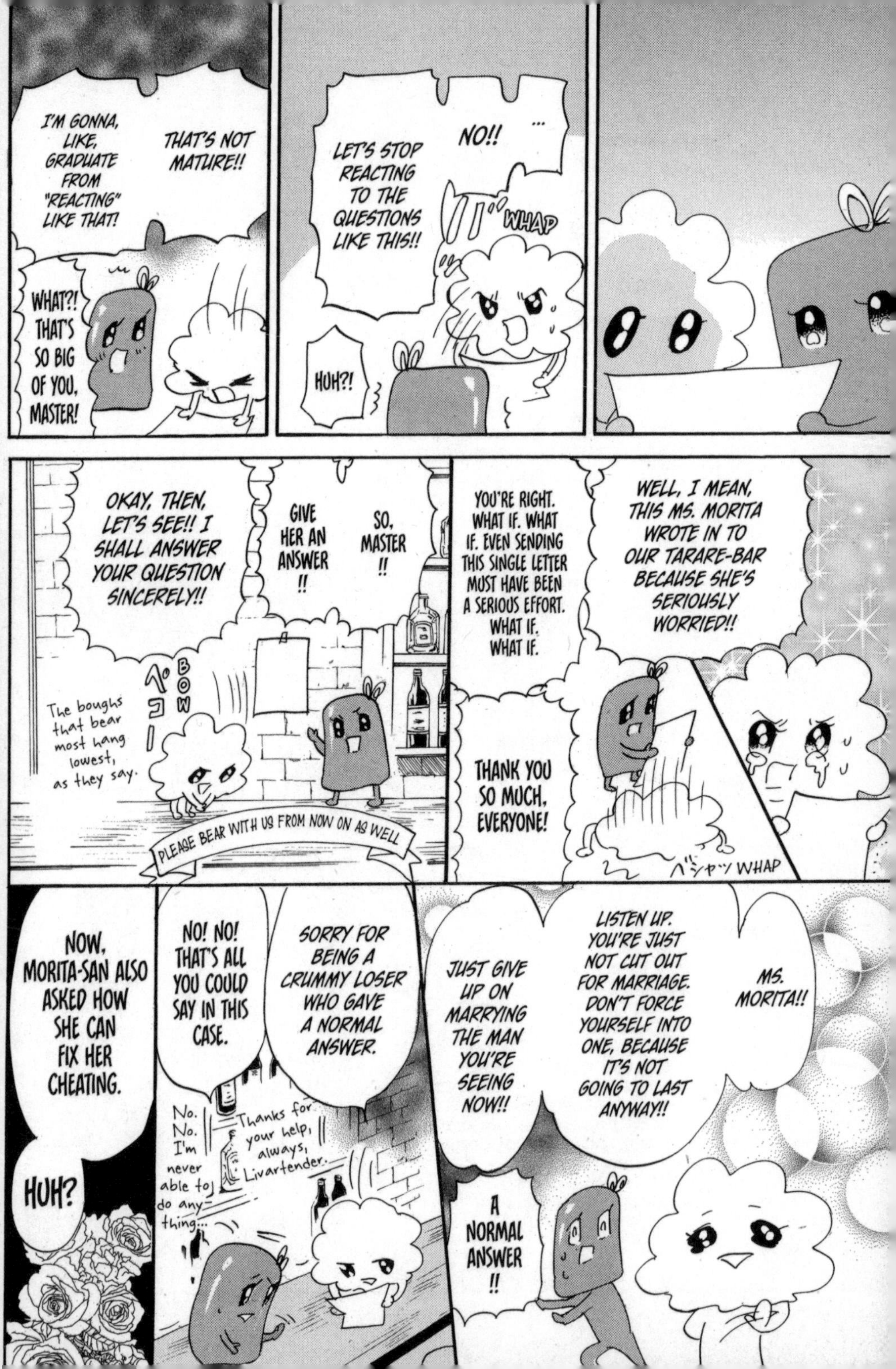

...
NO!!
LET'S STOP REACTING TO THE QUESTIONS LIKE THIS!!
WHAP
HUH?!
THAT'S NOT MATURE!!
I'M GONNA, LIKE, GRADUATE FROM "REACTING" LIKE THAT!
WHAT?! THAT'S SO BIG OF YOU, MASTER!
WELL, I MEAN, THIS MS. MORITA WROTE IN TO OUR TARARE-BAR BECAUSE SHE'S SERIOUSLY WORRIED!!
YOU'RE RIGHT. WHAT IF. WHAT IF. EVEN SENDING THIS SINGLE LETTER MUST HAVE BEEN A SERIOUS EFFORT. WHAT IF. WHAT IF.
THANK YOU SO MUCH, EVERYONE!
WHAP
SO, MASTER !!
GIVE HER AN ANSWER !!
OKAY, THEN, LET'S SEE!! I SHALL ANSWER YOUR QUESTION SINCERELY!!
BOW
The boughs that bear most hang lowest, as they say.
PLEASE BEAR WITH US FROM NOW ON AS WELL
MS. MORITA!!
LISTEN UP. YOU'RE JUST NOT CUT OUT FOR MARRIAGE. DON'T FORCE YOURSELF INTO ONE, BECAUSE IT'S NOT GOING TO LAST ANYWAY!!
JUST GIVE UP ON MARRYING THE MAN YOU'RE SEEING NOW!!
A NORMAL ANSWER !!
SORRY FOR BEING A CRUMMY LOSER WHO GAVE A NORMAL ANSWER.
NO! NO! THAT'S ALL YOU COULD SAY IN THIS CASE.
Thanks for your help, always, Livartender.
No. No. I'm never able to do anything...
NOW, MORITA-SAN ALSO ASKED HOW SHE CAN FIX HER CHEATING.
HUH?

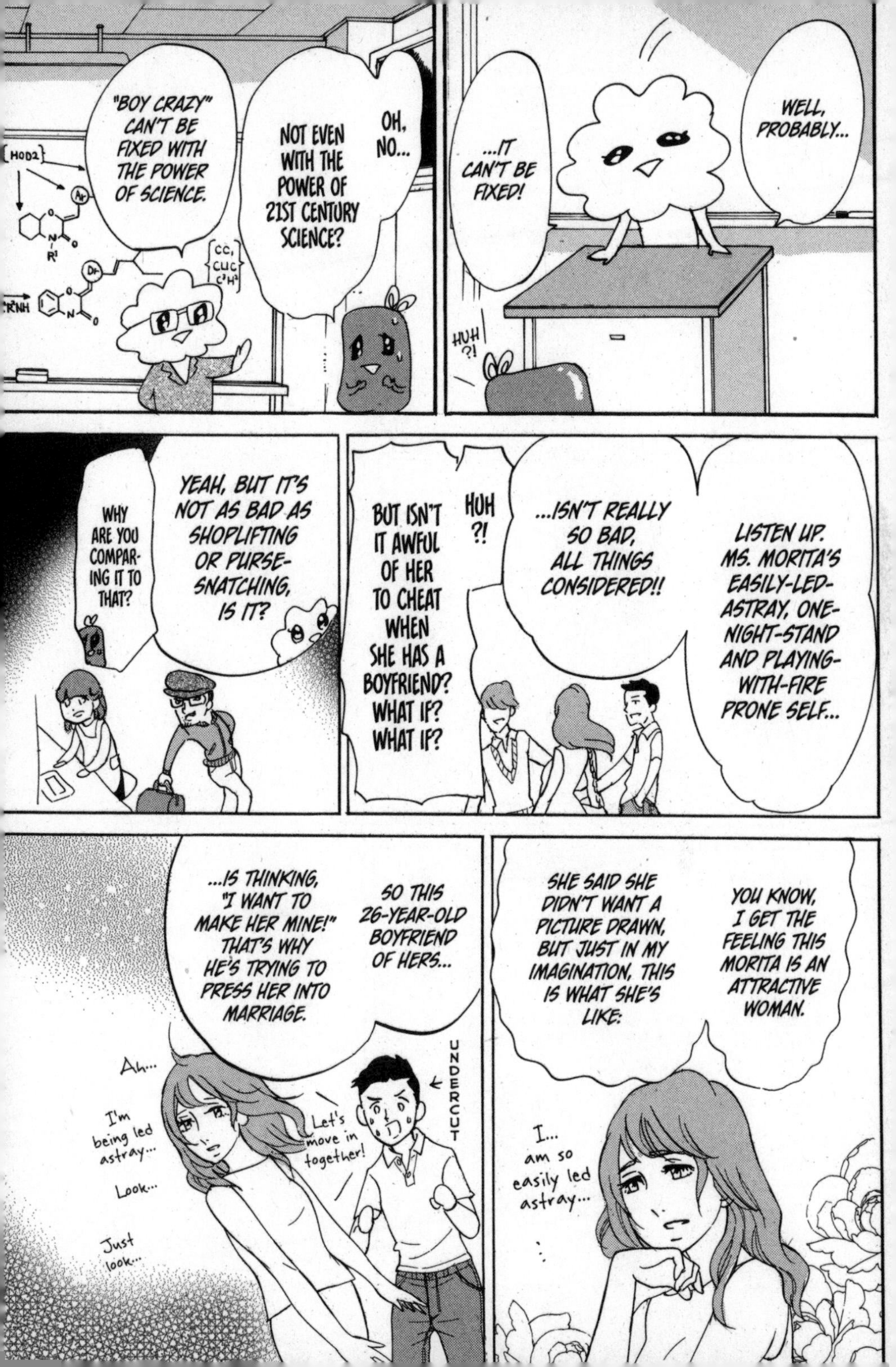
WELL, PROBABLY...
...IT CAN'T BE FIXED!
HUH ?!
OH, NO...
NOT EVEN WITH THE POWER OF 21ST CENTURY SCIENCE?
"BOY CRAZY" CAN'T BE FIXED WITH THE POWER OF SCIENCE.
LISTEN UP. MS. MORITA'S EASILY-LED-ASTRAY, ONE-NIGHT-STAND AND PLAYING-WITH-FIRE PRONE SELF...
...ISN'T REALLY SO BAD, ALL THINGS CONSIDERED!!
HUH ?!
BUT ISN'T IT AWFUL OF HER TO CHEAT WHEN SHE HAS A BOYFRIEND? WHAT IF? WHAT IF?
YEAH, BUT IT'S NOT AS BAD AS SHOPLIFTING OR PURSE-SNATCHING, IS IT?
WHY ARE YOU COMPARING IT TO THAT?
YOU KNOW, I GET THE FEELING THIS MORITA IS AN ATTRACTIVE WOMAN.
SHE SAID SHE DIDN'T WANT A PICTURE DRAWN, BUT JUST IN MY IMAGINATION, THIS IS WHAT SHE'S LIKE:
I... am so easily led astray...
...
SO THIS 26-YEAR-OLD BOYFRIEND OF HERS...
...IS THINKING, "I WANT TO MAKE HER MINE!" THAT'S WHY HE'S TRYING TO PRESS HER INTO MARRIAGE.
UNDERCUT
Let's move in together!
Ah...
I'm being led astray...
Look...
Just look...

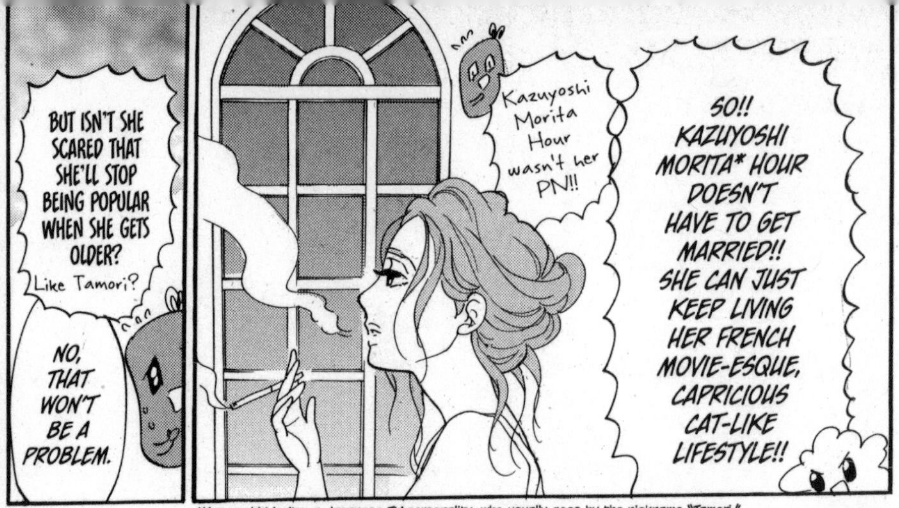

SO!! KAZUYOSHI MORITA* HOUR DOESN'T HAVE TO GET MARRIED!! SHE CAN JUST KEEP LIVING HER FRENCH MOVIE-ESQUE, CAPRICIOUS CAT-LIKE LIFESTYLE!!
Kazuyoshi Morita Hour wasn't her PN!!
BUT ISN'T SHE SCARED THAT SHE'LL STOP BEING POPULAR WHEN SHE GETS OLDER?
Like Tamori?
NO, THAT WON'T BE A PROBLEM.

*Kazuyoshi Morita: a Japanese TV personality, who usually goes by the nickname "Tamori."

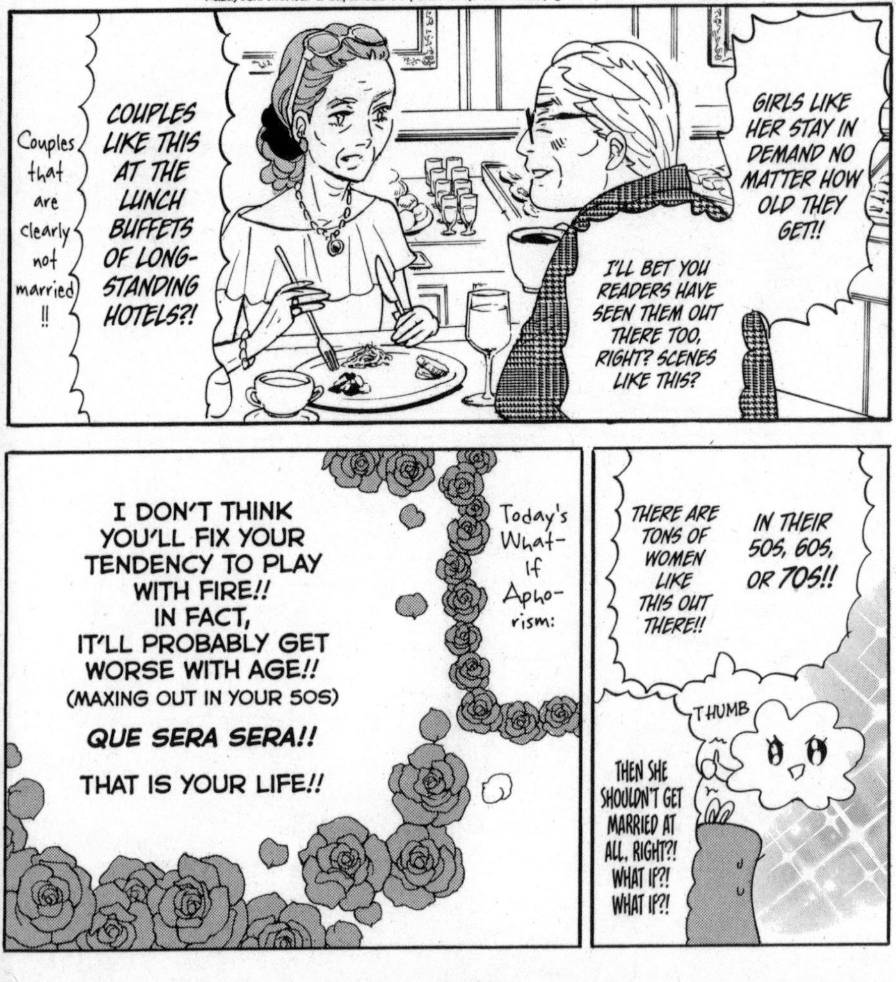

GIRLS LIKE HER STAY IN DEMAND NO MATTER HOW OLD THEY GET!!
I'LL BET YOU READERS HAVE SEEN THEM OUT THERE TOO, RIGHT? SCENES LIKE THIS?
COUPLES LIKE THIS AT THE LUNCH BUFFETS OF LONG-STANDING HOTELS?!
Couples that are clearly not married!!
THERE ARE TONS OF WOMEN LIKE THIS OUT THERE!! IN THEIR 50S, 60S, OR 70S!!
THUMB
THEN SHE SHOULDN'T GET MARRIED AT ALL, RIGHT?! WHAT IF?! WHAT IF?!
Today's What-If Aphorism:
I DON'T THINK YOU'LL FIX YOUR TENDENCY TO PLAY WITH FIRE!! IN FACT, IT'LL PROBABLY GET WORSE WITH AGE!! (MAXING OUT IN YOUR 50S)
QUE SERA SERA!!
THAT IS YOUR LIFE!!

★ NIGHT 13 ★

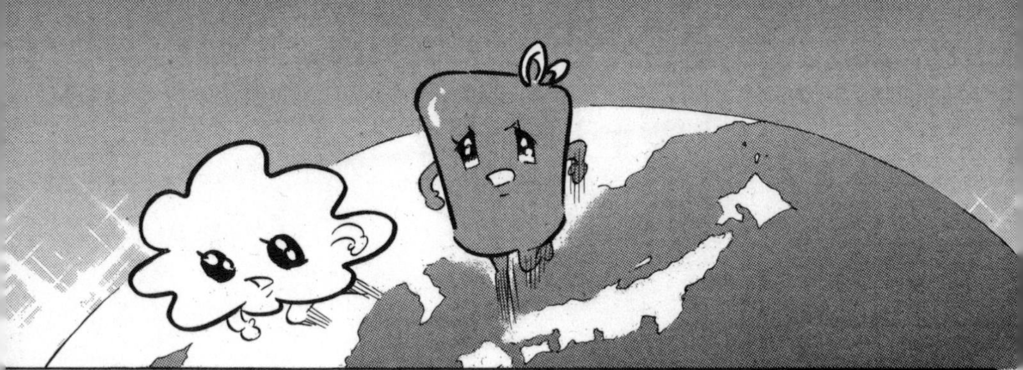

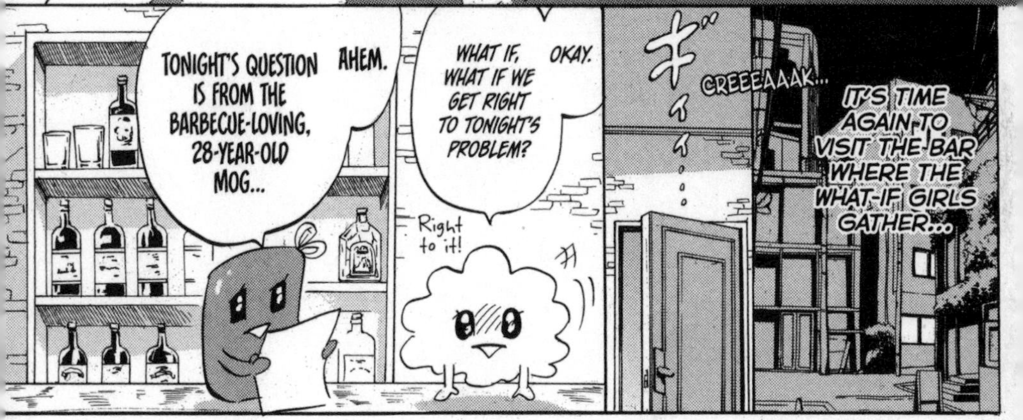

IT'S TIME AGAIN TO VISIT THE BAR WHERE THE WHAT-IF GIRLS GATHER...
ギィ
CREEEAAAK...
OKAY.
WHAT IF, WHAT IF WE GET RIGHT TO TONIGHT'S PROBLEM?
Right to it!
AHEM.
TONIGHT'S QUESTION IS FROM THE BARBECUE-LOVING, 28-YEAR-OLD MOG...

BECAUSE OF MY CAN'T-BE-BOTHERED PERSONALITY, I NEVER MANAGE TO PLAY THE "GOOD GIRL" IN FRONT OF MEN I DON'T CARE ABOUT. I SEEM TO REMEMBER ASKING MEN I WAS INTERESTED IN OUT ON DATES MYSELF BACK IN SCHOOL, BUT THAT WAS YEARS AGO.
SINCE THEN, NO ONE HAS REALLY STOOD OUT TO ME, SO WHEN I GO TO MIXERS AND SUCH, I NEVER FEEL LIKE EXCHANGING CONTACT INFO WITH ANYONE. IT FEELS LIKE I'M MISSING OUT ON A LOT OF OPPORTUNITIES TO MEET MEN, BUT MY "WHY BOTHER?" ATTITUDE ALWAYS WINS OUT IN THE END.
I CAN UNDERSTAND WANTING TO GO OUT WITH SOMEONE YOU DON'T REALLY LIKE JUST TO GIVE IT A SHOT, BUT IT SEEMS SO POINTLESS THAT I CAN'T ACTUALLY DO IT.

IS THAT AS BAD AN ATTITUDE TO TAKE AS I THINK IT IS?

PEN NAME: MOG (28)

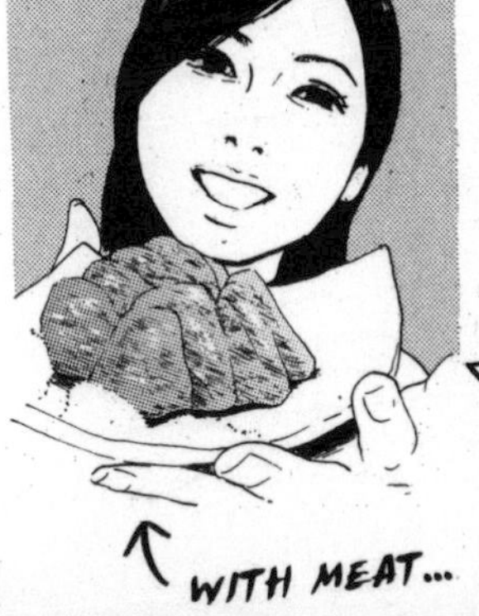

WITH MEAT...

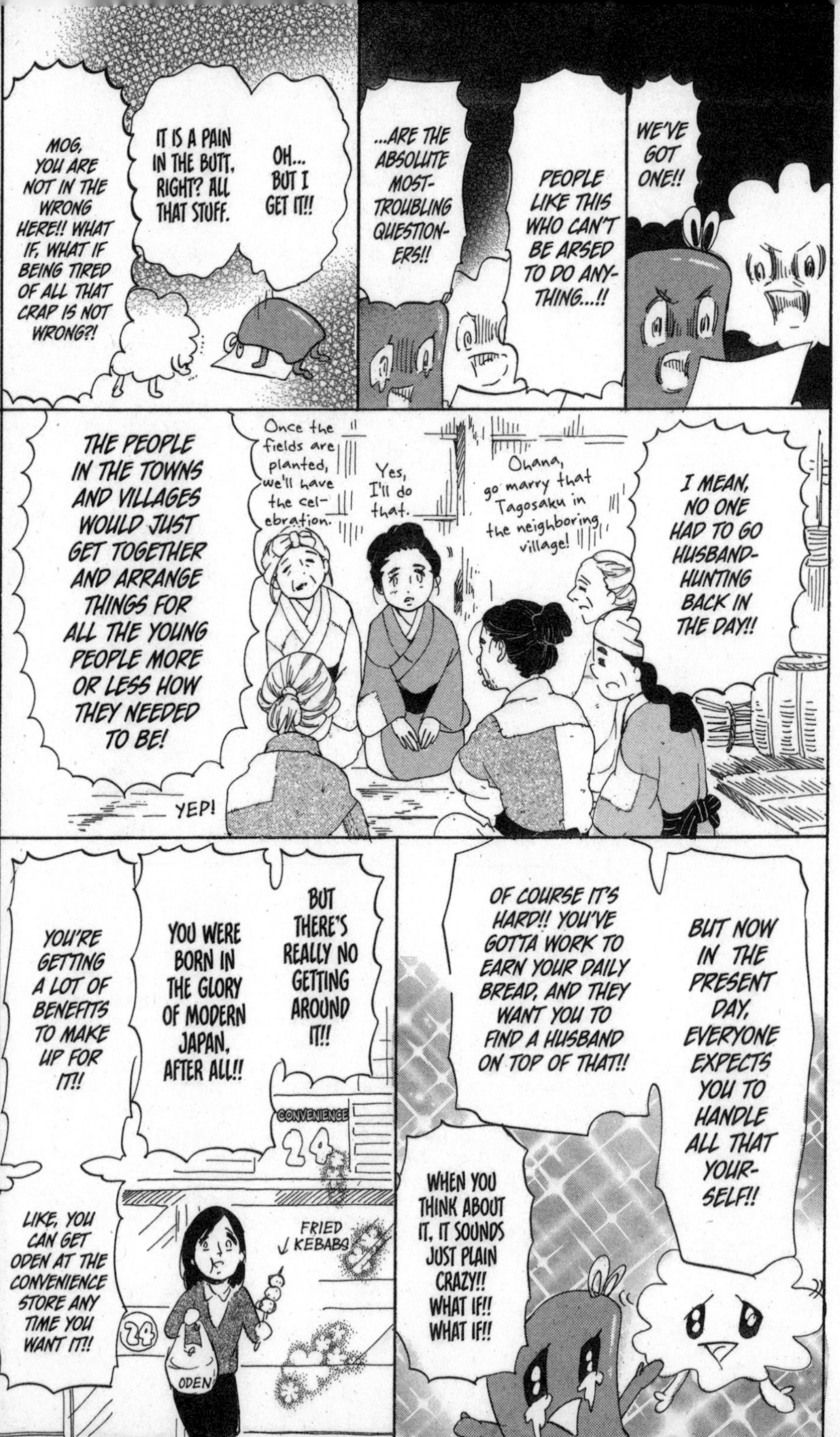

WE'VE GOT ONE!!
PEOPLE LIKE THIS WHO CAN'T BE ARSED TO DO ANYTHING...!!
...ARE THE ABSOLUTE MOST-TROUBLING QUESTIONERS!!
OH... BUT I GET IT!!
IT IS A PAIN IN THE BUTT, RIGHT? ALL THAT STUFF.
MOG, YOU ARE NOT IN THE WRONG HERE!! WHAT IF, WHAT IF BEING TIRED OF ALL THAT CRAP IS NOT WRONG?!
I MEAN, NO ONE HAD TO GO HUSBAND-HUNTING BACK IN THE DAY!!
Ohana, go marry that Tagosaku in the neighboring village!
Yes, I'll do that.
Once the fields are planted, we'll have the celebration.
THE PEOPLE IN THE TOWNS AND VILLAGES WOULD JUST GET TOGETHER AND ARRANGE THINGS FOR ALL THE YOUNG PEOPLE MORE OR LESS HOW THEY NEEDED TO BE!
YEP!
BUT NOW IN THE PRESENT DAY, EVERYONE EXPECTS YOU TO HANDLE ALL THAT YOURSELF!!
OF COURSE IT'S HARD!! YOU'VE GOTTA WORK TO EARN YOUR DAILY BREAD, AND THEY WANT YOU TO FIND A HUSBAND ON TOP OF THAT!!
WHEN YOU THINK ABOUT IT, IT SOUNDS JUST PLAIN CRAZY!! WHAT IF!! WHAT IF!!
BUT THERE'S REALLY NO GETTING AROUND IT!!
YOU WERE BORN IN THE GLORY OF MODERN JAPAN, AFTER ALL!!
YOU'RE GETTING A LOT OF BENEFITS TO MAKE UP FOR IT!!
CONVENIENCE
24
FRIED KEBABS
LIKE, YOU CAN GET ODEN AT THE CONVENIENCE STORE ANY TIME YOU WANT IT!!
24
ODEN

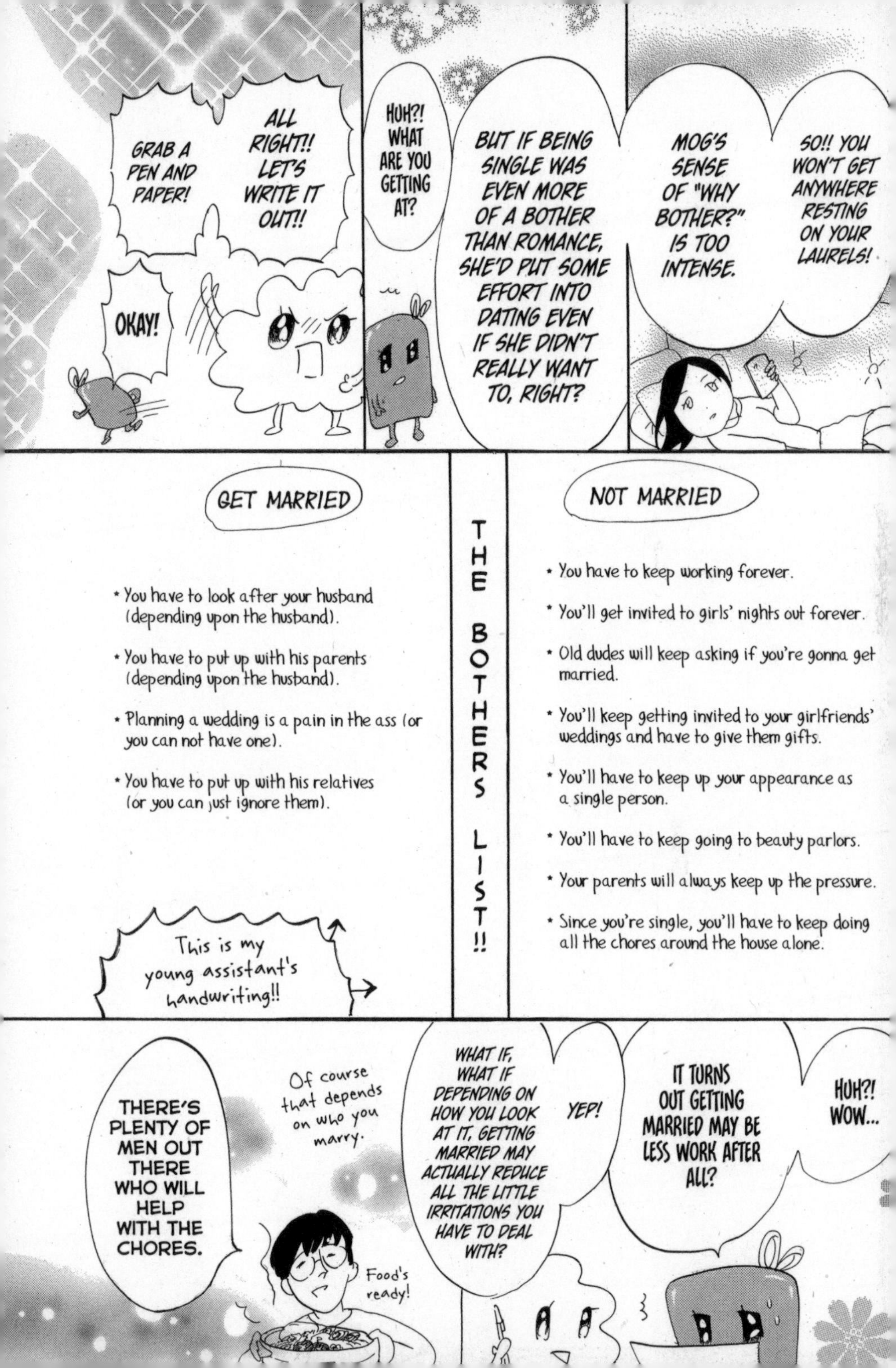

SO!! YOU WON'T GET ANYWHERE RESTING ON YOUR LAURELS!
MOG'S SENSE OF "WHY BOTHER?" IS TOO INTENSE.
BUT IF BEING SINGLE WAS EVEN MORE OF A BOTHER THAN ROMANCE, SHE'D PUT SOME EFFORT INTO DATING EVEN IF SHE DIDN'T REALLY WANT TO, RIGHT?
HUH?! WHAT ARE YOU GETTING AT?
ALL RIGHT!! LET'S WRITE IT OUT!!
GRAB A PEN AND PAPER!
OKAY!
THE BOTHERS LIST!!
NOT MARRIED
• You have to keep working forever.
• You'll get invited to girls' nights out forever.
• Old dudes will keep asking if you're gonna get married.
• You'll keep getting invited to your girlfriends' weddings and have to give them gifts.
• You'll have to keep up your appearance as a single person.
• You'll have to keep going to beauty parlors.
• Your parents will always keep up the pressure.
• Since you're single, you'll have to keep doing all the chores around the house alone.
GET MARRIED
• You have to look after your husband (depending upon the husband).
• You have to put up with his parents (depending upon the husband).
• Planning a wedding is a pain in the ass (or you can not have one).
• You have to put up with his relatives (or you can just ignore them).
This is my young assistant's handwriting!!
HUH?! WOW...
IT TURNS OUT GETTING MARRIED MAY BE LESS WORK AFTER ALL?
YEP!
WHAT IF, WHAT IF DEPENDING ON HOW YOU LOOK AT IT, GETTING MARRIED MAY ACTUALLY REDUCE ALL THE LITTLE IRRITATIONS YOU HAVE TO DEAL WITH?
Of course that depends on who you marry.
THERE'S PLENTY OF MEN OUT THERE WHO WILL HELP WITH THE CHORES.
Food's ready!

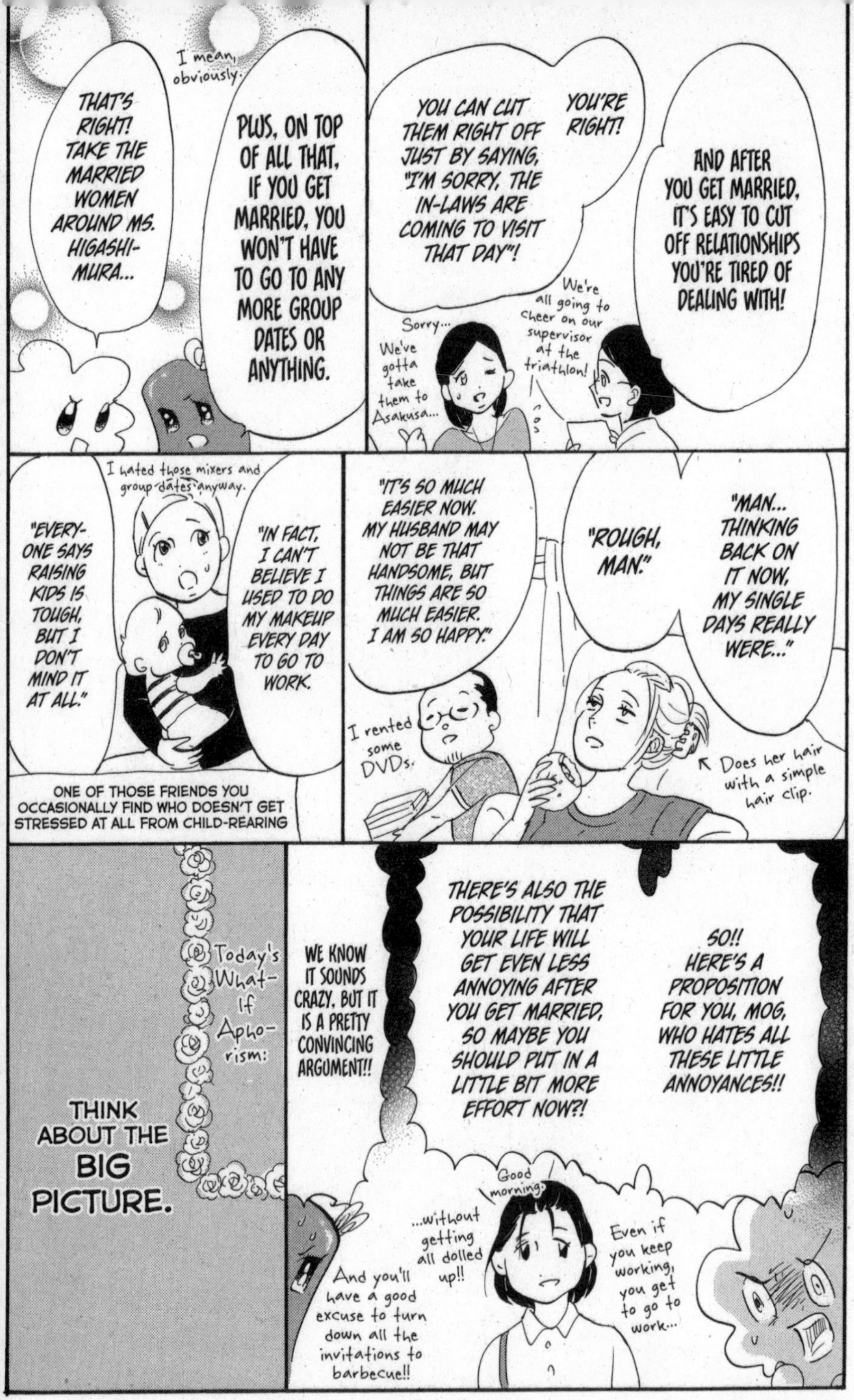
AND AFTER YOU GET MARRIED, IT'S EASY TO CUT OFF RELATIONSHIPS YOU'RE TIRED OF DEALING WITH!
YOU'RE RIGHT!
YOU CAN CUT THEM RIGHT OFF JUST BY SAYING, "I'M SORRY, THE IN-LAWS ARE COMING TO VISIT THAT DAY"!
We're all going to cheer on our supervisor at the triathlon!
Sorry... We've gotta take them to Asakusa...
PLUS, ON TOP OF ALL THAT, IF YOU GET MARRIED, YOU WON'T HAVE TO GO TO ANY MORE GROUP DATES OR ANYTHING.
I mean, obviously.
THAT'S RIGHT! TAKE THE MARRIED WOMEN AROUND MS. HIGASHIMURA...
"MAN... THINKING BACK ON IT NOW, MY SINGLE DAYS REALLY WERE..."
"ROUGH, MAN."
Does her hair with a simple hair clip.
"IT'S SO MUCH EASIER NOW. MY HUSBAND MAY NOT BE THAT HANDSOME, BUT THINGS ARE SO MUCH EASIER. I AM SO HAPPY."
I rented some DVDs.
"IN FACT, I CAN'T BELIEVE I USED TO DO MY MAKEUP EVERY DAY TO GO TO WORK.
I hated those mixers and group dates anyway.
"EVERYONE SAYS RAISING KIDS IS TOUGH, BUT I DON'T MIND IT AT ALL."
ONE OF THOSE FRIENDS YOU OCCASIONALLY FIND WHO DOESN'T GET STRESSED AT ALL FROM CHILD-REARING
SO!! HERE'S A PROPOSITION FOR YOU, MOG, WHO HATES ALL THESE LITTLE ANNOYANCES!!
THERE'S ALSO THE POSSIBILITY THAT YOUR LIFE WILL GET EVEN LESS ANNOYING AFTER YOU GET MARRIED, SO MAYBE YOU SHOULD PUT IN A LITTLE BIT MORE EFFORT NOW?!
WE KNOW IT SOUNDS CRAZY, BUT IT IS A PRETTY CONVINCING ARGUMENT!!
Good morning.
Even if you keep working, you get to go to work...
...without getting all dolled up!!
And you'll have a good excuse to turn down all the invitations to barbecue!!
Today's What-If Aphorism:
THINK ABOUT THE BIG PICTURE.

NIGHT 14

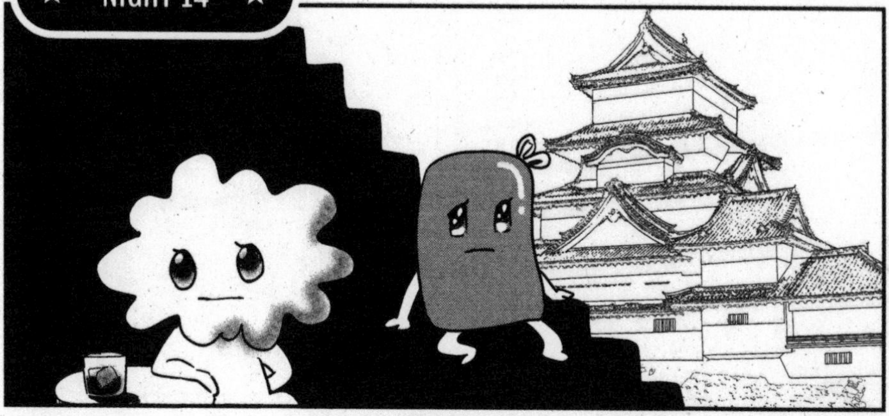

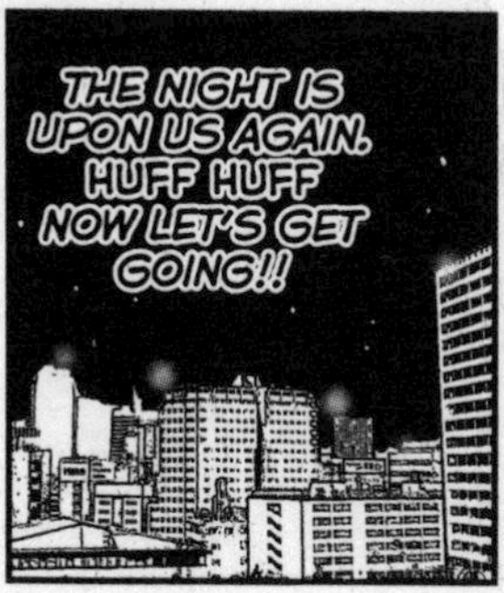
THE NIGHT IS UPON US AGAIN. HUFF HUFF NOW LET'S GET GOING!!

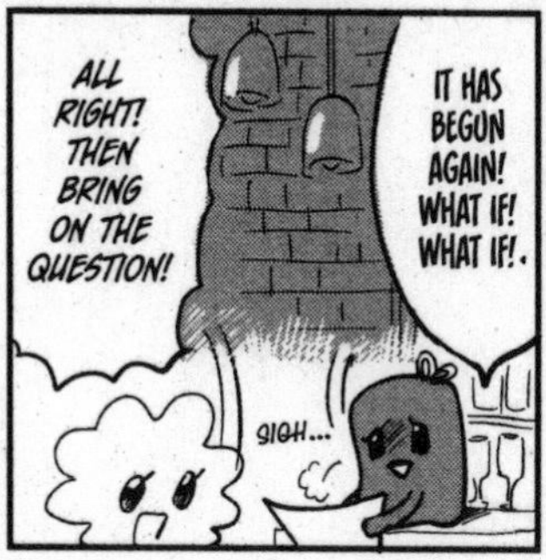
IT HAS BEGUN AGAIN! WHAT IF! WHAT IF!.
ALL RIGHT! THEN BRING ON THE QUESTION!
SIGH...

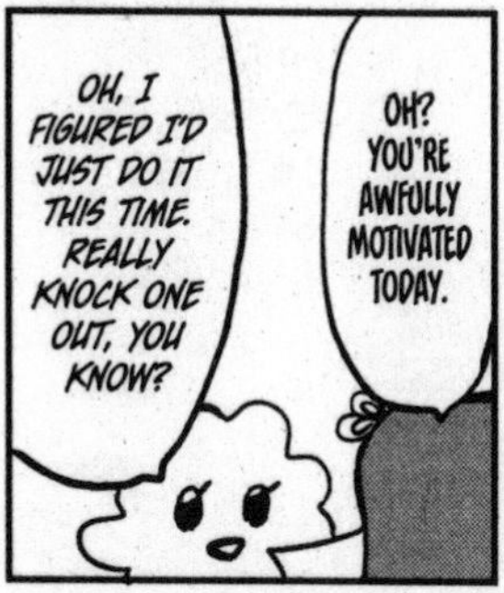
OH? YOU'RE AWFULLY MOTIVATED TODAY.
OH, I FIGURED I'D JUST DO IT THIS TIME. REALLY KNOCK ONE OUT, YOU KNOW?

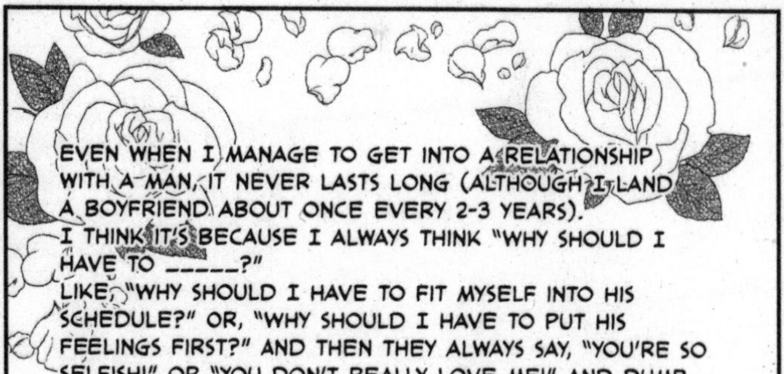
EVEN WHEN I MANAGE TO GET INTO A RELATIONSHIP WITH A MAN, IT NEVER LASTS LONG (ALTHOUGH I LAND A BOYFRIEND ABOUT ONCE EVERY 2-3 YEARS).
I THINK IT'S BECAUSE I ALWAYS THINK "WHY SHOULD I HAVE TO _____?"
LIKE, "WHY SHOULD I HAVE TO FIT MYSELF INTO HIS SCHEDULE?" OR, "WHY SHOULD I HAVE TO PUT HIS FEELINGS FIRST?" AND THEN THEY ALWAYS SAY, "YOU'RE SO SELFISH!" OR "YOU DON'T REALLY LOVE ME!" AND DUMP ME.
DO THE WOMEN WITH LONG-LASTING RELATIONSHIPS OR MARRIAGES JUST HAVE A DIFFERENT KIND OF PATIENCE THAN WHAT I HAVE? HOW CAN I BECOME A MORE BIG-HEARTED PERSON?
PEN NAME: ARINKO (30)

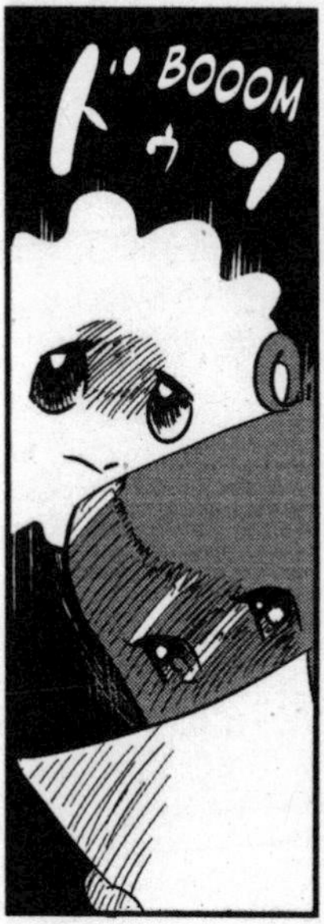
ドゥン
BOOOM

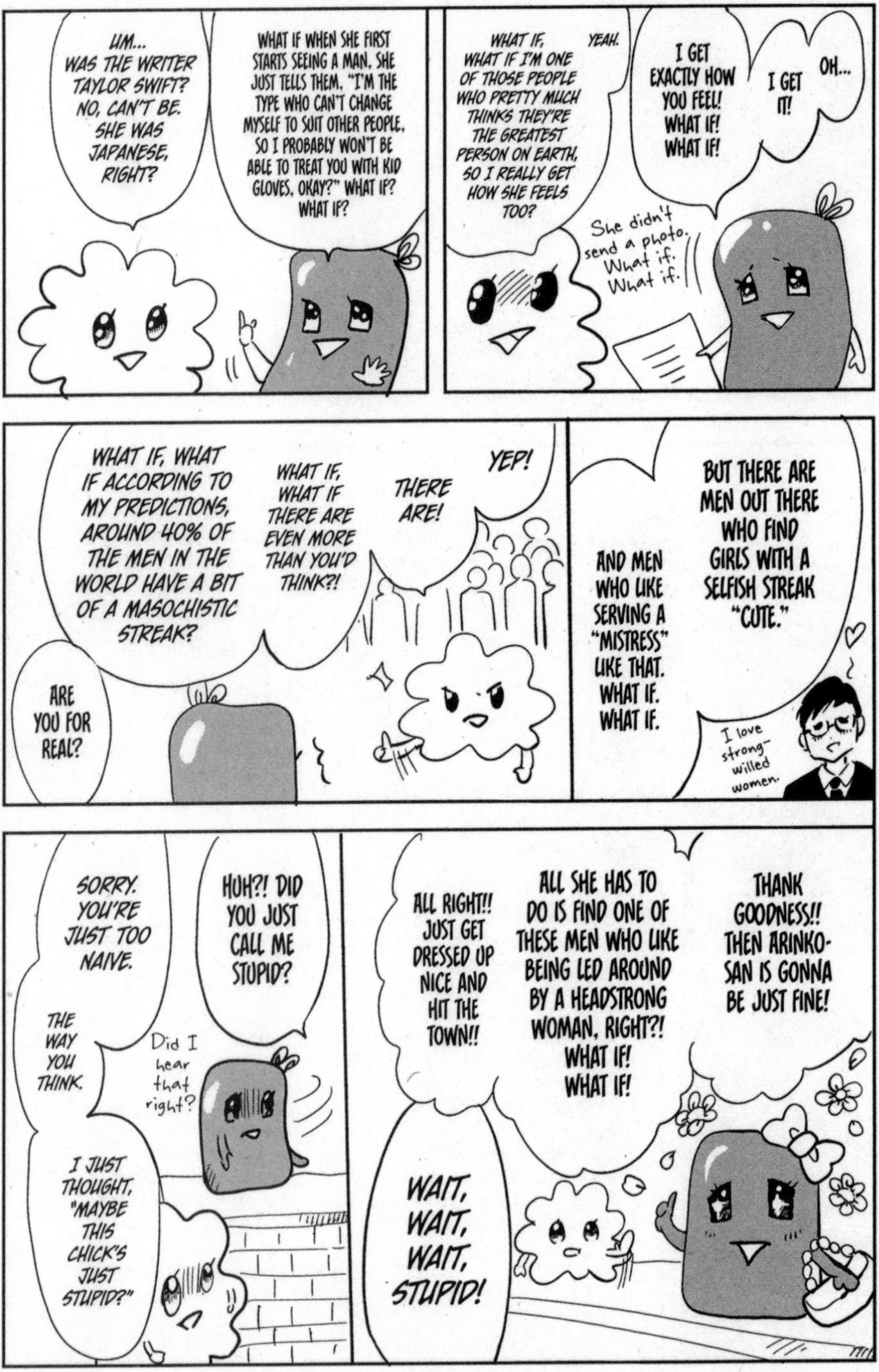
OH...
I GET IT!
I GET EXACTLY HOW YOU FEEL! WHAT IF! WHAT IF!
YEAH.
WHAT IF, WHAT IF I'M ONE OF THOSE PEOPLE WHO PRETTY MUCH THINKS THEY'RE THE GREATEST PERSON ON EARTH, SO I REALLY GET HOW SHE FEELS TOO?
She didn't send a photo. What if. What if.
WHAT IF WHEN SHE FIRST STARTS SEEING A MAN, SHE JUST TELLS THEM, "I'M THE TYPE WHO CAN'T CHANGE MYSELF TO SUIT OTHER PEOPLE, SO I PROBABLY WON'T BE ABLE TO TREAT YOU WITH KID GLOVES, OKAY?" WHAT IF? WHAT IF?
UM... WAS THE WRITER TAYLOR SWIFT? NO, CAN'T BE. SHE WAS JAPANESE, RIGHT?
BUT THERE ARE MEN OUT THERE WHO FIND GIRLS WITH A SELFISH STREAK "CUTE."
AND MEN WHO LIKE SERVING A "MISTRESS" LIKE THAT. WHAT IF. WHAT IF.
I love strong-willed women.
YEP!
THERE ARE!
WHAT IF, WHAT IF THERE ARE EVEN MORE THAN YOU'D THINK?!
WHAT IF, WHAT IF ACCORDING TO MY PREDICTIONS, AROUND 40% OF THE MEN IN THE WORLD HAVE A BIT OF A MASOCHISTIC STREAK?
ARE YOU FOR REAL?
THANK GOODNESS!! THEN ARINKO-SAN IS GONNA BE JUST FINE!
ALL SHE HAS TO DO IS FIND ONE OF THESE MEN WHO LIKE BEING LED AROUND BY A HEADSTRONG WOMAN, RIGHT?! WHAT IF! WHAT IF!
ALL RIGHT!! JUST GET DRESSED UP NICE AND HIT THE TOWN!!
WAIT, WAIT, WAIT, STUPID!
HUH?! DID YOU JUST CALL ME STUPID?
SORRY. YOU'RE JUST TOO NAIVE.
Did I hear that right?
THE WAY YOU THINK.
I JUST THOUGHT, "MAYBE THIS CHICK'S JUST STUPID?"

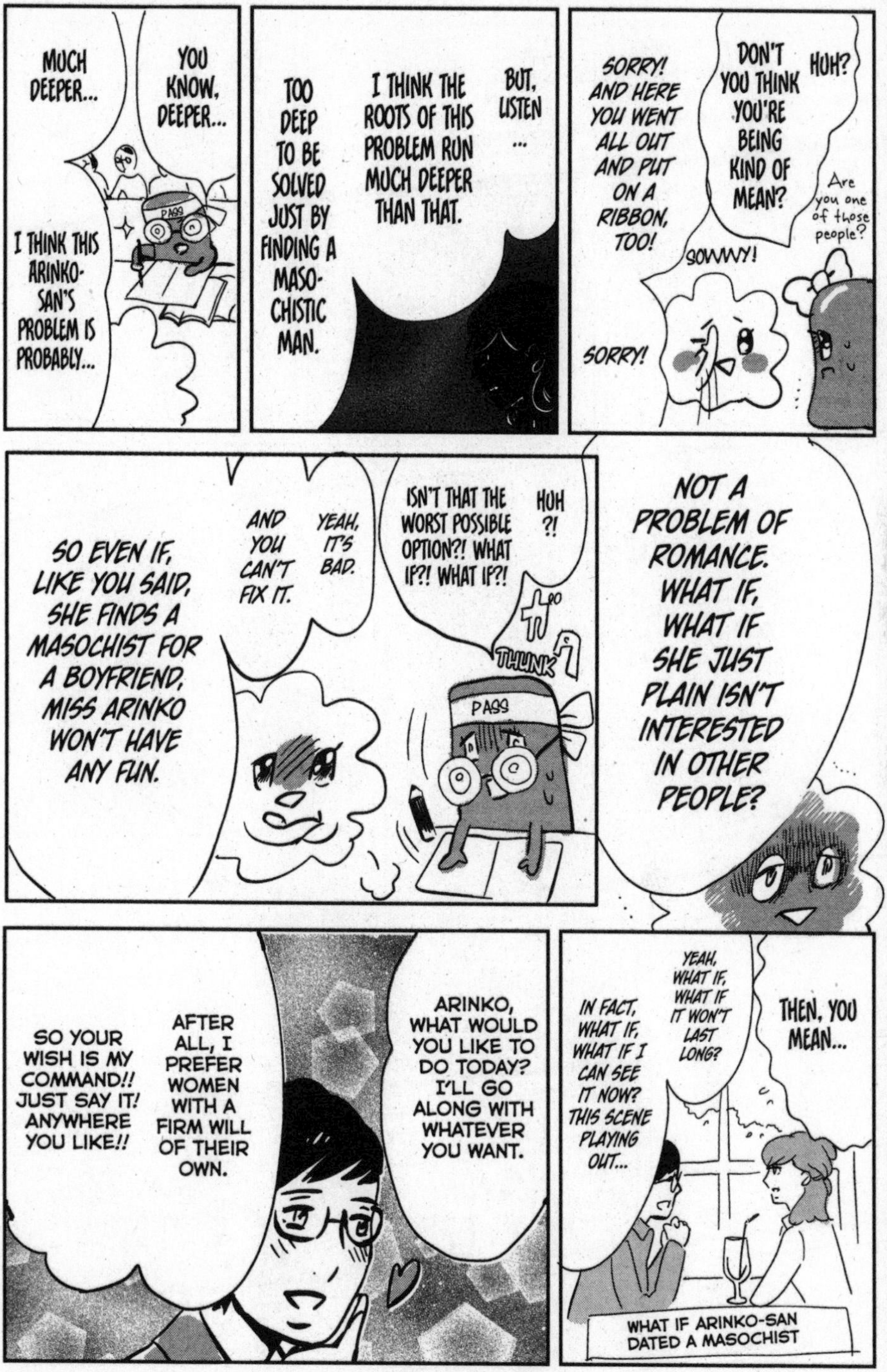
HUH?
DON'T YOU THINK YOU'RE BEING KIND OF MEAN?
Are you one of those people?
SORRY! AND HERE YOU WENT ALL OUT AND PUT ON A RIBBON, TOO!
SOWWY!
SORRY!
BUT, LISTEN ...
I THINK THE ROOTS OF THIS PROBLEM RUN MUCH DEEPER THAN THAT.
TOO DEEP TO BE SOLVED JUST BY FINDING A MASO-CHISTIC MAN.
YOU KNOW, DEEPER...
MUCH DEEPER...
I THINK THIS ARINKO-SAN'S PROBLEM IS PROBABLY...
NOT A PROBLEM OF ROMANCE. WHAT IF, WHAT IF SHE JUST PLAIN ISN'T INTERESTED IN OTHER PEOPLE?
HUH ?!
ISN'T THAT THE WORST POSSIBLE OPTION?! WHAT IF?! WHAT IF?!
THUNK
YEAH, IT'S BAD.
AND YOU CAN'T FIX IT.
SO EVEN IF, LIKE YOU SAID, SHE FINDS A MASOCHIST FOR A BOYFRIEND, MISS ARINKO WON'T HAVE ANY FUN.
THEN, YOU MEAN...
YEAH, WHAT IF, WHAT IF IT WON'T LAST LONG?
IN FACT, WHAT IF, WHAT IF I CAN SEE IT NOW? THIS SCENE PLAYING OUT...
WHAT IF ARINKO-SAN DATED A MASOCHIST
ARINKO, WHAT WOULD YOU LIKE TO DO TODAY? I'LL GO ALONG WITH WHATEVER YOU WANT.
AFTER ALL, I PREFER WOMEN WITH A FIRM WILL OF THEIR OWN.
SO YOUR WISH IS MY COMMAND!! JUST SAY IT! ANYWHERE YOU LIKE!!

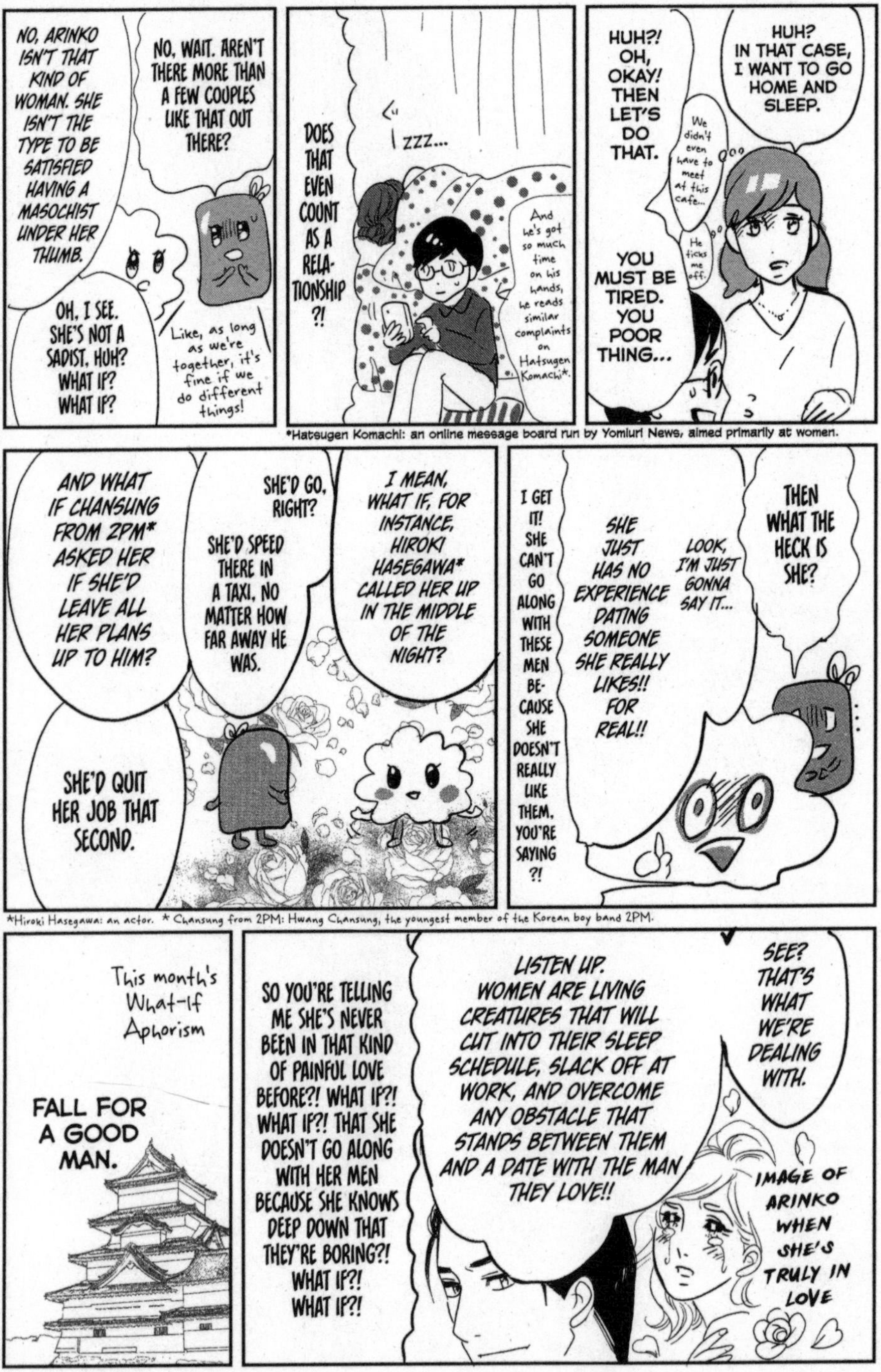
HUH? IN THAT CASE, I WANT TO GO HOME AND SLEEP.
We didn't even have to meet at this cafe...
He ticks me off.
HUH?! OH, OKAY! THEN LET'S DO THAT.
YOU MUST BE TIRED. YOU POOR THING...
DOES THAT EVEN COUNT AS A RELATIONSHIP?!
And he's got so much time on his hands, he reads similar complaints on Hatsugen Komachi*.
ZZZ...
NO, WAIT. AREN'T THERE MORE THAN A FEW COUPLES LIKE THAT OUT THERE?
NO, ARINKO ISN'T THAT KIND OF WOMAN. SHE ISN'T THE TYPE TO BE SATISFIED HAVING A MASOCHIST UNDER HER THUMB.
Like, as long as we're together, it's fine if we do different things!
OH, I SEE. SHE'S NOT A SADIST, HUH? WHAT IF? WHAT IF?
THEN WHAT THE HECK IS SHE?
LOOK, I'M JUST GONNA SAY IT...
SHE JUST HAS NO EXPERIENCE DATING SOMEONE SHE REALLY LIKES!! FOR REAL!!
I GET IT! SHE CAN'T GO ALONG WITH THESE MEN BECAUSE SHE DOESN'T REALLY LIKE THEM, YOU'RE SAYING?!
I MEAN, WHAT IF, FOR INSTANCE, HIROKI HASEGAWA* CALLED HER UP IN THE MIDDLE OF THE NIGHT?
SHE'D GO, RIGHT?
SHE'D SPEED THERE IN A TAXI, NO MATTER HOW FAR AWAY HE WAS.
AND WHAT IF CHANSUNG FROM 2PM* ASKED HER IF SHE'D LEAVE ALL HER PLANS UP TO HIM?
SHE'D QUIT HER JOB THAT SECOND.
SEE? THAT'S WHAT WE'RE DEALING WITH.
LISTEN UP. WOMEN ARE LIVING CREATURES THAT WILL CUT INTO THEIR SLEEP SCHEDULE, SLACK OFF AT WORK, AND OVERCOME ANY OBSTACLE THAT STANDS BETWEEN THEM AND A DATE WITH THE MAN THEY LOVE!!
IMAGE OF ARINKO WHEN SHE'S TRULY IN LOVE
SO YOU'RE TELLING ME SHE'S NEVER BEEN IN THAT KIND OF PAINFUL LOVE BEFORE?! WHAT IF?! WHAT IF?! THAT SHE DOESN'T GO ALONG WITH HER MEN BECAUSE SHE KNOWS DEEP DOWN THAT THEY'RE BORING?! WHAT IF?! WHAT IF?!
This month's What-If Aphorism
FALL FOR A GOOD MAN.

*Hatsugen Komachi: an online message board run by Yomiuri News, aimed primarily at women.

*Hiroki Hasegawa: an actor. * Chansung from 2PM: Hwang Chansung, the youngest member of the Korean boy band 2PM.

TOKYO

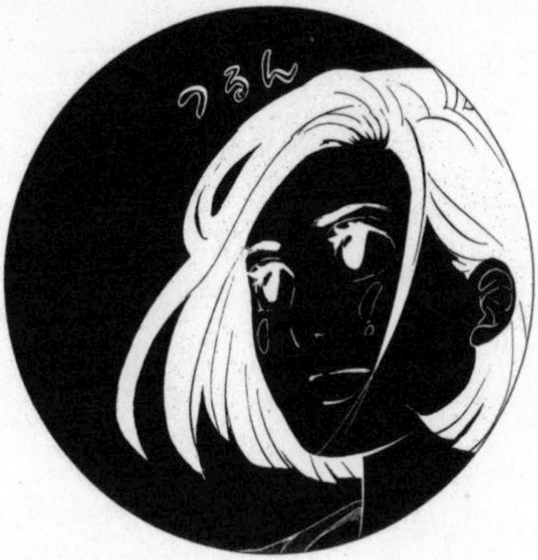
つるん

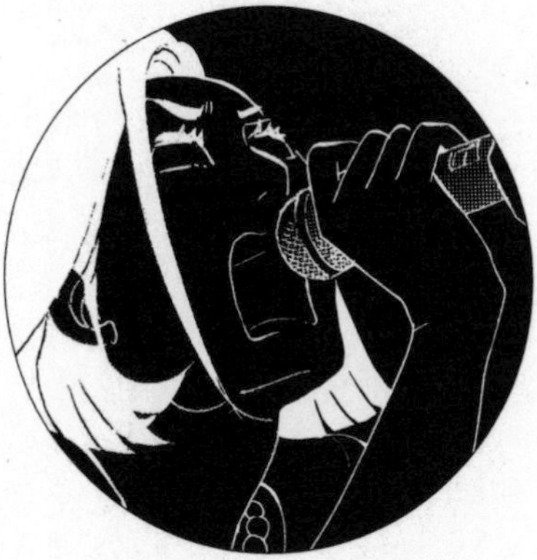

TARAREBA

GIRLS

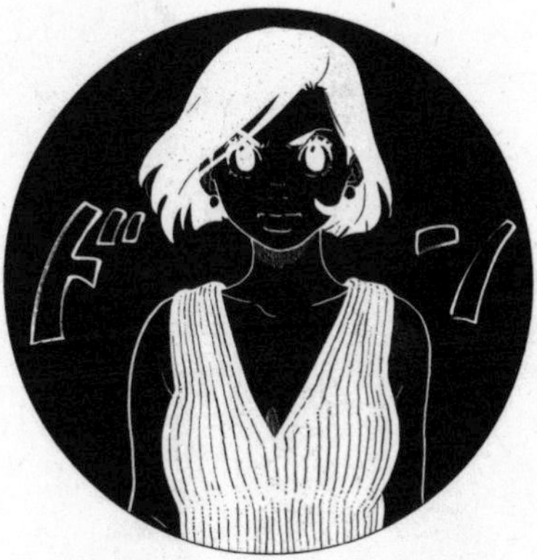

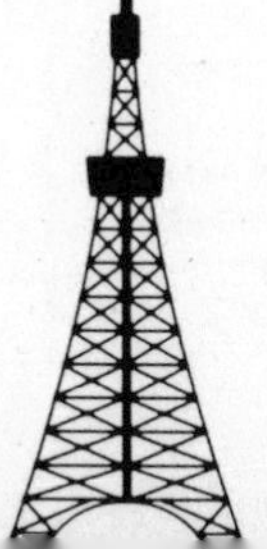

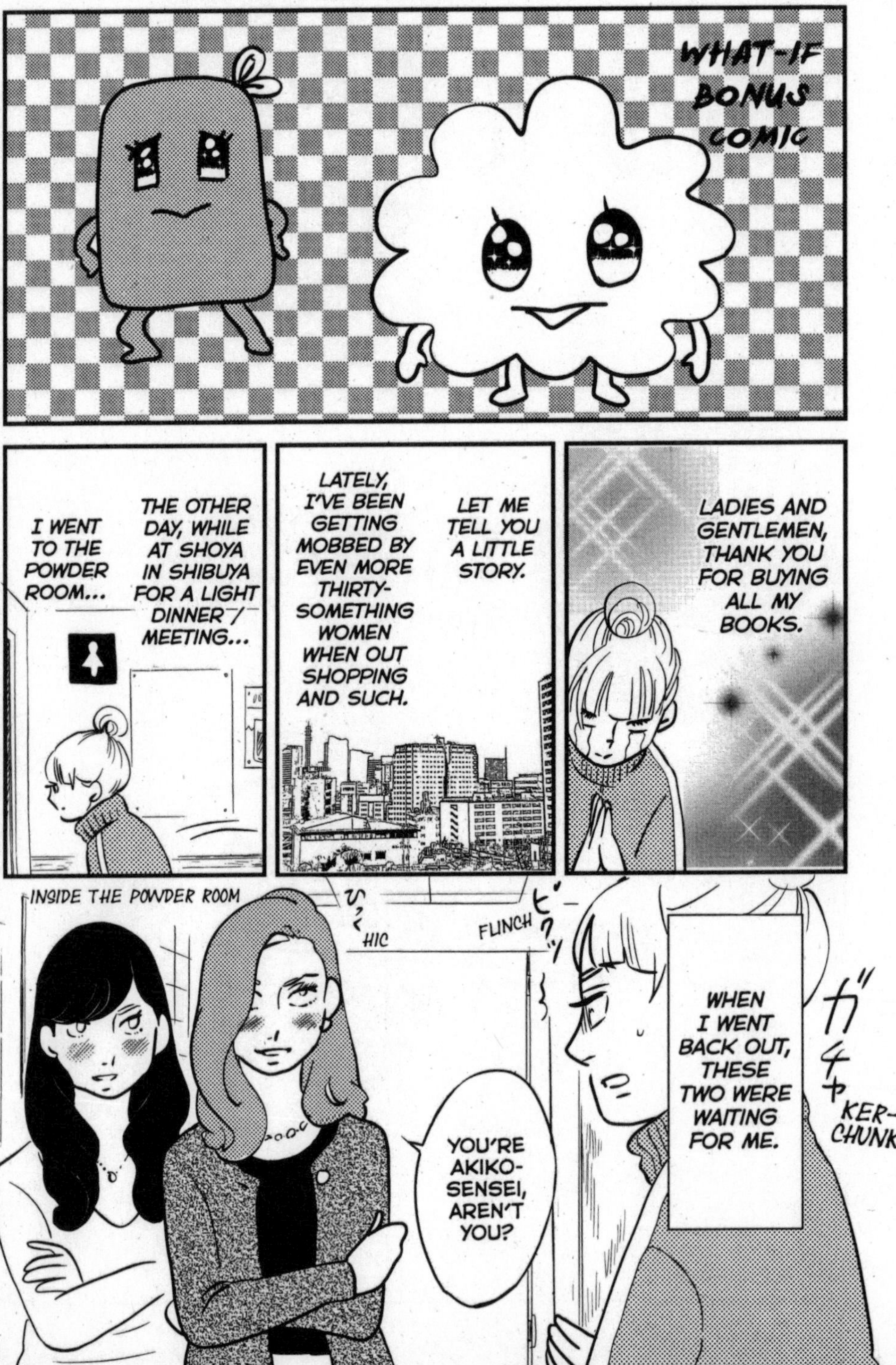
WHAT-IF BONUS COMIC
LADIES AND GENTLEMEN, THANK YOU FOR BUYING ALL MY BOOKS.
LET ME TELL YOU A LITTLE STORY.
LATELY, I'VE BEEN GETTING MOBBED BY EVEN MORE THIRTY-SOMETHING WOMEN WHEN OUT SHOPPING AND SUCH.
THE OTHER DAY, WHILE AT SHOYA IN SHIBUYA FOR A LIGHT DINNER / MEETING...
I WENT TO THE POWDER ROOM...
KER-CHUNK
WHEN I WENT BACK OUT, THESE TWO WERE WAITING FOR ME.
FLINCH
HIC
INSIDE THE POWDER ROOM
YOU'RE AKIKO-SENSEI, AREN'T YOU?

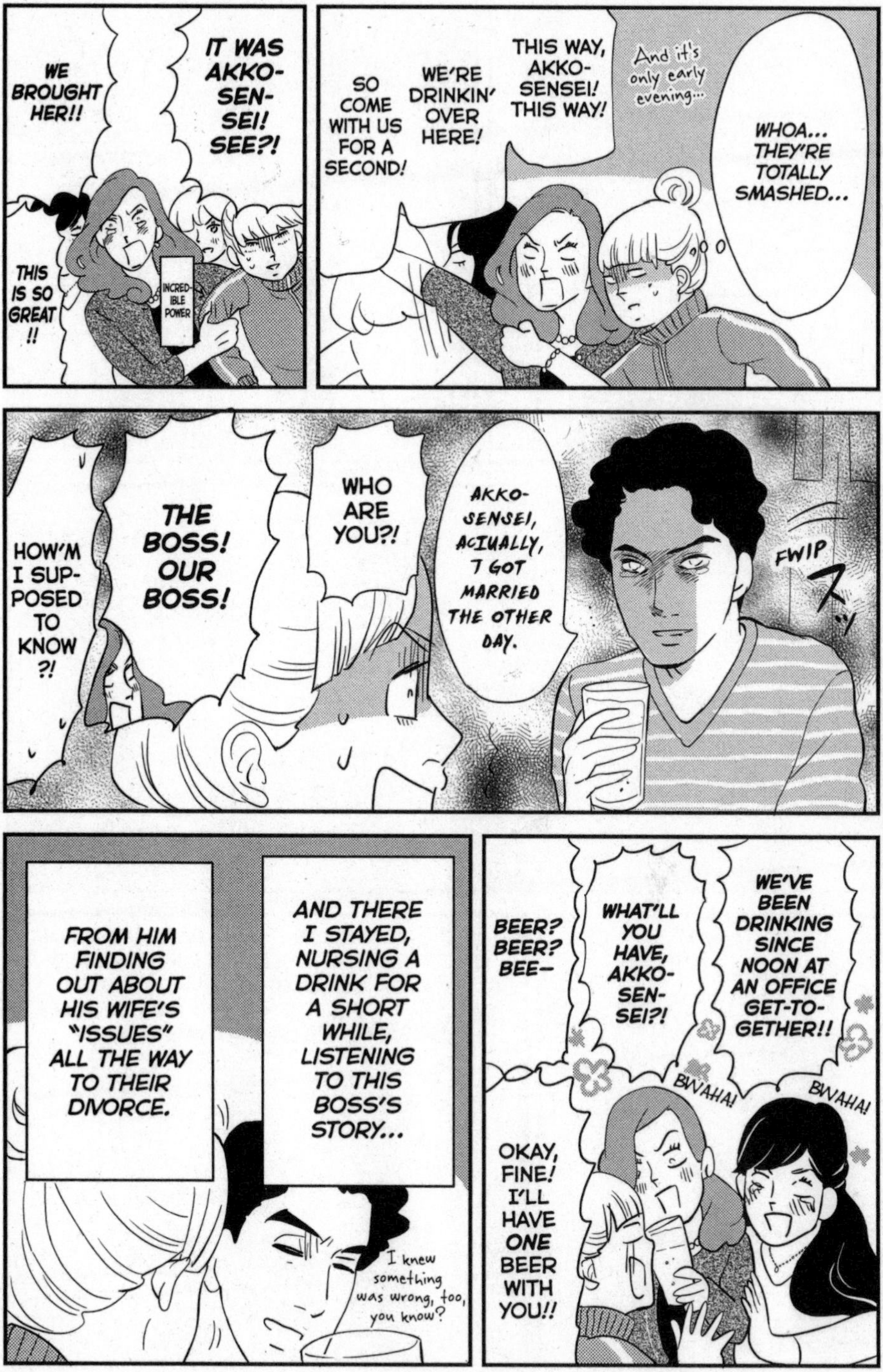
WHOA... THEY'RE TOTALLY SMASHED...
And it's only early evening...
THIS WAY, AKKO-SENSEI! THIS WAY!
WE'RE DRINKIN' OVER HERE!
SO COME WITH US FOR A SECOND!
IT WAS AKKO-SENSEI! SEE?!
WE BROUGHT HER!!
INCREDIBLE POWER
THIS IS SO GREAT!!
FWIP
AKKO-SENSEI, ACTUALLY, I GOT MARRIED THE OTHER DAY.
WHO ARE YOU?!
THE BOSS! OUR BOSS!
HOW'M I SUPPOSED TO KNOW?!
WE'VE BEEN DRINKING SINCE NOON AT AN OFFICE GET-TOGETHER!!
WHAT'LL YOU HAVE, AKKO-SENSEI?!
BEER? BEER? BEE–
BWAHA!
BWAHA!
OKAY, FINE! I'LL HAVE ONE BEER WITH YOU!!
AND THERE I STAYED, NURSING A DRINK FOR A SHORT WHILE, LISTENING TO THIS BOSS'S STORY...
FROM HIM FINDING OUT ABOUT HIS WIFE'S "ISSUES" ALL THE WAY TO THEIR DIVORCE.
I knew something was wrong, too, you know?

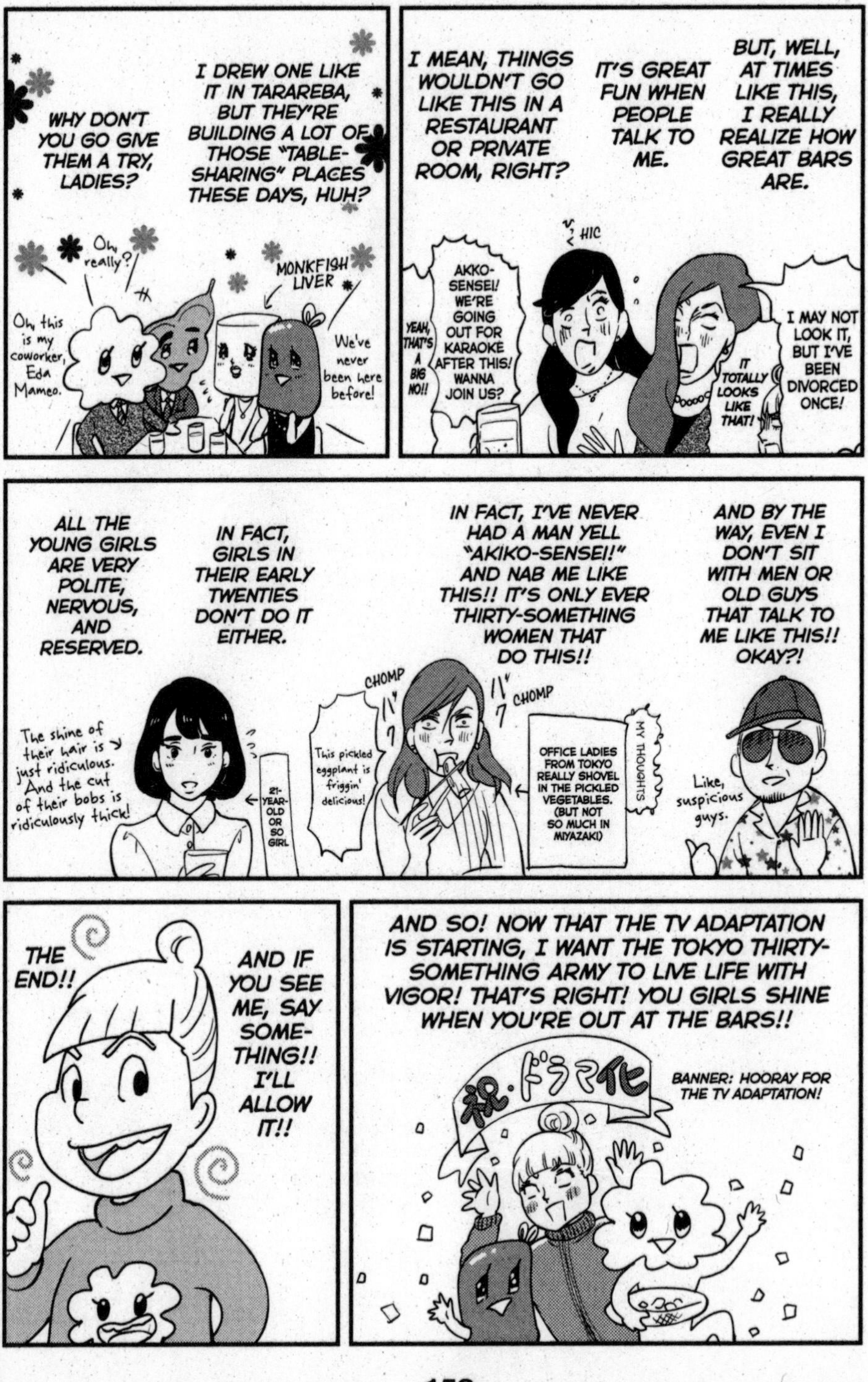
BUT, WELL, AT TIMES LIKE THIS, I REALLY REALIZE HOW GREAT BARS ARE.
IT'S GREAT FUN WHEN PEOPLE TALK TO ME.
I MEAN, THINGS WOULDN'T GO LIKE THIS IN A RESTAURANT OR PRIVATE ROOM, RIGHT?
I MAY NOT LOOK IT, BUT I'VE BEEN DIVORCED ONCE!
IT TOTALLY LOOKS LIKE THAT!
HIC
AKKO-SENSEI! WE'RE GOING OUT FOR KARAOKE AFTER THIS! WANNA JOIN US?
YEAH, THAT'S A BIG NO!!
I DREW ONE LIKE IT IN TARAREBA, BUT THEY'RE BUILDING A LOT OF THOSE "TABLE-SHARING" PLACES THESE DAYS, HUH?
WHY DON'T YOU GO GIVE THEM A TRY, LADIES?
MONKFISH LIVER
We've never been here before!
Oh, really?
Oh, this is my coworker, Eda Mameo.
AND BY THE WAY, EVEN I DON'T SIT WITH MEN OR OLD GUYS THAT TALK TO ME LIKE THIS!! OKAY?!
IN FACT, I'VE NEVER HAD A MAN YELL "AKIKO-SENSEI!" AND NAB ME LIKE THIS!! IT'S ONLY EVER THIRTY-SOMETHING WOMEN THAT DO THIS!!
IN FACT, GIRLS IN THEIR EARLY TWENTIES DON'T DO IT EITHER.
ALL THE YOUNG GIRLS ARE VERY POLITE, NERVOUS, AND RESERVED.
Like, suspicious guys.
MY THOUGHTS
OFFICE LADIES FROM TOKYO REALLY SHOVEL IN THE PICKLED VEGETABLES. (BUT NOT SO MUCH IN MIYAZAKI)
CHOMP
CHOMP
This pickled eggplant is friggin' delicious!
21-YEAR-OLD OR SO GIRL
The shine of their hair is just ridiculous. And the cut of their bobs is ridiculously thick!
AND SO! NOW THAT THE TV ADAPTATION IS STARTING, I WANT THE TOKYO THIRTY-SOMETHING ARMY TO LIVE LIFE WITH VIGOR! THAT'S RIGHT! YOU GIRLS SHINE WHEN YOU'RE OUT AT THE BARS!!
祝・ドラマ化
BANNER: HOORAY FOR THE TV ADAPTATION!
AND IF YOU SEE ME, SAY SOME-THING!! I'LL ALLOW IT!!
THE END!!

Tokyo Tarareba Girls Translation notes

The Fiend with Twenty Faces, page 34
A famous work by Edogawa Rampo, Japan's greatest writer of classic detective fiction.

I LOVED STUFF LIKE SHERLOCK HOLMES AND "THE FIEND WITH TWENTY FACES"...

Yuko Arimori, page 49
A marathon runner who placed bronze in the 1996 Olympics despite beating her prior record by 4 minutes.

I WANT TO PAT MYSELF ON THE BACK!
I FEEL JUST LIKE YUKO ARIMORI AT THE ATLANTA OLYMPICS!

Doutor, page 54
Doutor Coffee is a ubiquitous chain of coffee shops in Japan.

THEN STOP AT A NEARBY DOUTOR FOR COFFEE AND TALK ABOUT THE MOVIE!

Ame Talk, page 56
A talk / variety show hosted by the members of the Japanese comedy duo "Ame-Agari Kesshitai."

NO.
WE JUST WATCHED A MOVIE, SO...
WHY DON'T WE RELAX WITH A FEW DRINKS AND PUT ON A RECORDING OF AME TALK OR SOMETHING?

Yoshi Ikuzo, page 99

One of Japanese singer Yoshi Ikuzo's most famous songs is *Ora Tokyo sa Iguda* (roughly, "I'm Headin' t' Tokyo"). In the song, he complains that his tiny hometown is so small that "it doesn't even have any pianos / it doesn't have any bars." Rinko here uses the same grammatical construction when she muses about not having any pictures of Key to delete, or a LINE address to block—then catches herself doing it.

WAIT.
WHO DO I THINK I AM, YOSHI IKUZO?
はは HA HA...

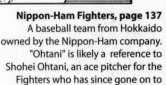

A HUSBAND WHO BARGES IN ON HIS WIFE'S GATHERINGS IS SO UNCOUTH!
I heard that in a rakugo story!
HE'S NOT MY HUSBAND YET!
Jeez! You guys!
WHEN WE DRINK, I WANT TO TALK ABOUT THE KINDS OF THINGS YOU CAN ONLY TALK ABOUT WHEN IT'S JUST US GIRLS!

Rakugo, page 105:

Rakugo is a type of traditional Japanese comic storytelling. While it is superficially similar to western stand-up comedy in that it involves a single performer telling humorous stories, it draws on a centuries-old canon of performance tradition. For more information, read *Descending Stories*, also from Kodansha Comics.

WAIT A SECOND. JUST LET ME SEE HOW THE NIPPON HAM-FIGHTERS GAME TURNS OUT...
WOW, OHTANI'S AWESOME.
HE'S THE KIND OF PLAYER YOU ONLY SEE ONCE IN A DECADE.
THIS IS NO TIME TO BE WATCHING BASEBALL NEWS! WHAT IF! WHAT IF!

Nippon-Ham Fighters, page 137

A baseball team from Hokkaido owned by the Nippon-Ham company. "Ohtani" is likely a reference to Shohei Ohtani, an ace pitcher for the Fighters who has since gone on to play for the Los Angeles Angels. Ohtani is notable for being both an effective pitcher and hitter, which is a rarity at the highest levels of baseball.

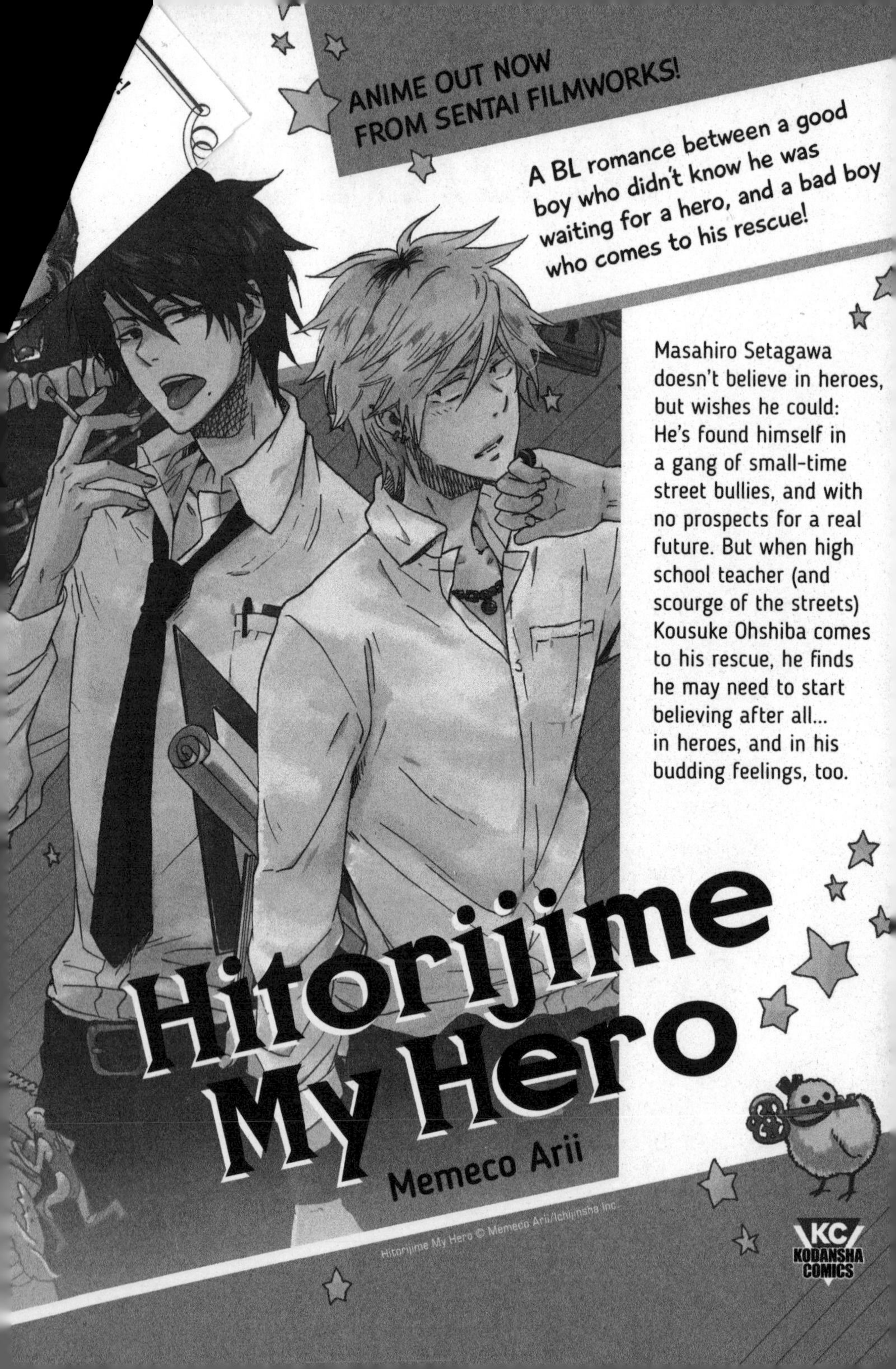
ANIME OUT NOW
FROM SENTAI FILMWORKS!
A BL romance between a good boy who didn't know he was waiting for a hero, and a bad boy who comes to his rescue!
Masahiro Setagawa doesn't believe in heroes, but wishes he could: He's found himself in a gang of small-time street bullies, and with no prospects for a real future. But when high school teacher (and scourge of the streets) Kousuke Ohshiba comes to his rescue, he finds he may need to start believing after all... in heroes, and in his budding feelings, too.
Hitorijime My Hero
Memeco Arii
Hitorijime My Hero © Memeco Arii/Ichijinsha Inc.
KC
KODANSHA COMICS